CASENOTE® Legal Briefs®

CRIMINAL PROCEDURE

Keyed to Courses Using

Kamisar, LaFave, and Israel's Modern Criminal Procedure Sixteenth Edition by King, Kerr, and Primus

Authored by: Publisher's Editorial Staff

ASPEN PUBLISHING

To contact Customer Service, e-mail customer.service@aspenpublishing.com, call 1-800-950-5259, or mail correspondence to:

Aspen Publishing
Attn: Order Department
1 Wall Street
Burlington, MA 01803

Printed in the United States of America.

1 2 3 4 5 6 7 8 9 0

ISBN 979-8-8890-6802-0

About Aspen Publishing

Aspen Publishing is a leading provider of educational content and digital learning solutions to law schools in the U.S. and around the world. Aspen provides best-in-class solutions for legal education through authoritative textbooks, written by renowned authors, and breakthrough products such as Connected eBooks, Connected Quizzing, and PracticePerfect.

The Aspen Casebook Series (famously known among law faculty and students as the "red and black" casebooks) encompasses hundreds of highly regarded textbooks in more than eighty disciplines, from large enrollment courses such as Torts and Contracts to emerging electives such as Sustainability and the Law of Policing. Study aids such as the *Examples & Explanations* and the *Emanuel Law Outlines* series, both highly popular collections, help law students master complex subject matter.

Major products, programs, and initiatives include:

- **Connected eBooks** are enhanced digital textbooks and study aids that come with a suite of online content and learning tools designed to maximize student success. Designed in collaboration with hundreds of faculty and students, the Connected eBook is a significant leap forward in the legal education learning tools available to students.
- **Connected Quizzing** is an easy-to-use formative assessment tool that tests law students' understanding and provides timely feedback to improve learning outcomes. Delivered through CasebookConnect.com, the learning platform already used by students to access their Aspen casebooks, Connected Quizzing is simple to implement and integrates seamlessly with law school course curricula.
- **PracticePerfect** is a visually engaging, interactive study aid to explain commonly encountered legal doctrines through easy-to-understand animated videos, illustrative examples, and numerous practice questions. Developed by a team of experts, PracticePerfect is the ideal study companion for today's law students.
- The **Aspen Learning Library** enables law schools to provide their students with access to the most popular study aids on the market across all of their courses. Available through an annual subscription, the online library consists of study aids in e-book, audio, and video formats with full text search, note-taking, and highlighting capabilities.
- Aspen's **Digital Bookshelf** is an institutional-level online education bookshelf, consolidating everything students and professors need to ensure success. This program ensures that every student has access to affordable course materials from day one.
- **Leading Edge** is a community centered on thinking differently about legal education and putting those thoughts into actionable strategies. At the core of the program is the Leading Edge Conference, an annual gathering of legal education thought leaders looking to pool ideas and identify promising directions of exploration.

Format for the Casenote® Legal Brief

Nature of Case: This section identifies the form of action (e.g., breach of contract, negligence, battery), the type of proceeding (e.g., demurrer, appeal from trial court's jury instructions) or the relief sought (e.g., damages, injunction, criminal sanctions).

Party ID: Quick identification of the relationship between the parties.

Fact Summary: This is included to refresh your memory and can be used as a quick reminder of the facts.

Rule of Law: Summarizes the general principle of law that the case illustrates. It may be used for instant recall of the court's holding and for classroom discussion or home review.

Facts: This section contains all relevant facts of the case, including the contentions of the parties and the lower court holdings. It is written in a logical order to give you a clear understanding of the case. The plaintiff and defendant are identified by their proper names throughout and are always labeled with a (P) or (D).

Issue: The issue is a concise question that brings out the essence of the opinion as it relates to the section of the casebook in which the case appears. Both substantive and procedural issues are included if relevant to the decision.

Concurrence/Dissent: All concurrences and dissents are briefed whenever they are included by the casebook author.

Analysis: This last paragraph gives you a broad understanding of where the case "fits in" with other cases in the section of the book and with the entire course. It is a hornbook-style discussion indicating whether the case is a majority or minority opinion and comparing the principal case with other cases in the casebook. It may also provide analysis from restatements, uniform codes, and law review articles.

Holding and Decision: This section offers a clear and in-depth discussion of the rule of the case and the court's rationale. It is written in easy-to-understand language and answers the issue presented by applying the law to the facts of the case. When relevant, it includes a thorough discussion of the exceptions to the case as listed by the court, any major cites to the other cases on point, and the names of the judges who wrote the decisions.

Quicknotes: Conveniently defines legal terms found in the case.

Palsgraf v. Long Island R.R. Co.

Injured bystander (P) v. Railroad company (D)

N.Y. Ct. App., 248 N.Y. 339, 162 N.E. 99 (1928).

NATURE OF CASE: Appeal from judgment affirming verdict for plaintiff seeking damages for personal injury.

FACT SUMMARY: Helen Palsgraf (P) was injured on R.R.'s (D) train platform when R.R.'s (D) guard helped a passenger aboard a moving train, causing his package to fall on the tracks. The package contained fireworks which exploded, creating a shock that tipped a scale onto Palsgraf (P).

RULE OF LAW

The risk reasonably to be perceived defines the duty to be obeyed.

FACTS: Helen Palsgraf (P) purchased a ticket to Rockaway Beach from R.R. (D) and was waiting on the train platform. As she waited, two men ran to catch a train that was pulling out from the platform. The first man jumped aboard, but the second man, who appeared as if he might fall, was helped aboard by the guard on the train who had kept the door open so they could jump aboard. A guard on the platform also helped by pushing him onto the train. The man was carrying a package wrapped in newspaper. In the process, the man dropped his package, which fell on the tracks. The package contained fireworks and exploded. The shock of the explosion was apparently of great enough strength to tip over some scales at the other end of the platform, which fell on Palsgraf (P) and injured her. A jury awarded her damages, and R.R. (D) appealed.

ISSUE: Does the risk reasonably to be perceived define the duty to be obeyed?

HOLDING AND DECISION: (Cardozo, C.J.) Yes. The risk reasonably to be perceived defines the duty to be obeyed. If there is no foreseeable hazard to the injured party as the result of a seemingly innocent act, the act does not become a tort because it happened to be a wrong as to another. If the wrong was not willful, the plaintiff must show that the act as to her had such great and apparent possibilities of danger as to entitle her to protection. Negligence in the abstract is not enough upon which to base liability. Negligence is a relative concept, evolving out of the common law doctrine of trespass on the case. To establish liability, the defendant must owe a legal duty of reasonable care to the injured party. A cause of action in tort will lie where harm, though unintended, could have been averted or avoided by observance of such a duty. The scope of the duty is limited by the range of danger that a reasonable person could foresee. In this case, there was nothing to suggest from the appearance of the parcel or otherwise that the parcel contained fireworks. The guard could not reasonably have had any warning of a threat to Palsgraf (P), and R.R. (D) therefore cannot be held liable. Judgment is reversed in favor of R.R. (D).

DISSENT: (Andrews, J.) The concept that there is no negligence unless R.R. (D) owes a legal duty to take care as to Palsgraf (P) herself is too narrow. Everyone owes to the world at large the duty of refraining from those acts that may unreasonably threaten the safety of others. If the guard's action was negligent as to those nearby, it was also negligent as to those outside what might be termed the "danger zone." For Palsgraf (P) to recover, R.R.'s (D) negligence must have been the proximate cause of her injury, a question of fact for the jury.

ANALYSIS

The majority defined the limit of the defendant's liability in terms of the danger that a reasonable person in defendant's situation would have perceived. The dissent argued that the limitation should not be placed on liability, but rather on damages. Judge Andrews suggested that only injuries that would not have happened but for R.R.'s (D) negligence should be compensable. Both the majority and dissent recognized the policy-driven need to limit liability for negligent acts, seeking, in the words of Judge Andrews, to define a framework "that will be practical and in keeping with the general understanding of mankind." The Restatement (Second) of Torts has accepted Judge Cardozo's view.

Quicknotes

FORESEEABILITY A reasonable expectation that change is the probable result of certain acts or omissions.

NEGLIGENCE Conduct falling below the standard of care that a reasonable person would demonstrate under similar conditions.

PROXIMATE CAUSE The natural sequence of events without which an injury would not have been sustained.

Note to Students

Aspen Publishing is proud to offer *Casenote® Legal Briefs*—continuing thirty years of publishing America's best-selling legal briefs.

Casenote® Legal Briefs are designed to help you save time when briefing assigned cases. Organized under convenient headings, they show you how to abstract the basic facts and holdings from the text of the actual opinions handed down by the courts. Used as part of a rigorous study regimen, they can help you spend more time analyzing and critiquing points of law than on copying bits and pieces of judicial opinions into your notebook or outline.

Casenote® Legal Briefs should never be used as a substitute for assigned casebook readings. They work best when read as a follow-up to reviewing the underlying opinions themselves. Students who try to avoid reading and digesting the judicial opinions in their casebooks or online sources will end up shortchanging themselves in the long run. The ability to absorb, critique, and restate the dynamic and complex elements of case law decisions is crucial to your success in law school and beyond. It cannot be developed vicariously.

In addition to *Casenote® Legal Briefs*, Aspen Publishing offers the following study aids:

- *Casenote® Legal Briefs*
- *Emanuel® Law Outlines*
- Emanuel® *Law in a Flash Flash Cards*
- Emanuel® *CrunchTime® Series*

Each of these series is designed to provide you with easy-to-understand explanations of complex points of law. Each volume offers guidance on the principles of legal analysis and, consulted regularly, will hone your ability to spot relevant issues. We have titles that will help you prepare for class, prepare for your exams, and enhance your general comprehension of the law along the way.

To find out more about our law school tools for success, visit us at *www.AspenPublishing.com* or e-mail us at *customer.service@aspenpublishing.com*. We'll be happy to assist you.

How to Brief a Case

A. Decide on a Format and Stick to It

Structure is essential to a good brief. It enables you to arrange systematically the related parts that are scattered throughout most cases, thus making manageable and understandable what might otherwise seem to be an endless and unfathomable sea of information. There are, of course, an unlimited number of formats that can be utilized. However, it is best to find one that suits your needs and stick to it. Consistency breeds both efficiency and the security that when called upon you will know where to look in your brief for the information you are asked to give.

Any format, as long as it presents the essential elements of a case in an organized fashion, can be used. Experience, however, has led *Casenote® Legal Briefs* to develop and utilize the following format because of its logical flow and universal applicability.

NATURE OF CASE: This is a brief statement of the legal character and procedural status of the case (e.g., "Appeal of a burglary conviction").

There are many different alternatives open to a litigant dissatisfied with a court ruling. The key to determining which one has been used is to discover *who is asking this court for what.*

This first entry in the brief should be kept as *short as possible.* Use the court's terminology if you understand it. But since jurisdictions vary as to the titles of pleadings, the best entry is the one that addresses who wants what in this proceeding, not the one that sounds most like the court's language.

RULE OF LAW: A statement of the general principle of law that the case illustrates (e.g., "An acceptance that varies any term of the offer is considered a rejection and counteroffer").

Determining the rule of law of a case is a procedure similar to determining the issue of the case. Avoid being fooled by red herrings; there may be a few rules of law mentioned in the case excerpt, but usually only one is *the* rule with which the casebook editor is concerned. The techniques used to locate the issue, described below, may also be utilized to find the rule of law. Generally, your best guide is simply the chapter heading. It is a clue to the point the casebook editor seeks to make and should be kept in mind when reading every case in the respective section.

FACTS: A synopsis of only the essential facts of the case, i.e., those bearing upon or leading up to the issue.

The facts entry should be a short statement of the events and transactions that led one party to initiate legal proceedings against another in the first place. While some cases conveniently state the salient facts at the beginning of the decision, in other instances they will have to be culled from hiding places throughout the text, even from concurring and dissenting opinions. Some of the "facts" will often be in dispute and should be so noted. Conflicting evidence may be briefly pointed up. "Hard" facts must be included. Both must be *relevant* in order to be listed in the facts entry. It is impossible to tell what is relevant until the entire case is read, as the ultimate determination of the rights and liabilities of the parties may turn on something buried deep in the opinion.

Generally, the facts entry should not be longer than three to five *short* sentences.

It is often helpful to identify the role played by a party in a given context. For example, in a construction contract case the identification of a party as the "contractor" or "builder" alleviates the need to tell that that party was the one who was supposed to have built the house.

It is always helpful, and a good general practice, to identify the "plaintiff" and the "defendant." This may seem elementary and uncomplicated, but, especially in view of the creative editing practiced by some casebook editors, it is sometimes a difficult or even impossible task. Bear in mind that the *party presently* seeking something from this court may not be the plaintiff, and that sometimes only the cross-claim of a defendant is treated in the excerpt. Confusing or misaligning the parties can ruin your analysis and understanding of the case.

ISSUE: A statement of the general legal question answered by or illustrated in the case. For clarity, the issue is best put in the form of a question capable of a "yes" or "no" answer. In reality, the issue is simply the Rule of Law put in the form of a question (e.g., "May an offer be accepted by performance?").

The major problem presented in discerning what is *the* issue in the case is that an opinion usually purports to raise and answer several questions. However, except for rare cases, only one such question is really the issue in the case. Collateral issues not necessary to the resolution of the matter in controversy are handled by the court by language known as *"obiter dictum"* or merely *"dictum."* While dicta may be included later in the brief, they have no place under the issue heading.

To find the issue, ask *who wants what* and then go on to ask *why did that party succeed or fail in getting it.* Once this is determined, the "why" should be turned into a question.

The complexity of the issues in the cases will vary, but in all cases a single-sentence question should sum up the issue. *In a few cases,* there will be two, or even more rarely, three issues of equal importance to the resolution of the case. Each should be expressed in a single-sentence question.

Since many issues are resolved by a court in coming to a final disposition of a case, the casebook editor will reproduce the portion of the opinion containing the issue or issues most relevant to the area of law under scrutiny. A noted law professor gave this advice: "Close the book; look at the title on the cover." Chances are, if it is Property, you need not concern yourself with whether, for example, the federal government's treatment of the plaintiff's land really raises a federal question sufficient to support jurisdiction on this ground in federal court.

The same rule applies to chapter headings designating sub-areas within the subjects. They tip you off as to what the text is designed to teach. The cases are arranged in a casebook to show a progression or development of the law, so that the preceding cases may also help.

It is also most important to remember to *read the notes and questions* at the end of a case to determine what the editors wanted you to have gleaned from it.

HOLDING AND DECISION: This section should succinctly explain the rationale of the court in arriving at its decision. In capsulizing the "reasoning" of the court, it should always include an application of the general rule or rules of law to the specific facts of the case. Hidden justifications come to light in this entry: the reasons for the state of the law, the public policies, the biases and prejudices, those considerations that influence the justices' thinking and, ultimately, the outcome of the case. At the end, there should be a short indication of thedisposition or procedural resolution of the case (e.g., "Decision of the trial court for Mr. Smith (P) reversed").

The foregoing format is designed to help you "digest" the reams of case material with which you will be faced in your law school career. Once mastered by practice, it will place at your fingertips the information the authors of your casebooks have sought to impart to you in case-by-case illustration and analysis.

B. Be as Economical as Possible in Briefing Cases

Once armed with a format that encourages succinctness, it is as important to be economical with regard to the time spent on the actual reading of the case as it is to be economical in the writing of the brief itself. This does not mean "skimming" a case. Rather, it means reading the case with an "eye" trained to recognize into which "section" of your brief a particular passage or line fits and having a system for quickly and precisely marking the case so that the passages fitting any one particular part of the brief can be easily identified and brought together in a concise and accurate manner when the brief is actually written.

It is of no use to simply repeat everything in the opinion of the court; record only enough information to trigger your recollection of what the court said. Nevertheless, an accurate statement of the "law of the case," i.e., the legal principle applied to the facts, is absolutely essential to class preparation and to learning the law under the case method.

To that end, it is important to develop a "shorthand" that you can use to make marginal notations. These notations will tell you at a glance in which section of the brief you will be placing that particular passage or portion of the opinion.

Some students prefer to underline all the salient portions of the opinion (with a pencil or colored underliner marker), making marginal notations as they go along. Others prefer the color-coded method of underlining, utilizing different colors of markers to underline the salient portions of the case, each separate color being used to represent a different section of the brief. For example, blue underlining could be used for passages relating to the rule of law, yellow for those relating to the issue, and green for those relating to the holding and decision, etc. While it has its advocates, thecolor-coded method can be confusing and time-consuming (all that time spent on changing colored markers). Furthermore, it can interfere with the continuity and concentration many students deem essential to the reading of a case for maximum comprehension. In the end, however, it is a matter of personal preference and style. Just remember, whatever method you use, underlining must be used sparingly or its value is lost.

If you take the marginal notation route, an efficient and easy method is to go along underlining the key portions of the case and placing in the margin alongside them the following "markers" to indicate where a particular passage or line "belongs" in the brief you will write:

N	(NATURE OF CASE)
RL	(RULE OF LAW)
I	(ISSUE)
HL	(HOLDING AND DECISION, relates to the RULE OF LAW behind the decision)
HR	(HOLDING AND DECISION, gives the RATIONALE or reasoning behind the decision)
HA	(HOLDING AND DECISION, applies the general principle(s) of law to the facts of the case to arrive at the decision)

Remember that a particular passage may well contain information necessary to more than one part of your brief, in which case you simply note that in the margin. If you are using the color-coded underlining method instead of marginal notation, simply make asterisks or checks in the margin next to the passage in question in the colors that indicate the additional sections of the brief where it might be utilized.

The economy of utilizing "shorthand" in marking cases for briefing can be maintained in the actual brief writing process itself by utilizing "law student shorthand" within the brief. There are many commonly used words and phrases for which abbreviations can be substituted in your briefs (and in your class notes also). You can develop abbreviations that are personal to you and which will save you a lot of time. A reference list of briefing abbreviations can be found on page x of this book.

C. Use Both the Briefing Process and the Brief as a Learning Tool

Now that you have a format and the tools for briefing cases efficiently, the most important thing is to make the time spent in briefing profitable to you and to make the most advantageous use of the briefs you create. Of course, the briefs are invaluable for classroom reference when you are called upon to explain or analyze a particular case. However, they are also useful in reviewing for exams. A quick glance at the fact summary should bring the case to mind, and a rereading of the rule of law should enable you to go over the underlying legal concept in your mind, how it was applied in that particular case, and how it might apply in other factual settings.

As to the value to be derived from engaging in the briefing process itself, there is an immediate benefit that arises from being forced to sift through the essential facts and reasoning from the court's opinion and to succinctly express them in your own words in your brief. The process ensures that you understand the case and the point that it illustrates, and that means you will be ready to absorb further analysis and information brought forth in class. It also ensures you will have something to say when called upon in class. The briefing process helps develop a mental agility for getting to the *gist* of a case and for identifying, expounding on, and applying the legal concepts and issues found there. The briefing process is the mental process on which you must rely in taking law school examinations; it is also the mental process upon which lawyers rely in serving their clients and in making a living.

Abbreviations for Briefs

acceptance	acp
affirmed	aff
answer	ans
assumption of risk	a/r
attorney	atty
beyond a reasonable doubt	b/r/d
bona fide purchaser	BFP
breach of contract	br/k
cause of action	c/a
common law	c/l
Constitution	Con
constitutional	con
contract	K
contributory negligence	c/n
cross	x
cross-complaint	x/c
cross-examination	x/ex
cruel and unusual punishment	c/u/p
defendant	D
dismissed	dis
double jeopardy	d/j
due process	d/p
equal protection	e/p
equity	eq
evidence	ev
exclude	exc
exclusionary rule	exc/r
felony	f/n
freedom of speech	f/s
good faith	g/f
habeas corpus	h/c
hearsay	hr
husband	H
injunction	inj
in loco parentis	ILP
inter vivos	I/v
joint tenancy	j/t
judgment	judgt
jurisdiction	jur
last clear chance	LCC
long-arm statute	LAS
majority view	maj
meeting of minds	MOM
minority view	min
Miranda rule	Mir/r
Miranda warnings	Mir/w
negligence	neg
notice	ntc
nuisance	nus
obligation	ob
obscene	obs
offer	O
offeree	OE
offeror	OR
ordinance	ord
pain and suffering	p/s
parol evidence	p/e
plaintiff	P
prima facie	p/f
probable cause	p/c
proximate cause	px/c
real property	r/p
reasonable doubt	r/d
reasonable man	r/m
rebuttable presumption	rb/p
remanded	rem
res ipsa loquitur	RIL
respondeat superior	r/s
Restatement	RS
reversed	rev
Rule Against Perpetuities	RAP
search and seizure	s/s
search warrant	s/w
self-defense	s/d
specific performance	s/p
statute	S
statute of frauds	S/F
statute of limitations	S/L
summary judgment	s/j
tenancy at will	t/w
tenancy in common	t/c
tenant	t
third party	TP
third party beneficiary	TPB
transferred intent	TI
unconscionable	uncon
unconstitutional	unconst
undue influence	u/e
Uniform Commercial Code	UCC
unilateral	uni
vendee	VE
vendor	VR
versus	v
void for vagueness	VFV
weight of authority	w/a
weight of the evidence	w/e
wife	W
with	w/
within	w/i
without	w/o
without prejudice	w/o/p
wrongful death	wr/d

Table of Cases

A
Ake v. Oklahoma . . . 11
Apprendi v. New Jersey . . . 251
Arizona v. Gant . . . 79
Armstrong, United States v. . . . 176
Ashe v. Swenson . . . 193
Atwater v. City of Lago Vista . . . 82

B
Bagley, United States v. . . . 207
Banks, United States v. . . . 65
Barker v. Wingo . . . 200
Batson v. Kentucky . . . 221
Berghuis v. Thompkins . . . 135
Betts v. Brady . . . 6
Bordenkircher v. Hayes . . . 210
Boyd v. United States . . . 166
Brewer v. Williams (Williams I) . . . 146

C
California v. Acevedo . . . 77
California v. Carney . . . 76
California v. Ciraolo . . . 47
California v. Greenwood . . . 46
Carpenter v. United States . . . 51
Chadwick, United States v. . . . 74
Chapman v. California . . . 256
Chavez v. Martinez . . . 144
Chimel v. California . . . 72
City of. *See name of city*
Clark, State v. . . . 178
Class v. United States . . . 216
Colorado v. Connelly . . . 158
Costello v. United States . . . 180
Cronic, United States v. . . . 18
Cuyler v. Sullivan . . . 31

D
Darden v. Wainwright . . . 238
Davis v. United States . . . 111, 138
Dickerson v. United States . . . 143
Dionisio, United States v. . . . 168
Dixon, United States v. . . . 191
Duckworth v. Eagan . . . 133
Dunn, United States v. . . . 44

E
Entick v. Carrington . . . 38

F
Faretta v. California . . . 13
Fernandez v. California . . . 99
Fisher v. United States . . . 169
Florida v. Bostick . . . 57
Florida v. Jardines . . . 55

G
Gideon v. Wainwright . . . 7
Gonzales-Lopez, United States v. . . . 14
Graham v. Conner . . . 93
Gray v. Maryland . . . 197
Griffin v. California . . . 236

H
Harrington v. Richter . . . 21, 264
Hoffa v. United States . . . 114
Horton v. California . . . 67
Howes v. Fields . . . 125
Hubbell, United States v. . . . 170

I
Illinois v. Allen . . . 232
Illinois v. Gates . . . 63
Illinois v. Somerville . . . 240
Illinois v. Wardlow . . . 87

J
Jacobson v. United States . . . 116
J.D.B. v. North Carolina . . . 124
Jones, United States v. . . . 54

K
Kansas v. Glover . . . 88
Katz v. United States . . . 42
Kentucky v. King . . . 70
Kyllo v. United States . . . 49

L
Lafler v. Cooper . . . 26
Leon, United States v. . . . 110
Lockhart v. Nelson . . . 246
Lovasco, United States v. . . . 202

M
Manson v. Brathwaite . . . 164
Mapp v. Ohio . . . 40
Maryland v. Pringle . . . 64
Maryland v. Shatzer . . . 140
McCoy v. Louisiana . . . 33
Merriman, People v. . . . 190
Michigan v. Bryant . . . 234
Michigan Department of State Police v. Sitz . . . 96
Miller v. Fenton . . . 155
Minnesota v. Carter . . . 105
Minnesota v. Dickerson . . . 91
Miranda v. Arizona . . . 121
Missouri v. Frye . . . 213
Missouri v. Seibert . . . 161
Montejo v. Louisiana . . . 150
Moran v. Burbine . . . 134
Murray v. United States . . . 108

N
Neder v. United States . . . 257
New York v. Quarles . . . 131
North Carolina v. Pearce . . . 254

O
Oregon v. Kennedy . . . 243

P
Patane, United States v. . . . 159
Patterson v. Illinois . . . 148

Payton v. New York . . . 68
Pennsylvania v. Muniz . . . 129
People v. *See name of opposing party*
Presley v. Georgia . . . 230
Puerto Rico v. Sánchez Valle et al. . . . 247

R
Rakas v. Illinois . . . 104
Renico v. Lett . . . 242
R. Enterprises, Inc., United States v. . . . 167
Resendiz-Ponce, United States v. . . . 185
Rhode Island v. Innis . . . 127
Robinson, United States v. . . . 83
Rodriguez-Moreno, United States v. . . . 188
Rompilla v. Beard . . . 23
Ross v. Moffitt . . . 10
Rothgery v. Gillespie County . . . 8
Ruiz, United States v. . . . 211
Russell v. United States . . . 184

S
Salerno, United States v. . . . 174
Salinas v. Texas . . . 141
Santobello v. New York . . . 215
Schaffer v. United States . . . 195
Schneckloth v. Bustamonte . . . 97
Scott, United States v. . . . 244
Sherman v. United States . . . 115
Skilling v. United States . . . 224
Smith v. Maryland . . . 50
Stone v. Powell . . . 260
Strickland v. Washington . . . 20

T
Tahlequah, City of v. Bond . . . 94
Taylor v. Illinois . . . 206
Taylor v. Louisiana . . . 220
Teague v. Lane . . . 263
Terry v. Ohio . . . 85
Texas v. Cobb . . . 153
Torres v. Madrid . . . 59

U
United States v. *See name of opposing party*
Utah v. Strieff . . . 2

W
Wainwright v. Sykes . . . 261
Warden v. Hayden . . . 69
Watson, United States v. . . . 81
Weaver v. Massachusetts . . . 28
Wheat v. United States . . . 32
Whren v. United States . . . 75
Williams v. Florida . . . 204
Williams v. New York . . . 250
Williams, United States v. . . . 181
Wong Sun v. United States . . . 107

Note: There are no principal cases in Chapters 1 and 2 of the casebook.

CHAPTER 3

Some General Reflections on the Constitutionalization of Criminal Procedure

Quick Reference Rules of Law

PAGE

1. *Utah v. Strieff.* Evidence remains admissible when the link between unconstitutional police action and the evidence obtained has been broken by an intervening circumstance, such that the protections of the Fourth Amendment that have been violated would not be furthered by the subsequent suppression of the evidence. 2

Utah v. Strieff

State (P) v. Suspected owner of drugs (D)

579 U.S. 232 (2016)

NATURE OF CASE: Appeal from Utah Supreme Court's decision in favor of the defendant.

FACT SUMMARY: Police suspected Strieff (D) of drug possession and stopped him in a parking lot. After learning his name, the officer discovered Strieff (D) had an outstanding arrest warrant. In a subsequent search incident to the arrest, the police found methamphetamine on Strieff's (D) person.

RULE OF LAW
Evidence remains admissible when the link between unconstitutional police action and the evidence obtained has been broken by an intervening circumstance, such that the protections of the Fourth Amendment that have been violated would not be furthered by the subsequent suppression of the evidence.

FACTS: Police in Utah suspected a certain house was the center of illegal drug activity. While conducting surveillance, officers observed Strieff (D) leave the house and walk to a nearby convenience store. A police officer, suspecting Strieff (D) of drug possession, stopped him in the parking lot and demanded his name. The officer then requested warrant information from his dispatchers. The dispatchers informed the officer that Strieff (D) had an outstanding arrest warrant for a traffic violation. In a subsequent search incident to the arrest, the police found methamphetamine on Strieff's (D) person. At trial Strieff (D) moved to suppress the evidence on the grounds the stop was without reasonable suspicion. The State (P) conceded the stop was illegal but argued the evidence should remain admissible. The trial court agreed. On appeal, the Utah Supreme Court reversed in favor of Strieff (D). The State (P) appealed to the United States Supreme Court.

ISSUE: Does evidence remain admissible when the link between unconstitutional police action and the evidence obtained has been broken by an intervening circumstance, such that the protections of the Fourth Amendment that have been violated would not be furthered by the subsequent suppression of the evidence?

HOLDING AND DECISION: (Thomas, J.) Yes. Evidence remains admissible when the link between unconstitutional police action and the evidence obtained has been broken by an intervening circumstance, such that the protections of the Fourth Amendment that have been violated would not be furthered by the subsequent suppression of the evidence. Three factors exist to determine if the discovery of a valid arrest warrant is an intervening cause to break the link between the unlawful stop of Strieff (D) and the discovery of drugs on his person. First, we examine the temporal proximity between the unconstitutional conduct and the discovery of the evidence. This factor favors suppressing the evidence. Here, the officer discovered the methamphetamine within minutes of learning of the outstanding arrest warrant. The second factor is the existence of the intervening circumstances. This factor favors the State (P). Here, the warrant was valid, and the officer had an obligation to arrest Strieff (D) once he became aware of it. The officer's actions were thus independently compelled. Once he made the arrest, the subsequent search incident to the arrest was lawful. The third factor is the purpose and flagrancy of the officer's conduct. This factor also favors the State (P). The exclusionary rule exists to deter officer's purposeful or flagrant conduct when carrying out a stop or search. In this matter, the officer was at most negligent. The officer made two good-faith errors. He failed to note when Strieff (D) entered the home and failed to inquire if Strieff (D) would speak with him voluntarily, as opposed to demanding his name. These errors do not rise to a flagrant violation of Strieff's (D) rights. Accordingly, we find the discovery of the valid warrant was an intervening cause between the illegal stop and the discovery of the drugs of Strieff's (D) person. Reversed.

DISSENT: (Sotomayor, J.) Unlawful "stops" have severe consequences much greater than the inconvenience suggested by the name. Police officers now have an array of instruments to probe and examine individuals, and if the use of these devices is condoned without adequate cause, officers have the potential to target pedestrians in an arbitrary manner, and to treat members of our communities as second-class citizens. Although many Americans have been stopped for speeding or jaywalking, few may realize how degrading a stop can be when the officer is looking for more. Under the Court's decisions, an officer is allowed to stop an individual for whatever reason the officer wants—so long as the officer can point to a pretextual justification after the fact. Although such justification must provide specific reasons why the officer suspected the individual was breaking the law, it may factor in ethnicity, residency, what the individual was wearing, and how the individual behaved. The officer need not even know which law might have been broken so long as the officer can later point to any possible infraction—even one that is minor, unrelated, or

Continued on next page.

ambiguous. The indignity of the stop is not limited to the officer's perception of the individual as a criminal, since the officer is permitted to make a thorough frisk of the individual if the officer thinks the individual is dangerous. Further, if the officer chooses, the officer may handcuff the individual and take him to jail for nothing more than a minor infraction, such as speeding or jaywalking. At the jail, the individual can be fingerprinted, swabbed for DNA, and forced to shower with a delousing agent while the individual is forced to lift his tongue, hold out his arms, turn around, and undergo a hand inspection of his genitals. Worse, even if the individual is innocent, the individual will join the 65 million Americans with an arrest record and experience the "civil death" of discrimination by employers, landlords, and whoever else conducts a background check. Moreover, if the individual fails to pay bail or appear for court, a judge will issue a warrant to render the individual "arrestable on sight" in the future. This case involves a suspicionless stop, one in which the officer initiated this chain of events without justification. Many innocent people are subjected to the humiliations of these unconstitutional searches but people of color are disproportionate victims of this type of scrutiny. By legitimizing the conduct that produces this double consciousness, this case tells everyone, White and Black, guilty and innocent, that an officer can verify your legal status at any time. It says that your body is subject to invasion while courts excuse the violation of your rights. It implies that you are not a citizen of a democracy but the subject of a carceral state, just waiting to be cataloged. These are not just isolated instances, as the majority claims. The people who have been subjected to such indignities and rights violations show us that unlawful police stops corrode all our civil liberties and threaten all our lives. Until their voices matter too, our justice system will continue to be anything but.

DISSENT: (Kagan, J.) The officer's investigatory stop was calculated. He knew there was a good chance that there would be a warrant on Strieff (D). The stop was so unjustified that the State (P) did not even defend it at trial. This decision will embolden police officers to make unlawful stops now that they are aware the discovery of a valid arrest warrant will forgive the unlawful stop or seizure.

ANALYSIS

Among the three factors to determine if the warrant was an intervening circumstance, the final factor regarding the officer's purposeful or flagrant conduct appears to give reviewing courts wide discretion. The majority and the dissents differed greatly in their interpretation of this factor. The majority felt the officer's errors were simply negligent while the dissenting justices clearly found them to be unconstitutional. It remains to be seen if future cases will further define this type of police conduct.

Quicknotes

ARREST WARRANT An order issued by a court directing an officer to arrest a particular individual.

INVESTIGATORY STOP A brief, non-intrusive stop requiring the police officer to have a reasonable suspicion that a crime has been committed based on specific and articulable facts.

CHAPTER 4

The Right to Counsel

Quick Reference Rules of Law

PAGE

1. *Betts v. Brady.* The right to counsel is not fully applicable to the states because the Sixth Amendment's guarantee of counsel is not completely incorporated by the Fourteenth Amendment, but the failure to appoint counsel is a violation of due process if, under the circumstances of the case, it results in a conviction that is lacking in fundamental fairness. *6*

2. *Gideon v. Wainwright.* The right to counsel is one of those rights that is "fundamental and essential to a fair trial" and is thus made obligatory upon the states by the Fourteenth Amendment. *7*

3. *Rothgery v. Gillespie County.* A criminal defendant's initial appearance before a judicial officer, where he learns of the charges against him, constitutes the start of adversarial proceedings that triggers the attachment of the Sixth Amendment's right to counsel. *8*

4. *Ross v. Moffitt.* There is no constitutional right to appointed counsel for discretionary appellate proceedings. *10*

5. *Ake v. Oklahoma.* An indigent criminal defendant who has made a preliminary showing that his or her sanity at the time of the offense is likely to be a significant factor at trial is entitled under the Fourteenth Amendment's Due Process Clause to have the state provide access to a psychiatrist's assistance on this issue at trial and sentencing. *11*

6. *Faretta v. California.* A criminal defendant has a Sixth Amendment right to conduct a pro se defense. *13*

7. *United States v. Gonzalez-Lopez.* A trial court's erroneous deprivation of a criminal defendant's choice of counsel entitles him to reversal of his conviction. *14*

Betts v. Brady

Farmhand (D) v. Court (P)

316 U.S. 455 (1942)

NATURE OF CASE: Criminal prosecution for robbery.

FACT SUMMARY: Betts (D) was indicted for robbery and his request to have counsel appointed for his trial was denied under a local law which allowed appointed counsel only for rape and murder cases.

RULE OF LAW

The right to counsel is not fully applicable to the states because the Sixth Amendment's guarantee of counsel is not completely incorporated by the Fourteenth Amendment, but the failure to appoint counsel is a violation of due process if, under the circumstances of the case, it results in a conviction that is lacking in fundamental fairness.

FACTS: Betts (D), an indigent, was indicted for robbery. He was an unemployed farmhand of ordinary intelligence but uneducated. He requested to have counsel appointed for him because he was too poor to afford an attorney, but his request was denied under a local rule that allowed the appointment of counsel only in rape and murder cases. Betts's (D) defense to the charge was the presentation of an alibi, so the only issue involved in the trial was the veracity of the prosecution and defense witnesses. Betts (D) elected to have a trial without a jury and didn't take the stand in his own defense; the trial resulted in a conviction and an eight-year sentence.

ISSUE: Is the state's failure to appoint counsel for an indigent defendant a violation of the Fourteenth Amendment a guarantee of due process?

HOLDING AND DECISION: (Roberts, J.) No. The Fourteenth Amendment's guarantee of due process does not require the appointment of counsel for indigent defendants in all criminal cases. Under the Sixth Amendment, which applies only to federal courts, appointment of counsel is required for all criminal cases if the defendant is unable to afford counsel and he does not intentionally and competently waive his right to counsel. But the Fourteenth Amendment does not incorporate all aspects of the Sixth Amendment, so the federal rule of appointment of counsel for all criminal cases is not applicable to the states. The Sixth Amendment is not fully incorporated because the appointment of counsel is not a fundamental right essential to preserve the fairness of all trials. In most states the appointment of counsel is not considered required for all cases but is essentially a question of legislative policy. However, in most states the court does have the power to appoint counsel where it is necessary in the interest of fairness. Affirmed.

DISSENT: (Black, J.) First, the Fourteenth Amendment makes the Sixth Amendment guarantee of counsel fully applicable to the states, but this view is not accepted by the majority. Nonetheless, even if the majority's view of incomplete incorporation is adopted, the nature of the offense and the circumstances of the trial show that the denial of counsel was a violation of due process.

ANALYSIS

This case is important only for historical reasons, because its holding that the Sixth Amendment is not fully applicable to the states through the Fourteenth Amendment was reversed in *Gideon v. Wainwright*, 372 U.S. 335 (1963). But the rule had vitality until 1963. Under the *Betts* rule, the Court was willing to find special circumstances that made the denial of appointed counsel violation of due process.

Quicknotes

PROCEDURAL DUE PROCESS The constitutional mandate that if the state or federal government acts so as to deny a citizen of a life, liberty, or property interest, the person is first entitled to notice and the right to be heard.

RIGHT TO COUNSEL Right conferred by the Sixth Amendment that the accused shall be provided effective legal assistance in a criminal proceeding.

Gideon v. Wainwright

Non-capital felon (D) v. Court (P)

372 U.S. 335 (1963)

NATURE OF CASE: Appeal of denial of petition for habeas corpus relief.

FACT SUMMARY: Gideon (D) appealed his criminal conviction for a noncapital felony on the grounds that the trial court's refusal to appoint counsel for him was unconstitutional.

RULE OF LAW

The right to counsel is one of those rights that is "fundamental and essential to a fair trial" and is thus made obligatory upon the states by the Fourteenth Amendment.

FACTS: Gideon (D) was convicted of a noncapital felony after the Florida trial court refused to appoint counsel for him because the law allowed such appointment only in capital cases. His petition for habeas corpus relief was denied, but the United States Supreme Court granted certiorari to consider his contention that the denial of appointed counsel had been unconstitutional.

ISSUE: Is the right to counsel one of those rights that is "fundamental and essential to a fair trial" and is thus made obligatory upon the states by the Fourteenth Amendment?

HOLDING AND DECISION: (Black, J.) Yes. The right to counsel is one of those rights that is "fundamental and essential to a fair trial" and is thus made obligatory upon the states by the Fourteenth Amendment. A provision of the Bill of Rights that is "fundamental and essential to a fair trial" is made obligatory upon the states by the Fourteenth Amendment. *Betts v. Brady*, 316 U.S. 455 (1942), was correct in so assuming. However, the *Betts* Court was wrong in concluding that the Sixth Amendment's guarantee of counsel is not one of those fundamental rights. It is. In deciding it was not, the *Betts* Court made an abrupt break with its own well-considered precedents. Today, this Court returns to these old precedents by recognizing that the right to counsel of one charged with a crime is deemed fundamental and essential to a fair trial in our country. Reversed.

CONCURRENCE: (Clark, J.) The Constitution makes no distinction between capital and noncapital cases. It requires due process for a deprivation of "liberty" just as for a deprivation of "life."

CONCURRENCE: (Harlan, J.) While *Betts* should be overruled, to say that it represented "an abrupt break with well-considered precedents" is wrong. *Betts* recognized that special circumstances similar to those that made denial of counsel unconstitutional in capital cases could exist in noncapital cases, but it required they be shown in order to establish a denial of due process. The special circumstances rule has been abandoned in capital cases and it is time it now be abandoned in noncapital cases that carry the possibility of a substantial prison sentence.

ANALYSIS

The flip side of the right to have counsel is the right not to have counsel, i.e., self-representation. The American Bar Association has taken the position that the right to counsel is so fundamental that except in the simplest trials the court should appoint "standby counsel" when a defendant chooses to represent himself or herself. Most courts that have addressed the issue have decided that a defendant need not specifically be informed of the right to represent himself or herself.

Quicknotes

PROCEDURAL DUE PROCESS The constitutional mandate that if the state or federal government acts so as to deny a citizen of a life, liberty, or property interest, the person is first entitled to notice and the right to be heard.

RIGHT TO COUNSEL Right conferred by the Sixth Amendment that the accused shall be provided effective legal assistance in a criminal proceeding.

Rothgery v. Gillespie County

Criminal defendant (P) v. State (D)

554 U.S. 191 (2008)

NATURE OF CASE: Appeal from lower court decision in favor of the State (D).

FACT SUMMARY: Using erroneous information, the State (D) charged Rothgery (P) with unlawful possession of a firearm by a felon. The State (D) arraigned Rothgery (P) without the assistance of counsel and subsequently jailed Rothgery (P) for a short time before he posted a security bond.

RULE OF LAW

A criminal defendant's initial appearance before a judicial officer, where he learns of the charges against him, constitutes the start of adversarial proceedings that triggers the attachment of the Sixth Amendment's right to counsel.

FACTS: Using erroneous information, Texas police arrested Rothgery (P) for unlawful possession of a firearm. The police brought him before a magistrate judge for an Article 15.17 hearing. At the hearing, the magistrate judge found probable cause existed and set bail at $5,000. The State (D) then jailed Rothgery (P) before he posted a security bond. Six months later, a grand jury formally indicted Rothgery (P) for the same charge. After his re-arrest, the State (D) jailed Rothgery (P) for three weeks until he was able to post bail. The State (D) then assigned him a lawyer. The lawyer proved to the State (D) that the charges were erroneous. The State (D) agreed and dismissed all charges. Rothgery (P) then brought this action against the State (D) under 42 U.S.C. 1983, alleging that the State's (D) unwritten policy of denying indigent defendants with counsel until a formal indictment is issued, well after initial arraignment, violated his Sixth Amendment right to counsel. The district court granted the State (D) summary judgment and the Fifth Circuit Court of Appeals affirmed. Rothgery (P) appealed to the United States Supreme Court.

ISSUE: Does a criminal defendant's initial appearance before a judicial officer, where he learns of the charges against him, constitute the start of adversarial proceedings that triggers the attachment of the Sixth Amendment's right to counsel?

HOLDING AND DECISION: (Souter, J.) Yes. A criminal defendant's initial appearance before a judicial officer, where he learns of the charges against him, constitutes the start of adversarial proceedings that triggers the attachment of the Sixth Amendment's right to counsel. The Court has previously held that the Sixth Amendment right to counsel attaches at the initiation of criminal proceedings, whether that initiation is in the form of an indictment, arraignment, preliminary hearing, or some other hearing wherein the defendant is formally charged. Typically, an arraignment is the initial appearance. The issue here is whether Texas's Article 15.17 hearing is an initial appearance. It clearly qualifies. At the hearing, the State (D) informed Rothgery (P) of the charges against him and set bail. Once attachment occurs, the state must appoint counsel during any critical stage of the post-attachment proceedings. The Court shall not consider at this time whether the six-month delay in appointment of counsel for Rothgery (P) specifically constituted a violation of his right to counsel. Reversed.

CONCURRENCE: (Roberts, C.J.) The Court is bound by multiple precedents which have found that the Sixth Amendment right attaches at the point of the initial hearing. Justice Alito, however, correctly points out in his concurrence the distinction between the time the right attaches and the circumstances when counsel must be provided to the defendant.

CONCURRENCE: (Alito, J.) The Court's opinion is correct that Rothgery's (P) right to counsel attached at the Article 15.17 hearing. However, there is a distinction between when the right to counsel attaches and the state's duty to supply counsel post-attachment. The moment of attachment is not the same as a criminal defendant's substantive entitlement to assistance of counsel. The state need only supply counsel at those pretrial and trial events that may prejudice the outcome of the defendant's prosecution. These are referred to as critical stages of the prosecution, such as a police lineup or pretrial interrogations and of course the trial itself.

DISSENT: (Thomas, J.) The commencement of a criminal prosecution referred to in the Sixth Amendment occurs when the state files formal criminal charges in court to try and punish the defendant. Rothgery's (P) appearance before the magistrate here did not commence a criminal prosecution. No formal charges were filed. The only document submitted at the time was an affidavit from a police officer. Our prior decisions have used the term "arraignment" as the usual time when the right to counsel attaches. However, there is a difference between an informal hearing before a magistrate after an arrest and a formal arraignment post-indictment where the defendant enters a plea. The latter proceeding should be when the right to counsel arises.

Continued on next page.

ANALYSIS

Justice Alito's concurrence is critical to an understanding of the Sixth Amendment's right to counsel. Eight of the nine judges agreed that the right attaches at the initial appearance, regardless of the form of that appearance. That was the sole question at issue here. It is a different analysis as to when the state must provide counsel to an indigent defendant throughout the prosecution.

Quicknotes

RIGHT TO COUNSEL Right conferred by the Sixth Amendment that the accused shall be provided effective legal assistance in a criminal proceeding.

SIXTH AMENDMENT Provides the right to a speedy and public trial by impartial jury, the right to be informed of the accusation, the right to confront witnesses, and the right to have the assistance of counsel in all criminal prosecutions.

Ross v. Moffitt

Forgery convict (D) v. Court (P)

417 U.S. 600 (1974)

NATURE OF CASE: Appeal from a conviction for forgery.

FACT SUMMARY: Ross (D) contended that he was entitled to appointed counsel to represent him in a petition for discretionary review by the state supreme court.

RULE OF LAW

There is no constitutional right to appointed counsel for discretionary appellate proceedings.

FACTS: Ross (D) was convicted of forgery in a North Carolina state court. He was represented at trial and in his appeal of right to the intermediate appellate court by a public defender. He was denied such representation in his discretionary appeal to the state supreme court. The United States Supreme Court granted review.

ISSUE: Is there a constitutional right to appointed counsel for discretionary appellate proceedings?

HOLDING AND DECISION: (Rehnquist, J.) No. There is no constitutional right to appointed counsel for discretionary appellate proceedings. At the trial stage, the state's responsibility is to ensure the defendant's rights are protected. The state has channeled resources toward convicting a defendant, thus in an adversarial arena it is only just that counsel be appointed. However, on appeal, the defendant initiates the process in order to overturn a lower court. The defendant is thus not in need of protection from state action. He is the aggressor. No constitutional right exists in this circumstance. Affirmed.

DISSENT: (Douglas, J.) The indigent defendant, whose liberty is at stake, is at a great disadvantage on appeal whether such is of right or discretionary. He is entitled to appointed counsel.

ANALYSIS

This case rejects the equal protection argument that wealthy defendants have a better chance in discretionary appeal than indigent defendants. Wealth is not a suspect classification and thus indigence does not necessarily entitle the defendant to increased access to appellate review.

Quicknotes

EQUAL PROTECTION Guarantee under the Fourteenth Amendment to the U.S. Constitution that the government must treat each person or class of persons the same as it treats other persons or classes of persons in like circumstances.

STRICT SCRUTINY Method by which courts determine the constitutionality of a law when a law affects a fundamental right; under the test, the legislature must have had a compelling interest to enact the law, and measures prescribed by the law must be the least restrictive means possible to accomplish its goal.

SUSPECT CLASSIFICATION A class of persons who have historically been subject to discriminatory treatment; statutes drawing a distinction between persons based on a suspect classification, i.e., race, nationality, or alienage, are subject to a strict scrutiny standard of review.

Ake v. Oklahoma

Indigent murderer claiming insanity (D) v. State (P)

470 U.S. 68 (1985)

NATURE OF CASE: Appeal from capital murder conviction and sentencing of indigent individual on grounds that the state's refusal to provide psychiatric assistance was a denial of due process in violation of the Fourteenth Amendment.

FACT SUMMARY: Ake (D), an indigent individual convicted of first-degree murder, who had asserted the insanity defense, but who was sentenced to death, contended that he was entitled under the Fourteenth Amendment's Due Process Clause to have the state provide him with the assistance of a psychiatrist at trial and at sentencing as to issues implicating his mental condition.

RULE OF LAW

An indigent criminal defendant who has made a preliminary showing that his or her sanity at the time of the offense is likely to be a significant factor at trial is entitled under the Fourteenth Amendment's Due Process Clause to have the state provide access to a psychiatrist's assistance on this issue at trial and sentencing.

FACTS: Ake (D), an indigent, was charged with first-degree murder. The trial judge found Ake's (D) behavior at arraignment so bizarre that the trial judge ordered him to be examined by a psychiatrist. The examining psychiatrist found Ake (D) to be incompetent to stand trial and suggested that he be committed, but six weeks later, after being committed to the state mental hospital, he was found to be competent on the condition that he continue to be sedated with an antipsychotic drug. The State (P) then resumed proceedings, and Ake's (D) attorney informed the court that he would raise an insanity defense and requested a psychiatric evaluation at state expense to determine petitioner's mental state at the time of the offense, claiming that petitioner was entitled to such an evaluation by the federal Constitution. This request was denied, and the jury found Ake (D) guilty on all counts. At the sentencing proceeding, the State (P) asked for the death penalty, relying on the examining psychiatrists' testimony to establish the likelihood of Ake's (D) future dangerous behavior. Ake (D) had no expert witness to rebut this testimony or to give evidence in mitigation of his punishment, and he was sentenced to death. The United States Supreme Court granted certiorari in the case.

ISSUE: Is an indigent criminal defendant who has made a preliminary showing that his or her sanity at the time of the offense is likely to be a significant factor at trial entitled under the Fourteenth Amendment's Due Process Clause to have the state provide access to a psychiatrist's assistance on this issue at trial and sentencing?

HOLDING AND DECISION: (Marshall, J.) Yes. An indigent criminal defendant who has made a preliminary showing that his or her sanity at the time of the offense is likely to be a significant factor at trial is entitled under the Fourteenth Amendment's Due Process Clause to have the state provide access to a psychiatrist's assistance on this issue at trial and sentencing. Due process requires that a state must provide indigent criminal defendants with a fair opportunity to present their defense fairly within the adversary system by providing them with the basic tools for an adequate defense or appeal when they cannot afford to pay for them. In those cases where a defendant is able to make an ex parte threshold showing to a trial court that his or her sanity is likely to be a significant factor in his or her defense, the need for the assistance of a psychiatrist is at its greatest because without such assistance, the risk of an inaccurate resolution of sanity issues is extremely high. With such assistance, the defendant is fairly able to present at least enough information to the jury, in a meaningful manner, as to permit it to make a sensible determination. In such a circumstance, where the potential accuracy of the jury's determination is so dramatically enhanced and where the interests of the individual and the state in an accurate proceeding are substantial, the state's monetary interest must yield, and it must pay for a competent psychiatrist to assist the defendant. Similarly, here Ake (D) was denied the means of presenting evidence to rebut the State's (P) evidence of his future dangerousness. The same interests implicated by a criminal trial regarding an indigent's mental condition are implicated in the context of a capital sentencing proceeding when the state presents psychiatric evidence of the defendant's future dangerousness. In sum, where the consequence of error is so great, the relevance of responsive psychiatric testimony so evident, and the burden on the state so slim, due process requires access to a psychiatric examination on relevant issues, to the testimony of the psychiatrist, and to assistance in preparation at the sentencing phase. [Reversed.]

ANALYSIS

Although the Court in *Ake* specified that before an indigent criminal defendant is entitled to a state-appointed

Continued on next page.

psychiatrist, the defendant must make a threshold showing that his or her sanity is likely to be a significant factor in his or her defense, the Court did not elucidate how that requirement was to be satisfied, nor did it set forth any standards for such a requirement. However, the Eleventh Circuit, in *Moore v. Kemp*, 809 F.2d 702 (11th Cir. 1987), interpreted the standard to require something more than a mere possibility of assistance from a psychiatrist and required the defendant to show that "there exists a reasonable probability both that an expert would be of assistance to the defense and that denial of expert assistance would result in a fundamentally unfair trial." This standard has been adopted by other federal circuits, as well as a majority of states.

Quicknotes

CAPITAL OFFENSE A crime in which the death penalty may be imposed.

DUE PROCESS The constitutional mandate requiring the courts to protect and enforce individuals' rights and liberties consistent with prevailing principles of fairness and justice and prohibiting the federal and state governments from such activities that deprive its citizens of life, liberty, or property interest.

EXPERT WITNESS A witness providing testimony at trial who is specially qualified regarding the particular subject matter involved.

FIRST-DEGREE MURDER The willful killing of a person with deliberation and premeditation; first-degree murder also encompasses those situations in which a person is killed within the perpetration of, or attempt to perpetrate, specified felonies.

INSANITY DEFENSE An affirmative defense to a criminal prosecution that the defendant suffered from a mental illness, thereby relieving the defendant of liability for his or her conduct.

Faretta v. California

Grand theft defendant (D) v. State (P)

422 U.S. 806 (1975)

NATURE OF CASE: Appeal from conviction for grand theft.

FACT SUMMARY: Faretta (D) was convicted following a trial court's refusal to allow him to represent himself.

RULE OF LAW

A criminal defendant has a Sixth Amendment right to conduct a pro se defense.

FACTS: Faretta (D) was charged with grand theft. Before trial, he indicated that he wished to conduct his own defense. Faretta (D) was a high school graduate and had once before represented himself. The trial court compelled him to allow an attorney to represent him, and he was convicted. Faretta's (D) appeals were rejected in the state courts. Faretta (D) appealed to the United States Supreme Court.

ISSUE: Does a criminal defendant have a Sixth Amendment right to conduct a pro se defense?

HOLDING AND DECISION: (Stewart, J.) Yes. A criminal defendant has a Sixth Amendment right to conduct a pro se defense. The protections afforded a defendant in the Sixth Amendment are personal to the defendant. The right to counsel is just that—a right. Rights may be waived. To thrust counsel upon an unwilling defendant would violate the language of the Amendment. So long as waiver of counsel is intelligently made, the state cannot force one upon a defendant. Reversed.

DISSENT: (Burger, C.J.) The Sixth Amendment guarantees a defendant a full defense; and allowing a defendant to waive the right to counsel violates this spirit.

DISSENT: (Blackmun, J.) The overriding interest in any criminal prosecution is that justice be done. Without counsel justice often will not be done to a defendant.

ANALYSIS

The rule here was later lessened somewhat. In *McKaskle v. Wiggins*, 465 U.S. 168 (1984), the Court held that a court could force a defendant to have counsel in a consultant role while conducting his defense. Obviously, where consultation ends and outright representation starts is not a distinction easily made.

Quicknotes

GRAND THEFT The illegal taking of another's property with the intent to deprive the owner thereof, the value of which is greater than the statutory amount.

PRO SE DEFENSE Representing oneself at trial rather than retaining a lawyer.

United States v. Gonzalez-Lopez

Federal government (P) v. Alleged drug distributor (D)

548 U.S. 140 (2006)

NATURE OF CASE: Appeal from vacated conviction for distribution of illegal drugs.

FACT SUMMARY: Gonzalez-Lopez (D) contended that the district court's erroneous denial of application for admission pro hac vice by Low, his counsel of choice, entitled him to a reversal of his conviction on drug charges.

RULE OF LAW

A trial court's erroneous deprivation of a criminal defendant's choice of counsel entitles him to reversal of his conviction.

FACTS: Gonzalez-Lopez (D) hired attorney Low, a California attorney, to represent him on a federal drug charge in federal court in Missouri. The district court denied Low's application for admission pro hac vice on the ground that he had violated a professional conduct rule in that jurisdiction and then, with one exception, prevented Gonzalez-Lopez (D) from meeting or consulting with Low throughout the trial. Instead, a local attorney represented Gonzalez-Lopez (D). The jury found Gonzalez-Lopez (D) guilty. The court of appeals reversed, holding that the district court erred in interpreting the disciplinary rule, that the court's refusal to admit Low therefore violated Gonzalez-Lopez's (D) Sixth Amendment right to paid counsel of his choosing, and that this violation was not subject to harmless error review. The Government (P) conceded that the district court had erroneously deprived Gonzalez-Lopez (D) of his counsel of choice. The United States Supreme Court granted certiorari.

ISSUE: Does a trial court's erroneous deprivation of a criminal defendant's choice of counsel entitle him to reversal of his conviction?

HOLDING AND DECISION: (Scalia, J.) Yes. A trial court's erroneous deprivation of a criminal defendant's choice of counsel entitles him to reversal of his conviction. Although the Government (P) conceded that the district court's error violated Gonzalez-Lopez's (D) Sixth Amendment right to counsel of choice, it nonetheless contends that the violation is not "complete" unless (1) the defendant can show that substitute counsel was ineffective to the extent that his performance was deficient and the defendant was prejudiced by it, or (2) the defendant can demonstrate that substitute counsel's performance, while not deficient, was not as good as what his counsel of choice would have provided, creating a "reasonable probability that. . .the result. . .would have been different." To support these propositions, the Government (P) emphasizes that the right to counsel is accorded to ensure that the accused receive a fair trial, and it asserts that a trial is not unfair unless a defendant has been prejudiced. The right to counsel of choice, however, does not require that a trial be fair, but that a particular guarantee of fairness be provided, namely, that the accused be defended by the counsel he believes to be best. The Due Process Clause requires that a trial be fair, but the elements of fairness can also be found in the Counsel Clause. The right provided in that Clause was violated here; no additional showing of prejudice is required to make the violation "complete." While prejudice is required for a showing of ineffective counsel, which is derived from the Sixth Amendment's purpose of ensuring a fair trial, choice of counsel does not derive from this purpose. Instead, it is a root constitutional principle, so that its violation does not require more than a showing that the defendant was deprived of his counsel of choice. This Sixth Amendment violation is also not subject to harmless-error analysis, as the court of appeals correctly held. The erroneous deprivation of the right to counsel of choice qualifies as structural error, "with consequences that are necessarily unquantifiable and indeterminate." Different attorneys will pursue different strategies with regard to myriad trial matters, and the choice of attorney will affect whether and on what terms the defendant cooperates with the prosecution, plea bargains, or decides to go to trial. It is impossible to know what different choices the rejected counsel would have made, and then to quantify the impact of those different choices on the outcome of the proceedings. To do so would require speculation. This inquiry is not comparable to that required to show that a counsel's deficient performance prejudiced a defendant. Notwithstanding these rulings, nothing in this opinion should be construed as casting any doubt, or qualifying in any way, the Court's previous holdings limiting the right to counsel of choice and recognizing trial courts' authority to establish criteria for admitting lawyers to argue before them. However broad a trial court's discretion may be, it is conceded here that the district court erred, and the ensuing choice of counsel violation is not subject to harmless-error review. Affirmed.

DISSENT: (Alito, J.) Instead of the per se rule that the majority adopts, defendants denied their first choice of counsel should be required to show that the error affected the quality of their representation. The majority errs in

Continued on next page.

concluding that the Sixth Amendment protects a defendant's choice of counsel; instead, it protects the right to have the assistance of that counsel. It follows, therefore, that if the quality of that assistance is not adversely affected, there is no constitutional violation. Such an interpretation is supported by the Sixth Amendment itself, which focuses on assistance of counsel, rather than on counsel's identity. Further, a defendant's right to counsel of choice has always been limited by various factors, as where the chosen counsel may not practice before the court hearing the case, or by conflict-of-interest rules. Under this understanding, a defendant would not have to show that the second-choice attorney was constitutionally ineffective but would be entitled to a new trial if he could show an identifiable difference in the quality of representation between the disqualified counsel and the attorney who represents the defendant at trial. Even if, however, the majority's rule is correct, it does not follow that it will always require reversal. Instead, reversal should occur only where fundamental unfairness has been shown—and such unfairness does not flow inexorably from the denial of first-choice counsel. The majority's focus on the trial error/structural defect dichotomy is misleading since the touchstone of structural error is fundamental unfairness. Thus, reversal should not be automatic where constitutional error does not necessarily result in such unfairness. Otherwise, the majority's per se rule gives the defendant a second bite at the apple even if second-choice counsel was "brilliant." Requiring some showing of prejudice or permitting harmless-error review would avoid such an anomalous result.

ANALYSIS

It should be kept in mind that the right to counsel of choice is not implicated where the defendant must have appointed counsel. In such situations, the court does not violate the defendant's choice of counsel right if it denies the appointment of a specifically requested attorney.

Quicknotes

DUE PROCESS CLAUSE Language in the Fifth and Fourteenth Amendments to the U.S. Constitution providing that no person shall be deprived of "life, liberty, or property, without due process of law."

HARMLESS ERROR An error taking place during trial that does not require the reviewing court to overturn or modify the trial court's judgment in that it did not affect the appellant's substantial rights or the disposition of the action.

PRO HAC VICE Applicable to a specific occasion; the use or application of a condition for the limited duration of a single situation.

CHAPTER 5

The Performance of Counsel

Quick Reference Rules of Law

PAGE

1. *United States v. Chronic.* The determination of whether a criminal defendant has received ineffective assistance of counsel must be made on the basis of specific attorney errors and shortcomings rather than on general standards applied inferentially to the circumstances surrounding a legal representation, where such circumstances do not justify a presumption of ineffectiveness. *18*

2. *Strickland v. Washington.* A defendant must, in order to show he was denied the effective assistance of counsel, establish that: (1) counsel's performance was deficient and (2) the deficient performance prejudiced the defense. *20*

3. *Harrington v. Richter.* Federal habeas relief may be granted when the earlier state court decision involved an unreasonable application of clearly established federal law. *21*

4. *Rompilla v. Beard.* Even when a capital defendant and the defendant's family members have suggested that no mitigating evidence is available, the defendant's lawyer is bound to make reasonable efforts to obtain and review material that the lawyer knows the prosecution will probably rely on as evidence of aggravation at the trial's sentencing phase, for the purpose of possibly rebutting the evidence of aggravation and possibly discovering evidence in mitigation. *23*

5. *Lafler v. Cooper.* When claiming ineffective assistance of counsel based on erroneous advice to reject a plea offer, a defendant must show there was a reasonable probability that the court would have accepted the plea agreement and that the conviction and sentence would have been less severe than those that were in fact imposed. *26*

6. *Weaver v. Massachusetts.* In the context of a public-trial violation during jury selection, where an error is neither preserved nor raised on direct review but is raised later via an ineffective-assistance-of-counsel claim, the defendant must demonstrate prejudice to secure a new trial. *28*

7. *Cuyler v. Sullivan.* (1) A state trial judge is under no duty to inquire into the propriety of multiple representation, absent objection. (2) The mere possibility of a conflict of interest does not create a Sixth Amendment violation. *31*

8. *Wheat v. United States.* A criminal defendant is not entitled to have counsel of his choice where his representation would create an inherent conflict of interest. *32*

9. *McCoy v. Louisiana.* The Sixth Amendment guarantees a defendant the right to choose the objective of his defense and to insist that his counsel refrain from admitting guilt, even when counsel's experienced-based view is that confessing guilt offers the defendant the best chance to avoid the death penalty. *33*

United States v. Cronic

Federal government (P) v. Individual convicted of mail fraud (D)

466 U.S. 648 (1984)

NATURE OF CASE: Appeal from ineffective assistance of counsel reversal of mail fraud conviction.

FACT SUMMARY: Cronic's (D) conviction for mail fraud was reversed on the presumption that Cronic (D) did not have effective assistance of counsel because the counsel that was appointed to him after his retained lawyer withdrew shortly before trial was young, practiced in real estate, had never participated in a jury trial, and had less than a month to prepare for trial in a case that took the Government (P) over four and one-half years and thousands of documents, to investigate. The Government (P) contended that it was error to base the reversal on a presumption, based on the surrounding circumstances, rather than an actual showing, of ineffective assistance of counsel.

RULE OF LAW

The determination of whether a criminal defendant has received ineffective assistance of counsel must be made on the basis of specific attorney errors and shortcomings rather than on general standards applied inferentially to the circumstances surrounding a legal representation, where such circumstances do not justify a presumption of ineffectiveness.

FACTS: Cronic (D) and two associates were indicted on mail fraud charges involving a "check kiting" scheme. When Cronic's (D) retained counsel withdrew shortly before the scheduled trial date, the federal district court appointed a young lawyer with a real estate practice who had never participated in a jury trial to represent Cronic (D), but allowed him only 25 days to prepare for trial, even though the Government (P) had taken over four and one-half years to investigate the case and had reviewed thousands of documents during that investigation. Cronic (D) was convicted, but the Tenth Circuit Court of Appeals reversed the conviction, because it inferred that Cronic's (D) right to the effective assistance of counsel under the Sixth Amendment had been violated. Finding it unnecessary to inquire into counsel's actual performance at trial, the court based its inference on the circumstances surrounding the representation, particularly (1) the time afforded for investigation and preparation, (2) the experience of counsel, (3) the gravity of the charge, (4) the complexity of possible defenses, and (5) the accessibility of witnesses to counsel. The Government (P) appealed the reversal, contending that it was error for the appellate court to have merely inferred ineffective assistance of counsel from the circumstances rather than requiring a showing that there had been an actual breakdown of the adversarial process. The United States Supreme Court granted certiorari.

ISSUE: Must the determination of whether a criminal defendant has received ineffective assistance of counsel be made on the basis of specific attorney errors and shortcomings rather than on general standards applied inferentially to the circumstances surrounding a legal representation, where such circumstances do not justify a presumption of ineffectiveness?

HOLDING AND DECISION: (Stevens, J.) Yes. The determination of whether a criminal defendant has received ineffective assistance of counsel must be made on the basis of specific attorney errors and shortcomings rather than on general standards applied inferentially to the circumstances surrounding a legal representation, where such circumstances do not justify a presumption of ineffectiveness. The right to the effective assistance of counsel is the right of the accused to require the prosecution's case to survive the crucible of meaningful adversarial testing. When a true adversarial criminal trial has been conducted—even if defense counsel may have made demonstrable errors—the kind of testing envisioned by the Sixth Amendment has occurred. If the process loses its character as a confrontation between adversaries, the constitutional guarantee is violated. Here, although the Tenth Circuit Court of Appeals purported to apply a standard of reasonable competence, it did not indicate that there had been an actual breakdown of the adversarial process during a trial. Instead, it concluded that the circumstances surrounding the representation of respondent mandated an inference that counsel was unable to discharge its duties. However, only when surrounding circumstances justify a presumption of ineffectiveness can a Sixth Amendment claim be sufficient without inquiry into counsel's actual performance at trial. The burden is on the accused to show that counsel's assistance was ineffective because it is presumed that counsel is competent to provide effective assistance. Here, the court of appeals did not find that Cronic (D) was denied the presence of counsel at a critical stage of the prosecution, nor did it find, based on the actual conduct of the trial, that there was a breakdown in the adversarial process that would justify a presumption that Cronic's (D) conviction was insufficiently reliable to satisfy the Constitution. The dispositive question, therefore, is whether the circumstances surrounding the representation—and in particular the

Continued on next page.

five criteria identified by the court of appeals—justified such a presumption. Although those factors are relevant to an evaluation of a lawyer's effectiveness in a particular case, they do not provide a basis for concluding that competent counsel was not able to provide Cronic (D) effective assistance, whether singly or taken together. Neither the period of time that the Government (P) spent investigating the case nor the number of documents involved is necessarily relevant to the question whether a competent lawyer could prepare to defend the case in 25 days. The Government's (P) task of finding and assembling admissible evidence that will carry its burden of proving guilt beyond a reasonable doubt is entirely different from the defendant's task in preparing to deny or rebut a criminal charge. Of course, in some cases the rebuttal may be equally burdensome and time consuming, but there is no necessary correlation between the two. Here, there were no grounds to dispute the factual record, only whether Cronic (D) had the request criminal intent. Therefore, the period of 25 days to consider the question whether those facts justified an inference of criminal intent was not so short that it even arguably justified a presumption that no lawyer could provide effective assistance of counsel. Similarly, the mere fact that counsel was young, practiced in real estate, and had never tried a jury case before does not raise a presumption of ineffective assistance. Every experienced criminal defense attorney once tried his or her first criminal case, and a lawyer's experience with real estate transactions might be more useful in preparing to try a criminal case involving financial transactions, as here, than would prior experience in handling, for example, armed robbery prosecutions. Thus, although the character of a particular lawyer's experience may shed light in an evaluation of the attorney's actual performance, it does not justify a presumption of ineffectiveness in the absence of such an evaluation. Finally, the three other criteria used by the court of appeals—the gravity of the charge, the complexity of the case, and the accessibility of witnesses—are all matters that may affect what a reasonably competent attorney could be expected to have done under the circumstances, but none identifies circumstances that in themselves make it unlikely that respondent received the effective assistance of counsel. For these reasons, the case must be remanded for a review of the record for an evaluation of whether counsel made any specific errors, or failed to function meaningfully as an adversary, that would, in fact, support an ineffective assistance claim. [Reversed and remanded.]

ANALYSIS

Circumstances that are so likely to prejudice the accused that ineffective assistance of counsel may be presumed include cases where there has been a complete denial of counsel at a critical stage of the trial. Similarly, if counsel entirely fails to subject the prosecution's case to meaningful adversarial testing, then there has been a denial of Sixth Amendment rights that makes the adversary process itself presumptively unreliable. Likewise, such circumstances may be present when, although counsel is available to assist the accused, the likelihood that any lawyer, even a fully competent one, could provide effective assistance is so small that a presumption of prejudice is appropriate without inquiry into the actual conduct of the trial. An example of such a circumstance occurred in *Powell v. Alabama*, 287 U.S. 45 (1932), where there had been a last-minute designation of counsel extremely close upon the trial, making it so unlikely that any lawyer could provide effective assistance that ineffectiveness was properly presumed without inquiry into actual performance at trial. However, as *Cronic* demonstrates, not every refusal to postpone a criminal trial will give rise to such a presumption.

Quicknotes

CRIMINAL INTENT An intent to commit a criminal offense plus an action taken toward commission of the crime.

INEFFECTIVE ASSISTANCE OF COUNSEL A claim brought by an accused in which it must be determined whether the attorney's rendering of representation was such that the ultimate disposition of the case may not be relied upon as fair.

Strickland v. Washington

Confessing convict (D) v. State (P)

466 U.S. 668 (1984)

NATURE OF CASE: Appeal from denial of writ of habeas corpus.

FACT SUMMARY: Strickland (D) contended that he was denied effective assistance of counsel when his attorney failed to present character evidence that might have reduced his sentence.

RULE OF LAW

A defendant must, in order to show he was denied the effective assistance of counsel, establish that: (1) counsel's performance was deficient and (2) the deficient performance prejudiced the defense.

FACTS: Strickland (D) confessed to several crimes including murder, torture, and kidnapping. After he was convicted, he stated at the sentencing hearing that he was sorry for and regretted his crimes. His appointed counsel chose not to introduce any character evidence and to allow the court to pass sentence based solely on Strickland's (D) statements. The attorney knew that the judge favored such repentance, and that introducing character evidence would subject Strickland (D) to cross-examination. Strickland (D) was sentenced to death. He petitioned the district court for a writ of habeas corpus, contending that he was denied effective assistance of counsel. The district court found that any errors made by counsel were not prejudicial and denied the writ. The court of appeals reversed, and the United States Supreme Court granted certiorari.

ISSUE: Must a defendant, in order to show he was denied the effective assistance of counsel, establish that: (1) counsel's performance was deficient and (2) the deficient performance prejudiced the defense?

HOLDING AND DECISION: (O'Connor, J.) Yes. In order to establish that he was denied effective assistance of counsel, a defendant must show: (1) counsel's performance was deficient and (2) the deficient performance prejudiced his defense. This requires that the defendant show that counsel's errors were so serious as to deprive him of a fair trial. In this case, Strickland's (D) counsel gave him reasonably effective assistance by pursuing a reasonable defense strategy. In addition, any further character evidence submitted at the hearing would have been cumulative and ineffective. Therefore, any errors committed were not prejudicial. As a result, Strickland (D) failed to establish that he was denied effective counsel. Reversed.

DISSENT: (Marshall, J.) The prejudice standard here established by the majority is so malleable that, in practice, it will either have no grip at all or will yield excessive variation in the manner in which the Sixth Amendment is interpreted and applied by different courts. To tell lawyers and lower courts that counsel for a criminal defendant must behave "reasonably" and must act like "a reasonably competent attorney" is to tell them almost nothing.

ANALYSIS

In this case, the Court stated that the "benchmark for judging any claim of ineffectiveness must be whether counsel's conduct so undermined the proper functioning of the adversarial process that the trial cannot be relied on as having produced a just result." From this point of departure, it broke the test down to two parts: performance and prejudice.

Quicknotes

CERTIORARI A discretionary writ issued by a superior court to an inferior court in order to review the lower court's decisions; the U.S. Supreme Court's writ ordering such review.

CHARACTER EVIDENCE Evidence of someone's moral standing in a community based on reputation.

WRIT OF HABEAS CORPUS A proceeding in which a defendant brings a writ to compel a judicial determination of whether he or she is lawfully being held in custody.

Harrington v. Richter

State (P) v. Convicted felon (D)

562 U.S. 86 (2011)

NATURE OF CASE: Review of petition for habeas corpus relief.

FACT SUMMARY: Richter (D) was convicted of several counts, including murder, but argued on appeal his criminal defense attorney provided ineffective assistance for failure to consult certain experts. Richter's (D) conviction was affirmed at each step. Richter (D) sought habeas corpus relief in the federal system after being denied relief in the state courts.

RULE OF LAW

Federal habeas relief may be granted when the earlier state court decision involved an unreasonable application of clearly established federal law.

FACTS: Joshua Johnson told police he was in bed and Patrick Klein was in the living room when two men broke into his house, shot him and Klein, and stole a gun safe, weapons, and cash. Evidence at the scene corroborated Johnson's account. Blood spatter and pools of blood were in the kitchen, the living room, and in the doorway to Johnson's bedroom. Investigators did not take samples from the bedroom doorway blood pool. When investigators searched Richter's (D) residence, they found a gun safe and ammunition that matched the caliber weapons used to shoot Johnson and Klein. Klein died of his injuries. Richter (P) initially denied involvement but then produced one of the weapons and told a version of events that differed from Johnson's. Richter (D) and Christian Branscombe were tried on several charges, including murder. In his opening statement, Richter's (D) defense attorney indicated Branscombe shot Johnson in self-defense and Klein was killed in the crossfire in the bedroom doorway. The prosecution had not intended to introduce forensic evidence related to the blood samples but changed course after the defense opening statement. Defense counsel elicited damaging testimony during cross-examination of the prosecution experts. Defense also called seven witnesses to testify to Richter's (D) version of events. The jury nonetheless convicted Richter (D) on all counts and the California Court of Appeals affirmed. The California Supreme Court denied review and Richter (D) did not file for review by the United States Supreme Court. As permitted under California law, Richter (D) later filed a direct petition with the California Supreme Court for habeas corpus relief. He argued ineffective assistance of counsel because defense counsel failed to consult experts in serology, pathology, or blood spatter patterns to confirm his account rather than Johnson's. The California Supreme Court denied Richter's (D) petition in a one-sentence summary order and Richter (D) filed in the United States District Court. The District Court denied his petition and a three-judge panel of the Court of Appeals for the Ninth Circuit affirmed. The Court of Appeals then granted rehearing en banc and reversed. The Court of Appeals considered preliminarily whether the federal habeas statute applied to Richter's (D) petition but determined the California decision was an unreasonable application of *Strickland v. Washington*, 466 U.S. 668 (1984), because Richter's (D) defense counsel was deficient for failing to consult blood experts. The United States Supreme Court granted review.

ISSUE: May federal habeas relief be granted when the earlier state court decision involved an incorrect application of clearly established federal law?

HOLDING AND DECISION: (Kennedy, J.) Yes. Federal habeas relief may be granted when the earlier state court decision involved an unreasonable application of clearly established federal law. When evaluating the application of the Strickland standard, the question is not whether the earlier state court incorrectly evaluated the merits of the claim but whether the state court unreasonably applied federal law. A state court determination on the merits precludes federal habeas relief so long as "fair-minded jurists could disagree" on the correctness of the state court decision. Here, the Court of Appeals disagreed with the state court's decision but determined that their disagreement equaled the state court's unreasonable application of *Strickland*. That is not correct. Federal habeas relief for persons in state custody is available pursuant to 28 U.S.C. § 2254, as amended by the Antiterrorism and Effective Death Penalty Act of 1996 (AEDPA). Richter (P) argued the summary order did not address the merits, but his arguments failed. Section 2254(d) applies to his petition; habeas relief is not available to him unless he demonstrates the earlier state court's decision was contrary to clearly established federal law, involved an unreasonable application of clearly established federal law, or was based on an unreasonable determination of facts in light of the record. The Ninth Circuit Court of Appeals relied on the second exception involving unreasonable application. The Court of Appeals determined the California Supreme Court's decision on Richter's (D) ineffective assistance of counsel claim unreasonably applied the holding in *Strickland*. The Court of Appeals reviewed the case de novo, found

Continued on next page.

a *Strickland* violation, and declared the state court's decision unreasonable. AEDPA requires more; the court must evaluate the basis for the state court's decision and then ask whether fair-minded jurists might disagree that the decision was inconsistent with clearly established federal law. The Court of Appeals ignored the second step. *Strickland* and § 2254(d) are "highly deferential" and the question is not whether counsel's actions were reasonable but whether there is any reasonable argument that counsel satisfied *Strickland* standards. There are reasons Richter's (D) counsel may have chosen not to consult blood experts. Perhaps counsel did not want to confirm his client's guilt or transform the case into a battle of the experts. Richter's (D) counsel made a mistake in thinking the prosecution would not present forensic evidence but the prosecution did not make that decision until trial began and that may not be so fundamental a mistake to call the trial's fairness into doubt. It was not unreasonable for the California Supreme Court to determine Richter's (D) evidence of prejudice fell short of showing a substantial likelihood of a different result but for counsel's actions. Further, there was sufficient evidence in support of guilt rather than Richter's (D) version. The California Supreme Court decision required more deference than it received. Reversed.

ANALYSIS

Federal habeas relief is not meant to be another opportunity to appeal the lower conviction but to correct serious deficiencies in a state court action. The Antiterrorism and Effective Death Penalty Act of 1996 (AEDPA) tightened review even further to ensure the thousands of habeas petitions filed each year do not result in an automatic federal relitigation of state court convictions. Even if the federal courts would have arrived at a different conclusion, the state court's decision is entitled to deference if it arises out of a legitimate basis.

Quicknotes

DE NOVO The review of a lower court decision by an appellate court, which is hearing the case as if it had not been previously heard and as if no judgment had been rendered.

HABEAS CORPUS A proceeding in which a defendant brings a writ to compel a judicial determination of whether he is lawfully being held in custody.

INEFFECTIVE ASSISTANCE OF COUNSEL A claim brought by an accused in which it must be determined whether the attorney's rendering of representation was such that the ultimate disposition of the case may not be relied upon as fair.

Rompilla v. Beard

Convicted murderer sentenced to death (P) v. State official (D)

545 U.S. 374 (2005)

NATURE OF CASE: Appeal from reversal of grant of habeas corpus petition challenging death sentence on the grounds of ineffective assistance of counsel.

FACT SUMMARY: Rompilla (P), who was sentenced to death, contended that he had ineffective assistance of counsel at his sentencing hearing, because his attorneys failed to review the materials in a prior conviction file that they knew the prosecution would use as evidence of aggravation in seeking the death penalty, and that, because of their failure to review those materials, they failed to discover evidence of mitigation. The State (D) countered that Rompilla's (P) lawyers' efforts to uncover mitigation from Rompilla (P), certain of his family members, and three mental health experts constituted effective assistance of counsel.

RULE OF LAW

Even when a capital defendant and the defendant's family members have suggested that no mitigating evidence is available, the defendant's lawyer is bound to make reasonable efforts to obtain and review material that the lawyer knows the prosecution will probably rely on as evidence of aggravation at the trial's sentencing phase, for the purpose of possibly rebutting the evidence of aggravation and possibly discovering evidence in mitigation.

FACTS: Rompilla (P) was convicted of murder and other crimes. At sentencing, in mitigation, five members of Rompilla's (P) family beseeched the jury for mercy, but he was sentenced to death. His new postconviction lawyers filed for state postconviction relief, claiming ineffective assistance by his trial counsel in failing to present significant mitigating evidence about Rompilla's (P) childhood, mental capacity and health, and alcoholism. Trial counsel knew that the State (D) would seek the death penalty by proving Rompilla (P) had a significant history of felony convictions indicating the use or threat of violence, an aggravator under state law. Trial counsel further knew that the State (D) would attempt to establish this history by proving Rompilla's (P) prior conviction for rape and assault and would emphasize his violent character by introducing a transcript of the rape victim's testimony given in that earlier trial. Apparently, trial counsel failed to obtain the prior conviction file or to look at the transcript until the eve of the sentencing hearing, notwithstanding that the file was readily available at the same courthouse at which Rompilla's (P) trial took place. Moreover, trial counsel did not examine any of the other materials in the prior conviction file once they had obtained it. Had trial counsel reviewed all the materials in the entire file, they would have discovered the mitigating evidence found by postconviction counsel. However, there was no indication as to the size of the file, which could have comprised several boxes of documents. In the same file with the transcript of the prior trial were the records of Rompilla's (P) imprisonment on the earlier conviction, which trial counsel testified to never having seen. The prison files pictured Rompilla's (P) childhood and mental health very differently from anything trial counsel had seen or heard. An evaluation by a corrections counselor in a 10-page document titled "Initial Transfer Petition," which was prepared to facilitate Rompilla's (P) transfer to a maximum-security prison, stated that Rompilla (P) was reared in a slum environment, came to the attention of juvenile authorities at a young age, quit school at 16, and started a series of incarcerations, often of an assaultive nature and commonly related to over-indulgence in alcoholic beverages. The same file disclosed test results that the defense's mental health experts would have viewed as pointing to schizophrenia and other disorders, and test scores showing a third-grade level of cognition after nine years of schooling. The state courts rejected the ineffective assistance of counsel claim, finding that trial counsel had sufficiently investigated the mitigation possibilities. Rompilla (P) then petitioned for habeas corpus relief in federal district court on grounds of inadequate representation. The federal District Court granted the petition. A majority of the Third Circuit Court of Appeals reversed, finding nothing unreasonable in the state's highest court's application of *Strickland v. Washington*, 466 U.S. 668 (1984), given trial counsel's efforts to uncover mitigation evidence from Rompilla (P), certain of his family members, and three mental health experts. A dissenting judge, however, concluded that trial counsels' failure to obtain relevant records on Rompilla's (P) background was owing to trial counsel's unreasonable reliance on family members and medical experts to tell them what records might be useful. The United States Supreme Court granted certiorari.

ISSUE: Even when a capital defendant and the defendant's family members have suggested that no mitigating evidence is available, is the defendant's lawyer bound to make reasonable efforts to obtain and review material that the lawyer knows the prosecution will probably rely on as evidence of aggravation at the trial's sentencing phase, for the purpose of possibly rebutting the evidence

Continued on next page.

of aggravation and possibly discovering evidence in mitigation?

HOLDING AND DECISION: (Souter, J.) Yes. Even when a capital defendant and the defendant's family members have suggested that no mitigating evidence is available, the defendant's lawyer is bound to make reasonable efforts to obtain and review material that the lawyer knows the prosecution will probably rely on as evidence of aggravation at the trial's sentencing phase, for the purpose of possibly rebutting the evidence of aggravation and possibly discovering evidence in mitigation. With every effort to view the facts as a defense lawyer would have done at the time, it is difficult to see how trial counsel could have failed to realize that without examining the readily available file they were seriously compromising their opportunity to respond to a case for aggravation. Without making reasonable efforts to review the file, trial counsel could have had no hope of knowing whether the prosecution was quoting selectively from the transcript, or whether there were circumstances extenuating the behavior described by the victim. The obligation to get the file was particularly pressing in Rompilla's (P) case, owing to the similarity of the violent prior offense to the crime charged and Rompilla's (P) sentencing strategy stressing residual doubt. Trial counsel's duty was not just common sense but was also described in the American Bar Association Standards for Criminal Justice, which have been held to be guides to determining what is reasonable. Contrary to the dissent's claim, requiring defense counsel to review a prior conviction file under circumstances such as those presented by the case at bar does not create a per se rule that requires defense counsel to do a complete review of the file on any prior conviction introduced. Instead, trial counsel fell short here because they failed to make reasonable efforts to review the prior conviction file, despite knowing that the prosecution intended to introduce Rompilla's (P) prior conviction not merely by entering a notice of conviction into evidence but by quoting damaging testimony of the rape victim in that case. The unreasonableness of attempting no more than they did was heightened by the easy availability of the file at the trial courthouse, and the great risk that testimony about a similar violent crime would hamstring trial counsel's chosen defense of residual doubt. It is owing to these circumstances that the state courts were objectively unreasonable in concluding that trial counsel could reasonably decline to make any effort to review the file. Other situations, where a defense lawyer is not charged with knowledge that the prosecutor intends to use a prior conviction in this way, might well warrant a different assessment. Because the state courts found trial counsel's representation adequate, they never reached the prejudice element of a *Strickland* claim, i.e., whether there is a reasonable probability that, but for counsel's unprofessional errors, the result would have been different. A de novo examination of this element shows that trial counsel's lapse was prejudicial. Had they looked at the prior conviction file, they would have found a range of mitigation leads that no other source had opened up. The imprisonment records contained in that file pictured Rompilla's (P) childhood and mental health very differently from anything they had seen or heard. The accumulated entries—e.g., that Rompilla (P) had a series of incarcerations, often related to alcohol; and test results that would have pointed the defense's mental health experts to schizophrenia and other disorders—would have destroyed the benign conception of Rompilla's (P) upbringing and mental capacity trial counsel had formed from talking to five family members and from the mental health experts' reports. With this information, trial counsel would have become skeptical of the impression given by the five family members and would unquestionably have gone further to build a mitigation case. The evidence they could have discovered would have added up to a mitigation case bearing no relation to the few naked pleas for mercy actually put before the jury. The undiscovered mitigating evidence, taken as a whole, might well have influenced the jury's appraisal of Rompilla's (P) culpability, and the likelihood of a different result had the evidence gone in is sufficient to undermine confidence in the outcome actually reached at sentencing. [Reversed; the State (D) must either retry the case on penalty or stipulate to a life sentence.]

DISSENT: (Kennedy, J.) The majority create a per se, rigid rule that requires defense counsel in every case to review the records of prior convictions used by the State (D) as aggravation evidence, contrary to the Court's precedents warning against the creation of such guidelines or checklists to evaluate attorney performance. The majority also fails to heed this admonition by treating the ABA Standards for Criminal Justice as binding statutory text. The majority's rule potentially imposes a heavy burden on defense counsel, as it seems to require defense counsel to review every document in a prior conviction file, and every page of every document in such a file, regardless of the prosecution's proposed use of the prior conviction. However, the majority ignores the reality that case files may comprise numerous boxes with numerous documents, so that a full review of even a single prior-conviction case file could be very time consuming, notwithstanding that many of the documents in a file are duplicative or irrelevant. The majority's decision also ignores the reality that states devote very limited resources to capital defenses, so that if defense attorneys dutifully comply with the Court's new rule, they will have to divert resources from other tasks. The net effect in many cases—instances where defense counsel reasonably can conclude that reviewing old case files is not an effective use of time—will be to diminish the

Continued on next page.

quality of representation, not improve it. Moreover, the majority disregards the sound strategic calculation supporting the decisions made by Rompilla's (P) attorneys, who were aware of Rompilla's (P) priors and the circumstances surrounding those convictions; the attorneys indicated that they had reviewed documents relating to the prior conviction. Based on this information, as well as their numerous conversations with Rompilla (P) and his family, trial counsel reasonably could conclude that reviewing the full prior-conviction case file was not the best allocation of resources. In any event, even accepting the majority's misguided analysis of the adequacy of trial counsel's representation, Rompilla (P) should not be entitled to habeas relief, because he cannot satisfy *Strickland's* prejudice requirement. The majority finds prejudice only through a remarkable leap that rests entirely on the serendipity of defense counsel somehow stumbling across "a range of mitigation leads" in the Initial Transfer Petition. However, nothing in the record indicates that Rompilla's (P) trial attorneys would have discovered the transfer petition, or the clues contained in it, if they had reviewed the file. The majority faults Rompilla's (P) attorneys for failing to learn what the State (D) knew about the crime, to discover any mitigating evidence the State (D) would downplay, and to anticipate the details of the aggravating evidence the State (D) would emphasize. The reality is that even if Rompilla's (P) attorneys had reviewed the case file with these purposes in mind, they almost surely would have attributed no significance to the transfer petition following only a cursory review. The majority claims that the transfer petition would have been discovered because it was in the same file with the transcript, but this characterization is misleading, and the conclusion the majority draws from it is accordingly fallacious. The record indicates only that the transfer petition was a part of the same case file, but Rompilla (P) provides no indication of the size of the file, which could have comprised several boxes of documents. For these reasons, Rompilla (P) cannot make out a case of ineffective assistance of counsel and should not be entitled to habeas relief.

ANALYSIS

In 1989, shortly after Rompilla's (P) trial, the American Bar Association (ABA) promulgated a set of guidelines specifically devoted to setting forth the obligations of defense counsel in death penalty cases—ABA Guidelines for the Appointment and Performance of Counsel in Death Penalty Cases (1989). The Guidelines applied the clear requirements for investigation set forth in the earlier ABA Standards for Criminal Justice to death penalty cases and imposed a forceful directive: "Counsel should make efforts to secure information in the possession of the prosecution or law enforcement authorities, including police reports." In 2003, the ABA amended those Guidelines, and set forth defense counsel's obligations in death penalty cases even more explicitly: "Later, and current, ABA Guidelines relating to death penalty defense are even more explicit: "Counsel must ... investigate prior convictions ... that could be used as aggravating circumstances or otherwise come into evidence. If a prior conviction is legally flawed, counsel should seek to have it set aside. Counsel may also find extenuating circumstances that can be offered to lessen the weight of a conviction." The Court's decision in *Rompilla* gives judicial effect and scope to the ABA Guidelines.

Quicknotes

AGGRAVATION Circumstances and facts adduced by the prosecution at a criminal defendant's sentencing designed to show that increasing the sentence is warranted.

HABEAS CORPUS A proceeding in which a defendant brings a writ to compel a judicial determination of whether he or she is lawfully being held in custody.

INEFFECTIVE ASSISTANCE OF COUNSEL A claim brought by an accused in which it must be determined whether the attorney's rendering of representation was such that the ultimate disposition of the case may not be relied upon as fair.

MITIGATING CIRCUMSTANCES OR EVIDENCE Circumstances that may be considered as extenuating or reducing the degree of moral culpability; although they do not constitute a justification or excuse for the offense in question, they are considered in fairness to a party.

MITIGATION Defense response at a criminal defendant's sentencing designed to reduce or lessen the effects of aggravating factors.

Lafler v. Cooper

State (P) v. Convicted individual seeking relief due to ineffective counsel (D)

566 U.S. 156 (2012)

NATURE OF CASE: State's (P) appeal from Sixth Circuit Court of Appeals' decision upholding plaintiff's post-conviction relief.

FACT SUMMARY: After the State (P) charged Anthony Cooper (D) with intent to murder and related charges, the State (P) offered a favorable plea agreement to Cooper (D). Cooper's (D) counsel advised him not to take it and proceed to trial. A jury convicted Cooper (D) and he received a sentence greater than that offered in the plea agreement.

RULE OF LAW

When claiming ineffective assistance of counsel based on erroneous advice to reject a plea offer, a defendant must show there was a reasonable probability that the court would have accepted the plea agreement and that the conviction and sentence would have been less severe than those that were in fact imposed.

FACTS: On March 25, 2003, Anthony Cooper (D) shot Kali Mundy multiple times, but Mundy survived. The State of Michigan (P) charged Cooper (D) with intent to murder, possession of a firearm by a felon, possession of a firearm in the commission of a felony, and for being a habitual offender. Prior to trial, the prosecution offered to dismiss two of the charges and to recommend a sentence of 51 to 85 months in prison in exchange for a guilty plea. Cooper's (D) counsel advised him to reject the offer because he felt the State (P) would be unable to prove intent at the trial. A jury convicted Cooper (D) of all charges. The trial court then sentenced him to 185 to 360 months in prison. Cooper (D) then filed a petition for habeas relief in federal district court. The basis for the petition was that the advice of Cooper's (D) counsel to reject the plea offer constituted ineffective assistance of counsel. The district court granted the writ and ordered the State (P) to impose a sentence consistent with the original plea offer. The Sixth Circuit Court of Appeals affirmed. The United States Supreme Court granted the State's (P) petition for review.

ISSUE: When claiming ineffective assistance of counsel based on erroneous advice to reject a plea offer, must a defendant show there was a reasonable probability that the court would have accepted the plea agreement and that the conviction and sentence would have been less severe than those that were in fact imposed?

HOLDING AND DECISION: (Kennedy, J.) Yes. When claiming ineffective assistance of counsel based on erroneous advice to reject a plea offer, a defendant must show there was a reasonable probability that the court would have accepted the plea agreement and that the conviction and sentence would have been less severe than those that were in fact imposed. In this appeal, all parties agree the advice of Cooper's (D) attorney constituted ineffective assistance of counsel. The issue here is whether that ineffective assistance prejudiced Cooper (D). The State (P) essentially argues that Cooper (D) and his counsel validly rejected the plea offer in the hopes the jury would return a verdict of not guilty. The State (P) argues that Cooper (D) went on to receive a full and fair trial and his subsequent conviction rendered the ineffective assistance of counsel moot. When examining ineffective assistance of counsel claims in the context of plea bargaining, the defendant must show a reasonable probability the court would have accepted the agreement. The defendant must also show the prosecutor would not have withdrawn the offer prior to trial. The State's (P) view of the protections of the Sixth Amendment is too narrow. The Sixth Amendment requires effective assistance of counsel at all critical stages of the criminal proceeding, especially including the plea-bargaining process. If a plea bargain is offered, the defendant has the right to effective counsel when considering whether to accept the offer. Cooper (D) has shown that he did not receive effective assistance of counsel and was prejudiced because he received a greater sentence than the sentence included in the plea offer. The task now is to determine the appropriate remedy. The Sixth Amendment requires that remedies should be tailored to the injuries suffered and should not infringe on competing interests. The remedy should not grant a windfall to the defendant. Essentially, the trial court has the discretion to review the matter and impose the sentence offered as part of the plea agreement or to retain the sentence imposed after the jury verdict. Courts should consider a defendant's willingness or unwillingness to accept responsibility for their actions. Here, the State (P) should reoffer the plea agreement to Cooper (D). The court can then exercise its discretion to accept the agreement, retain the sentence imposed post-conviction, or something between those two options. Reversed.

DISSENT: (Scalia, J.) Cooper (D) received a full and fair trial and received a sentence that the law prescribed. This Court has never held that a defendant is entitled to competent counsel when deciding to reject a plea offer. The Court effectively creates a new constitutional

Continued on next page.

right to effective plea bargaining. Moreover, the Sixth Amendment's focus is to ensure a fair trial. The inquiry is to determine if the ineffective assistance of counsel undermined the adversarial process and failed to produce a just result. Here, the error of Cooper's (D) attorney was unfortunate, but it was not of constitutional significance. The Court's remedy is also absurd. It is extraordinary that a trial judge has discretion to create a remedy where there is a constitutional violation and even more extraordinary that the judge has discretion to issue no remedy at all.

ANALYSIS

This decision expands on the companion case of *Missouri v. Frye*, 566 U.S. 134 (2012). In *Frye*, the United States Supreme Court held that defense counsel has the duty to communicate plea offers to their clients. The *Cooper* decision goes further and essentially constitutionalizes the entire plea-bargaining process. Both decisions are based on the reality that well over 90 percent of convictions in state and federal court are the result of plea bargains.

Quicknotes

INEFFECTIVE ASSISTANCE OF COUNSEL A claim brought by an accused in which it must be determined whether the attorney's rendering of representation was such that the ultimate disposition of the case may not be relied upon as fair.

PLEA BARGAIN An agreement between a prosecutor and a criminal defendant that is submitted to the court for approval; it generally involves the defendant's pleading guilty to a lesser charge or count in exchange for a more lenient sentence.

SIXTH AMENDMENT Provides the right to a speedy and public trial by impartial jury, the right to be informed of the accusation, the right to confront witnesses, and the right to have the assistance of counsel in all criminal prosecutions.

WRIT OF HABEAS CORPUS A proceeding in which a defendant brings a writ to compel a judicial determination of whether he or she is lawfully being held in custody.

Weaver v. Massachusetts

Convicted murderer (D) v. State (P)

137 S. Ct. 1899 (2017)

NATURE OF CASE: Appeal from murder conviction on grounds that the convict had been denied effective assistance of counsel because the convict's attorney had failed to object when the convict was denied the right to a public trial, including voir dire.

FACT SUMMARY: Weaver (D), who had been convicted of murder, contended five years later that he had been denied effective assistance of counsel because his defense counsel had failed to object to the courtroom's closure to the public during voir dire. The State (P) contended that Weaver (D) suffered no prejudice from such closure, and that, therefore, he could not prevail on his claim.

RULE OF LAW

In the context of a public-trial violation during jury selection, where an error is neither preserved nor raised on direct review but is raised later via an ineffective-assistance-of-counsel claim, the defendant must demonstrate prejudice to secure a new trial.

FACTS: When Weaver (D) was tried in a Massachusetts (P) trial court, the courtroom could not accommodate all the potential jurors. As a result, during jury selection, any member of the public who was not a potential juror was excluded, including Weaver's (D) mother and her minister. Defense counsel neither objected to the closure at trial nor raised the issue on direct review. Weaver (D) was convicted of murder and a related charge. Five years later, he filed a motion for a new trial in state court, arguing that his attorney had provided ineffective assistance by failing to object to the courtroom closure. The trial court ruled that he was not entitled to relief. The Massachusetts Supreme Judicial Court affirmed in relevant part. Although it recognized that the violation of the right to public trial was a structural error, it rejected Weaver's (D) ineffective assistance claim because he had not shown prejudice. The United States Supreme Court granted certiorari to resolve a split among the Circuits as to this issue.

ISSUE: In the context of a public-trial violation during jury selection, where an error is neither preserved nor raised on direct review but is raised later via an ineffective-assistance-of-counsel claim, must the defendant demonstrate prejudice to secure a new trial?

HOLDING AND DECISION: (Kennedy, J.) Yes. In the context of a public-trial violation during jury selection, where an error is neither preserved nor raised on direct review but is raised later via an ineffective-assistance-of-counsel claim, the defendant must demonstrate prejudice to secure a new trial. This case requires an examination of the proper application of the doctrines of structural error and ineffective assistance of counsel. They are intertwined, because the reasons an error is deemed structural may influence the proper standard used to evaluate an ineffective-assistance claim premised on the failure to object to that error. Generally, a constitutional error that does not contribute to the verdict obtained is deemed harmless, which means the defendant is not entitled to reversal. However, a structural error, which affects the framework within which the trial proceeds, defies harmless error analysis. Thus, when a structural error is objected to and then raised on direct review, the defendant is entitled to relief without any inquiry into harm. There are three broad rationales for finding an error to be structural. One is when the right at issue does not protect the defendant from erroneous conviction but instead protects some other interest—like the defendant's right to conduct his own defense—where harm is irrelevant to the basis underlying the right. Another is when the error's effects are simply too hard to measure—e.g., when a defendant is denied the right to select his or her own attorney—making it almost impossible for the government to show that the error was harmless beyond a reasonable doubt. Finally, some errors always result in fundamental unfairness, e.g., when an indigent defendant is denied an attorney. Moreover, it is important to keep in mind that an error can count as structural even if it does not lead to fundamental unfairness in every case. Although a public-trial violation counts as structural error, it does not always lead to fundamental unfairness. Though courtroom closure is to be avoided, there are some circumstances when it is justified. This suggests that not every public-trial violation results in fundamental unfairness. Indeed, a public-trial violation is structural because of the difficulty of assessing the effect of the error. The public-trial right also furthers interests other than protecting the defendant against unjust conviction, including the rights of the press and of the public at large. Thus, an unlawful closure could take place and yet the trial will still be fundamentally fair from the defendant's standpoint. The proper remedy for addressing the violation of the right to a public trial depends on when the objection was raised. If an objection is made at trial and the issue is raised on direct appeal, the defendant generally is entitled to "automatic reversal" regardless of the error's

Continued on next page.

actual effect on the outcome. If, however, the defendant does not preserve a structural error on direct review but raises it later in the context of an ineffective-assistance claim, the defendant generally bears the burden to show deficient performance and that the attorney's error prejudiced the defense. To demonstrate prejudice in most cases, the defendant must show a reasonable probability that the result of the proceeding would have been different but for attorney error. Here, for analytical purposes only, the Court will assume (without deciding the issue) that even if there is no showing of a reasonable probability of a different outcome, relief still must be granted if the defendant shows that attorney errors rendered the trial fundamentally unfair. Not every public-trial violation will lead to a fundamentally unfair trial. Also, the failure to object to that violation does not always deprive the defendant of a reasonable probability of a different outcome. Thus, a defendant raising a public-trial violation via an ineffective-assistance claim must show either a reasonable probability of a different outcome in the case or, as assumed here, that the particular violation was so serious as to render the trial fundamentally unfair. The reason for placing the burden on Weaver (D) here, however, derives from both the nature of the error and the difference between a public-trial violation preserved and then raised on direct review and a public-trial violation raised as an ineffective-assistance claim. When a defendant objects to a courtroom closure, the trial court can either order the courtroom opened or explain the reasons for keeping it closed, but when a defendant first raises the closure in an ineffective-assistance claim, the trial court has no chance to cure the violation. The costs and uncertainties of a new trial are also greater because more time will have elapsed in most cases. Additionally, the finality interest is more at risk. These differences justify a different standard for evaluating a structural error depending on whether it is raised on direct review or in an ineffective-assistance claim. Applying these principles here, Weaver (D) has not shown a reasonable probability of a different outcome but for counsel's failure to object, or that counsel's shortcomings led to a fundamentally unfair trial. Therefore, he is not entitled to a new trial. Although potential jurors might have behaved differently had his family or the public been present, Weaver (D) has offered no evidence suggesting a reasonable probability of a different outcome but for counsel's failure to object. He has also failed to demonstrate fundamental unfairness. His mother and her minister were indeed excluded during jury selection, but his trial was not conducted in secret or in a remote place; closure was limited to the jury voir dire; the courtroom remained open during the evidentiary phase of the trial; the closure decision apparently was made by court officers, not the judge; venire members who did not become jurors observed the proceedings; and the record of the proceedings indicates no basis for concern, other than the closure itself. There was no showing, furthermore, that the potential harms flowing from a courtroom closure came to pass in this case, e.g., misbehavior by the prosecutor, judge, or any other party. Thus, even though this case comes here on the assumption that the closure was a Sixth Amendment violation, the violation here did not pervade the whole trial or lead to basic unfairness. Affirmed.

CONCURRENCE: (Thomas, J.) Two of the Court's assumptions in this case are questionable. First, it is not clear that the Sixth Amendment right to a public trial extends to jury selection. Second, *Strickland v. Washington*, 466 U.S. 668 (1984), did not hold, as the Court assumes, that a defendant may establish prejudice by showing that counsel's errors "rendered the trial fundamentally unfair."

CONCURRENCE: (Alito, J.) *Strickland* requires that a defendant be prejudiced by defense counsel's deficient performance. The prejudice requirement—which is the one at issue in this case—arises from the very nature of the right to effective representation, so that counsel simply cannot be ineffective unless his mistakes have harmed the defense (or, at least, unless it is reasonably likely that they have). There are two ways of meeting the *Strickland* prejudice requirement. A defendant must demonstrate either that the error at issue was prejudicial or that it belongs to the narrow class of attorney errors that are tantamount to a denial of counsel, for which an individualized showing of prejudice is unnecessary. Weaver (D), however, attempts to escape this framework by stressing that the deprivation of the right to a public trial has been described as a "structural" error, but this is irrelevant under *Strickland*. The concept of "structural error" comes into play when it is established that an error occurred at the trial level, and it must be decided whether the error was harmless. The prejudice prong of *Strickland* is entirely different. It does not ask whether an error was harmless but whether there was an error at all, because unless counsel's deficient performance prejudiced the defense, there could not have been a Sixth Amendment violation in the first place. Weaver's theory conflicts with Strickland because it implies that an attorney's error can be prejudicial even if it had no effect, or only some conceivable effect, on the outcome of his trial, but that is precisely what *Strickland* rules out.

DISSENT: (Breyer, J.) A defendant who shows that his attorney's constitutionally deficient performance produced a structural error should not face the additional—and often insurmountable—*Strickland* hurdle of demonstrating that the error changed the outcome of the proceeding. The Court has recognized that structural errors' distinctive attributes make them defy analysis by harmless-error standards, which is why the Court has categorically

Continued on next page.

exempted structural errors from the case-by-case harmlessness review to which trial errors are subjected. Our precedent does not try to parse which structural errors are the truly egregious ones. It simply views all structural errors as intrinsically harmful and holds that any structural error warrants automatic reversal on direct appeal without regard to its effect on the outcome of a trial. The majority, however, departs from this approach, since it assumes that some structural errors, but not others, can warrant relief without a showing of actual prejudice. Even if some structural errors do not create fundamental unfairness, all structural errors nonetheless have features that make them defy analysis by harmless-error standards, which is why all structural errors—not just the "fundamental unfairness" ones—are exempt from harmlessness inquiry and warrant automatic reversal on direct review. Those same features mean that all structural errors defy an actual-prejudice analysis under *Strickland*. This problem is highlighted by this case with regard to public-trial violations, since, as the Court has observed, the benefits of a public trial are frequently intangible, difficult to prove, or a matter of chance. As a result, a requirement that prejudice be shown from the lack of a public trial would in most cases deprive the defendant of the public-trial guarantee, since it would be difficult to envisage a case in which any defendant would have evidence available of specific injury. To establish actual prejudice from an attorney's failure to object to a public-trial violation, a defendant would face the nearly impossible burden of establishing how the trial might have gone differently had it been open to the public. Thus, *Strickland* cannot be read as requiring defendants to prove what this Court has held cannot be proved. If courts do not presume prejudice when counsel's deficient performance leads to a structural error, then defendants may well be unable to obtain relief for incompetence that deprived them of basic protections without which a criminal trial cannot reliably serve its function as a vehicle for determination of guilt or innocence. This is precisely what *Strickland* sought to avoid.

ANALYSIS

Neither the reasoning nor the holding of this decision calls into question the Court's precedents determining that certain errors are deemed structural and require reversal because they cause fundamental unfairness, either to the defendant in the specific case or by the pervasive undermining of the systemic requirements of a fair and open judicial process. Those precedents include *Sullivan v. Louisiana*, 508 U.S. 275, 278–279 (1993) (failure to give a reasonable-doubt instruction); *Tumey v. Ohio*, 273 U.S. 510, 535 (1927) (biased judge); and *Vasquez v. Hillery*, 474 U.S. 254, 261-264 (1986) (exclusion of grand jurors on the basis of race). The Court, in addition, has granted automatic relief to defendants who prevailed on claims alleging race or gender discrimination in the selection of the petit jury, see *Batson v. Kentucky*, 476 U.S. 79, 100 (1986); *J.E.B. v. Alabama ex rel. T. B.*, 511 U.S. 127, 145–146, (1994), though the Court has yet to label those errors structural in express terms. The errors in those cases necessitated automatic reversal after they were preserved and then raised on direct appeal. It should also be noted that the decision in *Weaver* does not address whether the result should be any different if the errors were raised instead in an ineffective assistance claim on collateral review.

Quicknotes

INEFFECTIVE ASSISTANCE OF COUNSEL A claim brought by an accused in which it must be determined whether the attorney's rendering of representation was such that the ultimate disposition of the case may not be relied upon as fair.

PREJUDICIAL ERROR An error that affects the outcome of a trial, the judgment of which may be reversed, establishing a basis for a new trial.

Cuyler v. Sullivan

Warden (P) v. Convicted murderer (D)

446 U.S. 335 (1980)

NATURE OF CASE: Review of order granting federal habeas corpus relief.

FACT SUMMARY: Sullivan (D) contended that the trial court erred in not undertaking its own inquiry as to whether his attorney's multiple representation created a possibility of conflict.

RULE OF LAW

(1) A state trial judge is under no duty to inquire into the propriety of multiple representation, absent objection.
(2) The mere possibility of a conflict of interest does not create a Sixth Amendment violation.

FACTS: Sullivan (D) was indicted with two others for first-degree murder. Two private attorneys represented all three defendants, each tried separately. At no time during this trial did Sullivan (D) object that his counsel had a conflict of interest. After the trial, which resulted in a conviction, Sullivan (D) appealed, both directly and in a state collateral proceeding. The Pennsylvania Supreme Court upheld the conviction. Sullivan (D) then filed a federal habeas action. The district court denied the petition. The Third Circuit reversed, holding that the trial court should have inquired as to the possibility of a conflict. The United States Supreme Court granted review.

ISSUE:

(1) Is a state trial judge under a duty to inquire into the propriety of multiple representation?
(2) Does the possibility of a conflict of interest create a Sixth Amendment violation?

HOLDING AND DECISION: (Powell, J.)

(1) No. A state trial judge is under no duty to inquire into the propriety of multiple representation, absent objection.
(2) No. The mere possibility of a conflict of interest does not create a Sixth Amendment violation. Defense counsel has an ethical obligation to advise the court of conflicts, and such counsel is usually in a better position than the courts to see the conflict arise. Courts rely on counsel in this area, and nothing in this Court's precedent mandates anything to the contrary. With respect to whether the possibility of conflict gives rise to a Sixth Amendment violation, a Sixth Amendment violation occurs only when counsel is actually ineffective. The possibility of conflict, which exists in almost all cases of multiple representations, is not sufficient to give rise to a violation. The cause is vacated and remanded.

CONCURRENCE AND DISSENT: (Marshall, J.) The potential for conflict in multiple representation is so grave that a court should make its own inquiry as to possible conflicts. Furthermore, if an actual conflict of interest existed, that alone is sufficient evidence of a Sixth Amendment violation.

ANALYSIS

The level of the Court's analysis was that of the Constitution. It should be remembered that constitutional law only provides a minimum level of rights; statutes can go beyond this level. In the context of this case, Federal Rule of Criminal Procedure 44(c) provides for judicial inquiry as to conflicts in some limited instances.

Quicknotes

HABEAS CORPUS A proceeding in which a defendant brings a writ to compel a judicial determination of whether he or she is lawfully being held in custody.

SIXTH AMENDMENT Provides the right to a speedy and public trial by impartial jury, the right to be informed of the accusation, the right to confront witnesses, and the right to have the assistance of counsel in all criminal prosecutions.

Wheat v. United States

Drug conspirator (D) v. Federal government (P)

486 U.S. 153 (1988)

NATURE OF CASE: Appeal from conviction for conspiracy.

FACT SUMMARY: Wheat (D) contended he was deprived of his right to counsel when the district court disqualified his attorney of choice for conflict of interest.

RULE OF LAW

A criminal defendant is not entitled to have counsel of his choice where his representation would create an inherent conflict of interest.

FACTS: Wheat (D) was arrested along with Gomez-Barajas and Bravo on drug conspiracy charges. Iredale, an attorney, represented both Gomez-Barajas and Bravo. Bravo pled guilty, and Gomez-Barajas was acquitted. Gomez-Barajas was scheduled to be tried separately on the other charge; however, he offered to plead guilty pursuant to a plea bargain. After this agreement was made, but before it was accepted by the court, Wheat (D) sought to have Iredale represent him. The Government (P) moved to disqualify Iredale on the basis that such representation would require the cross-examination of Gomez-Barajas and Bravo and thus presented a conflict of interest. The court denied the request for Iredale to represent Wheat (D), rejecting Wheat's (D) contention that the denial violated his constitutional right to counsel. Wheat (D) was convicted and appealed. The court of appeals affirmed, and the United States Supreme Court granted a hearing.

ISSUE: Is a criminal defendant entitled to have counsel of his own choice where his representation would create an inherent conflict of interest?

HOLDING AND DECISION: (Rehnquist, C.J.) No. A criminal defendant is not entitled to have counsel of his choice where his representation creates an inherent conflict of interest. The right to counsel does not always include the right to counsel of choice. In this case, representation of all three co-conspirators would incurably compromise counsel's ability to represent all his clients. As a result, the representation was properly denied. Affirmed.

DISSENT: (Marshall, J.) A constitutional right to counsel of choice exists and is fully applicable in this case. The right to control the defense rests solely with the defendant. Thus, such right overcomes any potential conflict of interest.

DISSENT: (Stevens, J.) The majority here gives inadequate weight to the informed and voluntary character of the clients' waiver of their right to conflict-free representation. Specifically, the majority virtually ignores the fact that the additional counsel representing petitioner had provided him with sound advice concerning the wisdom of a waiver and would have remained available during the trial to assist in the defense.

ANALYSIS

In general, counsel may represent conflicting interests after full disclosure and a written waiver. Some cases, such as this one, present such a pronounced conflict that it cannot be waived. It is felt that while the right to counsel of choice is upheld, the right to effective counsel is sacrificed.

Quicknotes

CONFLICT OF INTEREST Ethical problems that arise, or may be anticipated to arise, between an attorney and his or her client if the interests of the attorney, another client, or a third-party conflict with those of the present client.

CROSS EXAMINATION The interrogation of a witness by an adverse party either to further inquire as to the subject matter of the direct examination or to call into question the witness's credibility.

McCoy v. Louisiana

Convicted murderer (D) v. State (P)

138 S. Ct. 1500 (2018)

NATURE OF CASE: Appeal from affirmance of denial of new trial in first-degree murder case, on grounds that trial court violated defendant's constitutional rights by permitting counsel to concede defendant's guilt over defendant's unambiguous objections.

FACT SUMMARY: Robert McCoy (D), who had received three death verdicts in a first-degree murder case, contended that the trial court violated his constitutional rights by permitting his attorney, over McCoy's (D) strenuous and unambiguous objections, to concede McCoy's (D) guilt in pursuing a mental-illness defense.

RULE OF LAW

The Sixth Amendment guarantees a defendant the right to choose the objective of his defense and to insist that his counsel refrain from admitting guilt, even when counsel's experienced-based view is that confessing guilt offers the defendant the best chance to avoid the death penalty.

FACTS: Robert McCoy (D) was charged with murdering his estranged wife's mother, stepfather, and son. McCoy (D) pleaded not guilty to first-degree murder, insisting that he was out of the state at the time of the killings and that corrupt police killed the victims when a drug deal went wrong. Although he vociferously insisted on his innocence and adamantly objected to any admission of guilt, the trial court permitted his counsel, Larry English, to tell the jury, during the trial's guilt phase, McCoy (D) "committed [the] three murders." English's strategy was to concede that McCoy (D) committed the murders but argue that McCoy's (D) mental state prevented him from forming the specific intent necessary for a first-degree murder conviction. Over McCoy's (D) repeated objection, English told the jury McCoy (D) was the killer. McCoy (D) testified in his own defense, maintaining his innocence, and pressing an alibi difficult to fathom. The jury found him guilty of all three first-degree murder counts. At the penalty phase, English again conceded McCoy's (D) guilt, but urged mercy in view of McCoy's (D) mental and emotional issues. The jury returned three death verdicts. Represented by new counsel, McCoy (D) unsuccessfully moved for a new trial. The Louisiana Supreme Court affirmed the trial court's ruling that English had authority to concede guilt, despite McCoy's (D) opposition. The United States Supreme Court granted certiorari to resolve a division of opinion among state courts of last resort on the question whether it is unconstitutional to allow defense counsel to concede guilt over the defendant's intransigent and unambiguous objection.

ISSUE: Does the Sixth Amendment guarantee a defendant the right to choose the objective of his defense and to insist that his counsel refrain from admitting guilt, even when counsel's experienced-based view is that confessing guilt offers the defendant the best chance to avoid the death penalty?

HOLDING AND DECISION: (Ginsburg, J.) Yes. The Sixth Amendment guarantees a defendant the right to choose the objective of his defense and to insist that his counsel refrain from admitting guilt, even when counsel's experienced-based view is that confessing guilt offers the defendant the best chance to avoid the death penalty. The Sixth Amendment guarantees to each criminal defendant "the Assistance of Counsel for his defence." The defendant does not surrender control entirely to counsel, since counsel is still the client's assistant. The lawyer's province is trial management, but some decisions are reserved for the client—including whether to plead guilty, waive the right to a jury trial, testify in one's own behalf, and forgo an appeal. Autonomy to decide that the objective of the defense is to assert innocence belongs in this reserved-for-the-client category. Refusing to plead guilty in the face of overwhelming evidence against her, rejecting the assistance of counsel, and insisting on maintaining her innocence at the guilt phase of a capital trial are not strategic choices; they are decisions about what the defendant's objectives in fact are. Counsel may reasonably assess a concession of guilt as best suited to avoiding the death penalty, as English did here. However, the client may not share that objective and may wish to avoid, above all else, the opprobrium attending admission that he killed family members, or he may hold life in prison not worth living and prefer to risk death for any hope, however small, of exoneration. Thus, when a client makes it clear that the objective of "his defence" is to maintain innocence of the charged criminal acts and pursue an acquittal, his lawyer must abide by that objective and may not override it by conceding guilt. If a client declines to participate in his defense, then an attorney may permissibly guide the defense pursuant to the strategy she believes to be in the defendant's best interest. Presented with express statements of the client's will to maintain innocence, as in the case at bar, however, counsel may not steer the ship the other way. Here, the Louisiana Supreme Court concluded that English's refusal to maintain McCoy's (D) innocence was necessitated by a Louisiana Rule of Professional Conduct that prohibits counsel from

Continued on next page.

suborning perjury. However, there was no avowed perjury involved in this case. English harbored no doubt that McCoy (D) believed what he was saying; English simply disbelieved that account in view of the prosecution's evidence. Louisiana's (P) ethical rules might have stopped English from presenting McCoy's (D) alibi evidence if English knew perjury was involved, but Louisiana (P) has identified no ethical rule requiring English to admit McCoy's (D) guilt over McCoy's (D) objection. The majority of state courts of last resort to consider this issue have held, unlike Louisiana (P), that counsel may not admit her client's guilt of a charged crime over the client's intransigent objection to that admission, where the disagreement between client and counsel is not over strategy, but over the fundamental objective of the defendant's representation. Moreover, ineffective-assistance-of-counsel jurisprudence does not apply here, where the client's autonomy, not counsel's competence, is in issue. To gain redress for attorney error, a defendant ordinarily must show prejudice, but here, the violation of McCoy's (D) protected autonomy right was complete when the court allowed counsel to usurp control of an issue within McCoy's (D) sole prerogative. Violation of a defendant's Sixth Amendment-secured autonomy has been ranked "structural" error; when present, such an error is not subject to harmless-error review. An error is structural if it is not designed to protect defendants from erroneous conviction, but instead protects some other interest, such as the fundamental legal principle that a defendant must be allowed to make his own choices about the proper way to protect his own liberty. Counsel's admission of a client's guilt over the client's express objection is error structural in kind because it blocks the defendant's right to make a fundamental choice about his own defense. Accordingly, McCoy (D) must be accorded a new trial without any need first to show prejudice. Reversed.

DISSENT: (Alito, J.) Contrary to the majority's statement of the facts, English did not concede that McCoy (D) was guilty of first-degree murder but conceded only one element of that crime—that McCoy (D) killed three victims. To the contrary, English argued that McCoy (D) was not guilty of first-degree murder because he lacked the intent (the mens rea) required for the offense. Also, the evidence against McCoy (D) was overwhelming, and McCoy (D) had been found competent to stand trial. Even assuming, arguendo, that the majority is correct in holding that English would not have violated state ethics rules, since no perjury was involved, had English abided by McCoy's (D) wishes the result would have been disastrous for McCoy (D). That approach stood no chance of winning an acquittal and would have severely damaged English's credibility in the eyes of the jury, thus undermining his ability to argue effectively against the imposition of a death sentence at the penalty phase of the trial. According to McCoy's (D) new counsel, it would have been constitutional for English to make out a case that McCoy (D) lacked the requisite intent for first-degree murder, without admitting—or even mentioning—that McCoy (D) had killed the victims. Such an approach, however, is negligibly different from one that concedes the killings. If English had conspicuously refrained from endorsing petitioner's story and had based his defense solely on McCoy's (D) dubious mental condition, the jury would surely have gotten the message that English was essentially conceding that McCoy (D) killed the victims. Moreover, the constitutional right that the majority has articulated—a criminal defendant's right to insist that his attorney contest his guilt with respect to all charged offenses—will rarely be implicated outside of capital cases, in which the jury must decide both guilt and punishment. Admitting guilt of all charged offenses in other types of cases will achieve nothing, and it is hard to imagine a situation in which a competent attorney might take that approach. So, the right that the majority has discovered is effectively confined to capital cases. Additionally, few rational defendants facing a possible death sentence are likely to insist on contesting guilt where there is no real chance of acquittal and where admitting guilt may improve the chances of avoiding execution. Further, where a capital defendant and his retained attorney cannot agree on a basic trial strategy, the attorney and client will generally part ways unless, as in this case, the court is not apprised until the eve of trial. Finally, if counsel is appointed, and unreasonably insists on admitting guilt over the defendant's objection, a capable trial judge will almost certainly grant a timely request to appoint substitute counsel. Even if all these conditions are met, the right that the majority identifies will not come into play unless the defendant expressly protests counsel's strategy of admitting guilt; where the defendant is advised of the strategy and says nothing, or is equivocal, the right is deemed to have been waived. For all these reasons, the right unearthed by the majority is likely to appear only rarely. Nevertheless, the related question of a defendant's rights in the face of counsel's unilateral decision to concede an element of the offense charged may arise more frequently and should be addressed. Some criminal offenses contain elements that the prosecution can easily prove beyond any shadow of a doubt. If a defendant insists on contesting those elements, must counsel go along? Does the same rule apply to all elements? If there are elements that may not be admitted over the defendant's objection, must counsel go further and actually contest those elements? Or is it permissible if counsel refrains from expressly conceding those elements but essentially admits them? What about conceding that a defendant is guilty, not of the offense charged, but of a lesser included offense? That is what English did in this case. Is admitting guilt of a lesser included offense over the defendant's objection always unconstitutional? These

Continued on next page.

are not easy questions, and the fact that they have not come up in this Court for more than two centuries suggests that they will arise infrequently in the future. In any event, given the situation in which English found himself when trial commenced, the Court should have held that he did not violate any fundamental right by expressly acknowledging that McCoy (D) killed the victims. Lastly, the majority summarily concludes that the violation of McCoy's (D) constitutional right is a structural error. However, the Louisiana Supreme Court did not address or decide this question—and neither should this Court, which is a court of review, not of first view.

ANALYSIS

This is the latest of the Court's opinions on the type of decision that is within the control of a criminal defendant or counsel when the defendant relinquishes the right to self-representation and accepts counsel's assistance. In *Jones v. Barnes*, 463 U.S. 745 (1983), for example, the Court held that defense counsel assigned to prosecute an appeal from a criminal conviction does not have a constitutional duty to raise every nonfrivolous issue requested by the defendant. Although the accused has the ultimate authority to make certain fundamental decisions regarding his case, including the decision whether to take an appeal, an indigent defendant has no constitutional right to compel appointed counsel to press nonfrivolous points requested by the client if counsel, as a matter of professional judgment, decides not to present those points.

Quicknotes

INTENT The state of mind that exists when one's purpose is to commit a criminal act.

MENS REA Criminal intent.

SIXTH AMENDMENT Provides the right to a speedy and public trial by impartial jury, the right to be informed of the accusation, the right to confront witnesses, and the right to have the assistance of counsel in all criminal prosecutions.

CHAPTER 6

Searches and Seizures

Quick Reference Rules of Law

PAGE

1. *Entick v. Carrington.* The government may not search a person's home and seize property in the absence of legal authority to do so. 38

2. *Mapp v. Ohio.* Evidence obtained in an unlawful search and seizure may not be used as evidence in a state trial of the accused. 40

3. *Katz v. United States.* The attachment of a listening device to the outside of a public telephone booth is a search and seizure within the meaning of the Fourth Amendment. 42

4. *United States v. Dunn.* For Fourth Amendment purposes, the area surrounding a barn that is 50 yards away from the fence surrounding a house is not within the house's curtilage. 44

5. *California v. Greenwood.* Garbage left in a public space for collection may be searched without a warrant. 46

6. *California v. Ciraolo.* A warrantless naked-eye aerial observation of a fenced-in backyard from 1,000 feet does not violate the Fourth Amendment. 47

7. *Kyllo v. United States.* Where the government uses a device that is not in general public use to explore details of the home that would previously have been unknowable without physical intrusion, the surveillance is a "search" and is presumptively unreasonable without a warrant. 49

8. *Smith v. Maryland.* The warrantless installation and use of a pen register to record numbers dialed from an individual's home telephone does not violate the individual's legitimate expectations of privacy. 50

9. *Carpenter v. United States.* An individual has a legitimate expectation of privacy in the record of his or her physical movements as captured through cell-site location information (CSLI), so that the government must generally obtain a search warrant supported by probable cause before acquiring CSLI. 51

10. *United States v. Jones.* The government's installation of a Global-Positioning-System (GPS) device on an individual's vehicle and the government's use of the device to track the location of that vehicle constitute a search under the Fourth Amendment. 54

11. *Florida v. Jardines.* The curtilage is part of a private home for Fourth Amendment purposes, and it is impermissible to enter the curtilage with a trained police dog for search purposes without express or implied permission from the homeowner. 55

12. *Florida v. Bostick.* Where the police conduct a suspicionless sweep of a bus, and ask passengers for consent to search their luggage, while informing the passengers that they are free to decline such request, the appropriate test for determining whether contraband discovered pursuant to such a sweep has been seized in violation of the Fourth Amendment is whether, taking into account all of the circumstances surrounding the encounter, a reasonable passenger would feel free to decline the officers' requests or otherwise terminate the encounter. 57

13. *Torres v. Madrid.* The application of physical force by a government agent to the body of a person with the intent to restrain is a seizure for Fourth Amendment purposes even if the person does not submit and is not subdued. 59

Entick v. Carrington

Homeowner suspected of seditious libel [P] v. State [D]

19 Howell's State Trials 1029 (1765)

NATURE OF CASE: Action in trespass challenging the search and seizure of property pursuant to a warrant for seditious libel as unlawful.

FACT SUMMARY: Entick (P), who had written "The Monitor," a pamphlet critical of King George III, contended that a search and seizure of his residence and property pursuant to a warrant issued by Lord Halifax, the King's Secretary of State, for seditious libel was unlawful, and Entick (P) sued those who conducted the search and seizure, including Carrington (D), for trespass.

RULE OF LAW
The government may not search a person's home and seize property in the absence of legal authority to do so.

FACTS: Entick (P) authored a pamphlet, "The Monitor," in which he strongly criticized King George III. Lord Halifax, the King's Secretary of State, issued a warrant to Carrington (D) and three other law enforcement officials known as "messengers" (D), to search and seize Entick's (P) belongings to be brought before Lord Halifax so he could examine them for the commission of seditious libel. The messengers (D) broke into Entick's (P) home with force and arms, and, over the course of four hours, they broke open locks and doors, boxes, chests, and drawers, and searched all of the rooms before taking away 100 charts and 100 pamphlets, causing £2,000 of damage. Entick (P) sued the messengers (D) for trespass. The messengers (D) defended by asserting they had acted lawfully pursuant to Lord Halifax's warrant, in the King's name, so that they could not be liable for trespass.

ISSUE: May the government search a person's home and seize their property in the absence of legal authority to do so?

HOLDING AND DECISION: [Judge not identified in casebook extract.] No. The government may not search a person's home and seize their property in the absence of legal authority to do so. The power that the Secretary of State claims for himself is not supported by any legal precedent or any statute or legal principle, and no other magistrate has claimed such a power, other than the lord chief justice of the court of King's Bench. The search and seizure here are made before a competent court has determined that the suspect whose property is invaded has committed the crime of which he is accused, and before there has been a conviction. Unless limited by a public law passed for the common good, people have the unabridged right to be secure in their property: "The great end, for which men entered into society, was to secure their property. That right is preserved sacred and incommunicable in all instances, where it has not been taken away or abridged by some public law for the good of the whole." In England, every invasion of property, no matter how small, is a trespass unless it is justified by positive law, and whether an asserted justification exists at law is a matter to be decided by a judge, after reviewing written statutes and case-law precedents of the common law. If, however, no justification can be found, there has been a trespass, and judgment must be rendered for the plaintiff. Accordingly, the defendants have the burden of showing that the search and seizure they engaged in was justified by law; otherwise, their actions comprise a trespass. Papers are a person's private property, and where they are seized and transported as part of a trespass, their private nature will give rise to greater damages for the transgression. There is no written law that empowers a magistrate to search for, and to remove, private property in the manner done here. Therefore, such a practice cannot be said to be legal, especially since such a practice would subvert "all the comforts of society." It stretches incredulity to assert that the government all along has had the right to search, seize, and carry away private property such as a person's private papers upon a first warrant, before any court has determined criminality, but that right has never been set down in a book of law. "The strongest evidence before a trial, being only ex parte, is but suspicion; it is not proof. Weak evidence is a ground of suspicion, though in a lower degree; and if suspicion at large should be a ground of search, especially in the case of libels, whose house would be safe?" For these reasons, the warrant is illegal and void.

ANALYSIS

Entick v. Carrington, written by Lord Camden, the Chief Justice of the Common Pleas, is considered a leading, landmark English civil liberties and constitutional case. It established that the executive's and the state's powers extend only as far as expressly permitted by public law, and that law enforcement may act only within the law. It also established the corollary principle that individuals may do anything except that which is forbidden by law. Lord Camden's judgment in Entick is credited with greatly influencing the enactment of the Fourth Amendment. In *Boyd v. United States*, 116 U.S. 616 (1886), the Supreme Court said of *Entick*: "The

Continued on next page.

principles laid down in this opinion affect the very essence of constitutional liberty and security. . . . It is not the breaking of [a man's] doors and the rummaging of his drawers that constitutes the essence of the offense, but it is the invasion of his indefeasible right of personal security, personal liberty, and private property, where that right has never been forfeited by his conviction of some public offense—it is the invasion of this sacred right which underlies and constitutes the essence of Lord Camden's judgment." The Court in *Boyd* also observed that it had no doubt that when the Fourth and Fifth Amendments were written and adopted, Lord Camden's language was relied on as expressing the true doctrine on the subject of searches and seizures and as furnishing the true criteria of the reasonable and unreasonable character of such seizures.

Quicknotes

SEARCH AND SEIZURE An inspection conducted in order to obtain evidence to be utilized for the prosecution of a crime and the subsequent taking of such evidence.

SEDITIOUS LIBEL Libel committed with an intent to incite people to overthrow the government by unlawful or violent means.

TRESPASS Unlawful interference with, or damage to, the real or personal property of another.

Mapp v. Ohio

Homeowner (D) v. State (P)

367 U.S. 643 (1961)

NATURE OF CASE: Certiorari from conviction of possession of lewd and lascivious materials.

FACT SUMMARY: Evidence obtained when officers broke into and conducted an unlawful search of Miss Mapp's (D) home was used for her conviction by an Ohio state court of possession of lewd and lascivious materials.

RULE OF LAW

Evidence obtained in an unlawful search and seizure may not be used as evidence in a state trial of the accused.

FACTS: On May 23, 1957, three Cleveland police officers arrived at Miss Mapp's (D) home pursuant to information that a person wanted for questioning in connection with a bombing and a large amount of "policy paraphernalia" could be found there. When Miss Mapp (D), after telephoning her attorney, refused to allow the officers in without a search warrant, they waited for more officers and then forcibly broke into the house. The officers then proceeded to conduct a warrantless search of Miss Mapp's (D) entire house. At her subsequent trial, evidence seized from this search was used to convict her of the possession of lewd and lascivious books, pictures, and photographs. The Supreme Court of Ohio found that her conviction was valid, even though it was based upon unlawfully seized evidence. Thereupon, Miss Mapp (D) was granted certiorari by the United States Supreme Court.

ISSUE: Can evidence obtained in an unlawful search and seizure be used as evidence in a state trial of the accused?

HOLDING AND DECISION: (Clark, J.) No. Evidence obtained in an unlawful search and seizure may not be uased as evidence in a state trial of the accused. The Fourth Amendment is incorporated in the Fourteenth Amendment Due Process Clause and requires that state courts exclude evidence obtained by unlawful searches and seizures. The Fourth Amendment right to be free from unreasonable searches and seizures was first extended to the states under the Fourteenth Amendment in *Wolf v. Colorado*, 338 U.S. 25 (1949). Although this Court refused in *Wolf* to apply the exclusionary rule to the states as essential to the protection of that right, it was well established even then, by this Court, in *Weeks*, 232 U.S. 383 (1914), that in federal prosecutions, the Fourth Amendment bars the use of any evidence secured through any illegal search and seizure. Today, for compelling reasons, the same sanction of exclusion must be applied to the states. First, as a minor consideration, it must be recognized that *Wolf* was based upon factual considerations no longer true today. At the time of *Wolf*, two-thirds of the states were opposed to the use of the exclusionary rule, but today more than half have wholly or partially adopted it. Second, and more important, the exclusionary rule is essential to the protection of the right to be free from unreasonable searches and seizures and to the integrity of the judiciary. The purpose of the exclusionary rule is "to compel respect for the constitutional guaranty in the only effectively available way—by removing the incentive to disregard it." Without this rule, the Fourth and Fourteenth Amendments' protection against unreasonable searches and seizures would be a valueless "form of words." Furthermore, the "judicial integrity" of our system requires that government, for its own preservation, observe its own laws, especially the charter of its own existence. Miss Mapp's (D) conviction must be reversed.

DISSENT: (Harlan, J.) There are several problems with the Court's decision today. First, the pivotal issue is not a reexamination of *Wolf*, but whether the "mere knowing possession of obscene materials" can be considered criminal, consistent with the rights of free thought and expression. Second, even if the issue is the reexamination of *Wolf*, this Court's reasoning that the basic federal remedy for a violation of the Fourth Amendment rights must apply to the states is unjustifiable. *Wolf* did not hold that the Fourth Amendment, as such, is applicable to the states through the Fourteenth Amendment, but only that problem does not involve the substantive commands of the Fourth Amendment, but the flexible Due Process Clause of the Fourteenth Amendment. The Court should refrain from hindering the states in their own criminal law enforcement with the adamant exclusionary rule.

ANALYSIS

This case illustrates the trend of the Supreme Court in incorporating the Bill of Rights into the Due Process Clause of the Fourteenth Amendment. However, the Court has not applied a "total incorporation theory," as it did here, to all those rights so far incorporated. For example, in the case of the right to a trial by jury, the federal requirement of a unanimous verdict of the twelve-man jury for conviction is not applicable to the states, although the right to a jury trial is, because such a requirement is not "essential" to the right. Note, finally,

Continued on next page.

that the Fourth Amendment applies only to the government (state or federal), and as such the prosecution may use evidence obtained by private parties even if the methods such parties used were illegal.

Quicknotes

BILL OF RIGHTS Refers to the first ten Amendments to the U.S. Constitution, setting forth individual rights and liberties.

EXCLUSIONARY RULE A rule precluding the introduction at trial of evidence unlawfully obtained in violation of the federal constitutional safeguards against unreasonable searches and seizures.

FOURTEENTH AMENDMENT DUE PROCESS CLAUSE Provides that protections mandated by the U.S. Constitution and observed by the federal government are equally applicable, and therefore must be observed by the states.

FOURTH AMENDMENT Provides that persons be secure as to their persons and private belongings against unreasonable searches and seizures.

PRIVILEGE AGAINST SELF-INCRIMINATION A privilege guaranteed by the Fifth Amendment to the U.S. Constitution in a criminal proceeding for communications made by an accused and protecting an accused or witness from having to give testimony that may incriminate him- or herself.

Katz v. United States

Telephone bettor (D) v. Federal government (P)

389 U.S. 347 (1967)

NATURE OF CASE: Appeal from criminal conviction for transmitting betting information over the phone.

FACT SUMMARY: Katz (D) was arrested for transmitting wagering information by telephone to another state. At his trial, the Government (P) introduced recordings of his conversation made by attaching a listening and recording device to the outside of a phone booth.

RULE OF LAW

The attachment of a listening device to the outside of a public telephone booth is a search and seizure within the meaning of the Fourth Amendment.

FACTS: Katz (D) was arrested and convicted for transmitting betting information by telephone to another state in violation of a federal statute. At his trial, the prosecution introduced recordings of phone conversations Katz (D) had made. These recordings were made by attaching a listening and recording device to the outside of a phone booth that Katz (D) used to make his calls. There was no search warrant. The Government (P) used this device only after it had made an investigation that indicated the phone booth was being used to transmit such information, and the Government (P) only recorded conversations that Katz (D) personally had.

ISSUE: Is the attachment of a listening device to the outside of a public telephone booth a search and seizure within the meaning of the Fourth Amendment?

HOLDING AND DECISION: (Stewart, J.) Yes. The attachment of a listening device to the outside of a public telephone booth is a search and seizure within the meaning of the Fourth Amendment. The Fourth Amendment protects a person from search and seizure if, under the circumstances, the person has a justifiable expectation of privacy, regardless of whether an actual physical trespass occurred. Whatever a person knowingly exposes to the public, even in his own home, is therefore not protected by the Fourth Amendment, but what a person keeps private, even in a public place, may be protected. Earlier cases stated that surveillance, without a trespass or seizure of a material object, is outside of the Fourth Amendment and now these cases must be overturned. Even though the phone booth was a public place, and there was no physical trespass (the device was on the outside of the booth), there was a search because the Government (P) violated the privacy upon which Katz (D) justifiably relied. There also is a seizure even though no tangible property was taken because the recording of a statement overheard, even if there is no trespass, is a seizure. The remaining question, then, is whether the Government (P) complied with the constitutional standards of the Fourth Amendment. Although the Government (P) reasonably believed that the phone booth was being illegally used, and their search and seizure was carefully limited both in scope and duration, the action cannot be upheld because there was no search warrant issued. A search warrant is a safeguard in several ways: a neutral magistrate, on the basis of information presented to him, determines whether a warrant should issue; the search warrant carefully limits the scope of the search; and the government must report back on the evidence it finds. Without such safeguards, even if the search was in fact reasonable, it cannot be upheld. Reversed.

CONCURRENCE: (Harlan, J.) In order to be protected by the Fourth Amendment, a person must have an actual subjective expectation of privacy and, also, that expectation of privacy must be reasonable.

DISSENT: (Black, J.) When the Fourth Amendment was adopted, eavesdropping was a common practice, and if the framers of the Constitution wished to limit that procedure, they would have used appropriate language. This case, then, goes against the plain meaning of the Fourth Amendment, which was solely aimed at limiting the practice of breaking into buildings and seizing tangible property. Therefore, wiretapping, which is a form of eavesdropping, is not subject to the Fourth Amendment.

ANALYSIS

Katz rejects the old rule that held that there was no search unless there was a physical trespass and substitutes a new rule based on the defendant's expectation of privacy. One facet of this privacy concept is the place involved—for example, if, unlike Katz (D), the defendant was engaged in conversation in a public place that was audible to others, there would be no search within the meaning of the Fourth Amendment. Also, the privacy concept turns on the action of the defendant. If the defendant had engaged in a loud conversation, even in his own home, which was audible to a person standing outside his door, there would be no search since the conversation was exposed by the defendant to the public.

Quicknotes

EXPECTATION OF PRIVACY Requirement that in order to invoke the Fourth Amendment's protection against unreasonable searches and seizures, the individual must have a reasonable expectation of privacy in respect to the location searched or thing seized.

FOURTH AMENDMENT Provides that persons be secure as to their person and private belongings against unreasonable searches and seizures.

United States v. Dunn

Federal government (P) v. Convicted drug felon (D)

480 U.S. 294 (1987)

NATURE OF CASE: Appeal from reversal of conviction for drug-related offenses.

FACT SUMMARY: Dunn (D) contended that a barn on his property and the area around it, which were 50 yards from a fence surrounding his house, were within the curtilage of his house and, therefore, within the Fourth Amendment's protective ambit, so that evidence of illegal drug manufacturing obtained as the result of a warrantless search of the barn area had to be suppressed.

RULE OF LAW

For Fourth Amendment purposes, the area surrounding a barn that is 50 yards away from the fence surrounding a house is not within the house's curtilage.

FACTS: Drug Enforcement Administration (DEA) agents discovered that Carpenter (D) had bought large quantities of chemicals and equipment used to make controlled substances. The agents then obtained a warrant for, and placed, tracking "beepers" in some of the equipment and one of the chemical containers, which, when transported in Carpenter's (D) truck, led the agents to Dunn's (D) ranch. Aerial photographs of the ranch showed the truck backed up to a barn behind the ranch house. The ranch was completely encircled by a perimeter fence, and contained several interior barbed wire fences, including one around the house approximately 50 yards from the barn, and a wooden fence enclosing the front of the barn, which had an open overhang and locked, waist-high gates. Without a warrant, police officers crossed the perimeter fence, several of the barbed wire fences, and the wooden fence in front of the barn. They were led there by the smell of chemicals used to make the controlled substances. They did not enter the barn but stopped at the locked gate and shined a flashlight inside, observing what they took to be a drug laboratory. They then left the ranch but entered it twice the next day to confirm the laboratory's presence. They obtained a search warrant and executed it, arresting Dunn (D) and seizing chemicals and equipment, as well as bags of amphetamines they discovered in the house. After the district court denied Dunn's (D) motion to suppress all evidence seized pursuant to the warrant, Dunn (D) and Carpenter (D) were convicted of conspiracy to manufacture controlled substances and related offenses. The court of appeals reversed, holding that the barn was within the residence's curtilage and therefore within the Fourth Amendment's protective ambit. The Supreme Court granted certiorari.

ISSUE: For Fourth Amendment purposes, is the area surrounding a barn that is 50 yards away from the fence surrounding a house within the house's curtilage?

HOLDING AND DECISION: (White, J.) No. For Fourth Amendment purposes, the area surrounding a barn that is 50 yards away from the fence surrounding a house is not within the house's curtilage. The question of the extent of curtilage should be resolved with particular reference to four factors, at least to the extent that they bear upon whether the area claimed to be curtilage is so intimately tied to the home itself that it should be placed under the home's "umbrella" of protection: (1) the proximity of the area to the home; (2) whether the area is within an enclosure surrounding the home; (3) the nature and uses to which the area is put; and (4) the steps taken by the resident to protect the area from observation by passersby. Applying the first factor, the barn's substantial distance from the fence surrounding the house (50 yards) and from the house itself (60 yards) supports no inference that it should be treated as an adjunct of the house. Second, the barn did not lie within the fence surrounding the house, which plainly demarcates the area that is part and parcel of the house, but it stands out as a distinct and separate portion of the ranch. Third, it is especially significant that the officers possessed objective data indicating that the barn was not being used as part of Dunn's (D) home. Fourth, Dunn (D) did little to protect the barn area from observation by those standing outside, the ranch's fences being of the type used to corral livestock, not to ensure privacy. Reversed.

DISSENT: (Brennan, J.) The Fourth Amendment was violated by the police officers for two reasons. First, the barn and its surrounding area were part of the curtilage of Dunn's (D) house. Second, Dunn (D) had a reasonable expectation of privacy that was infringed. Prior precedent, both federal and state, demonstrates that a barn is an integral part of a farmhouse and, therefore, within a farmhouse's curtilage, even where the barn is more than 60 yards away. The distance is not determinative, nor is the configuration of the fences. Here, there was a well-used path/road that connected the barn to the house, and the barn and house were clustered together with other buildings in a clearing. As to the third extent-of-curtilage factor used by the majority, the majority's reasoning misapplies this factor (the nature of the use). Merely because

Continued on next page.

the barn and barnyard were not in domestic use do not render those areas nondomestic. To hold otherwise is contrary to the Court's own precedent. Neither smells nor sounds that indicate nondomestic use take a structure or area outside a house's curtilage, since a barn, like a home, may simultaneously be put to domestic and nondomestic uses, even the manufacture of controlled substances; dual use does not strip a home or any building within the home's curtilage, of Fourth Amendment protection. Finally, as to the fourth extent-of-curtilage factor, the facts are contrary to the majority's conclusion that Dunn (D) did little to protect the barn's privacy. Assuming arguendo, the barn and barnyard were not within Dunn's (D) home's curtilage, his reasonable expectation of privacy would nonetheless trigger the Fourth Amendment's protections. It is settled that there the Amendment protects privacy expectations in commercial premises. Here, all the actions taken by the police officers without a warrant were constitutionally intolerable. Farmers' and ranchers' expectations of privacy in their barns and other outbuildings are expectations society would regard as reasonable, so that the police actions taken in this case clearly violate the Fourth Amendment's protections.

ANALYSIS

The extent-of-curtilage issue has also been raised in connection with a business. In *United States v. Swart*, 679 F.2d 698 (7th Cir. 1982), for example, the court of appeals utilized both a "business curtilage" concept and a *Katz* reasonable expectation-of-privacy analysis, 389 U.S. 347 (1967), to hold that the warrantless search of business premises violated the Fourth Amendment. In that case police officers searched the area surrounding a garage and sheds, which constituted a business for repairing and rebuilding cars and trucks. The Court held that the search violated the Fourth Amendment because the cars "may have been within the curtilage of the business buildings," and because the occupant of the premises had a reasonable expectation of privacy in the cars located on his property which was not diminished by the fact that the cars were on closed business premises. In this case, it is arguable that a barn, like a factory, a plant, or a warehouse, is a business place not open to the general public. Like these other business establishments, the barn, and any area immediately surrounding or adjacent to it from which the public is excluded, should receive protection. A business operator is indisputably entitled to constitutional protection within the premises when steps have been taken to ensure privacy. It is a compelling argument that he or she should be entitled to protection in those areas immediately surrounding the building when obvious efforts have been made to exclude the public.

Quicknotes

CURTILAGE The area immediately surrounding a dwelling.

EXPECTATION OF PRIVACY Requirement that in order to invoke the Fourth Amendment's protection against unreasonable searches and seizures, the individual must have a reasonable expectation of privacy in respect to the location searched or thing seized.

FOURTH AMENDMENT Provides that persons be secure as to their person and private belongings against unreasonable searches and seizures.

California v. Greenwood

State (P) v. Garbage owner (D)

486 U.S. 35 (1988)

NATURE OF CASE: Review of dismissal of charges of narcotics possession.

FACT SUMMARY: Greenwood (D) was caught in possession of narcotics when police searched his house on the authority of a warrant issued based on evidence obtained through a search of Greenwood's (D) garbage.

RULE OF LAW

Garbage left in a public space for collection may be searched without a warrant.

FACTS: Suspecting that Greenwood (D) was involved with narcotics, a police officer searched Greenwood's (D) garbage, which had been placed on the street for collection. Evidence of narcotics was found. Based on this evidence, a warrant was issued. Police searched Greenwood's (D) home, and narcotics were found. Greenwood (D) was arrested and charged. The superior court dismissed the charges; the court of appeal affirmed; and the California Supreme Court denied the State's (P) petition for review.

ISSUE: May garbage left in a public space for collection be searched without a warrant?

HOLDING AND DECISION: (White, J.) Yes. Garbage left in a public space for collection may be searched without a warrant. The necessity for a warrant in any given situation is based on whether an individual has a reasonable expectation of privacy. In the case of garbage left in a public space for collection, it is well known that animals, children, and scavengers can and do rummage through garbage. Therefore, it is not reasonable to expect the contents of a garbage bag to remain private. This being so, no reasonable expectation of privacy existed here, and no warrant was needed. The judgment of the court of appeal is reversed and the case remanded.

DISSENT: (Brennan, J.) Scrutiny of another's trash is contrary to commonly accepted notions of civilized behavior. A single bag of trash testifies eloquently to the social status and personal habits of the person who produced it and can relate intimate details about the person's sexual and health practices, professional status, political associations and inclinations, private thoughts, and personal relationships. It is just this intimate activity associated with the sanctities of home and the privacies of life that the Fourth Amendment is designed to protect from warrantless scrutiny. The bags used by Greenwood (D) should not be deprived of Fourth Amendment protections merely because they were used to discard rather than transport his personal effects. This is particularly true since Greenwood (D) was required by a municipal ordinance to leave trash on his curb for pickup and was prohibited from disposing of it any other way.

ANALYSIS

It appears that a rule that can be gleaned from this case, and others, such as *California v. Ciraolo*, 476 U.S. 207 (1986), is as follows: police are not to be expected to be less inquisitive than the most inquisitive members of the general public. Most individuals do not go through others' trash. Some, however, do. This being so, the police may reasonably be expected to do so as well.

Quicknotes

FOURTH AMENDMENT Provides that persons be secure as to their person and private belongings against unreasonable searches and seizures.

SEARCH An inspection conducted in order to obtain evidence to be utilized for the prosecution of a crime and the subsequent taking of such evidence.

WARRANT An order issued by a court directing an officer to undertake a certain act (e.g., arrest or search).

California v. Ciraolo

State (P) v. Marijuana grower (D)

476 U.S. 207 (1986)

NATURE OF CASE: Appeal from state action for offenses related to growing marijuana.

FACT SUMMARY: Ciraolo (D) contended that a warrantless naked-eye aerial observation of his fenced-in backyard, made at 1,000 feet, which revealed marijuana plants, violated the Fourth Amendment by encroaching on his reasonable expectations of privacy.

RULE OF LAW

A warrantless naked-eye aerial observation of a fenced-in backyard from 1,000 feet does not violate the Fourth Amendment.

FACTS: The police received an anonymous telephone tip that marijuana was growing in Ciraolo's (D) backyard, which was enclosed by two fences, one of which was 10 feet, and shielded from view at ground level. Officers who were trained in marijuana identification secured a private airplane, flew over Ciraolo's (D) house at an altitude of 1,000 feet, and made a naked-eye identification of marijuana plants growing in the yard. A search warrant was later obtained on the basis of the observations; a photograph of the surrounding area taken from the airplane was attached as an exhibit. The warrant was executed, and marijuana plants were seized. The State (P) brought a criminal action against Ciraolo (D) and the State (P) appealed the state appellate court's decision. The United States Supreme Court granted certiorari.

ISSUE: Does a warrantless naked-eye aerial observation of a fenced-in backyard from 1,000 feet violate the Fourth Amendment?

HOLDING AND DECISION: (Burger, C.J.) No. A warrantless naked-eye aerial observation of a fenced-in backyard from 1,000 feet does not violate the Fourth Amendment. The touchstone of Fourth Amendment analysis is whether a person has a constitutionally protected reasonable expectation of privacy, which involves the two inquiries of whether the individual manifested a subjective expectation of privacy in the object of the challenged search, and whether society is willing to recognize that expectation as reasonable. As to the first inquiry, it is undisputed that Ciraolo (D) had a subjective expectation of privacy, at least as to street-level observations, since he put up a 10-foot fence around his backyard. However, it is not clear that he could have expected privacy from all observations. As for the second inquiry, the test of legitimacy is not whether the individual chooses to conceal assertedly "private activity," but whether the government's intrusion infringes upon the personal and societal values protected by the Fourth Amendment. Here, Ciraolo's (D) expectation of privacy from all observations of his backyard was unreasonable. That the backyard and its crop were within the "curtilage" of Ciraolo's (D) home did not itself bar all police observation. The mere fact that an individual has taken measures to restrict some views of his activities does not preclude an officer's observation from a public vantage point where he has a right to be and which renders the activities clearly visible. The police observations here took place within public navigable airspace, in a physically nonintrusive manner. The police were able to observe the plants readily discernible to the naked eye as marijuana, and it was irrelevant that the observation from the airplane was directed at identifying the plants and that the officers were trained to recognize marijuana. Any member of the public flying in this airspace who cared to glance down could have seen everything that the officers observed. The Fourth Amendment simply does not require police traveling in the public airways at 1,000 feet to obtain a warrant in order to observe what is visible to the naked eye. Reversed.

DISSENT: (Powell, J.) Not only physical intrusions, but any technologically aided intrusions that violate a reasonable expectation of privacy are prohibited by the Fourth Amendment. Here, the surveillance was of a home, since the backyard is unquestionably part of the home's curtilage. It is also undisputed that Ciraolo (D) had an expectation of privacy in his backyard. The issue then—which the majority incorrectly decides—is whether the expectation was a reasonable one that society would protect. Merely because the public can fleetingly peer into a person's backyard from an airplane does not mean that a person's privacy expectations in the backyard are nullified by the possibility of such observations. Instead, the actual risk to privacy from commercial or pleasure aircraft is virtually nonexistent. That is why people build fences around their backyards, but not roofs over them. Thus, people do not knowingly expose their backyards to the public merely by failing to build barriers that prevent aerial surveillance. Because there is a qualitative difference between aerial police surveillance and remote public aerial observations, they are not equivalent. When, as here, an individual has a reasonable expectation of privacy in his backyard, aerial police surveillance of that yard constitutes a "search" under the Fourth Amendment.

Continued on next page.

ANALYSIS

This case raises the issue of how the reasonableness of privacy expectations can change with changes in commonly accepted technology. Much of the dissent's argument rests on the premise that the risk of public aerial observations of residential property is virtually nonexistent. Although this may have been true at the time this decision was rendered, modern satellite technology, combined with very powerful computers and the Internet, permits virtually anyone around the world to use a program such as Google Maps to observe anyone's backyard with a few clicks of a mouse. Thus, while most people still do not build roofs over their yards, it is arguable that an expectation of privacy in one's yard from aerial observation – police or otherwise – would not be adjudged reasonable by today's societal standards.

Quicknotes

CURTILAGE The area immediately surrounding a dwelling.

EXPECTATION OF PRIVACY Requirement that in order to invoke the Fourth Amendment's protection against unreasonable searches and seizures, the individual must have a reasonable expectation of privacy in respect to the location searched or thing seized.

SEARCH An inspection conducted in order to obtain evidence to be utilized for the prosecution of a crime and the subsequent taking of such evidence.

Kyllo v. United States

Suspected grower of marijuana (D) v. Federal government (P)

533 U.S. 27 (2001)

NATURE OF CASE: Appeal from indictment of manufacturing marijuana.

FACT SUMMARY: Federal agents suspected Kyllo (D) of growing marijuana in his residence and used a thermal scanner to prove he was doing so.

RULE OF LAW

Where the government uses a device that is not in general public use to explore details of the home that would previously have been unknowable without physical intrusion, the surveillance is a "search" and is presumptively unreasonable without a warrant.

FACTS: Federal agents suspected Kyllo (D) was growing marijuana in his home and used a thermal-imaging device to scan the residence. The agents concluded that Kyllo (D) was using halide lights to grow marijuana in his house and a magistrate issued a search warrant on the basis of the thermal scan, tips from informants, and Kyllo's (D) heating bills. Kyllo (D) was indicted and unsuccessfully moved to suppress the evidence. The court of appeals remanded the case for an evidentiary hearing regarding the intrusiveness of the thermal imaging. The district court upheld the warrant and affirmed denial of the motion. The court of appeals affirmed.

ISSUE: Where the government uses a device that is not in general public use to explore details of the home that would previously have been unknowable without physical intrusion, is the surveillance a "search" and is it presumptively unreasonable without a warrant.

HOLDING AND DECISION: (Scalia, J.) Yes. Where the government uses a device that is not in general public use to explore details of the home that would previously have been unknowable without physical intrusion, the surveillance is a "search" and is presumptively unreasonable without a warrant. Case remanded to the district court to determine whether probable cause existed independent of the evidence from the thermal visioning. Reversed and remanded.

DISSENT: (Stevens, J.) There is a distinction between "through-the-wall surveillance" that gives the observer direct access to information in a private area and the thought processes used to draw inferences from information in the public domain. The Court has crafted a rule that purports to deal with direct observation of the inside of the home. This case, however, involves indirect deductions from observations of the exterior of the home.

ANALYSIS

The Court upholds the test of "reasonableness" set forth in *Katz v. United States*, 389 U.S. 347 (1967), that whether the individual has an expectation of privacy depends on whether society is prepared to recognize such expectation as reasonable. The Court rejects the erosion of Fourth Amendment protection by technological advances, concluding that any such technological "intrusion into a constitutionally protected area" constitutes a search, especially if the product of the use of a device is not available to the general public.

Quicknotes

FOURTH AMENDMENT Provides that persons be secure as to their person and private belongings against unreasonable searches and seizures.

PROBABLE CAUSE A reasonable basis for believing that a crime has been committed.

REASONABLE EXPECTATION OF PRIVACY In order to invoke the Fourth Amendment's protection against unreasonable searches and seizures, an individual must have a reasonable expectation of privacy in respect to the location searched or thing seized.

SEARCH An inspection conducted in order to obtain evidence to be utilized for the prosecution of a crime and the subsequent taking of such evidence.

WARRANT An order issued by a court directing an officer to undertake a certain act (e.g., arrest or search).

Smith v. Maryland

Convicted robber (D) v. State (P)

442 U.S. 735 (1979)

NATURE OF CASE: On writ of certiorari from robbery conviction.

FACT SUMMARY: Using evidence obtained from a pen register, police obtained a warrant to search Smith's (D) home, leading to his eventual conviction for robbery.

RULE OF LAW

The warrantless installation and use of a pen register to record numbers dialed from an individual's home telephone does not violate the individual's legitimate expectations of privacy.

FACTS: McDonough was robbed; she described to police the robber and an automobile she observed near the crime. She later saw the car driving past her house and received obscene and threatening phone calls from a man identifying himself as the robber. The police spotted a man meeting the description McDonough had given them driving in McDonough's neighborhood. The police traced the license plate number and learned it was registered to Smith (D). At the request of the police, but without a warrant or court order, the phone company installed a device called a pen register at its offices to monitor and record numbers dialed from Smith's (D) home. The register revealed that Smith (D) had called McDonough, and on the basis of this and other evidence, police obtained a warrant to search his home. The trial court denied Smith's (D) motion to suppress the evidence derived from the pen register, and he was convicted of robbery. The United States Supreme Court granted review.

ISSUE: Does the warrantless installation and use of a pen register to record numbers dialed from an individual's home telephone violate his legitimate expectations of privacy?

HOLDING AND DECISION: (Blackmun, J.) No. The warrantless installation and use of a pen register to record numbers dialed from an individual's home phone does not violate legitimate expectations of privacy. Users of the telephone must realize that they are conveying information about the numbers they dial to the phone company. They typically realize that the phone company has facilities for recording such numbers for a variety of purposes, including billing, detecting fraud, and identifying obscene callers. The fact that Smith (D) dialed the numbers from his home phone is immaterial; the phone company obtains the information regarding numbers dialed in the same way, regardless of where the phone is located. This Court has held that an individual does not harbor a legitimate expectation of privacy in information he voluntarily turns over to third parties. Affirmed.

DISSENT: (Stewart, J.) The majority distinguishes between the numbers dialed and the content of conversations, in which we have held an individual enjoys an expectation of privacy from surveillance. It is incorrect to say that the numbers dialed are without content, as they can easily reveal the most intimate details of a person's life.

DISSENT: (Marshall, J.) The notion that those who reveal information to third parties assume the risk of disclosure implies choice. It is idle to speak of choice in the context of the use of a home telephone, an instrument that has become a necessity in our society, and one for which there is no practical alternative.

ANALYSIS

In response to *Smith*, Congress passed legislation prohibiting the installation of pen registers, except for maintenance and testing, without a court order. Likewise, Congress prohibited seizure of financial institution records without a subpoena or warrant, in response to *United States v. Miller*, 425 U.S. 435 (1976), a case cited by Justice Blackmun in *Smith*.

Quicknotes

CERTIORARI A discretionary writ issued by a superior court to an inferior court in order to review the lower court's decisions; the U.S. Supreme Court's writ ordering such review.

SUBPOENA A court-issued mandate to compel a witness to appear at trial.

WARRANT An order issued by a court directing an officer to undertake a certain act (e.g., arrest or search).

Carpenter v. United States

Convicted robber (D) v. Federal government (P)

138 S. Ct. 2206 (2018)

NATURE OF CASE: Appeal by convicted robber from affirmance of denial of motion to suppress cellular phone routing data, known as cell-site location information (CSLI), obtained without a warrant.

FACT SUMMARY: Carpenter (D), who was convicted of several counts of robbery, contended that cellular phone routing data, known as cell-site location information (CSLI), that the Federal Bureau of Investigation obtained without a warrant and that showed that his cell phone was near robbery locations at the time the robberies occurred, should have been suppressed on the grounds that the government's (P) seizure of that data without a warrant supported by probable cause violated the Fourth Amendment.

RULE OF LAW

An individual has a legitimate expectation of privacy in the record of his or her physical movements as captured through cell-site location information (CSLI), so that the government must generally obtain a search warrant supported by probable cause before acquiring CSLI.

FACTS: Each time a cell phone connects to a cell site, it generates a time-stamped record known as cell-site location information (CSLI). Wireless carriers collect and store this information for their own business purposes. After the Federal Bureau of Investigation (FBI) identified the cell phone numbers of several robbery suspects, prosecutors were granted court orders to obtain the suspects' cell phone records under the Stored Communications Act. Wireless carriers produced CSLI for Carpenter's (D) phone, and the Government (P) was able to obtain 12,898 location points cataloging Carpenter's movements over 127 days—an average of 101 data points per day. Carpenter (D) moved to suppress the data, arguing that the government's (P) seizure of the records without obtaining a warrant supported by probable cause violated the Fourth Amendment. The district court denied the motion, and prosecutors used the records at trial to show that Carpenter's (D) phone was near four of the robbery locations at the time those robberies occurred. Carpenter (D) was convicted. The court of appeals affirmed, holding that Carpenter (D) lacked a reasonable expectation of privacy in the location information collected by the FBI because he had shared that information with his wireless carriers. The United States Supreme Court granted certiorari.

ISSUE: Does an individual have a legitimate expectation of privacy in the record of his or her physical movements as captured through cell-site location information (CSLI), so that the government must generally obtain a search warrant supported by probable cause before acquiring CSLI?

HOLDING AND DECISION: (Roberts, C.J.) Yes. An individual has a legitimate expectation of privacy in the record of his or her physical movements as captured through cell-site location information (CSLI), so that the government must generally obtain a search warrant supported by probable cause before acquiring CSLI. The location information obtained from Carpenter's (D) wireless carriers was the product of a search. A person does not surrender all Fourth Amendment protection by venturing into the public sphere. To the contrary, the Court has recognized that what one seeks to preserve as private, even in an area accessible to the public, may be constitutionally protected, and that individuals have a reasonable expectation of privacy in the whole of their physical movements. Thus, when an individual seeks to preserve something as private, and his expectation of privacy is one that society is prepared to recognize as reasonable, official intrusion into that sphere generally qualifies as a search and requires a warrant supported by probable cause. Allowing Government (P) access to cell-site records—which "hold for many Americans the 'privacies of life'" [*Riley v. California*, 573 U.S. 373 (2014)]—contravenes that expectation, since the time-stamped data provides an intimate window into a person's life, revealing not only his particular movements, but through them his familial, political, professional, religious, and sexual associations. Moreover, cell phone tracking is remarkably easy, cheap, and efficient compared to traditional investigative tools, and, with just the click of a button, the Government (P) can access each carrier's deep repository of historical location information at practically no expense. Cell-site records raise great privacy concerns, given that cell phones have become almost a "feature of human anatomy" [*Riley*, 573 U.S. 373 (2014) (slip op., at 9)], in that individuals carry their phones with them at all times, beyond public thoroughfares and into private residences, doctor's offices, political headquarters, and other potentially revealing locales. Accordingly, when the Government (P) tracks the location of a cell phone it achieves near perfect surveillance, as if it had attached an ankle monitor to the phone's user, and it can do so retrospectively to retrace a person's whereabouts, subject only to the five-year retention policies of most wireless

Continued on next page.

carriers. Critically, location information is continually logged for all 400 million devices in the United States, not just those belonging to persons who might happen to come under investigation, so the tracking capacity of CSLI runs against everyone. Additionally, the precision of such information is rapidly increasing. For these reasons when the Government (P) accessed CSLI from the wireless carriers, it invaded Carpenter's (D) reasonable expectation of privacy in the whole of his physical movements, and was a search. Therefore, the Government (P) must generally obtain a warrant supported by probable cause before acquiring CSLI records. Nonetheless, as with other searches, case-specific exceptions may support a warrantless search of an individual's cell-site records under certain circumstances. One well-recognized exception applies when the exigencies of the situation make the needs of law enforcement so compelling that a warrantless search is objectively reasonable under the Fourth Amendment. Such exigencies include the need to pursue a fleeing suspect, protect individuals who are threatened with imminent harm, or prevent the imminent destruction of evidence. Absent such exigencies, the Government (P) will have to obtain a warrant, and merely because CSLI is gathered by a third party will not render it less deserving of Fourth Amendment protection. Reversed.

DISSENT: (Kennedy, J.) First, CSLI is not nearly as precise as the majority asserts it is, and it only reveals a person's location generally, within an area of between a dozen to several hundred city blocks. Second, the majority errs in finding that precedent establishes that an individual has an expectation of privacy in the sum of the individual's whereabouts, and that CSLI records therefore implicate greater privacy interests than financial or telephone records. In fact, the opposite is true, since a person's movements are not particularly private. The Court previously held that when an individual travels over the public streets, he voluntarily conveys to anyone who wants to look the fact that he was traveling over particular roads in a particular direction, the fact of whatever stops he made, and the fact of his final destination. Today expectations of privacy in one's location are, if anything, even less reasonable. Millions of Americans choose to share their location on a daily basis, whether by using a variety of location-based services on their phones, or by sharing their location with friends and the public at large via social media.

DISSENT: (Thomas, J.) The reasonable-expectation-of-privacy test has no place in Fourth Amendment analysis and involves prohibited judicial policymaking.

DISSENT: (Gorsuch, J.) The Court, in deciding this case, should have taken a more traditional Fourth Amendment approach to the issues raised here, rather than relying on a "reasonable expectation of privacy" approach. A person's cell-site data could qualify as his papers or effects under existing law. Although the carrier holds the information, the relevant statute (47 U.S.C. § 222) provides that a customer's CSLI is customer proprietary network information (CPNI) and gives customers certain rights to control use of and access to CPNI about themselves. Carriers are statutorily forbidden to use, disclose, or permit access to individually identifiable CPNI without the customer's consent, except as needed to provide the customer's telecommunications services. The statute also requires the carrier to disclose CPNI upon affirmative written request by the customer, to any person designated by the customer. Congress even afforded customers a private cause of action for damages against carriers who violate the Act's terms. Plainly, customers have substantial legal interests in this information, including at least some right to include, exclude, and control its use. Those interests might even rise to the level of a property right. Ostensibly, Carpenter (D) could have vindicated his Fourth Amendment rights by invoking the law of property or any analogies to the common law, but instead only relied on "reasonable expectations" arguments. Accordingly, Carpenter (D) may have forfeited his most promising line of argument.

ANALYSIS

As the Court in this case notes, a request for cell-site location information (CSLI) lies at the intersection of two lines of cases. The first addresses a person's expectation of privacy in his or her physical location and movements. Prior to this case, the Court held, in *United States v. Jones*, 565 U.S. 400 (2012), that warrantless GPS monitoring of a suspect's vehicle through a tracking device violated the Fourth Amendment, not only because of the Government's (P) physical trespass of the vehicle, but also because of the suspect's related privacy expectations. In the second line of cases, the Court has held that a person has no legitimate expectation of privacy in information he or she voluntarily turns over to third parties, even if the information is revealed on the assumption that it will be used only for a limited purpose. Thus, the Government (P) is typically free to obtain such information from the recipient without triggering Fourth Amendment protections. This third-party doctrine has been applied to bank records and records of landline telephone companies. In this case, the Court declined to extend this doctrine, given what it found are the unique characteristics of cell phone location records, i.e., the ability to infallibly chronicle a person's location for years. Thus, whether the Government (P) uses its own surveillance technology or leverages the technology of a wireless carrier, an individual maintains a legitimate expectation of privacy in the record of his physical movements as captured through CSLI. Nonetheless, the

Continued on next page.

Court's decision in *Carpenter* is a narrow one, and does not disturb the third-party doctrine or call into question conventional surveillance techniques and tools, such as security cameras. Nor does the decision address other business records that might incidentally reveal location information or other collection techniques involving foreign affairs or national security.

Quicknotes

EXPECTATION OF PRIVACY Requirement that in order to invoke the Fourth Amendment's protection against unreasonable searches and seizures, the individual must have a reasonable expectation of privacy in respect to the location searched or thing seized.

FOURTH AMENDMENT Provides that persons be secure as to their persons and private belongings against unreasonable searches and seizures.

PROBABLE CAUSE A reasonable basis for believing that a crime has been committed.

United States v. Jones

Federal government (P) v. Suspected drug trafficker (D)

565 U.S. 400 (2012)

NATURE OF CASE: Appeal from intermediate appellate court decision in favor of the defendant.

FACT SUMMARY: Government agents installed a Global-Positioning-System (GPS) tracking device on the undercarriage of a vehicle owned by Jones (D), who was suspected of trafficking in narcotics, and then monitored the vehicle's movements for a period of 28 days.

RULE OF LAW

The government's installation of a Global-Positioning-System (GPS) tracking device on an individual's vehicle and the government's use of the device to track the location of that vehicle constitute a search under the Fourth Amendment.

FACTS: Government agents installed a Global-Positioning-System (GPS) tracking device on the undercarriage of Jones's (D) vehicle for a period of 28 days. The device was able to track the location of the vehicle to within 50 feet. The district court judge denied Jones's (D) motion to suppress the GPS evidence and a jury convicted him. The Court of Appeals for the D.C. Circuit then reversed, finding that the evidence obtained by the use of the GPS device without a warrant violated the Fourth Amendment. The Government (P) appealed to the United States Supreme Court.

ISSUE: Does the government's installation of a Global-Positioning-System (GPS) tracking device on an individual's vehicle and the government's use of the device to track the location of that vehicle constitute a search under the Fourth Amendment?

HOLDING AND DECISION: (Scalia, J.) Yes. The government's installation of a Global-Positioning-System (GPS) tracking device on an individual's vehicle and the government's use of the device to track the location of that vehicle constitute a search under the Fourth Amendment. The Government (P) argues that no search occurred because Jones (D) had no reasonable expectation of privacy in the area of the vehicle accessed by government agents or in the location of the vehicle on public roads. However, this case need not be analyzed on the reasonable expectation of privacy theory. Instead, the government's physical trespass in the form of attaching a device to one's vehicle constitutes the search. One's private vehicle is protected by the Fourth Amendment's prohibition of unreasonable searches of one's "person, houses, papers, and effects." The more general unreasonable expectation of privacy theory did not replace the original trespass to property theory of unreasonable searches. Rather, it is supplemental to the original understanding of the Fourth Amendment. It is enough for this case to focus narrowly upon the government's trespass upon Jones's (D) "effects," i.e., his vehicle, to find that a search occurred. Affirmed.

CONCURRENCE: (Alito, J.) The Court should have analyzed this under the broader reasonable expectation of privacy theory rather than the simple trespass to property theory. Reliance on the narrow trespass theory will not provide any guidance to law enforcement for those surveillance cases where there is no physical intrusion.

ANALYSIS

While the judgment in this case was unanimous, the Court was split five to four on how to analyze the use of the Global-Positioning-System (GPS) tracking device. The federal agents' intrusion upon the personal property of Jones (D) was the significant factor in this case. As the concurring justices note, however, the issue remains undecided on how far law enforcement can go with electronic or even Internet searches that do not include a physical intrusion.

Quicknotes

FOURTH AMENDMENT Provides that persons be secure as to their persons and private belongings against unreasonable searches and seizures.

SEARCH AND SEIZURE An inspection conducted in order to obtain evidence to be utilized for the prosecution of a crime and the subsequent taking of such evidence.

Florida v. Jardines

State (P) v. Marijuana grower (D)

569 U.S. 1 (2013)

NATURE OF CASE: Review of Fourth Amendment search in a criminal case.

FACT SUMMARY: Police brought a drug-detection dog to Jardines's (D) home. The dog "alerted" to the scent of marijuana at the front door. Police then obtained a search warrant for Jardines's (D) home and seized marijuana plants.

RULE OF LAW

The curtilage is part of a private home for Fourth Amendment purposes, and it is impermissible to enter the curtilage with a trained police dog for search purposes without express or implied permission from the homeowner.

FACTS: Police observed Jardines's (D) home on an unverified tip. They brought a trained drug-sniffing dog and approached the home. The dog "alerted" at the front door. Police then obtained a warrant to search the residence. The search revealed marijuana plants, but the evidence was excluded in the lower court as fruit of an unreasonable search.

ISSUE: Is the curtilage part of a private home for Fourth Amendment purposes, and is it impermissible to enter the curtilage with a trained police dog for search purposes without express or implied permission from the homeowner?

HOLDING AND DECISION: (Scalia, J.) Yes. The curtilage is part of a private home for Fourth Amendment purposes, and it is impermissible to enter the curtilage with a trained police dog for search purposes without express or implied permission from the homeowner. The home is first among equals for Fourth Amendment purposes. Man's right to retreat to his home would have very little practical value if the state's agents could search side yards and porches for evidence with impunity. There is no doubt here the detectives entered the curtilage, which is the area immediately surrounding and associated with the home. The issue then becomes whether the intrusion into a constitutionally protected area occurred with leave from Jardines (D). It did not. The habits of the country may provide an implicit license to a visitor to approach a home. A front door knocker allows for "solicitors, hawkers and peddlers of all kinds." Officers can knock on a front door and speak with the homeowner. There is no customary invitation for a trained police dog to explore the area looking for incriminating evidence. The State (P) relies on this Court's cases finding that the subjective intent of the officer is irrelevant. Those cases, however, deal with objectively reasonable searches so the officer's real reason for the search does not vitiate the objective reasonableness. Here, the objective basis for the officers' behavior was to conduct a search and no one believes they had a license to do so. The Court need not consider whether the officers violated Jardines's (D) expectation of privacy under *Katz v. United States*, 389 U.S. 347 (1967), because the officers conducted a search by physically intruding on Jardines's (D) property. Katz's reasonable-expectations test adds to, not substitutes for, the property-based understanding of the Fourth Amendment.

CONCURRENCE: (Kagan, J.) The Court could have arrived at the same decision by considering Jardines's (D) privacy interests. Privacy expectations are heightened in the home and surrounding area and it was an invasion of Jardines's (D) privacy for the officers to invade those expectations when searching with a trained canine assistant.

DISSENT: (Alito, J.) The Court's decision relies on trespass law that is nowhere to be found in Anglo-American jurisprudence. The majority finds Detective Bartelt committed a trespass when he engaged in an otherwise lawful visit to Jardines's (D) home but brought his dog. Trespass law provides no support for such a holding. The police are permitted to "knock and talk." They are permitted to see, hear, and smell what can be detected from their lawful vantage point. The Court states Bartelt had the objective purpose of conducting a search. There is no meaningful way to distinguish between the objective purpose of a "knock and talk" and what occurred here. The dog is the difference here. There is not a single case that holds a visitor commits a trespass when accompanied by a dog on a leash. The Court's trespass rule today is a newly struck counterfeit.

ANALYSIS

The Court's decision was a narrow one involving drug-sniffing dogs, but technological advancements continue to change state agencies' ability to collect evidence. The Court acknowledges officers may approach a private residence for the purpose of speaking with a resident and may even gather evidence from that "knock and talk." In the future, officers may have technological advances providing a greater ability to see, hear, and smell. The Court may have to reconsider what

Continued on next page.

constitutes an impermissible intrusion resulting in an impermissible search.

Quicknotes

CURTILAGE The area immediately surrounding a dwelling.

SEARCH An inspection conducted in order to obtain evidence to be utilized for the prosecution of a crime and the subsequent taking of such evidence.

Florida v. Bostick

State (P) v. Individual charged with drug trafficking (D)

501 U.S. 429 (1991)

NATURE OF CASE: Appeal from state's highest court reversal of drug trafficking charges on grounds that police seizure of evidence violated the Fourth Amendment.

FACT SUMMARY: Pursuant to a suspicionless bus sweep, police requested, and received, permission to search Bostick's (D) luggage, and, when they searched the luggage, they discovered cocaine. After being arrested and charged with drug trafficking, Bostick (D) sought to have the cocaine suppressed on the grounds that it had been seized in violation of the Fourth Amendment.

RULE OF LAW

Where the police conduct a suspicionless sweep of a bus, and ask passengers for consent to search their luggage, while informing the passengers that they are free to decline such request, the appropriate test for determining whether contraband discovered pursuant to such a sweep has been seized in violation of the Fourth Amendment is whether, taking into account all of the circumstances surrounding the encounter, a reasonable passenger would feel free to decline the officers' requests or otherwise terminate the encounter.

FACTS: Pursuant to drug interdiction efforts, a sheriff's office conducted suspicionless sweeps of busses. During such a sweep, two officers, who were wearing badges, and displaying their guns, walked up to Bostick (D), who was sitting on a bus bound for another state, asked him a few questions, and asked if they could search his bags. The officers did not point guns at Bostick (D) or otherwise threaten him, and they specifically advised him that he could refuse consent. Bostick (D) consented to the search, and the officers discovered cocaine in his luggage. He was arrested and charged with drug trafficking. Bostick (D) sought to have the cocaine suppressed on the grounds that it had been seized in violation of the Fourth Amendment. The state's highest court agreed with Bostick (D), concluding that because no reasonable person would ever feel free to leave the encounter under such circumstances, the police had engaged in an unconstitutional seizure. The United States Supreme Court granted certiorari.

ISSUE: Where the police conduct a suspicionless sweep of a bus, and ask passengers for consent to search their luggage, while informing the passengers that they are free to decline such request, is the appropriate test for determining whether contraband discovered pursuant to such a sweep has been seized in violation of the Fourth Amendment whether, taking into account all of the circumstances surrounding the encounter, a reasonable passenger would feel free to decline the officers' requests or otherwise terminate the encounter?

HOLDING AND DECISION: (O'Connor, J.) Yes. Where the police conduct a suspicionless sweep of a bus, and ask passengers for consent to search their luggage, while informing the passengers that they are free to decline such request, the appropriate test for determining whether contraband discovered pursuant to such a sweep has been seized in violation of the Fourth Amendment is whether, taking into account all of the circumstances surrounding the encounter, a reasonable passenger would feel free to decline the officers' requests or otherwise terminate the encounter. A consensual encounter does not trigger Fourth Amendment scrutiny, and even when officers have no basis for suspecting a particular individual, they may generally ask the individual questions, ask to examine identification, and request consent to search luggage, provided they do not convey a message that compliance with their requests is required. Thus, there is no doubt that if this same encounter had taken place before Bostick (D) boarded the bus or in the bus terminal, it would not be a seizure. That this encounter took place in the cramped confines of the bus is just one relevant factor in determining whether or not it was of a coercive nature. Bostick (D) contends that the inquiry should be whether a reasonable person would believe he would be free to leave under such circumstances, and asserts that he would not. However, this inquiry is not an accurate measure of an encounter's coercive effect when a person is seated on a bus about to depart, has no desire to leave, and would not feel free to leave even if there were no police present. Bostick (D) was already constrained by his decision to take a bus, so such an inquiry under these circumstances says nothing about whether the police conduct was coercive. The more appropriate inquiry is whether a reasonable passenger would feel free to decline the officers' request or otherwise terminate the encounter. If a person refuses the officers' request, such a refusal alone, does not furnish the minimal level of objective justification needed for detention or seizure. [Reversed and remanded.]

DISSENT: (Marshall, J.) Although the test adopted by the majority is correctly framed, the majority's

Continued on next page.

application of that test here is flawed, and its conclusion incorrect. It is practically inconceivable that a reasonable passenger who is approached by police during a bus sweep "would feel free to decline the officers' requests or otherwise terminate the encounter." Although it is true that a passenger could refuse to respond to the officers, or to give consent, it is likewise true that a passenger would reasonably believe that such refusal would only arouse the officers' suspicions and intensify their interrogation. Indeed, officers who carry out bus sweeps like the one at issue here frequently admit that this is the effect of a passenger's refusal to cooperate. The majority's observation that a mere refusal to answer questions, "without more," does not give rise to a reasonable basis for seizing a passenger, is utterly beside the point, because a passenger unadvised of his rights and otherwise unversed in constitutional law has no reason to know that the police cannot hold his refusal to cooperate against him. Additionally, even if Bostick (D) attempted to leave the bus, he would have had to squeeze by the gun-wielding officers. Although nothing in the record indicates that the officers pointed their weapons at Bostick (D) or the other passengers, the Court's precedents recognize that even the mere display of weapons by police during an encounter exerts significant coercive pressure on the confronted citizen. Further, even if Bostick (D) had perceived that the officers would let him leave the bus, he could not reasonably have been expected to resort to this means of evading their intrusive questioning, because, as far as he knew, the bus's departure from the terminal was imminent. Unlike a person approached by the police on the street, or at a bus or airport terminal after reaching its destination, a passenger approached by the police at an intermediate point in a long bus journey cannot simply leave the scene and repair to a safe haven to avoid unwanted probing by law-enforcement officials.

ANALYSIS

The *Bostick* test relies on a "reasonable person" standard. However, with the increased awareness that police-citizen encounters affect Black Americans differently than White Americans, with Black Americans on the whole several times more likely to be shot and killed by police officers than White Americans, some judges have stressed that it is important that the hypothetical "reasonable innocent person" standard must account for a person's race. Thus, for example, Judge Rosenbaum, concurring in *United States v. Knights*, 989 F.3d 1281 (11th Cir. 2021), has noted that regarding the reality of police-citizen interactions, race can and does affect whether a citizen feels "free to leave" a police encounter. Specifically, according to Judge Rosenbaum, Black Americans' lived experiences make them materially less likely than White Americans to believe they have the freedom to leave an interaction with the police, because, for Black citizens, the fear of violence often overlays the entire law-enforcement encounter. Blacks do not view themselves as having a choice to leave or end a police encounter, because historically, Blacks who have walked, run, or raced away from inquisitive police officers have ended up beaten and battered and sometimes dead. To address this racial disparity, Judge Rosenbaum proposes adopting a bright-line rule to evaluate police-citizen encounters under the Fourth Amendment, whereby officers who wish to engage in consensual interactions—at the very least with respect to those individuals an officer wants, without reasonable suspicion, to investigate in some way—at the outset, inform the approached individual that he may decline or end the interaction without penalty. According to Judge Rosenbaum, such a bright-line, race-neutral rule would provide a clear framework for citizens, officers, and courts to determine when a seizure has occurred, and would take a big step towards reflecting the realities of police-civilian interactions and making them safer for both officers and citizens.

Quicknotes

BRIGHT-LINE RULE A legal rule of decision to help resolve ambiguous issues simply and in a straightforward manner, sometimes sacrificing equity for certainty.

Torres v. Madrid

Individual injured by police (P) v. Police officer (D)

141 S.Ct. 989 (2021)

NATURE OF CASE: Appeal from affirmance of summary judgment in action brought under 42 U.S.C. § 1983 for damages resulting from alleged excessive police force.

FACT SUMMARY: State police officers Janice Madrid (Madrid) (D) and Richard Williamson (Williamson) (D) (collectively, "officers" (D)) arrived at an apartment complex to execute an arrest warrant and approached Roxanne Torres (Torres) (P). The officers (D) attempted to speak with Torres (P) as she drove away because she believed the officers (D) were carjackers. The officers (D) fired their service pistols to stop Torres (P), striking her twice. Torres (P) subsequently brought suit against the officers (D) under 42 U.S.C. § 1983 for damages, contending that that the officers (D) used excessive force against her and that the shooting constituted an unreasonable seizure under the Fourth Amendment.

RULE OF LAW

The application of physical force by a government agent to the body of a person with the intent to restrain is a seizure for Fourth Amendment purposes even if the person does not submit and is not subdued.

FACTS: State police officers Janice Madrid (Madrid) (D) and Richard Williamson (Williamson) (D) (collectively, "officers" (D)) arrived at an apartment complex to execute an arrest warrant and approached Roxanne Torres (Torres) (P), then standing near a Toyota FJ Cruiser. Although they determined that Torres (P) was not the target of the warrant, the officers (D) attempted to speak with her as she got into the driver's seat. Believing the officers (D) to be carjackers, Torres (P) hit the gas pedal to escape. The officers (D) fired their service pistols 13 times to stop Torres (P), striking her twice. Torres (P), who managed to escape and receive care at a hospital, subsequently brought suit against the officers (D) under 42 U.S.C. § 1983 for damages, contending that the officers (D) used excessive force against her and that the shooting constituted an unreasonable seizure under the Fourth Amendment. Affirming the District Court's grant of summary judgment to the officers (D), the Tenth Circuit Court of Appeals held that a suspect's continued flight after being shot by police negates a Fourth Amendment excessive-force claim. The United States Supreme Court granted certiorari.

ISSUE: Is the application of physical force by a government agent to the body of a person with the intent to restrain a seizure for Fourth Amendment purposes even if the person does not submit and is not subdued?

HOLDING AND DECISION: (Roberts, C.J.) Yes. The application of physical force by a government agent to the body of a person with the intent to restrain is a seizure for Fourth Amendment purposes even if the person does not submit and is not subdued. The Fourth Amendment protects "[t]he right of the people to be secure in their persons, houses, papers, and effects, against unreasonable searches and seizures." In *California v. Hodari D.*, 499 U.S. 621 (1991), the Court explained that common-law arrests are Fourth Amendment seizures, and that the common law considered the application of physical force to the body of a person with the intent to restrain to be an arrest—not an attempted arrest—even if the person does not yield and escapes. A review of the pertinent English and American decisions confirms that the slightest touching—or laying of hands—was a constructive detention that would complete the arrest. The analysis does not change merely because the officers (D) used force from a distance to restrain Torres (P). The required touching of the defendant's body can be as readily accomplished by a bullet as by the end of a finger. However, not every physical contact between a government employee and a member of the public is a Fourth Amendment seizure. A seizure requires the use of force with intent to restrain. Accidental force does not qualify, nor does force intentionally applied for some other purpose. The appropriate inquiry is whether the challenged conduct objectively manifests an intent to restrain. Thus, the test does not depend on either the subjective motivation of the officer or the subjective perception of the suspect. Finally, a seizure by force lasts only as long as the application of force unless the suspect submits. Applying these principles to the facts viewed in the light most favorable to Torres (P), the officers' (D) shooting applied physical force to her body and objectively manifested an intent to restrain her from driving away. Therefore, the officers (D) seized Torres (P) for the instant that the bullets struck her. Of course, a seizure is just the first step in the analysis. The Fourth Amendment does not forbid all or even most seizures—only unreasonable ones. Thus, the case is remanded to address questions regarding the reasonableness of the seizure, the damages caused by the seizure, and the officers' (D) entitlement to qualified immunity. Reversed.

Continued on next page.

DISSENT: (Gorsuch, J.) The majority holds that a criminal suspect can be simultaneously seized and roaming at large. The majority's view, that a Fourth Amendment "seizure" takes place whenever an officer "merely touches" a suspect, even if the suspect refuses to stop, evades capture, and is never to be seen again, is as mistaken as it is novel. Until now, a Fourth Amendment "seizure" has required taking possession of someone or something. To reach its contrary judgment, the majority must conflate a seizure with its attempt and confuse an arrest with a battery.

ANALYSIS

The Court took this case to resolve a split among the circuits, whereby some lower courts held that a "mere touch" constitutes a Fourth Amendment "seizure," whereas others, adhered to the view that the word "seizure" means "taking possession." The Court explained that this split occurred because courts were not careful to distinguish between seizures by control and seizures by force, and that each type of seizure enjoys a separate common-law pedigree. Unlike a seizure by force, a seizure by acquisition of control involves either voluntary submission to a show of authority or the termination of freedom of movement. The requirement of control or submission never extended to seizures by force, however, because, as the common-law courts recognized, any such requirement of control would be difficult to apply in cases involving the application of force. For example, at a basic level, it will often be unclear when an officer succeeds in gaining control over a struggling suspect, and courts would have to puzzle over whether an officer exercised control when the officer grabbed a suspect, when the officer tackled the suspect, or only when the officer secured handcuffs on the suspect. In cases involving seizures by force, the common law avoided such line-drawing problems by clearly fixing the moment of the seizure at the moment of touch.

Quicknotes

FOURTH AMENDMENT Provides that persons be secure as to their person and private belongings against unreasonable searches and seizures.

QUALIFIED IMMUNITY An affirmative defense relieving officials from civil liability for the performance of activities within their discretion so long as such conduct is not in violation of an individual's rights pursuant to law as determined by a reasonable person standard.

CHAPTER 7

Fourth Amendment Reasonableness

Quick Reference Rules of Law

PAGE

1. *Illinois v. Gates.* A magistrate must evaluate the totality of the circumstances presented to him, including, but not limited to, the reliability of an informant and the basis of his knowledge, in determining whether probable cause exists to issue a search warrant. *63*

2. *Maryland v. Pringle.* The passenger of a vehicle, even if separated from the drugs, has sufficient constructive possession of drugs located in the vehicle to give rise to probable cause for the passenger's arrest. *64*

3. *United States v. Banks.* Where law enforcement has a warrant to search a premises for illegal drugs that are susceptible of easy disposal, law enforcement's wait of 15 to 20 seconds after performing a knock-and-announce, and before forcibly entering the premises, is reasonable for purposes of the Fourth Amendment and 18 U.S.C. § 3109. *65*

4. *Horton v. California.* Where the police have a warrant or other justification for a search, and evidence of an immediately apparent incriminating nature is in plain view in a place where the officers have a lawful right of access, the police may seize the evidence whether or not they came upon it inadvertently. *67*

5. *Payton v. New York.* Absent exigent circumstances, the police may not make a warrantless, nonconsensual entry into a private residence to make a routine felony arrest. *68*

6. *Warden v. Hayden.* The Fourth Amendment allows all types of evidence to be seized pursuant to a valid search. *69*

7. *Kentucky v. King.* The exigent circumstances rule may be used to uphold a warrantless search only if police officers do not gain entry to a residence by an actual or threatened violation of the Fourth Amendment. *70*

8. *Chimel v. California.* Under the Fourth and Fourteenth Amendments, when a suspect is lawfully arrested in one room of his house, a search of his entire house cannot be constitutionally justified as incident to that arrest. *72*

9. *United States v. Chadwick.* The "automobile exception" permitting warrantless searches of vehicles in certain narrow circumstances does not apply to searches of luggage. *74*

10. *Whren v. United States.* The temporary detention of a motorist who the police have probable cause to believe has committed a civil traffic violation is consistent with the Fourth Amendment's prohibition against unreasonable seizures. *75*

11. *California v. Carney.* The "automobile exception" to the warrant requirement applies to motor homes. *76*

12. *California v. Acevedo.* The warrantless search of an automobile or any closed containers within it is reasonable under the Fourth Amendment if there is probable cause for the search. *77*

13. *Arizona v. Gant.* Police may search the passenger compartment of a vehicle incident to an occupant's arrest only if the occupant may have access to the vehicle or if it is reasonable to believe the vehicle contains evidence of the offense for which the occupant was arrested. *79*

14. *United States v. Watson.* A law officer may arrest a suspect without a warrant for a felony committed in his presence as well as for a felony not committed in his presence if he has reasonable grounds for making the arrest. *81*

CHAPTER 7

15. *Atwater v. City of Lago Vista.* The Fourth Amendment does not forbid a warrantless arrest for a minor criminal offense, such as a misdemeanor seatbelt violation punishable only by a fine. *82*

16. *United States v. Robinson.* The fact of a lawful arrest establishes the authority to conduct a full-scale, reasonable search under the Fourth Amendment. *83*

17. *Terry v. Ohio.* Where a police officer observes unusual conduct that leads him reasonably to conclude in light of his experience that criminal activity may be afoot and that the persons with whom he is dealing may be armed and presently dangerous, the officer is entitled for the protection of himself and others in the area to conduct a carefully limited search of the outer clothing of such persons in an attempt to discover weapons that might be used to assault him. *85*

18. *Illinois v. Wardlow.* Flight from police is sufficient to support a finding of reasonable suspicion and to justify a police officer's further investigation. *87*

19. *Kansas v. Glover.* When a law enforcement officer lacks information negating an inference that the owner of a vehicle is driving the vehicle, an investigative traffic stop made after running the vehicle's license plate and learning that the registered owner's driver's license has been revoked is reasonable under the Fourth Amendment. *88*

20. *Minnesota v. Dickerson.* The Fourth Amendment does not permit the warrantless seizure of contraband detected through a police officer's sense of touch during a protective patdown search where the search exceeds the bounds of what is necessary to determine if the detainee has a weapon. *91*

21. *Graham v. Connor.* All claims that law enforcement officers have used excessive force—deadly or not—in the course of arrest, investigatory stop, or other seizure of a free citizen should be analyzed under the Fourth Amendment and its "reasonableness" standard. *93*

22. *City of Tahlequah v. Bond.* A law enforcement officer will be shielded from civil liability for the officer's conduct so long as that conduct does not violate clearly established statutory or constitutional rights of which a reasonable person would have known. *94*

23. *Michigan Dept. of State Police v. Sitz.* A state's use of highway sobriety checkpoints does not violate the Fourth Amendment. *96*

24. *Schneckloth v. Bustamonte.* Whether a consent to a search was "voluntary" or was the product of duress or coercion, express or implied, is a question of fact to be determined from the totality of all the circumstances. *97*

25. *Fernandez v. California.* (1) An individual who objects to a warrantless search of his or her premises but is later lawfully removed from the premises on objectively reasonable grounds, can have his or her objection to the search superseded by a co-occupant who has common authority over the premises. (2) An individual's objection to a warrantless search of his or her premises does not remain effective indefinitely, even after the individual is no longer physically present at the premises, until the objection is withdrawn. *99*

Illinois v. Gates

State (P) v. Drug trafficker (D)

462 U.S. 213 (1983)

NATURE OF CASE: Appeal of an order to suppress evidence gained through an illegal search.

FACT SUMMARY: The Illinois Supreme Court suppressed evidence seized from Lance and Sue Gates (D) holding that the information in an anonymous letter failed to adequately show the reliability of the informant and his basis of knowledge and therefore showed insufficient probable cause to issue the search warrant.

RULE OF LAW

A magistrate must evaluate the totality of the circumstances presented to him, including, but not limited to, the reliability of an informant and the basis of his knowledge, in determining whether probable cause exists to issue a search warrant.

FACTS: An Illinois magistrate issued a search warrant for the car and residence of Larry and Sue Gates (D) based on an affidavit prepared by Mader, a Bloomingdale police detective, that stated he had initiated an investigation of the Gateses (D) based on information received in an anonymous letter that alleged in some detail the Gateses' (D) drug trafficking activities between Florida and Illinois (P) and said that on a particular date, the Gateses would follow this procedure and pick up over $100,000 in drugs. The affidavit further stated Mader's investigation had corroborated this information, in that among other things, the Gateses (D) had traveled to Florida on the day predicted and had left the next morning travelling toward Chicago. Pursuant to the warrant, the Bloomingdale police searched the Gateses' (D) car and residence upon their return and seized drugs, weapons, and other contraband. The trial court suppressed the evidence and the appellate court affirmed. The Illinois Supreme Court affirmed on the basis that probable cause could be found only if sufficient facts were presented to show both the relationship of the informant and the basis of his knowledge. It found the affidavit insufficient in this regard and held there was no probable cause to issue the warrant. Illinois (P) appealed.

ISSUE: Must a magistrate evaluate the totality of the circumstances presented to him, including, but not limited to, the reliability of the informant and the basis of his knowledge, in determining whether probable cause exists to issue a search warrant?

HOLDING AND DECISION: (Rehnquist, J.) Yes. A magistrate must evaluate the totality of the circumstances presented to him, including, but not limited to, the reliability of an informant and his basis of knowledge, in determining whether probable cause exists to issue a search warrant. In determining probable cause, reliability and basis of knowledge are more useful as interacting issues, where a weak showing of one can be compensated for by a strong showing in the other, than as separate requirements. To require strict adherence to the two-pronged test would severely curtail the use of anonymous information essential to effective police investigations. In this case, the affidavit showing corroboration of the letter coupled with the specificity of detail contained in the letter adequately show the reliability of the informant based on a totality of the circumstances, and, therefore, it was within the power of the issue magistrate to find that probable cause existed and to issue the warrant. Reversed.

DISSENT: (Stevens, J.) The facts and circumstances in this case show nothing more than a corroboration of events that are just as easily explainable as innocent travel as they are of criminal activity. Because of the lack of sufficient specificity of detail in the letter, it cannot itself be said to show reliability, and therefore no probable cause existed to issue the warrant using either the two-pronged test or the totality of the circumstances test.

ANALYSIS

This case shows the Court encouraging the issuance of search warrants by lowering the standards required to find probable cause. The two-pronged test derived from the cases of *Aguilar v. Texas*, 378 U.S. 108 (1964), and *Spinelli v. United States*, 393 U.S. 410 (1969), had evolved to the point where the Court felt that effective police functions were being undercut by overly expansive interpretations of Fourth Amendment rights. It is argued that the adoption of the totality of the circumstances test is actually retention of the two-pronged test with recognition of a good-faith exception to the exclusionary rule.

Quicknotes

AFFIDAVIT A declaration of facts written and affirmed before a witness.

PROBABLE CAUSE A reasonable basis for believing that a crime has been committed.

TOTALITY OF THE CIRCUMSTANCES TEST Standard that focuses on all the circumstances of a particular case, instead of individual factors.

Maryland v. Pringle

State (P) v. Convicted drug possessor (D)

540 U.S. 366 (2003)

NATURE OF CASE: Appeal by state from reversal of conviction for cocaine possession.

FACT SUMMARY: When Pringle (D) was arrested for cocaine possession when he was a front-seat passenger in a vehicle and the cocaine was found in the back seat, he argued that he did not have sufficient possession of the cocaine to show probable cause for his arrest; hence any confession resulting from such arrest would be invalid.

RULE OF LAW

The passenger of a vehicle, even if separated from the drugs, has sufficient constructive possession of drugs located in the vehicle to give rise to probable cause for the passenger's arrest.

FACTS: A police officer stopped an automobile for speeding. There were three occupants in the car. Pringle (D) was the front-seat passenger. When the driver opened the glove compartment to get the registration, the officer observed a large amount of rolled-up cash. The driver consented to a vehicle search, which yielded $763 from the glove compartment and cocaine from behind the back-seat armrest. Pringle (D) and both other occupants were arrested. Pringle (D) waived his *Miranda* rights [*Miranda v. Arizona*, 384 U.S. 436 (1966)] and confessed the cocaine belonged to him. The trial court denied Pringle's (D) motion to suppress the confession as fruit of an illegal arrest, holding the officer had probable cause for the arrest. Pringle (D) was convicted of cocaine possession; however, the Court of Appeals of Maryland reversed, holding that the mere finding of cocaine behind the back seat armrest when Pringle (D) was simply a passenger in the front seat failed to establish probable cause to arrest Pringle (D) for possession. Maryland (P) appealed.

ISSUE: Does the passenger of a vehicle, even if separated from the drugs, have sufficient constructive possession of drugs located in the vehicle to give rise to probable cause for the passenger's arrest?

HOLDING AND DECISION: (Rehnquist, C.J.) Yes. The passenger of a vehicle, even if separated from the drugs, has sufficient constructive possession of drugs located in the vehicle to give rise to probable cause for the passenger's arrest. Maryland law authorizes police officers to execute warrantless arrests, inter alia, for felonies committed in an officer's presence or where the officer has probable cause to believe a felony has been or is being committed. Here, the officer, upon recovering the plastic bags of cocaine, had probable cause to believe a felony had been committed. As to whether there was probable cause to believe Pringle (D) had committed that crime, Maryland law defines "possession" as the exercise of actual or constructive dominion over a thing by one or more persons. The probable cause standard is incapable of precise definition or quantification into percentages because it deals with probabilities and depends on the totality of the circumstances. In the instant case, Pringle (D) was one of three men riding in the car in the early morning hours when a large amount of rolled-up cash and five baggies of cocaine were found. The cocaine was "accessible" to all three of the occupants, including Pringle (D). It was an entirely reasonable inference from these facts that any or all three of the occupants had knowledge of, and exercised dominion and control over, the cocaine. Thus, a reasonable officer could conclude there was probable cause to believe Pringle (D) committed the crime of possession of cocaine, either solely or jointly. Reversed and remanded.

ANALYSIS

As the Supreme Court makes clear in *Pringle*, the probable cause standard is a practical, nontechnical conception that deals with the factual and practical considerations of everyday life on which reasonable and prudent persons, "not legal technicians," act. Probable cause is a "fluid concept"–turning on the assessment of probabilities in particular factual contexts, not readily, or even usually, reduced to a neat set of legal rules.

Quicknotes

FELONY A criminal offense of greater seriousness than a misdemeanor; felonies are generally defined pursuant to statute as any crime that is punishable by death or by a term of imprisonment exceeding one year.

INTER ALIA Among other things.

United States v. Banks

Federal government (P) v. Individual convicted on firearms and drug trafficking charges (D)

540 U.S. 31 (2003)

NATURE OF CASE: Appeal from reversal of conviction for illegal firearms possession and drug trafficking.

FACT SUMMARY: Banks (D), who was convicted of illegal firearms possession and drug trafficking on the basis of cocaine and weapons found in his residence, had successfully contended that law enforcement's wait of only 15 to 20 seconds after making a knock-and-announce pursuant to a search warrant and before forcibly entering his residence, was an unreasonably short time that violated the Fourth Amendment and 18 U.S.C. § 3109, thus requiring suppression of the evidence found in his residence. The Government (P) contended that law enforcement's wait had been reasonable under the circumstances.

RULE OF LAW

Where law enforcement has a warrant to search a premises for illegal drugs that are susceptible of easy disposal, law enforcement's wait of 15 to 20 seconds after performing a knock-and-announce, and before forcibly entering the premises, is reasonable for purposes of the Fourth Amendment and 18 U.S.C. § 3109.

FACTS: When federal and local law enforcement officers went to Banks's (D) apartment to execute a warrant to search for cocaine, they called out "police search warrant" and rapped on the front door hard enough to be heard by officers at the back door, waited for 15 to 20 seconds with no response, and then broke open the door. Banks (D) was in the shower and testified that he heard nothing until the crash of the door. The search produced weapons, crack cocaine, and other evidence of drug dealing. In response to drug and firearms charges, Banks (D) moved to suppress the evidence, arguing that the officers executing the search warrant waited an unreasonably short time before forcing entry, and, so, violated the Fourth Amendment and 18 U.S.C. § 3109, which permits an officer to enter by force if after notice of the officer's authority and purpose, the officer is refused admittance. After Banks (D) was convicted, the Ninth Circuit Court of Appeals reversed his conviction using a four-part, categorical scheme for vetting knock-and-announce entries. The United States Supreme Court granted certiorari.

ISSUE: Where law enforcement has a warrant to search a premises for illegal drugs that are susceptible of easy disposal, is law enforcement's wait of 15 to 20 seconds after performing a knock-and-announce, and before forcibly entering the premises, reasonable for purposes of the Fourth Amendment and 18 U.S.C. § 3109?

HOLDING AND DECISION: (Souter, J.) Yes. Where law enforcement has a warrant to search a premises for illegal drugs that are susceptible of easy disposal, law enforcement's wait of 15 to 20 seconds after performing a knock-and-announce, and before forcibly entering the premises, is reasonable for purposes of the Fourth Amendment and 18 U.S.C. § 3109. The standards bearing on whether officers can legitimately enter after knocking are the same as those for requiring or dispensing with knock and announce altogether. This Court's precedents have fleshed out the notion of reasonable execution on a case-by-case basis, and have pointed out factual considerations of unusual, albeit not dispositive, significance. The obligation to knock and announce before entering gives way when officers have reasonable grounds to expect futility or to suspect that an exigency, such as evidence destruction, will arise instantly upon knocking. Since most people keep their doors locked, a no-knock entry will normally do some damage, a fact too common to require a heightened justification when a reasonable suspicion of exigency already justifies an unwarned entry. This case turns on the exigency revealed by the circumstances known to the officers after they knocked and announced, which the Government (P) contends was the risk of losing easily disposable evidence. After 15 to 20 seconds without a response, officers could fairly have suspected that Banks (D) would flush away the cocaine if they remained reticent. Each of Banks's (D) counterarguments—that he was in the shower and did not hear the officers, and that it might have taken him longer than 20 seconds to reach the door—rests on a mistake about the relevant enquiry. As to the first argument, the facts known to the police are what count in judging a reasonable waiting time, and there is no indication that they knew that Banks (D) was in the shower, and, thus, unaware of an impending search. As to the second, the crucial fact is not the time it would take Banks (D) to reach the door but the time it would take him to destroy the cocaine. It is not unreasonable to think that someone could get in a position to destroy the drugs within 15 to 20 seconds. Once the exigency had matured, the officers were not bound to learn anything more or wait any longer before entering, even though the entry entailed some harm to the building. The four-part, categorical scheme

Continued on next page.

for vetting knock-and-announce entries crafted and used by the Court of Appeals is rejected in favor of a totality-of-the-circumstances approach. Under such a totality analysis, not only may damage to the building be a factor in assessing reasonableness, the speed with which contraband may be disposed of is also a factor. Thus, since one point of making an officer knock and announce is to give a person inside the chance to save their door, where there is no reason to suspect an immediate risk of frustration or futility in waiting at all, the reasonable wait time may well be longer when police make a forced entry, since they ought to be more certain the occupant has had time to answer the door. The need to damage property in the course of getting in is a good reason to require more patience than it would be reasonable to expect if the door were open. "Police seeking a stolen piano may be able to spend more time to make sure they really need the battering ram." Finally, the entry here also satisfied 18 U.S.C. § 3109, which permits entry by force "if, after notice of his authority and purpose, [an officer] is refused admittance." Because § 3109 implicates the exceptions to the common-law knock-and-announce requirement that informs the Fourth Amendment itself, § 3109 is also subject to an exigent circumstance exception, which qualifies the requirement of refusal after notice, just as it qualifies the obligation to announce in the first place. [Reversed.]

ANALYSIS

At common law, the knock-and-announce rule was traditionally justified in part by the belief that law enforcement's announcement generally would avoid the destruction or breaking of any house by which great damage and inconvenience might ensue. Thus, as the Court notes, one purpose in making a law enforcement officer announce his or her presence and purpose is to give a person inside the chance to save their door. In keeping with this original purpose, in cases where only minor offenses or misdemeanors, rather than felonies, are involved, the Court has held that the risk of losing evidence of a minor offense is insufficient to make it reasonable to enter a dwelling to make a warrantless arrest. See *Welsh v. Wisconsin*, 466 U.S. 740 (1984). Courts of Appeals have applied *Welsh* to warrantless entries simply to search for evidence, considering the gravity of the offense in determining whether exigent circumstances exist. Also, a few years after deciding *Banks*, the Court in *Hudson v. Michigan*, 547 U.S. 586 (2006), held that evidence should not be suppressed notwithstanding a violation of the knock-and-announce rule. Since *Hudson* was decided, the knock-and-announce rule has only rarely been the subject of litigation related to motions to suppress.

Quicknotes

EXIGENT CIRCUMSTANCES Circumstances requiring an extraordinary or immediate response; an exception to the prohibition on a warrantless arrest or search when police officers believe probable cause to exist and there is no time for obtaining a warrant.

KNOCK AND ANNOUNCE RULE Requirement that a police officer must first knock and announce his or her intention before entering an individual's home in the execution of a valid warrant.

Horton v. California

Convicted felon (D) v. State (P)

496 U.S. 128 (1990)

NATURE OF CASE: Appeal from criminal conviction upon denial of motion to suppress evidence.

FACT SUMMARY: Sergeant LaRault searched the home of Horton (D) with a search warrant for proceeds of a crime, found weapons in plain view, and seized them.

RULE OF LAW

Where the police have a warrant or other justification for a search, and evidence of an immediately apparent incriminating nature is in plain view in a place where the officers have a lawful right of access, the police may seize the evidence whether or not they came upon it inadvertently.

FACTS: Sergeant LaRault swore out an affidavit describing the proceeds of a crime and the weapons used. A search warrant was issued for the proceeds only. When LaRault searched Horton's (D) home he did not find the proceeds, but he discovered the weapons in plain view and seized them. At trial, Horton (D) argued that the weapons could not be introduced as evidence because LaRault's admission that he found other evidence while searching for the proceeds he was interested in meant that the discovery of the weapons was not inadvertent and, therefore, under *Coolidge v. New Hampshire*, 403 U.S. 443 (1971), not covered by the "plain view" doctrine. The trial judge disagreed and admitted the evidence. Horton (D) was convicted, and he appealed to the United States Supreme Court.

ISSUE: Where the police have a warrant or other justification for a search, and evidence of an immediately apparent incriminating nature is in plain view in a place where the officers have a lawful right of access, may the police seize the evidence whether or not they came upon it inadvertently?

HOLDING AND DECISION: (Stevens, J.) Yes. Where the police have a warrant or other justification for a search, and evidence of an immediately apparent incriminating nature is in plain view in a place where the officers have a lawful right of access, the police may seize the evidence whether or not they came upon it inadvertently. Evenhanded law enforcement is best achieved by application of objective standards, rather than standards depending on the subjective state of mind of the officer. There is no danger of officers using specific warrants or exigent circumstances to conduct general searches because the scope of the search is proscribed by the warrant's description of the place to be searched or the exigencies that justify the intrusion. This decision overrules the part of *Coolidge* that requires that an officer inadvertently come upon an object to seize it under the "plain view" doctrine. Affirmed.

DISSENT: (Brennan, J.) The Fourth Amendment not only protects privacy interests by requiring that a warrant describe the place to be searched, but also protects possessory interests by requiring that a warrant particularly describe the things to be seized. Eliminating the inadvertency requirement excuses officers from obtaining a warrant particularly describing evidence, giving them discretion to invade possessory interests in property.

ANALYSIS

The remaining requirements for "plain view" seizure have also come under United States Supreme Court review. In Coolidge v. *New Hampshire*, 403 U.S. 443 (1971), automobiles were in plain view, but they were parked on private property to which the police did not have legal access, so their seizure was unconstitutional. In *Arizona v. Hicks*, 480 U.S. 321 (1987), an officer lawfully searching an apartment for evidence of a shooting noticed expensive stereo components that seemed out of place in the badly furnished apartment. He moved the components to read the serial numbers, one serial number matched a stolen property list, and he seized the item. The seizure was ruled unconstitutional because the fact that the item was stolen was not immediately apparent and the moving of the components amounted to a separate search without probable cause.

Quicknotes

FOURTH AMENDMENT Provides that persons be secure as to their person and private belongings against unreasonable searches and seizures.

PLAIN VIEW DOCTRINE Exception to the requirement of a valid warrant for a search or seizure so long as the officer is lawfully in the location where the evidence is obtained and it is apparent that the thing seized is evidence.

Payton v. New York

Murder convict (D) v. State (P)

445 U.S. 573 (1980)

NATURE OF CASE: Appeal from convictions for murder.

FACT SUMMARY: Without a warrant, the police entered Payton's (D) apartment to arrest him for murder and, even though he was not there, seized a shell casing that was in plain sight and was later admitted into evidence at his trial.

RULE OF LAW

Absent exigent circumstances, the police may not make a warrantless, nonconsensual entry into a private residence to make a routine felony arrest.

FACTS: Having probable cause to believe Payton (D) had murdered a gas station manager the police entered his apartment to effect a routine felony arrest. Although he was not home, the police found a 30-caliber shell casing in plain sight in the apartment and seized it for ultimate use as evidence at his trial. Payton's (D) motions to suppress the evidence were denied and he was convicted of murder. On appeal, he argued that the statute authorizing warrantless entries to make routine felony arrests violated the Fourth Amendment. The court of appeals affirmed the conviction.

ISSUE: Absent exigent circumstances, may the police make a warrantless, nonconsensual entry into a private residence to make a routine felony arrest?

HOLDING AND DECISION: (Stevens, J.) No. Absent exigent circumstances, the police may not make a warrantless, nonconsensual entry into a private residence to make a routine felony arrest. The Fourth Amendment, made applicable to the states by the Fourteenth Amendment, draws a firm line at the entrance to the house. Absent exigent circumstances, that threshold may not reasonably be crossed without a warrant. Inasmuch as no warrant was obtained, the police acted impermissibly in entering Payton's (D) apartment, and the evidence found therein should not have been admitted into evidence at trial. Reversed and remanded.

DISSENT: (White, J.) Instead of adopting a rule that will severely hamper effective law enforcement, the Court should embrace a clear and simple rule comporting with the carefully crafted restrictions on the common-law power of arrest entry. That is, after knocking and announcing their presence, police may enter the home to make a daytime arrest without a warrant when there is a probable cause to believe that the person to be arrested committed a felony and is present in the house.

ANALYSIS

At the time this case was decided, some states had already passed laws requiring a warrant as a precondition to a felony arrest in the home. The Court noted that no proof had been offered that such a requirement had caused law enforcement in those states to suffer.

Quicknotes

EXIGENT CIRCUMSTANCES Circumstances requiring an extraordinary or immediate response; an exception to the prohibition on a warrantless arrest or search when police officers believe probable cause to exist and there is no time for obtaining a warrant.

KNOCK AND ANNOUNCE RULE Requirement that a police officer must first knock and announce his or her intention before entering an individual's home in the execution of a valid warrant.

Warden v. Hayden

State (P) v. Convicted robber (D)

387 U.S. 294 (1967)

NATURE OF CASE: Appeal from conviction for armed robbery.

FACT SUMMARY: Hayden's (D) personal items were seized from his home during a search and introduced as evidence at his trial.

RULE OF LAW
The Fourth Amendment allows all types of evidence to be seized pursuant to a valid search.

FACTS: Hayden's (D) home was searched without a warrant, but the search was justified by exigent circumstances. Items of his clothing (cap, jacket, and trousers) were seized during the search and were admitted at his trial for armed robbery. Hayden (D) was convicted and then appealed, claiming that the Fourth Amendment prohibited the seizure of items that were mere evidence rather than the instrumentalities of crime. The Court of Appeals for the Fourth Circuit agreed with Hayden (D) and the State (P) appealed to the United States Supreme Court.

ISSUE: Does the Fourth Amendment allow all types of evidence to be seized pursuant to a valid search?

HOLDING AND DECISION: (Brennan, J.) Yes. The Fourth Amendment allows all types of evidence to be seized pursuant to a valid search. Previously, this Court has supported a distinction between items that were "mere evidence" from instrumentalities, fruits of crime, or contraband. This rule was based on the premise that the right to search for and seize property depended on the assertion of the government of a superior interest. The purpose of apprehending and convicting criminals was not considered sufficient. Thus, stolen property and contraband were subject to seizure, but other items were not. This premise that property interests control the right of governmental searches has subsequently been discredited. The Fourth Amendment is designed to protect privacy, and a search directed at purely evidentiary objects is no more intrusive than one for instrumentalities of crime. The "mere evidence" limitation has also spawned exceptions so numerous that there has been extreme confusion. As long as requirements of the Fourth Amendment are followed, i.e., probable cause and the intervention of a neutral and detached magistrate, there is no viable reason for maintaining the "mere evidence" limitation. Accordingly, Hayden's (D) personal items were properly seized. The Court of Appeals is reversed.

DISSENT: (Douglas, J.) The personal effects of an individual are sacrosanct from the prying eyes of the government.

ANALYSIS

The majority decision noted the practical problems implicit in distinguishing between mere evidence and instrumentalities of crime. Moreover, nothing in the language of the Fourth Amendment supports the distinction. It should be noted, however, that without the mere evidence limitation it is much easier for the government to meet the particularity requirement for a warrant.

Quicknotes

FOURTH AMENDMENT Provides that persons be secure as to their person and private belongings against unreasonable searches and seizures.

Kentucky v. King

State (P) v. Subject of a warrantless search (D)

563 U.S. 452 (2011)

NATURE OF CASE: Appeal from state high court decision in favor of defendant.

FACT SUMMARY: After observing suspect purchase cocaine, police officers followed him to a breezeway in an apartment complex. The officers did not know which apartment the suspect entered. Smelling marijuana from one apartment and hearing things moving around in the apartment, the officers entered that apartment and discovered King (D) with drugs, cash, and other drug paraphernalia.

RULE OF LAW

The exigent circumstances rule may be used to uphold a warrantless search only if police officers do not gain entry to a residence by an actual or threatened violation of the Fourth Amendment.

FACTS: Police officers were following a suspect involved in a controlled purchase of cocaine. The suspect entered the breezeway of an apartment complex. The officers following the suspect into the breezeway did not know into which apartment he disappeared, the one on the left or the right. The officers smelled the odor of marijuana emanating from the apartment on the left. The officers knocked on the door of that apartment and announced their presence. They then heard things being moved around quickly in the apartment. This led the officers to believe that evidence was about to be destroyed. The officers then entered the apartment and found King (D), who was not the original suspect, with drugs, cash, and other drug paraphernalia. Before trial, King (D) moved to suppress the evidence on the grounds that the officers' search was an illegal warrantless search and no exceptions existed to uphold the search. The trial court denied the motion and a jury convicted King (D) on various drug charges. The Kentucky Supreme Court then overturned the decision, holding that the police could not rely upon the exigent circumstances exception when the police themselves created the emergency. The State (P) appealed to the United States Supreme Court.

ISSUE: May the exigent circumstances rule be used to uphold a warrantless search only if police officers do not gain entry to a residence by an actual or threatened violation of the Fourth Amendment?

HOLDING AND DECISION: (Alito, J.) Yes. The exigent circumstances rule may be used to uphold a warrantless search only if police officers do not gain entry to a residence by an actual or threatened violation of the Fourth Amendment. First, the exigent circumstances rule allows officers to conduct a search without a warrant if exigent circumstances exist which precludes officers from first obtaining a warrant. Such circumstances include the imminent destruction of evidence. However, lower federal courts have developed the "police created exigency" doctrine that holds that police may not conduct a search without a warrant if the police themselves create or manufacture the exigent circumstances. This Court now holds that the exigent circumstances exception may still be used as long as the police do not gain entry by an actual or threatened violation of the Fourth Amendment. A review of the officers' actions in exigent circumstance cases must be objective, and the Kentucky Supreme Court's use of a subjective test is inappropriate under the Fourth Amendment. Rather than ruminate whether the officers subjectively created the emergency by loudly knocking on the door of the apartment, the facts must be viewed objectively in light of all circumstances. Another test posited by the lower courts, whether it was reasonably foreseeable that the officers' actions would create the exigent circumstances, is also unworkable. There is always some possibility a suspect in the drug trade may have drugs in the residence. Use of the reasonable foreseeability test would include an analysis of the level of predictability that must be reached before the exigent circumstances rule would apply. Lastly, some courts have faulted police when circumstances supporting probable cause exist but the police fail to stop their activities and obtain a warrant. This approach interferes with law enforcement strategies. The police are under no obligation to halt their activities and obtain a search warrant once the minimum standard for probable cause has been reached. Reversed and remanded.

ANALYSIS

This decision reaffirms the original exigent circumstances rule and severely limits the "police created exigency" exception to that rule. In essence, as long as police do not gain entry by means of an actual or threatened violation of the Fourth Amendment, the warrantless search may be upheld. Note that here the Supreme Court did not engage in a specific analysis as to whether exigent circumstances were present. It assumed this for the purposes of its review but remanded the case

Continued on next page.

to the Kentucky Supreme Court for a determination of whether exigent circumstances were actually present.

Quicknotes

EXIGENT CIRCUMSTANCES Circumstances requiring an extraordinary or immediate response; an exception to the prohibition on a warrantless arrest or search when police officers believe probable cause to exist and there is no time for obtaining a warrant.

Chimel v. California

Burglary convict (D) v. State (P)

395 U.S. 752 (1969)

NATURE OF CASE: Appeal from burglary conviction.

FACT SUMMARY: Police officers, after lawfully arresting Chimel (D) in his house, conducted a search, over his objections, of his entire house, which produced evidence used to obtain his conviction on two charges of burglary.

RULE OF LAW

Under the Fourth and Fourteenth Amendments, when a suspect is lawfully arrested in one room of his house, a search of his entire house cannot be constitutionally justified as incident to that arrest.

FACTS: Late one afternoon, police officers arrived at Chimel's (D) home with a warrant authorizing his arrest for the burglary of a coin shop. Chimel's (D) wife allowed the officers to enter the house and wait for Chimel (D) to return from work. When Chimel (D) entered his home, the officers arrested him and then conducted a search, over his objection, of his entire three-bedroom house, including the attic, the garage, and a small workshop. During this search, the officers seized numerous coins, several medal tokens, and other objects used subsequently at Chimel's (D) trial to obtain his conviction on two charges of burglary. Upon affirmation of this conviction, Chimel (D) brought a petition for certiorari to this court.

ISSUE: Under the Fourth and Fourteenth Amendments, when a suspect is lawfully arrested in one room of his house, can a search of his entire house be constitutionally justified as incident to that arrest?

HOLDING AND DECISION: (Stewart, J.) No. Under the Fourth and Fourteenth Amendments, when a suspect is lawfully arrested in one room of his house, a search of his entire house cannot be constitutionally justified as incident to that arrest. Under the Fourth and Fourteenth Amendments, a warrantless search conducted incident to a lawful arrest may only extend to a search of the arrestee's person and to the area "within his immediate control" (i.e., the area within which he might obtain a weapon or destructible evidence). The past decisions of this Court on such searches have been far from consistent, and this case marks the final determination of which one of two divergent lines of cases applies. On one hand, the *Harris v. United States*, 331 U.S. 145 (1947), and *United States v. Rabinowitz*, 339 U.S. 56 (1950), line of cases has given a broad scope to warrantless searches conducted incident to arrest. Under these cases, anything within the "possession" of the arrestee (as broadly defined to include a search of the arrestee's entire apartment in *Harris*, and to include a search of the arrestee's one-room business office in *Rabinowitz*) may be searched at the time of his arrest, in order to seize any evidence connected with his suspected crime. On the other hand, the *Go-Bart Importing Co. et al. v. United States*, 282 U.S. 344 (1931), *United States v. Lefkowitz*, 285 U.S. 452 (1932), and *Trupiano v. United States*, 334 U.S. 699 (1948), line of cases limits warrantless charges incident to arrest. In both *Go-Bart* and *Lefkowitz*, such searches were limited to evidence that was "visible and accessible and in the offender's immediate custody." In *Trupiano*, the Court stated that a search warrant is always required absent some showing of "necessity" and that there must be something more of a necessity for a warrantless search than mere arrest. The decision of this Court today is an attempt to define, along the line of the *Trupiano* case, when such necessity exists. As this Court stated in *Trupiano*, the burden is upon those seeking an exemption from the warrant requirement to show that it is justified by necessity. Such justification in the case of warrantless searches incident to arrest may extend no further than the arrestee's person and the area within his immediate control. It is reasonable for an officer to search the arrestee's person for his own safety, since the arrestee may have concealed weapons, and it is reasonable to search the area within the arrestee's control to prevent him from reaching a weapon or destroying evidence. But any extension beyond such an area would lead to the "evaporation" of the Fourth Amendment's right against unreasonable searches and seizures. Here, the search of Chimel's (D) house was far beyond that area considered reasonable. As such, the judgment is reversed.

ANALYSIS

This case illustrates the limited scope of a warrantless search conducted incident to a lawful arrest. Whenever police take an arrested person into custody, it is "reasonable" to make a "full search" of his person, regardless of the reason for his arrest. But this decision leaves open the question of whether a "full search," or only a limited search for weapons, may be conducted when the person is not taken into custody after his arrest. Note, however, that after a lawful arrest, when the suspect is taken into custody, a warrantless search of his clothing and the property in his immediate possession may be done "after he has been brought to the station

Continued on next page.

house" and "after a substantial period of time during his incarceration" – at least when there is probable cause linking the clothes to his crime.

Quicknotes

EXIGENT CIRCUMSTANCES Circumstances requiring an extraordinary or immediate response; an exception to the prohibition on a warrantless arrest or search when police officers believe probable cause to exist and there is no time for obtaining a warrant.

PLAIN VIEW Exception to the requirement of a valid warrant for a search or seizure so long as the officer is lawfully in the location where the evidence is obtained and it is apparent that the object seized is evidence.

SEARCH INCIDENT TO A LAWFUL ARREST EXCEPTION Exception to the requirement of a valid warrant for a search or seizure so long as the officer is lawfully in the location where the evidence is obtained and it is apparent the thing seized is evidence.

United States v. Chadwick

Federal government (P) v. Accused drug trafficker (D)

433 U.S. 1 (1977)

NATURE OF CASE: Appeal from district court judgment dismissing charges of marijuana possession.

FACT SUMMARY: Chadwick (D) and his confederates were arrested by federal narcotics agents; an hour and a half later, their footlocker was opened and found to contain marijuana.

RULE OF LAW

The "automobile exception" permitting warrantless searches of vehicles in certain narrow circumstances does not apply to searches of luggage.

FACTS: Narcotics agents in San Diego observed the suspicious behavior of two persons (D) carrying a footlocker on a train bound for Boston. They alerted agents in Boston, who had a dog sniff the footlocker upon its arrival. The dog indicated the presence of drugs without alerting the owners of the locker. Chadwick (D) then joined the two suspects (D), and they placed the footlocker in the trunk of Chadwick's (D) car. The agents then arrested the three suspects (D) and took possession of the footlocker. An hour and a half later, the agents opened the footlocker and discovered large quantities of marijuana. Prior to their trial for drug possession, Chadwick et al. (D) successfully moved to suppress the marijuana. The Government (P) sought review.

ISSUE: Does the "automobile exception" permitting warrantless searches of vehicles in certain narrow circumstances apply to searches of luggage?

HOLDING AND DECISION: (Burger, C.J.) No. The "automobile exception" permitting warrantless searches of vehicles in certain narrow circumstances does not apply to searches of luggage. Luggage and automobiles are not analogous for Fourth Amendment purposes. Luggage contents are not open to public view, and the expectation of privacy is greater in luggage than in an automobile. Once the footlocker was transferred to the agents' control, there was no longer a danger that it would be moved before a warrant could be obtained. Moreover, the search, occurring more than an hour after the arrest of Chadwick et al. (D), was not incident to their arrest. The judgment is affirmed.

ANALYSIS

Justice Blackmun in his dissent in *Chadwick* suggests that the automobile exception would have applied if the agents had stopped Chadwick's (D) vehicle "on the highway" rather than making the arrest before the car was started. However, two years later, in *Arkansas v. Sanders,* 442 U.S. 753 (1979), implicitly addressing Justice Blackmun's concerns, the Court extended *Chadwick* and held that, in the absence of exigent circumstances, police are required to obtain a warrant before searching luggage taken from an automobile properly stopped and searched "on the highway." Nevertheless, several years later, the Court abrogated *Sanders* in *California v. Acevedo,* 500 U.S. 565 (1991), an opinion written by Justice Blackmun (now in the majority), that held that police, in a search extending only to a container within an automobile, may search the container without a warrant where they have probable cause to believe that it holds contraband or evidence. Thus, under *Acevedo,* the automobile exception applies to containers and luggage found inside a car.

Quicknotes

SEARCH INCIDENT TO LAWFUL ARREST Exception to the requirement of a valid warrant for a search or seizure so long as the officer is lawfully in the location where the evidence is obtained and it is apparent that the thing seized is evidence.

Whren v. United States

Driver of truck (D) v. Federal government (P)

517 U.S. 806 (1996)

NATURE OF CASE: Appeal challenging determinations that a police search was constitutional under the Fourth Amendment.

FACT SUMMARY: Whren (D) challenged the constitutionality of a police search of his truck, wherein narcotics were found, when the police stopped him for a traffic violation.

RULE OF LAW

The temporary detention of a motorist who the police have probable cause to believe has committed a civil traffic violation is consistent with the Fourth Amendment's prohibition against unreasonable seizures.

FACTS: On June 10, 1993, plainclothes vice-squad officers patrolled a "high drug area" of Washington, D.C. The police saw Whren (D) sitting at a stop sign in a truck for an unusually long time. When the police approached, Whren (D) turned right without signaling and sped off at an "unreasonable" speed. When the police stopped Whren (D), they looked in the car and saw bags of crack cocaine. When Whren (D) was arrested on narcotics charges, he challenged the legality of the stop, stating the police had no probable cause to search the car. Whren (D) claimed the police's reasons for the stop—traffic violations—were pretextual and that in this circumstance, a stricter, "objective officer" rule should govern whether the search was legal. The district court convicted Whren (D) of the narcotics charges and the appellate court affirmed. Whren (D) appealed.

ISSUE: Is the temporary detention of a motorist who the police have probable cause to believe has committed a civil traffic violation inconsistent with the Fourth Amendment's prohibition against unreasonable seizures?

HOLDING AND DECISION: (Scalia, J.) No. The temporary detention of a motorist who the police have probable cause to believe has committed a civil traffic violation is not inconsistent with the Fourth Amendment's prohibition against unreasonable seizures. Here, Whren (D) had violated traffic laws and, as such, the police had the right to stop him to give him a citation. The fact that such violations occur routinely does not warrant a different standard as to whether the search was constitutional. Even though the police were plainclothes officers, they still had the right to stop a motorist who violates traffic laws. An officer's motive does not automatically invalidate objectively justifiable behavior under the Fourth Amendment. Intentional discrimination in the application of a law is a Fifth Amendment Equal Protection question, not a Fourth Amendment search and seizure question, and does not apply to the case at hand. Searches are subject to a reasonableness standard, but where probable cause has existed, balancing tests have been applied only where the search and seizure has been extraordinary. Here, the traffic violation warranted the probable cause and the police properly seized the narcotics in plain view. Affirmed.

ANALYSIS

This case highlights certain Fourth Amendment search and seizure issues in the context of automobiles. While the Fourth Amendment usually requires police to obtain search warrants before conducting a search, the easy mobility of automobiles often permits searches without warrants if the police have probable cause to search the vehicle. Occasions where warrantless searches have been allowed involved searches incident to arrest and searches to prevent the loss of evidence. See *Application of Kiser*, 419 F.2d 1134 (8th Cir. 1969); *Carroll v. U.S.*, 267 U.S. 132 (1925).

Quicknotes

AUTOMOBILE STOP A police officer may stop an automobile and conduct a search of the vehicle without a valid warrant if he or she has probable cause to believe the vehicle contains evidence of a crime or contraband.

PROBABLE CAUSE A reasonable basis for believing that a crime has been committed.

California v. Carney

State (P) v. Drug dealer (D)

471 U.S. 386 (1985)

NATURE OF CASE: Appeal from conviction for drug trafficking.

FACT SUMMARY: Carney (D) was accused of trading drugs for sexual favors.

RULE OF LAW

The "automobile exception" to the warrant requirement applies to motor homes.

FACTS: A Drug Enforcement Agency (DEA) agent placed the motor home of Carney (D) under surveillance. When a youth exited the motor home, he was stopped by Williams, a DEA agent. The youth told Williams that he had received marijuana in return for sexual favors. Williams and other agents searched the motor home and found marijuana and related paraphernalia. Carney (D) was charged with possession for sale. He moved to suppress the evidence as the agents did not have a search warrant. The trial court denied the motion, but the California Supreme Court reversed.

ISSUE: Does the "automobile exception" to the warrant requirement apply to motor homes?

HOLDING AND DECISION: (Burger, C.J.) Yes. The "automobile exception" to the warrant requirement applies to motor homes. The reason for the exception is twofold. Autos are inherently mobile and can be taken away before a warrant is issued. Also, autos, unlike homes, are subject to regulations that lower the owner's expectation of privacy. The motor home here, while having homelike qualities, is also inherently mobile and is subject to the same state licensing as a regular automobile. Therefore, the rationales for the auto exception apply to mobile homes. Reversed.

DISSENT: (Stevens, J.) Where, as here, agents have the element of surprise on their side, and the motor home is parked, the exigencies justifying the auto exception do not apply.

ANALYSIS

While auto searches do not require warrants, probable cause is still necessary. For this reason, the scope of an auto search is limited. It may not be more intrusive than that necessary to obtain the required evidence.

Quicknotes

AUTOMOBILE EXCEPTION Exception to the requirement of a valid warrant if a police officer has probable cause to believe that a vehicle contains evidence of a crime or contraband; the officer may search the entire vehicle.

EXIGENT CIRCUMSTANCES Circumstances requiring an extraordinary or immediate response; an exception to the prohibition on a warrantless arrest or search when police officers believe probable cause to exist and there is no time for obtaining a warrant.

EXPECTATION OF PRIVACY Requirement that in order to invoke the Fourth Amendment's protection against unreasonable searches and seizures, the individual must have a reasonable expectation of privacy in respect to the location searched or thing seized.

PROBABLE CAUSE A reasonable basis for believing that a crime has been committed.

California v. Acevedo

State (P) v. Contraband possessor (D)

500 U.S. 565 (1991)

NATURE OF CASE: Appeal from acceptance of motion to suppress evidence.

FACT SUMMARY: In California's (P) criminal action against Acevedo (D) for possession of contraband, the appellate court, reversing the district court's ruling, accepted Acevedo's (D) motion to suppress evidence relating to his contraband possession.

RULE OF LAW
The warrantless search of an automobile or any closed containers within it is reasonable under the Fourth Amendment if there is probable cause for the search.

FACTS: Officers who had probable cause to believe that contraband was in a residence which they had under surveillance watched Acevedo (D) enter the address, stay for ten minutes, and reappear carrying a full, brown paper bag. Subsequently, Acevedo (D) placed this bag in the trunk of his car and started to drive away. However, the officers, fearing loss of evidence, stopped him, opened his trunk and the bag without a warrant, and found contraband. At the criminal proceedings brought against Acevedo (D) for possession of contraband, Acevedo (D) moved to suppress the contraband evidence, arguing that since the officers' probable cause was directed specifically at the bag and not at his car, common law dictated that the officers obtain a warrant prior to searching the bag's contents. Notwithstanding Acevedo's (D) argument, the district court denied his motion. On appeal, however, the California Court of Appeal reversed, and the Supreme Court denied review. California (P) appealed.

ISSUE: Is the warrantless search of an automobile or any closed containers within it reasonable under the Fourth Amendment if there is probable cause for the search?

HOLDING AND DECISION: (Blackmun, J.) Yes. The warrantless search of an automobile or any closed containers within it is reasonable under the Fourth Amendment if there is probable cause for the search. This rule rectifies the two apparently dichotomous common-law rules governing the warrantless search of an automobile and the warrantless search of a closed container within the automobile. The dichotomy dictates that if there is probable cause to search a car, then the entire car—including any closed container found therein—may be searched without a warrant, but if there is probable cause only as to a container in the car, the container may be held but not searched until a warrant is obtained. However, the line between probable cause to search a vehicle and probable cause to search a package in that vehicle is not always clear, and separate rules that govern the two objects to be searched may enable police to broaden their power to make warrantless searches to the detriment of privacy interests. Furthermore, the protection of privacy interests afforded by disallowing the warrantless search of a closed container contained within an automobile is minimal since, in an overwhelming majority of cases, a warrant is routinely given after a closed container is seized. Finally, the discrepancy between the two rules has led to confusion for law enforcement officers. Hence, to avoid these anomalous results, necessity dictates that the common-law rule requiring a warrant to search closed containers within an automobile be overruled. In the instant case, although the police merely had probable cause as to the contraband, their search of the paper bag was reasonable under the Fourth Amendment. Reversed.

DISSENT: (Stevens, J.) It is a cardinal principle that searches conducted outside the judicial process, without prior approval by judge or magistrate, are per se unreasonable under the Fourth Amendment—subject only to a few specifically established and well-delineated exceptions. Moreover, the circumstances in the present case are not so exceptional as to justify invasion of an individual's privacy interest outside the presence of a neutral magistrate.

ANALYSIS

In considering the above rule, the next logical step for the court may be to permit warrantless searches of luggage or personal belongings being transported on foot as opposed to within a motor vehicle, since there is a possibility that evidence can be lost, i.e., through the transporter taking flight or through the evidence being hidden, only to be retrieved later. Obviously, the possibility of these two things happening dictates whether such a rule would be adopted. Moreover, a significant increase in drug activity across the country may also make such a rule thinkable.

Continued on next page.

Quicknotes

AUTOMOBILE EXCEPTION Exception to the requirement of a valid warrant; if a police officer has probable cause to believe that a vehicle contains evidence of a crime or contraband; the officer may search the entire vehicle.

CONTRABAND Items that are illegal to have in one's possession or to trade or produce.

PROBABLE CAUSE A reasonable basis for believing that a crime has been committed.

Arizona v. Gant

State (P) v. Arrested individual, whose vehicle was subject to search (D)

556 U.S. 332 (2009)

NATURE OF CASE: Appeal from state high court decision in favor of defendant.

FACT SUMMARY: Local police arrested Gant (D) for an outstanding warrant for driving without a license. After the police placed Gant (D) in a police vehicle, a subsequent search of Gant's (D) vehicle revealed cocaine and a handgun.

RULE OF LAW
Police may search the passenger compartment of a vehicle incident to an occupant's arrest only if the occupant may have access to the vehicle or if it is reasonable to believe the vehicle contains evidence of the offense for which the occupant was arrested.

FACTS: After receiving a tip that a house was being used to distribute drugs, Tucson police officers approached the house and spoke to Gant (D). The police then left the house and conducted a records-check on Gant (D), which revealed he had an outstanding warrant for driving with a suspended license. The police went back to the house. While they were there, Gant (D) drove into the driveway. Upon recognizing Gant (D), the police immediately arrested him on the outstanding warrant. The arrest took place 10 to 15 feet away from Gant's (D) vehicle. The police then placed Gant (D) in a patrol car and searched his vehicle. The search revealed a handgun and cocaine. At trial, Gant (D) moved to suppress the evidence on the grounds police did not have probable cause for the search. The trial court denied his motion, but the Arizona Supreme Court found the search was unreasonable. The State (P) appealed.

ISSUE: May police search the passenger compartment of a vehicle incident to an occupant's arrest if the occupant may have access to the vehicle or if it is reasonable to believe the vehicle contains evidence of the offense for which the occupant was arrested?

HOLDING AND DECISION: (Stevens, J.) Yes. Police may search the passenger compartment of a vehicle incident to an occupant's arrest only if the occupant may have access to the vehicle or if it is reasonable to believe the vehicle contains evidence of the offense for which the occupant was arrested. In *New York v. Belton*, 453 U.S. 454 (1981), this Court held that searches incident to arrest may include the interior of a vehicle because of the assumption that the interior includes an area that an arrestee may reach, to either destroy evidence or retrieve a weapon. Over the past 28 years, however, *Belton* has been construed to allow all searches of a motor vehicle incident to an arrest, regardless of whether an arrestee may actually have access to the interior of the vehicle. *Belton* should not be interpreted so broadly. Rather, a search of a vehicle may only be conducted where the arrestee has actual access to the vehicle or if there is reason to believe the vehicle contains evidence related to the offense of the arrest. Here, Gant (D) was already handcuffed and in the patrol car at the time of the search. There was no way he could access the vehicle. Second, the police arrested Gant (D) for driving with a suspended license. The vehicle would not contain any additional evidence related to that offense. Accordingly, the search was unreasonable. Affirmed.

CONCURRENCE: (Scalia, J.) This case concerns only those searches conducted after police make an arrest. There is some fear that the Court's abandonment of *Belton's* bright-line rule may actually invite officers to leave a scene unsecured in order to conduct a search. *Belton* should be overruled in its entirety and the following new rule should be followed: Vehicle searches following arrests are reasonable only when the object of the search is evidence of the crime related to the arrest. Because there could be no evidence related to Gant's (D) arrest in the vehicle, the search of his vehicle was unlawful. The majority opinion will also better protect citizens from possible unlawful searches, which would likely occur if the dissent's view of the case was adopted.

DISSENT: (Alito, J.) The *Belton* holding was clear and unequivocal. That case held that whenever an officer makes an arrest of a person from a vehicle, the officer may search the passenger compartment of the arrestee's vehicle. The Court adopted that course because it established a bright-line rule that was easily followed by law enforcement. The Court did not limit its holding with reference to when a search was made. This Court should adhere to *Belton* because of law enforcement's reliance on the rule for the past 28 years. Circumstances have not changed since *Belton* that dictates a change in the law, nor has the *Belton* rule become unworkable. For these reasons, this Court is bound by stare decisis. The Court should have found the search of Gant's (D) vehicle reasonable and consistent with the *Belton* rule.

Continued on next page.

ANALYSIS

This decision limited the holding of *New York v. Belton*, 453 U.S. 454 (1981), regarding the ability to search vehicles incident to arrests. However, Justice Scalia's point regarding the limited applicability of the decision is significant. This decision only applies to searches following arrests. It does not apply to those situations where officers ask an occupant to step out of a vehicle and a search is conducted without an arrest being made. Those types of searches are not implicated here.

Quicknotes

BRIGHT-LINE RULE A legal rule of decision to help resolve ambiguous issues simply and in a straightforward manner, sometimes sacrificing equity for certainty.

PROBABLE CAUSE A reasonable basis for believing that a crime has been committed.

SEARCH INCIDENT TO A LAWFUL ARREST Exception to the requirement of a valid warrant for a search or seizure so long as the officer is lawfully in the location where the evidence is obtained and it is apparent that the thing seized is evidence.

STARE DECISIS Doctrine whereby courts follow legal precedent unless there is good cause for departure.

United States v. Watson

Federal government (P) v. Credit card thief (D)

423 U.S. 411 (1976)

NATURE OF CASE: Appeal from reversal of a conviction for theft of credit cards from the malls.

FACT SUMMARY: Watson (D) was arrested without a warrant by a Government (P) postal inspector who, on the basis of information from a reliable informant, had time to obtain an arrest warrant for theft of credit cards from the malls.

RULE OF LAW

A law officer may arrest a suspect without a warrant for a felony committed in his presence as well as for a felony not committed in his presence if he has reasonable grounds for making the arrest.

FACTS: A reliable informant told a Government (P) postal inspector that Watson (D) had supplied him with a stolen credit card and had agreed to furnish more cards later. Subsequently, the informant met with Watson (D) in a restaurant. When Watson (D) indicated that he had the cards, the informant signaled to the inspector, who arrested Watson (D) without a warrant. Watson's (D) conviction was reversed by the court of appeals on the grounds that the inspector had time to obtain an arrest warrant but failed to do so. The Government (P) appealed.

ISSUE: May a law officer arrest a suspect without a warrant for a felony committed in his presence as well as for a felony not committed in his presence if he has reasonable grounds for making the arrest?

HOLDING AND DECISION: (White, J.) Yes. A law officer may arrest a suspect without a warrant for a felony committed in his presence as well as for a felony not committed in his presence if he has reasonable grounds for making the arrest. Never has any case indicated that an arrest warrant is required under the Fourth Amendment to make an arrest for a felony. At common law, no such warrant was required, and in 1792, the Second Congress saw no inconsistency between the Fourth Amendment and giving federal marshals the same power as state officers to make warrantless arrests. Reversed.

CONCURRENCE: (Powell, J.) The holding creates an anomaly because great discretion is given in making warrantless arrests while rarely can a warrantless search be made even though it would appear an arrest is a greater personal invasion. "But logic sometimes must defer to history and experience."

DISSENT: (Marshall, J.) The case should have simply been decided on the ground that the inspector had probable cause to believe that an offense was taking place in his presence (at the restaurant), and that the suspect was then in possession of the evidence. The Court need not have gone beyond that; having done so, it must be said that the common-law rule provides no support for the far-reaching modern rule fashioned here. And, as a matter of doctrine, the longstanding existence of a government practice does not immunize it from scrutiny under the Constitution.

ANALYSIS

The American Law Institute's (ALI's) Model Code of Pre-Arraignment Procedure (1975) § 120.1 provides that a law officer, if he has reasonable cause, may make warrantless arrests for felonies and, under certain circumstances, for misdemeanors. The commentary to that section states: "This section does not require an officer to arrest under a warrant even if a reasonable opportunity to obtain a warrant exists. As to arrests on the street, such a requirement would be entirely novel."

Quicknotes

FELONY A criminal offense of greater seriousness than a misdemeanor; felonies are generally defined pursuant to statute as any crime that is punishable by death or by a term of imprisonment exceeding one year.

MISDEMEANOR A crime that does not constitute a felony; generally less severe than a felony and results in lesser punishment.

Atwater v. City of Lago Vista

Driver (P) v. City (D)

532 U.S. 318 (2001)

NATURE OF CASE: Civil rights claim stemming from arrest for misdemeanor traffic violation.

FACT SUMMARY: Atwater (P) claimed that her arrest for a misdemeanor seatbelt violation violated her Fourth Amendment rights against warrantless searches and seizures.

RULE OF LAW

The Fourth Amendment does not forbid a warrantless arrest for a minor criminal offense, such as a misdemeanor seatbelt violation punishable only by a fine.

FACTS: Atwater (P) was driving in a pickup truck with her three-year-old son and five-year-old daughter in the front seat. None of them was wearing a seatbelt. Texas law made it a misdemeanor for a driver, in a car equipped with a seatbelt, not to wear a seatbelt or not to secure any small child riding in the front seat with one. She ultimately pled no contest to the seatbelt charge and paid the fine. She then filed a 42 U.S.C. § 1983 action against the police officer, City of Lago Vista and chief of police (D), alleging her Fourth Amendment rights were violated. The district court granted summary judgment for the City (D), concluding the claim was meritless. A panel of the court of appeals reversed, but the court en banc vacated the previous decision and affirmed the summary judgment.

ISSUE: Does the Fourth Amendment forbid a warrantless arrest for a minor criminal offense, such as a misdemeanor seatbelt violation punishable only by a fine?

HOLDING AND DECISION: (Souter, J.) No. The Fourth Amendment does not forbid a warrantless arrest for a minor criminal offense, such as a misdemeanor seatbelt violation punishable only by a fine. We confirm what prior cases have suggested, that probable cause applies to all arrests. There is no need to apply a balancing test of interests involved in the particular situation. If an official has probable cause to believe that an individual has committed even a very minor criminal offense in his presence, he may arrest the offender without violating the Fourth Amendment. Affirmed.

DISSENT: (O'Connor, J.) The Court's position is inconsistent with the Fourth Amendment's guarantees. A custodial arrest, such as the one here, is a seizure. When it is affected without a warrant, the Fourth Amendment requires such search to be reasonable. The record here shows that Atwater's (P) arrest was unreasonable. The police officer (D) was not justified by law or reason in his decision to arrest Atwater (P) rather than to give her a citation, and severely infringed Atwater's (P) liberty and privacy interests.

ANALYSIS

Atwater (P) argued that common-law principles prohibited police officers from making warrantless misdemeanor arrests except in cases of "breach of the peace," a narrow category only including non-felony offenses "involving or tending toward violence." The Court rejects this argument stating that neither the legislative history of the Fourth Amendment nor subsequent decisions supported this position.

Quicknotes

BREACH The violation of an obligation imposed pursuant to contract or law, by acting or failing to act.

CIVIL RIGHTS ACT OF 1871, 42 U.S.C. § 1983 Enforces basic personal rights guaranteed by the U.S. Constitution.

COMMON LAW A body of law developed through the judicial decisions of the courts as opposed to the legislative process.

FOURTH AMENDMENT Provides that persons be secure as to their person and private belongings against unreasonable searches and seizures.

MISDEMEANOR A crime that does not constitute a felony; generally less severe than a felony and results in lesser punishment.

PROBABLE CAUSE A reasonable basis for believing that a crime has been committed.

SEARCH AND SEIZURE An inspection conducted in order to obtain evidence to be utilized for the prosecution of a crime and the subsequent taking of such evidence.

WARRANT An order issued by a court directing an officer to undertake a certain act (e.g., arrest or search).

United States v. Robinson

Federal government (P) v. Heroin possessor (D)

414 U.S. 218 (1973)

NATURE OF CASE: Action against Robinson (D) for possession and facilitation of concealment of heroin.

FACT SUMMARY: A police officer arrested Robinson (D) for a traffic violation. It was conceded that he had probable cause for the arrest. During his search of Robinson (D), the officer found a cigarette package containing heroin.

RULE OF LAW

The fact of a lawful arrest establishes the authority to conduct a full-scale, reasonable search under the Fourth Amendment.

FACTS: As a result of a previous investigation of Robinson's (D) driver's permit, Officer Jenks decided that there was reason to believe that Robinson (D) was driving without a license. Jenks signaled Robinson (D) to stop his car, and when he did, Jenks arrested him. It was conceded that Jenks had probable cause for the arrest. In accordance with police department procedures, Jenks searched Robinson (D). He felt an object in Robinson's (D) coat but could not tell its size or what it was. He pulled it out and found a crumbled cigarette package. He opened it and found heroin capsules inside. The court of appeals held that since no further evidence could have been obtained from a search in this case, Jenks should have only conducted a search for weapons.

ISSUE: Does the fact of a lawful arrest establish the authority to conduct a full- scale, reasonable search under the Fourth Amendment?

HOLDING AND DECISION: (Rehnquist, J.) Yes. The fact of a lawful arrest establishes the authority to conduct a full-scale, reasonable search under the Fourth Amendment. The validity of the search of the person of the arrestee is well established and is considered a reasonable search under the Fourth Amendment. The court of appeals felt that in a case involving a traffic violation, the principles of *Terry v. Ohio*, 392 U.S. 1 (1968), should be applied and only a search for weapons could be justified. *Terry v. Ohio* held that a frisk incident to an investigative stop based on less than probable cause must be limited to a search for weapons. That decision recognizes a sharp distinction between such frisks and searches incident to arrests for probable cause. That case affords no basis for extending the limitation placed on a stop-and-frisk search without probable cause to a probable cause arrest. The court of appeals, in effect, determined that the only reason supporting a full search incident to a lawful arrest was the possibility of discovering evidence. However, the reason for a full search rests equally on the need to disarm the arrestee. The danger to the officer is far greater in the case of the extended proximity that follows the custodial arrest of a suspect than in a stop-and-frisk encounter. Further, the danger to the officer flows from the arrest itself, rather than from the grounds for arrest. The search of Robinson's (D) person conducted by Jenks and the seizure of the heroin were permissible under the Fourth Amendment. Officer Jenks was not required to limit the search to a search for weapons. Reversed.

DISSENT: (Marshall, J.) The vast majority of the several state and federal courts which have considered this question have held that absent special circumstances, a police officer has no right to conduct a full search of the person incident to a lawful arrest for violation of a motor vehicle violation. Here, the majority attempts to avoid case-by-case adjudication of Fourth Amendment issues. However, "there is no formula for the determination of reasonable. Each case is to be decided on its own facts and circumstances." Further, the powers granted to the police in this case are strong ones, subject to potential abuse. There is always the possibility that a police officer, lacking probable cause to obtain a search warrant, will use a traffic arrest as a pretext to conduct a search. In this case, Jenks's removal of the cigarette package, which he said he did not believe was a weapon, exceeded the limitation of the *Terry* frisk for weapons. May a police officer, when effecting an arrest of a traffic offender, make a fuller search of the person than *Terry* permits? To answer this question, the individual's interest in remaining free from unnecessarily intrusive invasions of privacy must be balanced with society's interest that police officers refrain from taking unnecessary risks in performing their duties. It is not necessary to solve this balancing question here, but empirical evidence does support the court of appeals' decision rather than the result reached by the majority. This evidence indicates that "virtually all of the killings of officers in the line of duty are caused by guns and weapons, the very type of weapons which will not go undetected in a properly conducted weapons search." In this case, however, Jenks's search extended beyond Robinson's (D) person to a separate search of effects found on his person. Assuming, arguendo, that it was reasonable for Jenks to remove the cigarette package from Robinson's (D) person, there was no justification consistent with the Fourth Amendment for his looking inside the package.

Continued on next page.

Once in Jenks's hands, even if the package did contain a weapon, it was out of Robinson's (D) reach. Opening the package, therefore, did not further the protective purpose of the search.

ANALYSIS

Most courts have upheld inventory of the items found on the arrestee's person as a part of the booking process, on the grounds it is a reasonable means of safeguarding the accused's property while they are in jail, and ensuring weapons and contraband are not introduced into the jail. Some courts have limited the inventory authority somewhat by ruling that evidence found in an inventory must be suppressed if the police conducted the inventory without a correct determination of whether the arrestee would, of necessity, be held in jail. As to an officer's power to seize items uncovered in a search incident to an arrest, in *State v. Elkins*, 245 Ore. 279 (1966), it was held that before an officer can seize implements of a crime other than that for which the arrest was made, he must have reasonable grounds to believe that the article is contraband.

Quicknotes

CONTRABAND Items that are illegal to have in one's possession or to trade or produce.

INVESTIGATORY STOP A brief, nonintrusive stop requiring the police officer to have a reasonable suspicion that a crime has been committed based on specific and articulable facts.

PROBABLE CAUSE A reasonable basis for believing that a crime has been committed.

Terry v. Ohio

Armed suspect (D) v. State (P)

392 U.S. 1 (1968)

NATURE OF CASE: Certiorari from conviction for carrying a concealed weapon.

FACT SUMMARY: When Officer McFadden became suspicious of the behavior of three men in downtown Cleveland, he stopped them, identified himself, and, believing they were armed and dangerous, frisked them (i.e., patted their outer clothing) and found a concealed weapon on Terry (D).

RULE OF LAW

Where a police officer observes unusual conduct that leads him reasonably to conclude in light of his experience that criminal activity may be afoot and that the persons with whom he is dealing may be armed and presently dangerous, the officer is entitled for the protection of himself and others in the area to conduct a carefully limited search of the outer clothing of such persons in an attempt to discover weapons that might be used to assault him.

FACTS: Officer McFadden, a Cleveland plainclothes detective, became suspicious of two men (one of whom was Terry (D)) who were repeatedly peering into a store down the street and then returning to a corner. When a third man joined these two suspects, Officer McFadden, surmising that the suspects were "casing" a stickup and, therefore, might be armed and dangerous, stopped them. Upon identifying himself as a policeman and receiving only mumbling replies to his questions, McFadden patted (i.e., "frisked") their outer clothing and, upon feeling a pistol under Terry's (D) clothing, removed it. Terry (D) was charged with carrying a concealed weapon. At his trial, Terry (D) moved to suppress the evidence, but the trial court denied his motion and Terry (D) was convicted. Upon affirmation of his conviction by the Ohio Court of Appeals and dismissal of his appeal by the state supreme court, Terry (D) filed a petition for certiorari with this court.

ISSUE: Where a police officer observes unusual conduct that leads him reasonably to conclude in light of his experience that criminal activity may be afoot and that the persons with whom he is dealing may be armed and presently dangerous, is the officer entitled for the protection of himself and others in the area to conduct a carefully limited search of the outer clothing of such persons in an attempt to discover weapons that might be used to assault him?

HOLDING AND DECISION: (Warren, C.J.) Yes. Where a police officer observes unusual conduct that leads him reasonably to conclude in light of his experience that criminal activity may be afoot and that the persons with whom he is dealing may be armed and presently dangerous, the officer is entitled for the protection of himself and others in the area to conduct a carefully limited search of the outer clothing of such persons in an attempt to discover weapons that might be used to assault him. Stop-and-frisk conduct, although covered by the Fourth Amendment, should not be subjected to the warrant requirement as well. The wide variety of street encounters found by the police requires "necessarily swift action upon on-the-spot observations of the officer on the beat," which historically has not, and practically cannot, be subjected to the warrant requirement. As such, the brief intrusion on the suspect's freedom is more properly tested under the Fourth Amendment's general proscription against "unreasonable" searches and seizures. Under this test of reasonableness, the need to search must be balanced against the invasion involved. In the stop-and-frisk situation, the government has a need to search to promote effective crime control and to protect the police officer's safety. Furthermore, if (1) the stop-and-frisk is based upon "specific inferences" (not on "unparticularized suspicion or hunches"), so that the officer's behavior can later be objectively reviewed, and if (2) the stop-and-frisk is limited to a frisk for weapons, the invasion is justified and reasonable. Here, Officer McFadden legitimately investigated suspicious behavior, acted under "reasonable suspicion" that the suspects might be armed and dangerous, and frisked only their outer garments. As such, the search was reasonable, and the evidence is admissible. Judgment affirmed.

CONCURRENCE: (Harlan, J.) There are a few gaps in the decision of the Court, although its ultimate conclusion is sound. If a frisk is to be justified in order to protect the officer, the officer must first have constitutional grounds to make a forcible "stop" (i.e., reasonable suspicion), but a limited frisk incident to such a lawful stop requires no additional justification. There is no reason why an officer should risk a bullet by first questioning the suspect.

CONCURRENCE: (White, J.) There is no need for interrogation during an investigative stop before the officer frisks the suspect. Although an officer may question the suspects briefly, when a temporary detention is justified by a fear for the officer's and others' safety,

Continued on next page.

a protective frisk for weapons is justified regardless of whether any questions are asked.

DISSENT: (Douglas, J.) A search and seizure cannot be justified by Fourth Amendment standards unless there is "probable cause" to believe that a crime has been committed or is about to be committed. Here, however, since there was no "probable cause" for the issuance of a warrant, the Court's holding allows police greater freedom to search and seize than even a judge could authorize.

ANALYSIS

This case illustrates the less stringent rule applicable to stop-and-frisk than that applicable to arrest and search. This rule was further clarified in *Sibron v. New York*, 392 U.S. 40 (1968), in which the court stated than an officer "must be able to point to particular facts from which he reasonably inferred that the individual was armed and dangerous." However, in *Adams v. Williams*, 407 U.S. 143 (1972), the Court stated that this "reasonable inference" need not be based upon the officer's personal observation. Rather, it may be based upon an unnamed informer's tip that "carries some indicia of reliability," even though the unverified tip is not so reliable as to constitute "probable cause" for an arrest or search warrant.

Quicknotes

REASONABLE SUSPICION That which would cause an ordinary prudent person under the circumstances to suspect that a crime has been committed based on specific and articulable facts.

STOP AND FRISK A brief, nonintrusive stop requiring the police officer to have a reasonable suspicion that a crime has been committed based on specific and articulable facts, and involving a search for a concealed weapon that is conducted by patting down the clothes of the person.

Illinois v. Wardlow

State (P) v. Convicted felon (D)

528 U.S. 119 (2000)

NATURE OF CASE: Appeal from conviction for unlawful use of a weapon by a felon.

FACT SUMMARY: Wardlow (D) sought to suppress introduction of a .38-caliber handgun at trial on the basis that the gun was recovered during an unlawful stop and frisk.

RULE OF LAW

Flight from police is sufficient to support a finding of reasonable suspicion and to justify a police officer's further investigation.

FACTS: Officers Nolan and Harvey were working as uniformed officers in the special operations section of the Chicago Police Department. They observed Wardlow (D) standing next to a building holding an opaque bag. When he saw the officers, he fled. The officers eventually cornered him and conducted a pat-down search for weapons. During the frisk, Nolan felt a hard object and opened the bag to discover a .38-caliber handgun with five live rounds of ammunition. The officers arrested Wardlow (D). The trial court denied Wardlow's (D) motion to suppress, concluding the gun was recovered during a lawful stop and frisk, and convicted Wardlow (D) of unlawful use of a weapon by a felon. The appellate court reversed on the basis that Nolan did not have reasonable suspicion sufficient to justify an investigative stop under *Terry v. Ohio*, 392 U.S. 1 (1968). The Illinois Supreme Court agreed, and the United States Supreme Court granted review.

ISSUE: Is flight from police sufficient to support a finding of reasonable suspicion justifying a police officer in further investigation?

HOLDING AND DECISION: (Rehnquist, C.J.) Yes. Flight from police is sufficient to support a finding of reasonable suspicion justifying a police officer in further investigation. This case is governed by this Court's analysis in *Terry*. Nolan and Harvey were among eight other officers in a four-car caravan converging on an area known for drug trafficking. While an individual's presence in an area of expected criminal activity is not sufficient, without more, to support a reasonable, particularized suspicion that the person is committing a crime, the officers may take into consideration the relevant characteristics of a location in determining whether the circumstances are sufficiently suspicious to warrant further investigation. Moreover, nervous, evasive behavior is another pertinent factor in determining reasonable suspicion, such as Wardlow's (D) unprovoked flight upon seeing the police. Thus, Nolan was justified in suspecting Wardlow (D) was involved in criminal activity and in investigating further. Reversed.

CONCURRENCE AND DISSENT: (Stevens, J.) The State (P) asks the Court to announce a per se rule authorizing the temporary detention of anyone who flees at the mere sight of a police officer, while Wardlow (D) asks the Court to adopt the opposite per se rule—the fact that a person flees upon seeing the police can never justify a temporary investigative stop. While I agree with the Court's rejection of both per se rules, the testimony of the officer who seized Wardlow (D) does not support the conclusion that he had reasonable suspicion to make the stop.

ANALYSIS

Compare the result in this case with that in *Florida v. J.L.*, 529 U.S. 266 (2000). There the police responded to an anonymous call that a young Black male would be at a particular location, wearing particular clothing and carrying a gun. While nothing in the youth's behavior aroused suspicion, the police officer frisked him and discovered a gun. The Court held that an "anonymous tip" was insufficient to establish reasonable suspicion justifying the police to make an investigatory stop.

Quicknotes

REASONABLE SUSPICION That which would cause an ordinary prudent person under the circumstances to suspect that a crime has been committed based on specific and articulable facts.

STOP AND FRISK A brief, non-intrusive stop requiring the police officer to have a reasonable suspicion that a crime has been committed or is contemplated being committed based on specific and articulable facts and involving a search for a concealed weapon that is conducted by patting down the clothes of the person.

***TERRY* STOP** A search of a person suspected of intending to commit a crime that is conducted by patting down the clothes of the person; the search must be limited to the reason for which the individual was lawfully stopped.

Kansas v. Glover

State (P) v. Vehicle driver charged as habitual violator (D)

140 S. Ct. 1183 (2020)

NATURE OF CASE: Appeal from reversal of decision reversing grant of motion to suppress evidence obtained after traffic stop in prosecution of a vehicle driver as a habitual violator.

FACT SUMMARY: A deputy sheriff ran a license plate check on a pickup truck and discovered that the truck belonged to Charles Glover, Jr. (Glover) (D) and that Glover's (D) driver's license had been revoked. The deputy pulled the truck over because he assumed that Glover (D) was driving impermissibly. Glover (D), who was in fact driving and who was subsequently charged with driving as a habitual violator, moved to suppress all evidence from the stop, claiming that the deputy lacked reasonable suspicion for the stop, in violation of the Fourth Amendment.

RULE OF LAW

When a law enforcement officer lacks information negating an inference that the owner of a vehicle is driving the vehicle, an investigative traffic stop made after running the vehicle's license plate and learning that the registered owner's driver's license has been revoked is reasonable under the Fourth Amendment.

FACTS: Deputy Mark Mehrer (Deputy Mehrer), a Kansas (P) law enforcement officer, ran a license plate check on a pickup truck and discovered that the truck belonged to Charles Glover, Jr. (Glover) (D) and that Glover's (D) driver's license had been revoked. Based solely on that information, Deputy Mehrer pulled the truck over. Deputy Mehrer did not observe any traffic infractions and did not attempt to identify the truck's driver. Once the vehicle was stopped, Deputy Mehrer was able to identify Glover (D) as the driver and then charged Glover (D) with driving as a habitual violator. Glover (D) filed a motion to suppress all evidence seized during the stop, claiming that Deputy Mehrer lacked reasonable suspicion for the seizure, and, therefore, violated the Fourth Amendment. The state's trial court granted the motion. The state's intermediate appellate court reversed, concluding that the facts gave rise to a reasonable suspicion. The Kansas Supreme Court reversed, finding that Deputy Mehrer did not have reasonable suspicion because his inference that Glover (D) was behind the wheel amounted to "only a hunch" that Glover (D) was engaging in criminal activity, and that this "hunch" involved "applying and stacking unstated assumptions that are unreasonable without further factual basis," namely, that "the registered owner was likely the primary driver of the vehicle" and that "the owner will likely disregard the suspension or revocation order and continue to drive." The United States Supreme Court granted certiorari.

ISSUE: When a law enforcement officer lacks information negating an inference that the owner of a vehicle is driving the vehicle, is an investigative traffic stop made after running the vehicle's license plate and learning that the registered owner's driver's license has been revoked reasonable under the Fourth Amendment?

HOLDING AND DECISION: (Thomas, J.) Yes. When a law enforcement officer lacks information negating an inference that the owner of a vehicle is driving the vehicle, an investigative traffic stop made after running the vehicle's license plate and learning that the registered owner's driver's license has been revoked is reasonable under the Fourth Amendment. Under the Court's precedents, a law enforcement officer may initiate a brief investigative traffic stop when the officer has a particularized and objective basis to suspect legal wrongdoing. The level of suspicion required is less than that necessary for probable cause and depends on considerations of everyday life on which reasonable and prudent people act. The reasonable-suspicion standard thus permits officers to make commonsense judgments and inferences about human behavior. Here, Deputy Mehrer's commonsense inference that the owner of a vehicle was likely the vehicle's driver provided more than reasonable suspicion to initiate the stop. Such an inference is not made unreasonable merely because a vehicle's driver is not always its registered owner or because Glover (D) had a revoked license. Though common sense suffices to justify the officer's inference, empirical studies demonstrate that drivers with suspended or revoked licenses frequently continue to drive. Moreover, Kansas's (P) license-revocation scheme, which covers drivers who have already demonstrated a disregard for the law or are categorically unfit to drive, reinforces the reasonableness of the inference that an individual with a revoked license will continue to drive. Glover's (D) counterarguments are unpersuasive. Glover (D) argues that Deputy Mehrer's inference was unreasonable because it was not grounded in his law enforcement training or experience. Such a requirement, however, is inconsistent with this Court's Fourth Amendment jurisprudence. It would also place the burden on police officers to justify their inferences by referring to training materials or experience, and it would foreclose their ability to rely on common sense obtained outside of their work

Continued on next page.

duties. Glover's (D) argument that Kansas's (D) view would permit officers to base reasonable suspicion exclusively on probabilities also carries little force. Officers, like jurors, may rely on probabilities in the reasonable suspicion context. Moreover, the deputy here did more than that: He combined facts obtained from a database and commonsense judgments to form a reasonable suspicion that a specific individual was potentially engaged in specific criminal activity. The scope of this holding is narrow. The reasonable suspicion standard takes into account the totality of the circumstances. Although the presence of additional facts might dispel reasonable suspicion, here Deputy Mehrer possessed no information sufficient to rebut the reasonable inference that Glover (D) was driving his own truck with a revoked license. Reversed.

CONCURRENCE: (Kagan, J.) In this case, Deputy Mehrer had reasonable suspicion to stop Glover's (D) truck. First, as a matter of common sense, it is reasonable to suspect that a vehicle's registered owner is driving the vehicle. Although it is not similarly a matter of common sense that a vehicle's registered owner whose license is revoked will flout the law and drive the vehicle on pain of criminal penalties, such an inference is reasonable for a Kansas (P) law officer because Kansas (P) almost never revokes a license except for serious or repeated driving offenses. Thus, Deputy Mehrer had information about the registered owner's proclivity to break driving laws. Because a person with a revoked license in Kansas (P) has already shown a willingness to flout driving restrictions, that fact gives rise to a reasonable inference that such a person will drive without a license—at least often enough to warrant an investigatory stop. No such inference would be warranted, however, if Kansas (P) had barred Glover (D) from driving on a ground that provided no similar evidence of his penchant for ignoring driving laws. For example, Kansas (P) suspends driving licenses for matters having nothing to do with road safety, such as not paying child support. In such a case, the inference that the driver has a history of disregarding driving rules would no longer apply. Even where, as here, that inference at first is deemed reasonable, the inference may be rebutted by a showing that an officer knew of additional facts, such as where an officer knows the registered owner of a vehicle is an elderly man but can see the driver is a young woman, or where there is more than one registered owner. There are many such fact-specific situations that could negate reasonable suspicion notwithstanding an initial license-revocation alert. Additionally, a defendant may challenge the reasonableness of an officer's suspicion by adducing statistical evidence regarding "hit rates," i.e., the frequency with which vehicle stops such as the one made by the officer in a given case lead to the discovery of unlicensed drivers behind the wheel. Defendants may question testifying officers about such information, and, in fact, an officer may have an individual hit rate that if low enough could itself negate reasonable suspicion. In other words, in fully litigated cases, the license-revocation alert does not (as it did here) end the inquiry, but serves as the first step in assessing the reasonableness of the officer's suspicion.

DISSENT: (Sotomayor, J.) Under the majority's approach, a state's burden of proving reasonable suspicion for a vehicle stop is impermissibly reduced when viewed against the Court's precedents in this area. The state, until now, needed to show more than a mere hunch; a police officer needed to explain rational inferences from particular facts as viewed from the lens of the officer's experience and training. The Court's reasonable-suspicion jurisprudence not only required an objective reasonable officer's assessment of the facts, but also required that a stop be individualized, meaning there is a suspicion that the particular person being stopped is engaged in wrongdoing, rather than a suspicion based on a class to which the person belongs. Moreover, the majority flips the burden of proof by permitting police officers to make roadside stops whenever they do not have information that negates an inference that a vehicle's unlicensed owner is its driver. In the case at bar, Deputy Mehrer never indicated he had any informed belief about the propensity of unlicensed drivers to operate vehicles in the area, let alone that he relied on such a belief when seizing Glover (D). The majority thus absolves officers from any responsibility to investigate the identity of a driver where feasible. Cases are replete with instances where officers have been able to do just that, or at least ascertain a driver's age and gender from afar. The majority gives officers free rein to stop a vehicle involved in no suspicious activity merely because the vehicle is registered to a person with a revoked license. Such a stop, then, is (impermissibly) based on a mere hunch about the driver's identity. With no basis in the record to presume that unlicensed drivers routinely continue driving, the majority endeavors to fill the gap with its own "common sense." However, simply labeling an inference "common sense" does not make it so. To the contrary, whether a driver is likely to be its unlicensed owner is not at all obvious. Also, contrary to the majority's assertion, the reasonable-suspicion inquiry does not accommodate the average person's intuition, but only permits reliance on a particular type of common sense—that of the reasonable officer, developed through the officer's experiences and training in law enforcement. Such specialized knowledge, including knowledge of a geographical area's inhabitants and their customs, leads to the types of inferences and deductions that the police are permitted to make. However, allowing judges to offer their own brand of common sense where a state's proffered justifications for a search come up short shifts police work to the judiciary and, thereby, promotes broad, inflexible rules that overlook regional differences.

Continued on next page.

Finally, the majority cites empirical studies to bolster its claim that its inferences are grounded in "common experience." However, those studies do no such thing, since the studies do not provide information regarding the percentage of vehicle owners with revoked licenses in Kansas (P) who continue to drive their cars, and that might ostensibly inform an officer's inferences about driver identity. To the contrary, permitting the state to rely on large-data studies demonstrates the danger of relying on generalized data because it permits law enforcement to make seizures without particularized suspicion of wrongdoing or observed violations of law. In other words, the majority paves "the road to finding reasonable suspicion on nothing more than a demographic profile." That has never been the law, and it never should be.

ANALYSIS

As this case demonstrates, reasonable suspicion is a less demanding standard than probable cause not only in the sense that reasonable suspicion can be established with information that is different in quantity or content than that required to establish probable cause, but also in the sense that reasonable suspicion can arise from information that is less reliable than that required to show probable cause. The "reasonable suspicion" necessary to justify a vehicle stop until *Glover* was dependent upon both the content of information possessed by police and its degree of reliability. The standard took into account the totality of the circumstances. Although a mere hunch cannot create reasonable suspicion, the level of suspicion the standard has required is considerably less than proof of wrongdoing by a preponderance of the evidence, and obviously less than is necessary for probable cause. Arguably, *Glover* has reduced even that standard to where the government no longer needs to articulate individualized suspicion in certain vehicle stop cases, but only needs to connect a suspect's demographic class (i.e., the class of vehicle owners whose licenses have been revoked) to an inference of wrongdoing, with nothing more.

Quicknotes

FOURTH AMENDMENT Provides that persons be secure as to their person and private belongings against unreasonable searches and seizures.

PROBABLE CAUSE A reasonable basis for believing that a crime has been committed.

REASONABLE SUSPICION That which would cause an ordinary prudent person under the circumstances to suspect that a crime has been committed based on specific and articulable facts.

Minnesota v. Dickerson

State (P) v. Convicted narcotics possessor (D)

508 U.S. 366 (1993)

NATURE OF CASE: Appeal from reversal of conviction for possession of narcotics.

FACT SUMMARY: The State (P) contended that its police officer's detection of cocaine during a patdown of Dickerson (D) for weapons during a stop-and-frisk did not violate the Fourth Amendment.

RULE OF LAW

The Fourth Amendment does not permit the warrantless seizure of contraband detected through a police officer's sense of touch during a protective patdown search where the search exceeds the bounds of what is necessary to determine if the detainee has a weapon.

FACTS: Based on Dickerson's (D) seemingly evasive actions when approached by police officers and the fact that he had just left a building known for cocaine traffic, the officers decided to investigate further and ordered Dickerson (D) to submit to a patdown search. The search revealed no weapons, but the officer conducting it felt a small lump in Dickerson's (D) jacket pocket, believed it to be a lump of crack cocaine upon examining it with his fingers, and then reached into the pocket and retrieved a small bag of cocaine. Dickerson (D) was arrested and charged with possession of a controlled substance. The state trial court denied Dickerson's (D) motion to suppress the cocaine, and he was found guilty. The state's intermediate appellate court reversed; and the state's highest court affirmed. In doing so, the state supreme court held that both the stop and the frisk of Dickerson (D) were valid under *Terry v. Ohio*, 392 U.S. 1 (1968), but found the seizure of the cocaine to be unconstitutional. The United States Supreme Court granted certiorari.

ISSUE: Does the Fourth Amendment permit the warrantless seizure of contraband detected through a police officer's sense of touch during a protective patdown search where the search exceeds the bounds of what is necessary to determine if the detainee has a weapon?

HOLDING AND DECISION: (White, J.) No. The Fourth Amendment does not permit the warrantless seizure of contraband detected through a police officer's sense of touch during a protective patdown search where the search exceeds the bounds of what is necessary to determine if the detainee has a weapon. Under certain circumstances, police officers may without a warrant seize nonthreatening contraband during the lawful execution of a search, including a patdown search that is limited to searching for weapons. The seizure of contraband other than weapons during a lawful patdown search is justified by analogy to the "plain-view" doctrine, which permits police to seize an object without a warrant if they are lawfully in a position to view it, if its incriminating character is immediately apparent, and if they have a lawful right of access to it. Thus, if an officer lawfully pats down a suspect's outer clothing and feels an object whose contour or mass makes its identity immediately apparent, there has been no invasion of the suspect's privacy beyond that already authorized by the officer's search for weapons. If the object is contraband, its warrantless seizure would be justified by the realization that resort to a neutral magistrate under such circumstances would be impracticable and would do little to promote the Fourth Amendment's objectives. Applying these principles here, the dispositive question becomes whether the police officer in this case who was searching Dickerson (D) was acting within the bounds authorized by the Fourth Amendment. The answer is that he was not acting within those bounds. That is because the officer's continued exploration of the pocket after he concluded that it contained no weapon was unrelated to the sole justification for the search—to protect the officer and others nearby. The officer's search exceeded the "strictly circumscribed" search for weapons allowed under *Terry* and went on to become the type of search expanded into the equivalent of a general warrant to rummage and seize at will. Affirmed.

ANALYSIS

As this and other cases make clear, it must be immediately apparent that a seized item is illegal. If it is not apparent that the item is contraband, the police must have probable cause to seize it. If, however, the police lack probable cause to believe that the item is contraband without conducting some further search of the object–i.e., if its incriminating character is not immediately apparent–the seizure cannot be justified. Here, the officer did not have probable cause to believe the item in Dickerson's (D) jacket was a controlled substance and it was not immediately apparent what the object was; it was only through continued touching (searching) that the officer discovered the item's true nature. It was this continued searching that was offensive to the Fourth Amendment.

Continued on next page.

Quicknotes

FOURTH AMENDMENT Provides that persons be secure as to their person and private belongings against unreasonable searches and seizures.

PROBABLE CAUSE A reasonable basis for believing that a crime has been committed.

STOP AND FRISK A brief, non-intrusive stop requiring the police officer to have a reasonable suspicion that a crime has been committed or is contemplated being committed based on specific and articulable facts and involving a search for a concealed weapon that is conducted by patting down the clothes of the person.

Graham v. Connor

Civil rights plaintiff (P) v. Officer (D)

490 U.S. 386 (1989)

NATURE OF CASE: Appeal from grant of directed verdict in 42 U.S.C. § 1983 claim of excessive force.

FACT SUMMARY: Police officers were physically abusive in making an investigatory stop, seizure, and arrest of a free citizen.

RULE OF LAW

All claims that law enforcement officers have used excessive force—deadly or not—in the course of an arrest, investigatory stop, or other seizure of a free citizen should be analyzed under the Fourth Amendment and its "reasonableness" standard.

FACTS: Dethorne Graham (P), a diabetic, was suffering from an insulin reaction when he contacted a friend, Berry, to take him to the convenience store to purchase some juice to counteract the attack. Upon entering the store, Graham (P) noted how busy the store was and how long the line was and made a quick decision to go to another friend's house instead. Thus, Graham (P) rushed out of the store and into Berry's waiting car. Police officer Connor (D) witnessed this, and, suspicious about Graham's activities within the store, followed Graham (P) and Berry. About one-half mile from the store, Connor made an investigatory stop. Berry explained that Graham (P) was a diabetic and was having an episode, but Connor (D) ignored his pleas to get Graham (P) some sugar. Connor (D) ordered the two men to wait while he determined, what, if anything occurred at the convenience store. While Connor (D) returned to his car to call for backup assistance, Graham (P) ran twice around the car and finally sat down on the curb, where he passed out. Backup officers arrived on the scene amid the confusion, rolled Graham (P) over on the sidewalk, and cuffed him. They later dragged him over to a cruiser, slammed his head against its hood twice, and threw him headfirst into the cruiser. The officers eventually learned that nothing had occurred at the convenience store and drove Graham (P) home. Graham (P) sustained a broken foot, cuts on his wrists, an injured shoulder, and a ringing in his ears from his encounter with police. He filed a § 1983 claim against the officers for excessive force. The district court found no excessive force and granted the officers' motion for directed verdict. The Fourth Circuit Court of Appeals affirmed.

ISSUE: What constitutional standard governs a free citizen's claim that law enforcement officials used excessive force in the course of making an arrest, investigatory stop, or other seizure of his person?

HOLDING AND DECISION: (Rehnquist, C.J.) All claims that law enforcement officers have used excessive force—deadly or not—in the course of arrest, investigatory stop, or other seizure of a free citizen, should be analyzed under the Fourth Amendment and its "reasonableness" standard. The Fourth Amendment "reasonableness" standard requires balancing the intrusion on an individual's Fourth Amendment rights against the countervailing government interests at issue. The reasonableness of a particular use of force must be judged from the perspective of an officer on the scene. An officer's evil intentions will not make a Fourth Amendment violation out of an objectively reasonable use of force. The court of appeals erred in applying the four-part due process test. Vacated and remanded for reconsideration of the issue under the Fourth Amendment "reasonableness" standard.

ANALYSIS

Graham rejects using an officer's subjective intent as part of Fourth Amendment analysis in excessive force cases.

Quicknotes

FOURTH AMENDMENT Provides that persons be secure as to their person and private belongings against unreasonable searches and seizures.

City of Tahlequah v. Bond

Municipality (D) v. Estate administrator (P)

142 S. Ct. 9 (2021)

NATURE OF CASE: Appeal from reversal of grant of summary judgment to defendant police officers in action brought under 42 U.S.C. § 1983.

FACT SUMMARY: The estate (P) of Dominic Rollice (Rollice), who was fatally shot by police, brought suit for civil liability under 42 U.S.C. § 1983 against the police officers (D) who had shot Rollice. The officers asserted qualified immunity, claiming they had not violated any clearly established law.

RULE OF LAW

A law enforcement officer will be shielded from civil liability for the officer's conduct so long as that conduct does not violate clearly established statutory or constitutional rights of which a reasonable person would have known.

FACTS: Dominic Rollice's (Rollice's) ex-wife, Joy, called for police help because Rollice, who did not live with her but kept tools in her garage, was intoxicated and would not leave. The three officers (D) who arrived initially spoke with Rollice in the garage doorway, telling him they were there to get him a ride. He refused to be patted down for weapons, however. As the officers (D) approached the doorway, Rollice started to head to the back of the garage, disregarding the officer's command to stop. Rollice kept walking. He then grabbed a hammer from the back wall and turned around to face the officers (D). He grasped the handle of the hammer with both hands, as if preparing to swing a baseball bat, and pulled it up to shoulder level. The officers (D) backed up, drawing their guns. At this point, the officers (D) were yelling at Rollice to drop the hammer, which he did not do. Instead, he came out from behind a piece of furniture so that he had an unobstructed path to one of the officers (D). He then raised the hammer higher back behind his head and took a stance as if he was about to throw the hammer or charge at the officers (D). In response, two officers fired their weapons, killing Rollice. Rollice's estate (P) filed suit against, among others, the officers (D) who shot Rollice, alleging that the officers (D) were liable under 42 U.S.C. § 1983 for violating Rollice's Fourth Amendment right to be free from excessive force. The officers (D) moved for summary judgment, both on the merits and on qualified immunity grounds. The District Court granted their motion. The Tenth Circuit Court of Appeals reversed, finding that the Circuit's precedents allow an officer to be held liable for a shooting that is itself objectively reasonable if the officer's reckless or deliberate conduct created a situation requiring deadly force. Applying that rule, the Circuit Court concluded that a jury could find that one of the officer's initial step toward Rollice and the officers' (D) subsequent "cornering" of him in the back of the garage recklessly created the situation that led to the fatal shooting such that their ultimate use of deadly force was unconstitutional. As to qualified immunity, the Circuit Court concluded that several cases clearly established that the officers' (D) conduct was unlawful. The United States Supreme Court granted certiorari.

ISSUE: Will a law enforcement officer be shielded from civil liability for the officer's conduct so long as that conduct does not violate clearly established statutory or constitutional rights of which a reasonable person would have known?

HOLDING AND DECISION: (Per curiam) Yes. A law enforcement officer will be shielded from civil liability for the officer's conduct so long as that conduct does not violate clearly established statutory or constitutional rights of which a reasonable person would have known. On this record, the officers clearly did not violate any clearly established law. Therefore, it need not be decided whether they violated Rollice's constitutional rights, or whether recklessly creating a situation that requires deadly force can itself violate the Fourth Amendment. The doctrine of qualified immunity shields officers from civil liability so long as their conduct does not violate clearly established statutory or constitutional rights of which a reasonable person would have known. In the qualified immunity context, courts must not define clearly established law at too high a level of generality. It is not enough that a rule be suggested by then-existing precedent; the rule's contours must be so well defined that it is clear to a reasonable officer that the officer's conduct was unlawful in the situation the officer confronted. Here, the Circuit Court contravened these principles, and a review of the cases relied on shows clearly that none of those decisions comes close to establishing that the officers' (D) conduct was unlawful. All the cases the Circuit Court cited in support of its decision can easily be distinguished and do not set forth the clearly established law required to remove qualified immunity. [Reversed.]

ANALYSIS

With its rejection of all the cases relied on by the Tenth Circuit as comprising "clearly established law," the Court in *Bond* demonstrates the difficulty of meeting

Continued on next page.

the "clearly established law" standard, because, as the Court has formulated the standard, it requires not just a clear legal rule, but a prior case that has functionally identical facts. Based on this difficulty, critics of the standard have argued that the standard makes it extremely difficult to hold public officials accountable for unlawful conduct in most cases, because it is extremely difficult to find decided cases with effectively identical facts. The Court-made doctrine has also been criticized as being the product of judicial activism, rather than legislated law, and as serving as a virtual shield for police brutality.

Quicknotes

DEADLY FORCE That degree of force that is likely to result in death or great bodily injury.

QUALIFIED IMMUNITY An affirmative defense relieving officials from civil liability for the performance of activities within their discretion so long as such conduct is not in violation of an individual's rights pursuant to law as determined by a reasonable person standard.

REASONABLE PERSON STANDARD The standard of care exercised by one who possesses the intelligence, education, knowledge, attention, and judgment required by society of its members when governing behavior; the standard applies to a person's judgment when determining breach of a duty under the theory of negligence.

Michigan Dept. of State Police v. Sitz

State police (D) v. Licensed drivers (P)

496 U.S. 444 (1990)

NATURE OF CASE: Appeal from judgment for plaintiffs in a declaratory and injunctive relief action challenging the constitutionality of a state police highway sobriety checkpoint program.

FACT SUMMARY: Licensed drivers (P) contended that a state police highway sobriety checkpoint program violated the Fourth Amendment.

RULE OF LAW

A state's use of highway sobriety checkpoints does not violate the Fourth Amendment.

FACTS: The state police (D) established a highway sobriety checkpoint program with guidelines governing checkpoint operations, site selection, and publicity. Under the guidelines, checkpoints would be set up at selected sites along state roads. All vehicles passing through a checkpoint would be stopped and their drivers briefly examined for signs of intoxication. In cases where a checkpoint officer detected signs of intoxication, the motorist would be directed to a location out of the traffic flow and further sobriety testing would be conducted. All other drivers would be permitted to resume their journey immediately. During the only operation of the 75-minute checkpoint, 126 vehicles passed through the checkpoint, the average delay per vehicle was 25 seconds, and two drivers were arrested for driving under the influence. Licensed drivers (P) filed suit seeking declaratory and injunctive relief from potential subjection to the checkpoints. A court ruled for the drivers (P), and the state police appealed. The United States Supreme Court granted certiorari.

ISSUE: Does a state's use of highway sobriety checkpoints violate the Fourth Amendment?

HOLDING AND DECISION: (Rehnquist, C.J.) No. A state's use of highway sobriety checkpoints does not violate the Fourth Amendment. The vehicle stops at issue here are searches, so the question is whether such searches are reasonable under the Fourth Amendment. There is no dispute about the magnitude of, and the state's interest in eradicating, the drunken driving problem. On the other side of the balancing scale is the brief intrusion on the motorist, which is slight. In fact, the circumstances surrounding a checkpoint stop are much less intrusive than ones attendant to a roving-patrol stop and are potentially less frightening to the motorist. In sum, the balance weighs in favor of the state checkpoint program. Reversed.

DISSENT: (Stevens, J.) The majority misapplies the Fourth Amendment's balancing test. The record indicates that the net effect of sobriety checkpoints is infinitesimal, if not negative, and the record supports the inference that more conventional police efforts would have resulted in more driving under the influence arrests. The checkpoints are made at night, are random, and require surprise. In light of these considerations, it seems the majority overvalues the law enforcement interest in using sobriety checkpoints, undervalues the citizen's interest in freedom from random, unannounced investigatory seizures, and mistakenly assumes that there is "virtually no difference" between a routine stop at a permanent, fixed checkpoint and a surprise stop at a sobriety checkpoint. Accordingly, the majority's decision goes against precedents condemning suspicionless random stops of motorists for investigatory purposes.

ANALYSIS

The Court addressed only the initial stop of each motorist passing through a checkpoint and the associated preliminary questioning and observation by checkpoint officers. The opinion did not extend to the part of the checkpoint program involving detention of particular motorists for more extensive field sobriety testing, which the Court indicated might require satisfaction of an individualized suspicion standard. Arguably, however, an officer who questions a motorist at a sobriety checkpoint has virtually unlimited discretion to detain the driver on the basis of the slightest suspicion. For example, a ruddy complexion, an unbuttoned shirt, bloodshot eyes or a speech impediment may suffice to prolong the detention, and, ostensibly, any driver who had just consumed a glass of beer, or even a sip of wine, would almost certainly have the burden of demonstrating to the officer that her driving ability was not impaired.

Quicknotes

CHECKPOINT AUTOMOBILE STOP Exception to the requirement that a police officer have a reasonable suspicion that an automobile contains illegal evidence or contraband for automobile stops, made at a fixed checkpoint for the purpose of questioning the occupants of the vehicle; the officers must have probable cause or consent of the occupants prior to conducting a search of the vehicle.

FOURTH AMENDMENT Provides that persons be secure as to their person and private belongings against unreasonable searches and seizures.

Schneckloth v. Bustamonte

Court (P) v. Car passenger (D)

412 U.S. 218 (1973)

NATURE OF CASE: Petition for writ of habeas corpus, after conviction.

FACT SUMMARY: An officer stopped a car carrying Bustamonte (D) and five other men because it had a burned-out headlight. The one man who had identification said that the car belonged to his brother. When the officer asked if he could search it, the man replied, "Sure." The officer found some stolen checks in the car.

RULE OF LAW

Whether a consent to a search was "voluntary" or was the product of duress or coercion, express or implied, is a question of fact to be determined from the totality of all the circumstances.

FACTS: Officer Rand stopped an automobile when he observed that its headlight and license plate light were burned out. There were six men, including Bustamonte (D), in the car. Only one of the men had identification, and he said that the car belonged to his brother. When Rand asked if he could search the car, the man replied, "Sure, go ahead," and helped Rand with the search. Rand found some stolen checks in the car. Bustamonte (D), whose motion to suppress the evidence was denied, was convicted on the basis of the checks and other evidence. His conviction was affirmed on appeal; the federal district court denied his petition for a writ of habeas corpus. The Ninth Circuit Court of Appeals vacated the order denying the writ and remanded the case for further proceedings, holding that when a prosecutor relies upon consent to justify a search, it is an essential part of the state's burden to prove that the person knew of his right to refuse consent. The United States Supreme Court granted certiorari.

ISSUE: Is the question of whether consent to a search was "voluntary" or was the product or duress or coercion, express or implied, a question of fact to be determined from the totality of all the circumstances?

HOLDING AND DECISION: (Stewart, J.) Yes. Whether a consent to a search was "voluntary" or was the product of duress or coercion, express or implied, is a question of fact to be determined from the totality of all the circumstances. When the state seeks to rely on consent to justify a search, it has the burden of showing that the consent was freely and voluntarily given. Knowledge of the right to refuse consent to a search is one factor to be considered, the state need not establish such knowledge as the *sine qua non* of an effective, voluntary consent. Searches authorized by consent are of unquestioned benefit to the police. However, such consent must not be coerced. "To approve such searches without the most careful scrutiny would sanction the possibility of official coercion; to place artificial restrictions upon such searches would jeopardize their basic validity." To require that proof that the person consenting to the search knew of his/her right to refuse consent would seriously impair such searches. In many cases where there was no evidence of coercion, the state would still be unable to show that the person knew of the right to refuse. Likewise, a person who consented to a search could prevent the use of the fruits of the search as evidence by failing to testify to having knowledge of the right to refuse consent. It is suggested that subjects of searches be advised of their right to refuse. However, "it would be thoroughly impracticable to impose on the informal and unstructured conditions of the normal consent search the detailed requirements of an effecting warning." These conditions are far removed from the structured atmosphere of a trial or even "custodial interrogation." It is contended that consent is a waiver of a person's Fourth and Fourteenth Amendment rights, and that only knowing and intelligent waivers are valid. However, the knowing and intelligent waiver requirement is almost always only applied to those rights guaranteed to a criminal defendant in order to preserve a fair trial, such as rights to counsel, to confrontation, to a jury trial, and to a speedy trial. These rights are aimed at promoting the fair ascertainment of truth at trial. Fourth Amendment rights are quite different and protect one's privacy against arbitrary police intrusion. It would be unrealistic to expect that in the informal, unstructured context of a consent search, an officer could make the detailed type of examination demanded by the intelligent and knowing waiver requirements. Also, a waiver approach to consent searches would be inconsistent with decisions approving third party consents. It is inconceivable that the Constitution could countenance the waiver of a defendant's right to counsel or to confrontation by a third party. Yet, such consents to searches by third parties have been held valid. Here, there was no evidence of any coercive tactics by the police, either from the nature of the police questioning or the environment in which it took place. "Our decision today is a narrow one. We hold only that when the subject of a search is not in custody and the state attempts to justify a search on the basis of his consent, the Fourth and Fourteenth Amendments require that it demonstrate that the consent was in fact voluntarily given, and not the result of duress or coercion, express or implied. Voluntariness is a question of fact to

Continued on next page.

be determined from all the circumstances, and while the subject's knowledge of a right to refuse is a factor to be taken into account, the prosecution is not required to demonstrate such knowledge as a prerequisite to establishing a voluntary consent. Because the California court followed these principles in affirming [Bustamonte's (D)] conviction, and because the Ninth Circuit Court of Appeals, in remanding for an evidentiary hearing required more, its judgment must be reversed."

DISSENT: (Marshall, J.) This case deals not with "coercion" but with "consent," a subtly different concept. Freedom from coercion is a substantive right, guaranteed by the Fifth and Fourteenth Amendments. Consent is a mechanism by which substantive requirements are avoided. Consent searches are submitted not because such an exception to the requirements of probable cause and warrant is essential to law enforcement, but because citizens are permitted to choose whether they wish to exercise their constitutional rights. Our prior decisions do not support the view that a meaningful choice has been made simply because no coercion was used. Consent means a knowing choice. How can a decision made without knowledge of the available alternatives be called a choice? I would hold that the state may not rely on a purported consent to a search if the subject of the search did not know of his right to refuse consent. The subject's knowledge of this right could be shown by his demonstration of such knowledge at the time of the search, by having him testify under oath (if he is not the defendant), by the subject's prior experience or training, or if the police, at the time of the search, told the subject of his right to refuse consent. There is nothing impractical about this latter method, and the decision to employ it would lie with the officers. "I doubt that a simple statement by an officer of an individuals' right to refuse consent would do much to alter the informality of this exchange, except to alert the subject to a fact that he is entitled to know. For many years, Federal Bureau of Investigtion agents have routinely informed subjects of their right to refuse consent. I must conclude, with some reluctance, that when the court speaks of practicality, what it really is talking of is the continued ability of the police to capitalize on the ignorance of citizens so as to accomplish by subterfuge what they could not achieve by relying only on the knowing relinquishment of constitutional rights."

ANALYSIS

A search based upon a valid consent may be conducted without a warrant and without probable cause. Most federal courts have applied the light standards normally applicable to the waiver of constitutional rights to determine the validity of consent to a search. It is said that a consent, in order to be voluntary, must be unequivocal, specific, and intelligently given, uncontaminated by any duress or coercion, and is not lightly to be inferred. In *Bumper v. North Carolina*, 391 U.S. 543 (1968), consent for a search was given after the officer had stated that he had a search warrant. The Court held that the consent was not valid, since the officer's claim of authority was, in effect, an announcement that the occupant had no right to resist the search. Under such circumstances, acquiescence could not be construed as consent.

Quicknotes

CONSENT A voluntary and willful agreement by an individual possessing sufficient mental capacity to undertake an action suggested by another.

DURESS Unlawful threats or other coercive behavior by one person that causes another to commit acts he or she would not otherwise do.

PROBABLE CAUSE A reasonable basis for believing that a crime has been committed.

Fernandez v. California

Individual convicted of robbery and other felonies (D) v. State (P)

571 U.S. 292 (2014)

NATURE OF CASE: Appeal from conviction for robbery and other felonies.

FACT SUMMARY: Walter Fernandez (D), a robbery suspect, contended that because he had objected to a warrantless search of his apartment but was subsequently removed by police on the suspicion that he had violently assaulted his co-occupant, Roxanne Rojas, Rojas did not have the authority to consent to a search in his absence. Fernandez (D) also contended that the objection he had made while at the threshold to his apartment remained effective indefinitely until he changed his mind and withdrew it.

RULE OF LAW

(1) An individual who objects to a warrantless search of his or her premises but is later lawfully removed from the premises on objectively reasonable grounds, can have his or her objection to the search superseded by a co-occupant who has common authority over the premises.

(2) An individual's objection to a warrantless search of his or her premises does not remain effective indefinitely, even after the individual is no longer physically present at the premises, until the objection is withdrawn.

FACTS: Police officers observed Walter Fernandez (D), a suspect in a violent robbery, run into an apartment building, and they heard screams coming from one of the apartments. They knocked on the apartment door, which was answered by Roxanne Rojas, who appeared to be battered and bleeding. When the officers asked her to step out of the apartment so that they could conduct a protective sweep, Fernandez (D) came to the door and objected to the sweep. Suspecting that he had violently assaulted Rojas, the officers removed Fernandez (D) from the apartment and placed him under arrest. He was then identified as the perpetrator in the earlier robbery and taken to the police station. An officer later returned to the apartment and, after obtaining Rojas's oral and written consent, searched the premises, where he found several items linking Fernandez (D) to the robbery. The trial court denied Fernandez's (D) motion to suppress that evidence, and he was convicted. The conviction was not overturned on appeal at the state level, and the United States Supreme Court granted certiorari.

ISSUE:

(1) Can an individual who objects to a warrantless search of his or her premises but is later lawfully removed from the premises on objectively reasonable grounds, have his or her objection to the search superseded by a co-occupant who has common authority over the premises?

(2) Does an individual's objection to a warrantless search of his or her premises remain effective indefinitely, even after the individual is no longer physically present at the premises, until the objection is withdrawn?

HOLDING AND DECISION: (Alito, J.)

(1) Yes. An individual who objects to a warrantless search of his or her premises but is later lawfully removed from the premises on objectively reasonable grounds, can have his or her objection to the search superseded by a co-occupant who has common authority over the premises. Consent searches are permissible warrantless searches, and it would be unreasonable to require police officers to obtain a warrant when a sole owner or occupant voluntarily consents to a search of the premises. When multiple occupants are involved, the rule extends to the search of the premises or effects of an absent, nonconsenting occupant so long as "the consent of one who possesses common authority over [the] premises or effects" is obtained. *United States v. Matlock*, 415 U.S. 164 (1974). A narrow exception to this rule, announced in *Georgia v. Randolph*, 547 U.S. 103 (2006), is that when a physically present inhabitant refuses to consent, that refusal is dispositive as to the objector, regardless of a fellow occupant's consent. A controlling factor in *Randolph* was the objecting occupant's physical presence. Fernandez (D) contends that, notwithstanding that he was not present when Rojas consented, *Randolph* nevertheless controls. This contention is flawed. Fernandez (D) argues that his absence should not matter since it occurred only because the police had taken him away. Dictum in *Randolph* suggesting that consent by one occupant might not be sufficient if there is evidence that the police have removed the potentially objecting tenant from the entrance for the sake of avoiding a possible objection, is best understood to refer to situations in which the removal of the potential objector is not objectively reasonable. Fernandez (D) does not contest that the police had reasonable grounds for his removal or the existence of probable cause for his arrest. He was thus in the same position as an occupant absent for any other reason.

Continued on next page.

(2) No. An individual's objection to a warrantless search of his or her premises does not remain effective indefinitely, even after the individual is no longer physically present at the premises, until the objection is withdrawn. Fernandez's (D) argument that the objection he made while at the threshold remained effective until he changed his mind and withdrew it is inconsistent with *Randolph* in at least two important ways. First, it cannot be squared with the "widely shared social expectations" or "customary social usage" upon which *Randolph's* holding was based—that people usually do not enter a shared premises when one occupant invites them in, but another occupant tells them to stay out. If, however, only the inviting occupant is present, people are much more likely to accept the invitation to enter. Second, it also creates a plethora of practical complications that *Randolph* sought to avoid. One problem with the rule proposed by Fernandez (D) is that the indefiniteness of the objection's duration would lead to unreasonable results. Even holding that an objection lasted for a "reasonable" time would be unworkable, as it would not be readily apparent what such a "reasonable" interval time would be in any given context. Additionally, Fernandez's (D) rule would require the police and ultimately the courts to determine whether, after the passage of time, an objector still had "common authority" over the premises. Another problem would concern the procedure needed to register a continuing objection. Yet another would be which police officers would be bound by the objection. However, if *Randolph* is taken at its word—that it applies only when the objector is standing in the door saying "stay out" when officers propose to make a consent search—all of these problems disappear. Fernandez (D) strenuously claims that his expansive interpretation of *Randolph* would not hamper law enforcement, because in most cases where officers have probable cause to arrest a physically present objector, they also have probable cause to obtain a warrant to search the premises that the objector does not want them to enter. But this misunderstands the constitutional status of consent searches, which are permissible irrespective of the availability of a warrant. Even with modern technological advances, the warrant procedure imposes burdens on the officers who wish to search, the magistrate who must review the warrant application, and the party willing to give consent. Thus, requiring officers to obtain a warrant when a warrantless search is justified may interfere with law enforcement strategies and impose an unmerited burden on the person willing to consent to an immediate search. Denying someone in Rojas's position the right to allow the police to enter her home would also show disrespect for her independence. Having beaten Rojas, Fernandez (D) would bar her from controlling access to her own home until such time as he chose to relent. The Fourth Amendment does not give him that power.

CONCURRENCE: (Thomas, J.) A warrantless search is reasonable if police obtain the voluntary consent of a person authorized to give it, because co-occupants have assumed the risk that one of their number might permit a common area to be searched. Here, the trial court found that Rojas's consent was voluntary, and Fernandez (D) does not contest that Rojas had common authority over the premises. That, therefore, should be the end of the analysis.

DISSENT: (Ginsburg, J.) By reducing *Randolph* to a narrow exception, the majority minimizes the warrant's role as the bulwark of Fourth Amendment protection. And, by declaring that the principal rule is that consent by one resident of jointly occupied premises is generally sufficient to justify a warrantless search, the majority puts the law in this area on its head, given that consent searches themselves are a narrow, carefully drawn exception to the Fourth Amendment rule that warrantless entry of a person's home is unreasonable per se. Regarding the majority's view of Rojas's autonomy, which the majority seems to think is best served by allowing her consent to trump an abusive cohabitant's objection to a warrantless search, although domestic abuse is a serious problem, it should be addressed by means other than diminishing Fourth Amendment rights.

ANALYSIS

The majority asserts that when a consent search is available, requiring the police to obtain a warrant, even when they readily can do so, is burdensome and might entail delay, "[e]ven with modern technological advances." Justice Ginsburg, dissenting, takes the majority to task regarding this assertion, noting that the majority ignores the ease and speed with which search warrants nowadays can be obtained through various means, including telephonic or radio communication, electronic communication, and video conferencing. In light of such developments, Justice Ginsburg argues that the dilution of the warrant requirement should be vigilantly resisted, explaining that when the police have probable cause and can get a warrant with dispatch, as was the case in *Fernandez,* the law should insist on the formality of a warrant notwithstanding that the police can gain a co-occupant's consent to search, because the Framers "saw the neutral magistrate as an essential part of the criminal process shielding all of us, good or bad, saint or sinner, from unchecked police activity." Justice Ginsburg also observes, as the Court

Continued on next page.

already has in its precedents, that although the investigation of crime would always be simplified if warrants were unnecessary, the privacy of a person's home and property, under the Fourth Amendment, may not be totally sacrificed in the name of maximum simplicity in enforcement of the criminal law, so that a generalized interest in expedient law enforcement cannot, without more, justify a warrantless search.

Quicknotes

PROBABLE CAUSE A reasonable basis for believing that a crime has been committed.

REASONABLE EXPECTATION OF PRIVACY In order to invoke the Fourth Amendment's protection against unreasonable searches and seizures, an individual must have a reasonable expectation of privacy in respect to the location searched or thing seized.

WARRANT An order issued by a court directing an officer to undertake a certain act (e.g., arrest or search).

CHAPTER 8

The Scope of the Fourth Amendment Exclusionary Rule

Quick Reference Rules of Law

	PAGE
1. *Rakas v. Illinois.* A person may not move to suppress evidence in which he had no proprietary interest or expectation of privacy.	*104*
2. *Minnesota v. Carter.* An overnight guest in a home may claim the protection of the Fourth Amendment, but one who is merely present with the consent of the householder may not.	*105*
3. *Wong Sun v. United States.* Statements made by a defendant directly as the result of lawless police conduct are inadmissible against the defendant.	*107*
4. *Murray v. United States.* Under the "independent source" doctrine, "evidence initially uncovered, but not seized, during an illegal search will not be suppressed if the police later obtain a search warrant that does not rely on any facts discovered during the illegal search, and then seize the evidence during a second search pursuant to the warrant."	*108*
5. *United States v. Leon.* The Fourth Amendment does not require exclusion of evidence seized pursuant to a facially valid warrant where the police have acted in good faith.	*110*
6. *Davis v. United States.* Searches conducted by the police in reliance upon binding legal precedent existing at the time of the search are not subject to the exclusionary rule.	*111*

Rakas v. Illinois

Auto passenger (D) v. State (P)

439 U.S. 128 (1978)

NATURE OF CASE: Appeal of criminal convictions.

FACT SUMMARY: Various defendants sought to suppress evidence in which they had no proprietary interest seized from a vehicle in which they were passengers.

RULE OF LAW

A person may not move to suppress evidence in which he had no proprietary interest or expectation of privacy.

FACTS: Police stopped a vehicle that matched the description of a getaway car. After a search, a shotgun and shotgun shells were found. These belonged to the owner of the vehicle, who was also the driver. Charged with various crimes [not specified in the casebook excerpt], the passengers (D) moved to suppress the gun and shells. This was denied, and the passengers (D) were convicted, along with the driver. The Illinois appellate courts affirmed. The United States Supreme Court accepted the passengers' (D) writ for certiorari.

ISSUE: May a person move to suppress evidence in which he has no proprietary interest or expectation of privacy?

HOLDING AND DECISION: (Rehnquist, J.) No. A person may not move to suppress evidence in which he has no proprietary interest or expectation of privacy. The rights secured by the Fourth Amendment are personal; a person cannot move to suppress evidence seized in violation of another's rights. For a person to have a personal interest in the evidence sufficient to confer a right to seek suppression, one of two things must occur. One, the movant may have some sort of ownership or possessory interest in the evidence; such a seizure would violate a personal interest. In the alternative, the party seeking suppression must demonstrate that the items were seized from some sort of area in which he had a legitimate expectation of privacy. Absent these circumstances, a person cannot make a Fourth Amendment claim. Here, the passengers (D) had no proprietary interest in the seized articles. Further, they had no expectation of privacy in the interior of another person's vehicle. Consequently, they suffered no Fourth Amendment violation. Affirmed.

DISSENT: (White, J.) The majority holds that the Fourth Amendment protects property, not people. The ruling undercuts the force of the exclusionary rule in its deterrence of bad-faith Fourth Amendment violations. The police are now invited to engage in patently unreasonable searches every time an automobile contains more than one person.

ANALYSIS

Prior to this case, the Court considered the type of analysis made here to be one of standing. The Court believed this to be an inappropriate focus on procedure. In the opinion, the Court takes pains to point out that it was dealing with substantive Fourth Amendment law, not procedure.

Quicknotes

EXPECTATION OF PRIVACY Requirement that in order to invoke the Fourth Amendment's protection against unreasonable searches and seizures, the individual must have a reasonable expectation of privacy in respect to the location searched or thing seized.

FOURTH AMENDMENT Provides that persons be secure as to their person and private belongings against unreasonable searches and seizures.

Minnesota v. Carter

State (P) v. Accused (D)

525 U.S. 83 (1998)

NATURE OF CASE: Appeal from an order holding that an illegal search had occurred.

FACT SUMMARY: When a police officer saw people packaging cocaine through a window and later arrested the occupants of the apartment, they alleged that their Fourth Amendment rights had been violated and sought to have the evidence excluded.

RULE OF LAW

An overnight guest in a home may claim the protection of the Fourth Amendment, but one who is merely present with the consent of the householder may not.

FACTS: A confidential informant told the police that when walking by the window of a ground floor apartment, he had seen people putting a white powder into bags. The police officer looked through the same window, saw the men, and notified headquarters to prepare affidavits for a search warrant. When Carter (D) and Johns (D) left the building, they were arrested while in a motor vehicle, and cocaine was later found in the vehicle and in the apartment. Carter (D) and Johns (D) had never been in that apartment before and had been there for two hours to package the cocaine. Carter (D) and Johns (D) were convicted of state drug offenses. The trial court held that since they were only temporary out-of-state visitors, they could not challenge the legality of the government intrusion into the apartment, and that the police officer's observation through the window was not a "search" within the meaning of the Fourth Amendment. The Minnesota Supreme Court reversed, holding that Carter (D) and Johns (D) did have "standing" because they had a legitimate expectation of privacy in the invaded place, and that the officer's observation constituted an unreasonable "search" of the apartment. Minnesota (P) appealed.

ISSUE: If an overnight guest in a home may claim the protection of the Fourth Amendment, may one who is merely present with the consent of the householder also do so?

HOLDING AND DECISION: (Rehnquist, C.J.) No. An overnight guest in a home may claim the protection of the Fourth Amendment, but one who is merely present with the consent of the householder may not. The purely commercial nature of the transaction engaged in here, the relatively short time on the premises, and the lack of any previous connection between Carter (D) and the householder all lead to the conclusion that their situation is closer to that of one simply permitted on the premises, rather than that of an overnight guest. Therefore, any search that may have occurred did not violate their Fourth Amendment rights. Reversed.

CONCURRENCE: (Scalia, J.) Whereas it is plausible to regard a person's overnight lodging as at least his "temporary" residence, it is entirely impossible to give that characterization to an apartment that he uses to package cocaine.

CONCURRENCE: (Kennedy, J.) Almost all social guests have a legitimate expectation of privacy, and hence protection against unreasonable searches, in their host's home. In this case, Carter (D) and Johns (D) have established nothing more than a fleeting and insubstantial connection with Thompson's home.

DISSENT: (Ginsberg, J.) The Court's decision undermines not only the security of short-term guests but also the security of the home resident herself. When a homeowner chooses to share the privacy of her home and her company with a short-term guest, both host and guest have exhibited an actual (subjective) expectation of privacy, and that expectation is one that our society is prepared to recognize as reasonable.

ANALYSIS

Property used for commercial purposes is treated differently for Fourth Amendment purposes than residential property. While Carter (D) and Johns (D) were present in a "home," it was not their home. Only the Dissent argued that a short-term guest in a home should share her host's shelter against unreasonable searches and seizures. Since there was no violation of the Fourth Amendment, the evidence seized by the police was used against Carter (D) and Johns (D).

Quicknotes

EXPECTATION OF PRIVACY Requirement that in order to invoke the Fourth Amendment's protection against unreasonable searches and seizures, the individual must have a reasonable expectation of privacy in respect to the location searched or thing seized.

FOURTH AMENDMENT Provides that persons be secure as to their person and private belongings against unreasonable searches and seizures.

Continued on next page.

SEARCH An inspection conducted in order to obtain evidence to be utilized for the prosecution of a crime.

SEIZURE Under the Fourth Amendment, the application of physical force to the body of a person, or a show of force or authority, intended to restrain a person's liberty Also, as relates to property, the meaningful interference with an individual's possessory interests in that property. Only "unreasonable" seizures by the government are prohibited by the Fourth Amendment.

Wong Sun v. United States

Drug dealer (D) v. Federal government (P)

371 U.S. 471 (1963)

NATURE OF CASE: On certiorari from appellate court judgment upholding conviction for dealing in heroin.

FACT SUMMARY: Wong Sun's (D) co-defendant was unlawfully arrested and made incriminating statements to police.

RULE OF LAW

Statements made by a defendant directly as the result of lawless police conduct are inadmissible against the defendant.

FACTS: Federal agents went to the Chinese laundry operated by Wong Sun's (D) co-defendant, James Wah Toy. Toy told the agent that he was not open for business and to come back. The agent identified himself as a narcotics agent, and Toy ran into his living quarters at the back of the laundry. The agents broke open the door, followed Toy into his bedroom, and arrested him. A search of the premises revealed no narcotics. Toy told the agents that he and another man had been smoking the drug the night before and where the other man lived. Toy and two others were indicted on drug charges, and his statements to the agents in his bedroom were admitted against him.

ISSUE: May statements made by a defendant directly as the result of lawless police conduct be admitted against the defendant?

HOLDING AND DECISION: (Brennan, J.) No. Statements made by a defendant directly as the result of lawless police conduct are inadmissible against the defendant. The court of appeals held that there was neither reasonable grounds nor probable cause for Toy's arrest. We have held that physical evidence obtained during an unlawful invasion must be excluded. Today we hold that verbal evidence that derives so immediately from an unlawful entry is no less the fruit of official illegality than the more tangible fruits of the unwarranted intrusion. There was no intervening independent act to purge the illegality of its taint; therefore, the judgment of the court of appeals is reversed.

ANALYSIS

Wong Sun (D) made a confession as well, but his confession took place when he voluntarily returned several days after being arraigned to make the statement. Given his independent intervening voluntary act, the Court held that the taint of Toy's unlawful arrest was purged as to Wong Sun's (D) confession.

Quicknotes

EXCLUSIONARY RULE A rule precluding the introduction at trial of evidence unlawfully obtained in violation of the federal constitutional safeguards against unreasonable searches and seizures.

Murray v. United States

Convicted drug possessor (D) v. Federal government (P)

487 U.S. 533 (1988)

NATURE OF CASE: Appeal from conviction for marijuana possession.

FACT SUMMARY: Agents saw marijuana when they illegally entered a warehouse, then obtained a search warrant without using any information discovered during the illegal entry, reentered the warehouse, and seized the marijuana that was used to convict Murray (D).

RULE OF LAW

Under the "independent source" doctrine, "evidence initially uncovered, but not seized, during an illegal search will not be suppressed if the police later obtain a search warrant that does not rely on any facts discovered during the illegal search, and then seize the evidence during a second search pursuant to the warrant."

FACTS: Federal agents saw Murray (D) and others driving vehicles in and out of a warehouse which the agents believed contained drugs. Two drivers were lawfully arrested and their vehicles were found to contain marijuana. The agents entered the warehouse illegally and saw bales of marijuana, but without seizing the drugs they left the warehouse and applied for a search warrant. The warrant was issued despite the application making no mention of any information discovered during the illegal entry of the warehouse. The agents reentered the warehouse with the warrant and seized marijuana and other evidence. At trial, Murray (D) moved to suppress the evidence as fruit of the illegal search, the motion was denied, and Murray (D) was convicted. The court of appeals affirmed, and Murray (D) appealed to the United States Supreme Court.

ISSUE: Will evidence initially uncovered, but not seized, during an illegal search be suppressed if the police later obtain a search warrant that does not rely on any facts discovered during the illegal search, and then seize the evidence during a second search pursuant to the warrant?

HOLDING AND DECISION: (Scalia, J.) No. Under the "independent source" doctrine, "evidence initially uncovered, but not seized, during an illegal search will not be suppressed if the police later obtain a search warrant that does not rely on any facts discovered during the illegal search, and then seize the evidence during a second search pursuant to the warrant." Society's interest in deterring unlawful police behavior and society's interest in having juries review all probative evidence of a crime are properly balanced by putting the police in the same position they would have been in but for their illegal conduct. If, as here, police discover evidence illegally, but later acquire it through a lawful, independent source, suppressing the evidence would put the police in a worse position than they would have been absent the illegal conduct. This rule does not encourage officers to first search unlawfully and then get a warrant because if they already have probable cause they risk suppression of the evidence should they be unable to satisfy the independent source doctrine. If they do not already have probable cause, no information obtained during the illegal search can be used to establish probable cause, and, moreover, if a court does not believe that the officers would have sought a search warrant absent the illegal search, then the evidence will be suppressed. Judgment vacated and remanded for determination of whether the warrant-authorized search was an independent source of the challenged evidence.

DISSENT: (Marshall, J.) Under this ruling, officers have an incentive to search illegally first, then seek a warrant. If the illegal search turns up no evidence, the officers have saved the substantial time and inconvenience of obtaining a search warrant. If the illegal search does turn up evidence, it is a simple matter to exclude from the warrant application any information gained from the illegal entry. The defendant then will be reduced to the nearly unwinnable argument that the officers are lying when they testify that they would have sought the warrant absent the illegal search.

ANALYSIS

Closely related to the "independent source" doctrine, and another limit on "fruit of the poisonous tree" analysis, is the "inevitable discovery" doctrine announced in *Nix v. Williams*, 467 U.S. 431 (1984), which is discussed at length in *Murray*. In *Nix*, police learned the whereabouts of the victim's body by questioning the defendant in violation of his Sixth Amendment right to counsel. A search for the body had been under way but was called off when the defendant revealed the body's location. The Supreme Court, using much the same reasoning it used in *Murray*, held that evidence concerning the body was admissible because it inevitably would have been discovered by the searchers without the unlawful interrogation.

Continued on next page.

Quicknotes

FRUIT OF THE POISONOUS TREE Doctrine that evidence obtained as a result of illegal procedures is tainted and is usually inadmissible at trial.

INDEPENDENT SOURCE Pertaining to evidence derived from another source, independent of the evidence obtained with a defective warrant.

United States v. Leon

Federal government (P) v. Owner of illegally seized evidence (D)

468 U.S. 897 (1984)

NATURE OF CASE: Appeal from the suppression of evidence.

FACT SUMMARY: The court of appeals held that evidence seized pursuant to a facially valid warrant had to be suppressed due to a lack of probable cause to issue the warrant even though the police had acted in good faith.

RULE OF LAW
The Fourth Amendment does not require exclusion of evidence seized pursuant to a facially valid warrant where the police have acted in good faith.

FACTS: The district court granted Leon's (D) motion to suppress evidence seized on good faith pursuant to a facially valid warrant issued by the neutral magistrate which was subsequently found to be based on an affidavit that did not sufficiently establish probable cause. The court of appeals affirmed, refusing to recognize a good-faith exception to the exclusionary rule. The United States Supreme Court granted certiorari.

ISSUE: Does the Fourth Amendment require exclusion of evidence seized pursuant to a facially valid warrant where the police have acted in good faith?

HOLDING AND DECISION: (White, J.) No. The Fourth Amendment does not require exclusion of evidence seized pursuant to a facially valid warrant where the police have acted in good faith. The exclusionary rule is applied only in cases where it would be consistent with its rationale. The rule is imposed to deter police conduct that denies the defendant his constitutional rights. Where the police act in good faith, under the authorization of a neutral and detached magistrate, the deterrent purpose does not apply. As a result, the rule should not be applied in this case. Reversed.

DISSENT: (Brennan, J.) The exclusionary rule is indirectly compelled by the Fourth Amendment. Also, the good-faith exception will simply allow police to infringe on constitutional rights by limiting the information included in affidavits supporting search warrants.

ANALYSIS

The Court stated in this case that suppression remains a viable tool if the magistrate or judge, in issuing a warrant, was misled by information in an affidavit that the affiant knew was false. Suppression will also be allowed where the police could not have acted in good faith because the warrant was obviously invalid.

Quicknotes

AFFIDAVIT A declaration of facts written and affirmed before a witness.

EXCLUSIONARY RULE A rule precluding the introduction at trial of evidence unlawfully obtained in violation of the federal constitutional safeguards against unreasonable searches and seizures.

GOOD-FAITH EXCEPTION TO WARRANT REQUIREMENT The exception to the rule that evidence obtained as the result of an unlawful search and seizure is nevertheless admissible at trial if the officers had a reasonable, good-faith belief that they acted pursuant to legal authority.

PROBABLE CAUSE A reasonable basis for believing that a crime has been committed.

Davis v. United States

Passenger subject to a warrantless search (D) v. Federal government (P)

564 U.S. 229 (2011)

NATURE OF CASE: Appeal from intermediate appellate court decision in favor of the government.

FACT SUMMARY: Davis (D) was a passenger in a vehicle during a routine traffic stop. After the police arrested Davis (D) for giving a false name, the officers conducted a warrantless search of the vehicle incident to the arrest. The search produced an illegal firearm.

RULE OF LAW

Searches conducted by the police in reliance upon binding legal precedent existing at the time of the search are not subject to the exclusionary rule.

FACTS: During a routine traffic stop, police arrested Davis (D) for giving a false name. After the arrest, police conducted a warrantless search of the vehicle. The search produced a firearm in the pocket of Davis's coat. The Government (P) charged Davis (D) with one count of possession of a firearm by a convicted felon. A jury convicted Davis (D). While his appeal was pending at the Eleventh Circuit Court of Appeals, the United States Supreme Court decided *Arizona v. Gant*, 556 U.S. 332 (2009). *Arizona v. Gant* essentially held that law enforcement officers must demonstrate either a continuing threat to their safety or the need to preserve evidence before conducting a warrantless search of a vehicle incident to an arrest. The Eleventh Circuit Court of Appeals upheld the conviction of Davis (D), however, on the grounds that penalizing the officers for conduct in compliance with existing law at the time of the search would not deter officers from future Fourth Amendment violations. The United States Supreme Court granted Davis's (D) petition for review.

ISSUE: Are searches conducted by the police in reliance upon binding legal precedent existing at the time of the search subject to the exclusionary rule?

HOLDING AND DECISION: (Alito, J.) No. Searches conducted by the police in reliance upon binding legal precedent existing at the time of the search are not subject to the exclusionary rule. The reliance upon the binding precedent must be objectively reasonable. The sole purpose of the exclusionary rule is to deter future Fourth Amendment violations by other law enforcement personnel. Where the suppression of evidence will not yield deterrence, exclusion of the evidence is unwarranted. In addition to deterrence, courts must also weigh the substantial social costs generated by the rule. The deterrence benefits must outweigh the heavy costs of releasing criminals upon the community. The deterrence benefits of exclusion depend upon the culpability of the law enforcement conduct at issue in the case. Where police act deliberately or recklessly, the deterrent value of exclusion is strong. When police act in accordance with an objective good-faith belief in the legality of the search, the deterrence rationale carries much less weight. Here, the officers' search followed prior Eleventh Circuit precedent. However, the *Arizona v. Gant* decision has now made such searches illegal without a warrant. Davis (D) argues that prior precedent requires that the *Arizona* decision be applied retroactively to his case. The Court agrees *Arizona* should be retroactively applied. However, the existence of a Fourth Amendment violation does not mean Davis (D) is entitled to the remedy of exclusion of evidence. The remedy only applies where its purpose, deterrence, is effectively advanced. That is not the case here. Applying the good-faith exception to binding legal precedent as we have here will not prevent judicial consideration of prior Fourth Amendment decisions. This Court will continue to review criminal convictions from the twelve circuit courts of appeal and from the states. Affirmed.

CONCURRENCE: (Sotomayor, J.) The majority is correct that where the officers acted in compliance with binding legal precedence, application of the exclusionary rule will not yield appreciable deterrence. The test for legality of searches remains one, whether exclusion results in deterrence, and two, whether the benefits of exclusion outweigh the costs.

DISSENT: (Breyer, J.) While agreeing that *Arizona* applies retroactively to this case, the majority improperly and implausibly denies Davis (D) the remedy of exclusion to which he is entitled. Under this decision, the Court gives improper weight to the culpability of law enforcement. The majority will now only apply the exclusionary rule where the officers' conduct was deliberate or reckless. This will essentially swallow the exclusionary rule and weaken its deterrent effect.

ANALYSIS

Under the case of *Teague v. Lane*, 489 U.S. 288 (1989), any new constitutional rule must be applied retroactively to all pending state or federal cases that have not been completely resolved.

Quicknotes

EXCLUSIONARY RULE A rule precluding the introduction at trial of evidence unlawfully obtained in violation of the federal constitutional safeguards against unreasonable searches and seizures.

CHAPTER 9

Undercover Investigations

Quick Reference Rules of Law

PAGE

1. *Hoffa v. United States.* The government's use of an undercover informant without a warrant is not a violation of the Fourth Amendment. *114*

2. *Sherman v. United States.* The government may not originate a criminal design and implant it in the mind of an innocent person so that the government may prosecute that person. *115*

3. *Jacobson v. United States.* Where government actions create a person's disposition to commit a crime, and then government suggests the crime that the person commits, it is entrapment. *116*

Hoffa v. United States

Teamster (D) v. Federal government (P)

385 U.S. 293 (1966)

NATURE OF CASE: Appeal from a criminal conviction based on a Fourth Amendment violation.

FACT SUMMARY: While Hoffa (D) was on trial in Tennessee, the Government (P) sent a paid undercover informant to gather information about Hoffa (D) and report to the Government (P).

RULE OF LAW

The government's use of an undercover informant without a warrant is not a violation of the Fourth Amendment.

FACTS: Jimmy Hoffa (D) was on trial in Nashville, Tennessee. During the two-month trial, Edward Partin was a constant companion of Hoffa (D), visiting Hoffa (D) repeatedly at his suite in the Andrew Jackson Hotel. Partin was also frequently in the company of Hoffa's (D) associates at the hotel, around town, and in the courthouse. Also, during this time Partin was a paid Government (P) informant. Hoffa (D) argues that Partin's failure to disclose his role as an informant vitiated the consent that Hoffa (D) gave Partin to enter the hotel suite repeatedly, and the information given to the Government (P) as a result of Hoffa's (D) confidence was, therefore, a violation of the Fourth Amendment.

ISSUE: Is the government's use of an undercover informant without a warrant a violation of the Fourth Amendment?

HOLDING AND DECISION: (Stewart, J.) No. The government's use of an undercover informant without a warrant is not a violation of the Fourth Amendment. Hoffa (D) was not relying on the safety of his hotel room when Hoffa (D) made incriminating statements. Rather, he relied on a misplaced confidence in an informant. Affirmed.

DISSENT: (Warren, C.J.) Whether the government's use of an undercover agent violates the Constitution must be determined on a case-by-case basis. Here, Partin was a "jailbird" who had serious federal charges pending against him, so that his motives for becoming an informant are suspect. This type of informer and the way the Government (P) used him present a serious potential for undermining the integrity of the truth-finding process. Given his incentives and background, no conviction should be allowed to stand if it is based heavily on his testimony. Here, but for Partin's testimony, it is unlikely Hoffa (D) would have been convicted. Thus, the Fourth Amendment issues should not even have been reached; instead, the testimony should have been discredited as an affront to the quality and fairness of federal law enforcement, which is subject to the Court's supervisory powers. If a criminal defendant had in a similar fashion planted an informer in the prosecution's camp, he would be guilty of obstructing justice. Therefore, the conviction cannot stand.

ANALYSIS

In the companion case of *Osborn v. United States*, 385 U.S. 323 (1996), according to Justice Douglas, the Fourth Amendment issue should turn on whether the informant was a "turncoat friend" or a "government spy." Justice Douglas stressed that a person taking the risk that a friend will turn on him and report to the police is far different from a government plant.

Quicknotes

FOURTH AMENDMENT Provides that persons be secure as to their person and private belongings against unreasonable searches and seizures.

Sherman v. United States

Convicted drug dealer (D) v. Federal government (P)

356 U.S. 369 (1958)

NATURE OF CASE: On certiorari from appellate court judgment upholding narcotics conviction.

FACT SUMMARY: Sherman (D), upon the repeated entreaties of a Government (P) informant, supplied the informer with narcotics.

RULE OF LAW

The government may not originate a criminal design and implant it in the mind of an innocent person so that the government may prosecute that person.

FACTS: Sherman (D) met another man at a doctor's office where apparently both were seeking treatment of a narcotics addiction. Sherman's (D) acquaintance informed him that he was not responding to treatment and that he was suffering greatly, and asked Sherman (D) if he knew a source of narcotics. Sherman (D) tried to avoid the issue, but the acquaintance repeatedly prevailed on Sherman's (D) sympathy. Sherman (D) finally obtained a quantity of narcotics, which he shared with his acquaintance. The acquaintance, who turned out to be a government (P) informant, then advised police that Sherman (D) had sold him drugs. Sherman (D) was arrested and convicted, and the court of appeals affirmed. The United States Supreme Court granted certiorari.

ISSUE: May the government originate a criminal design and implant it in the mind of an innocent person so that the government may prosecute that person?

HOLDING AND DECISION: (Warren, C.J.) No. The government may not originate a criminal design and implant it in the mind of an innocent person so that the government may prosecute him. In considering whether entrapment has occurred, we look not only to the conduct of government agents, but to the subjective willingness of the defendant to commit the crime. If a person is predisposed to commit an offense, and the government merely affords him an opportunity to do that wrong which he was ready and willing to do, then the conduct of the government does not constitute entrapment. However, in this case the testimony of the prosecution's witnesses indicates that Sherman (D) was anything but ready and willing, and that only repeated entreaties by the informer, who claimed to be in great suffering, caused Sherman (D) to supply him with narcotics. Reversed and remanded.

CONCURRENCE: (Frankfurter, J.) Conduct is not less criminal because it is the result of temptation. The better test for entrapment would focus solely on the conduct of the police. As Justice Holmes wrote, "[F]or my part I think it a less evil that some criminals should escape than that the government should play an ignoble part."

ANALYSIS

In addition to disagreeing with the majority over whether the predisposition of the defendant should be considered in evaluating an entrapment defense, Justice Frankfurter argued that entrapment should be a question of law for the judge, not a jury issue. "It is the province of the court and the court alone," he wrote, "to protect itself and the government from such prostitution of the criminal law."

Quicknotes

ENTRAPMENT An act by public officers that induces a defendant into committing a criminal act.

Jacobson v. United States

Pornography buyer (D) v. Federal government (P)

503 U.S. 540 (1992)

NATURE OF CASE: Appeal of conviction for receiving child pornography.

FACT SUMMARY: Jacobson (D) claimed the Government (P) had entrapped him into violating a child pornography law.

RULE OF LAW

Where government actions create a person's disposition to commit a crime, and then government suggests the crime that the person commits, it is entrapment.

FACTS: At a time when it was legal, Jacobson (D) ordered from an adult bookstore two magazines picturing nude boys, though he later testified he thought he was ordering photos of young men over 17. Congress subsequently passed the Child Protection Act of 1984, criminalizing receipt by mail of sexually explicit depictions of children. The Postal Service found Jacobson's (D) name on the store's mailing list and began mailing Jacobson (D) letters and questionnaires from fictitious research and lobbying organizations and a fake pen pal. The mailings discussed and asked about Jacobson's (D) tastes in pornography and views on censorship. Each time he answered the next mailing was fit more to his tastes. After two years, the Customs Service, through a fake company, sent Jacobson (D) a child pornography brochure. He placed an order, but it was never filled. The Postal Service, using a fake company, sent Jacobson (D) a letter decrying censorship and claiming the media and government were trying to keep its material out of the country. Jacobson (D) requested a catalogue, from which he later ordered child pornography. Jacobson (D) was arrested upon controlled delivery of the magazine. He unsuccessfully raised an entrapment defense and was convicted under the 1984 Act. The court of appeals affirmed, and Jacobson (D) appealed.

ISSUE: Where government actions create a person's disposition to commit a crime, and then government suggests the crime that the person commits, is it entrapment?

HOLDING AND DECISION: (White, J.) Yes. Where government acts create a person's disposition to commit a crime, and then government suggests the crime that the person commits, it is entrapment. Jacobson (D) had become predisposed to break the law by the time he ordered a magazine from the Government (P). However, the Government (P) did not prove this disposition was not the product of years of Government (P) targeting. The magazines Jacobson (D) ordered from the bookstore were legal when bought. Evidence of predisposition to do what was once legal is not sufficient to show predisposition to do what now is illegal, since most people obey laws with which they disagree. Jacobson's (D) claim that he did not know he was ordering photos of minors from the bookstore was unchallenged. His answers to Government (P) mailings showed predisposition to view child pornography and to support a given agenda through lobbying groups but did not support an inference of predisposition to commit the alleged crime. The strong arguable inference is that by waving the banner of individual rights and disparaging efforts to restrict pornography, the Government (P) excited Jacobson's (D) interest in banned materials and exerted substantial pressure on him to fight censorship by obtaining such materials. The Government (P) may not play on an innocent man's weaknesses and beguile him into committing crimes he would not otherwise commit. Reversed.

DISSENT: (O'Connor, J.) Both times the Government (P) offered Jacobson (D) a chance to buy pornography he responded enthusiastically. Thus, a reasonable jury could find a predisposition to commit the crime. Predisposition should be assessed as of the time the government suggested the crime, not when the government first became involved; the government does not need a reasonable suspicion before it can investigate. Moreover, the two-year investigation of Jacobson (D) involved no threats, coercion, or "substantial pressure" to commit the crime. Finally, the Government (P) did not have to prove Jacobson (D) was predisposed to break the law, only that he was predisposed to receive child pornography. The 1984 Act does not require specific intent to break the law, only knowing receipt. Since the requirement of predisposition is designed to eliminate the entrapment defense for those who would have committed the crime absent government inducement, the elements of predisposition should track the elements of the crime.

ANALYSIS

The Court follows the subjective test for entrapment, i.e., whether the defendant was predisposed to commit the crime, as opposed to the objective test, i.e., whether police conduct created a substantial risk that an innocent person would commit the crime. However, as the dissent points out, the Court's main concern "is that the Government (P) went too far and 'abused' the

Continued on next page.

'processes of detection and enforcement' by luring an innocent person to violate the law." *Jacobson* illustrates how the subjective and objective tests are blurred in application. In analyzing an entrapment claim, courts must look to the conduct of both the defendant and the police.

Quicknotes

ENTRAPMENT An act by public officers that induces a defendant into committing a criminal act.

PREDISPOSITION Defendant's inclination to engage in the illegal activity for which he has been charged.

CHAPTER 10

Police Interrogation and Confessions

Quick Reference Rules of Law

PAGE

1. *Miranda v. Arizona (No. 759).* When a person has been taken into police custody or otherwise deprived of his freedom of action in any significant way, the following warnings must be given prior to questioning: (1) that he has the right to remain silent; (2) that any statement he does make may be used as evidence against him; (3) that he has the right to have an attorney present; and (4) that if he cannot afford an attorney, one will be appointed for him. *121*

2. *J.D.B. v. North Carolina.* When determining whether a suspect is in custody, thus requiring the police to inform the suspect of his *Miranda* rights, police must take into account the age of the suspect. *124*

3. *Howes v. Fields.* An interrogation of a prisoner, in private and in isolation from the general prison population, about events outside the prison, is not a per se custodial interrogation for *Miranda* purposes. *125*

4. *Rhode Island v. Innis.* Any words or actions on the part of the police that they should know are reasonably likely to elicit an incriminating response from the suspect constitute "interrogation" under *Miranda* and bring the *Miranda* safeguards into play. *127*

5. *Pennsylvania v. Muniz.* During a custodial interrogation, the response to the question "Do you know what the date was of your sixth birthday?" is testimonial and, therefore, excludable from evidence if made prior to the giving of *Miranda* warnings. *129*

6. *New York v. Quarles* Police need not give *Miranda* warnings where the need for such warnings is outweighed by the need to protect the public safety. *131*

7. *Duckworth v. Eagan.* Informing a suspect that an attorney would be appointed for him "if and when you go to court" does not render *Miranda* warnings inadequate. *133*

8. *Moran v. Burbine.* A voluntary confession obtained by police who fail to inform a defendant that an attorney attempted to contact him is not an invalid intrusion upon the defendant's *Miranda* rights. *134*

9. *Berghuis v. Thompkins.* (1) A criminal suspect's silence during an interrogation does not invoke his right to remain silent. (2) A criminal suspect waives his right to remain silent when he knowingly and voluntarily makes a statement to the police. (3) The police are not required to obtain a waiver of a criminal suspect's *Miranda* rights before interrogating him. *135*

10. *Davis v. United States.* After a suspect has waived his *Miranda* rights and talked to law-enforcement officers, the officers may keep questioning him unless and until he unambiguously asserts his right to counsel. *138*

11. *Maryland v. Shatzer.* When a criminal suspect who had previously invoked his right to an attorney is then released from custody for a period of 14 days, his subsequent waiver of his right to an attorney at a follow-up interrogation shall be deemed valid. *140*

12. *Salinas v. Texas.* A witness must expressly claim the Fifth Amendment privilege against self-incrimination during noncustodial police questioning. *141*

13. *Dickerson v. United States.* When a decision of the court involves interpretation and application of the Constitution, Congress may not legislatively supersede such decision. *143*

14. *Chavez v. Martinez.* The Fifth Amendment protection against self-incrimination applies only in criminal cases. *144*

15. *Brewer v. Williams (Williams I).* Police questioning of a suspect without the presence of known counsel during a critical stage of the proceedings is violative of the Sixth and Fourteenth Amendments. *146*

16. *Patterson v. Illinois.* Interrogation of a criminal defendant after indictment does not violate the Sixth Amendment right to counsel so long as the defendant knowingly and voluntarily waives his right to counsel at that stage. *148*

17. *Montejo v. Louisiana.* When a court automatically appoints counsel for an indigent defendant or when the defendant has requested counsel, there is no longer a presumption that any subsequent waiver of the defendant's right to counsel will be involuntary. *150*

18. *Texas v. Cobb.* The Sixth Amendment right to counsel does not extend to crimes that are "factually related" to those that have actually been charged. *153*

19. *Miller v. Fenton.* Where the totality of circumstances, including a suspect's susceptibility to interrogation pressures and the interviewing officer's demeanor and statements, indicate that the suspect's will was not overborne during a custodial interview, the suspect's confession is "voluntary" and, therefore, admissible in a criminal prosecution of the suspect. *155*

20. *Colorado v. Connelly.* Coercive police activity is a necessary predicate to the finding that a confession is not "voluntary" within the meaning of the Due Process Clause of the Fourteenth Amendment. *158*

21. *United States v. Patane.* The Self-Incrimination Clause is not violated by the admission into evidence of the physical fruit of a voluntary statement. *159*

22. *Missouri v. Seibert.* The police technique of interrogating in successive, unwarned and warned phases violates the requirements of *Miranda.* *161*

Miranda v. Arizona (No. 759)

Interrogated suspect (D) v. State (P)

384 U.S. 436 (1966)

NATURE OF CASE: Certiorari from various convictions and from the reversal of one.

FACT SUMMARY: Convictions resulted in several cases from confessions obtained through incommunicado-interrogation in a police-dominated atmosphere, without full warnings of constitutional rights.

RULE OF LAW

When a person has been taken into police custody or otherwise deprived of his freedom of action in any significant way, the following warnings must be given prior to questioning: (1) that he has the right to remain silent; (2) that any statement he does make may be used as evidence against him; (3) that he has the right to have an attorney present; and (4) that if he cannot afford an attorney, one will be appointed for him.

FACTS: Convictions in the cases of *Miranda v. Arizona* [No. 759], *Vignera v. New York* [No. 760], *Westover v. United States* [No. 761], and *California v. Stewart* [No. 584] are brought before this Court through petitions of certiorari. In each of these cases, confessions resulted after incommunicado-interrogation in a police-dominated atmosphere, without full warning of constitutional rights (or without any indication in the police records that such warnings were given). And in each of these cases, the confessions obtained from such interrogation were used as the basis for the resulting convictions. Only in the case of *Stewart* was the conviction reversed by the Supreme Court of California on the basis that Stewart (D) had not been informed of his rights. Because of the related nature of these cases, the United States Supreme Court granted certiorari to determine the central issue involved.

ISSUE: When a person is taken into custody, is it necessary that his constitutional rights to remain silent and to have an attorney present be explained to him before questioning?

HOLDING AND DECISION: (Warren, C.J.) Yes. When a person has been taken into police custody or otherwise deprived of his freedom of action in any significant way, the following warnings must be given prior to questioning: (1) that he has the right to remain silent; (2) that any statement he does make may be used as evidence against him; (3) that he has the right to have an attorney present; and (4) that if he cannot afford an attorney, one will be appointed for him. "[T]he prosecution may not use statements, whether exculpatory or inculpatory, stemming from custodial interrogation of the defendant unless it demonstrates the use of procedural safeguards effective to secure the privilege against self-incrimination. By custodial interrogation, we mean questioning initiated by law enforcement officers after a person has been taken into custody or otherwise deprived of his freedom of action in any significant way. As for the procedural safeguards to be employed, unless other fully effective means are devised to inform accused persons of their right to silence and to assure a continuous opportunity to exercise it, the following measures are required. Prior to any questioning, the person must be warned that he has a right to remain silent, that any statement he does make may be used as evidence against him, and that he has the right to the presence of an attorney, either retained or appointed (if he cannot afford one). The defendant may waive effectuation of these rights, provided the waiver is made voluntarily, knowingly and intelligently. If, however, he indicates in any manner and at any stage of the process that he wishes to consult with an attorney before speaking, there can be no questioning. Likewise, if the individual is alone and indicates in any manner that he does not wish to be interrogated, the police may not question him. The mere fact that he may have answered some questions or volunteered some statements on his own does not deprive him of the right to refrain from answering any further inquiries until he has consulted with an attorney and thereafter consents to be questioned." The rationale for this decision is based upon the nature of custodial interrogation and its relationship to the Fifth Amendment's Self-Incrimination Clause. The true nature of custodial interrogation clearly is described in standard police manuals and texts, which teach "psychologically oriented coercive techniques" (e.g., incommunicado detention, prolonged questioning). Such practices are inherently contrary to the principle that an individual may not be compelled to incriminate himself. And freedom from self-incrimination is "one of our nation's most cherished principles," based upon our accusatory system of justice which protects the "dignity and integrity of its citizens" by requiring that government may only produce incriminating evidence "by its own independent labors." It is elementary that, unless there are sufficient safeguards (i.e., those announced in this decision) to ensure the right against self-incrimination in custodial interrogation, its recognition at trial is meaningless. Here, in each case, the accused was put through custodial interrogations without the appropriate safeguards and the prosecution has not demonstrated any "knowing and intelligent waiver" of

Continued on next page.

rights in any of the cases. It is true that Westover (D) was informed of his rights by the FBI before his statement, but he had been subjected to police interrogation for over 14 hours prior to that time (i.e., before he was handed over to the Federal Bureau of Investigation (FBI)). Since the FBI questioning immediately followed the police interrogation, from Westover's (D) point of view at least, there had, in fact, been one continuous period of questioning with the warning of his rights only at the end of the process. Convictions are reversed in *Miranda*, in *Vignera*, and in *Westover*, and the reversal of the conviction in *Stewart* is affirmed.

DISSENT AND CONCURRENCE: (Clark, J.) (Dissent in the cases of *Vignera*, *Westover*, and *Miranda*; concurrence in the case of *Stewart*.) The Court should have been more restrained in these cases. There is a decided lack of information and empirical data on the practical operation of requirements comparable to those announced today. Furthermore, custodial interrogation has long been recognized as an "essential tool in effective law enforcement," and the rule, prior to today, recognized this fact by judging the voluntariness from the "totality of all the circumstances" (including whether an accused had been advised of his rights). The rule today, however, is too rigid.

DISSENT: (Harlan, J.) The decision of the Court today in abandoning its historical case-by-case approach represents poor constitutional law. The Court's new rules are designed to "ultimately discourage any confession at all." Such an approach cannot be sustained by constitutional or policy considerations. First, constitutionally there is no basis for extending the Fifth Amendment to the police station. Historically, the ban against self-incrimination has applied only in criminal proceedings, not in "extra-legal" situations, such as interrogations. Furthermore, even if it can be applied to custodial interrogations, it has never been held to forbid all pressures on an accused, as the Court today attempts to do. Similarly, there is no constitutional basis for applying the right to counsel to custodial interrogations. The danger of injustice by allowing an untrained person to defend himself in a technical court situation is the basis for this right, and that rationale is not applicable to custodial situations. Second, in considering policy issues, although it is true that police questioning will inherently entail some pressure on the suspect, until today the role of the Constitution has been to "sift out" only "undue pressure." The inflexible rules today, however, ignore this. Those who use coercive tactics may simply lie in court about having given the required warnings. Nothing is gained and many voluntary confessions will be lost. In conclusion, neither the constitutional interpretations nor the consequence of today's ruling is justifiable.

DISSENT: (White, J.) First, the Fifth Amendment forbids self-incrimination only if it is "compelled." Yet, the Court today has no factual basis for concluding that custodial interrogations are so inherently coercive as to make any statements arising from them, if there is no warning of rights, compelled. In fact, the Court has not examined a single transcript of any police interrogation. Furthermore, even if it is assumed that "all" such interrogations are coercive, the rule adopted today is irrational. If such interrogations are so "coercive," how can a suspect ever voluntarily waive his rights as the Court indicates he can? Second, and more importantly, the Court overlooks the ominous consequences of its decision. Although the Court states that the rule adopted is necessary to preserve the "integrity" of the individual, it overlooks the fact that without effective prevention of crime (or personal violence) there can be no human dignity. The most basic function of any government is to provide for the security of an individual and his property, but after today's decision, effective law enforcement will be impaired, in that more who are guilty may go free and many who could easily explain their innocence will waste police time while waiting for their attorneys.

ANALYSIS

Miranda illustrates the rule applicable to evidence sought to be admitted against an accused as "part of the prosecution's case," but a statement obtained in violation of the *Miranda* rule "may be used to impeach" an accused's testimony if he takes the stand at trial and if the statement is otherwise "voluntary and trustworthy." *Miranda* also does not apply to mere on-the-scene questioning, general fact-finding inquiries of citizens, or spontaneous admissions volunteered before the police began interrogation. Furthermore, it must be noted that several issues or problems have been raised in the wake of *Miranda*. First, while a waiver of rights will not be inferred from silence, the type of expression required remains open to question. However, the lower courts are in general agreement that a warning of rights need not be repeated at the beginning of each successive interrogation for a valid waiver to occur. Second, the Supreme Court has not addressed itself to the question of whether automatic reversal of a conviction based upon a confession obtained in violation of *Miranda* is required. Third, the Supreme Court has also left open the question of whether the "fruits" (*Wong Sun*, 371 U.S. 471 (1963)) derived from statements obtained in violation of *Miranda* are admissible. Finally, fourth, although the Court in *Miranda* states that the warnings are necessary "unless other full effective means are devised to inform accused persons" of their rights, it is questionable what would be considered "effective." The Crime Control Act of 1968, applicable to federal criminal trials, seeks to substitute for the *Miranda* warnings a test of "voluntariness" based

Continued on next page.

upon the totality of circumstances. However, the Court in *Miranda* does seem to indicate that something more than a test of voluntariness is required, although the constitutionality of this legislation is presently undetermined.

Quicknotes

CERTIORARI A discretionary writ issued by a superior court to an inferior court in order to review the lower court's decisions; the U.S. Supreme Court's writ ordering such review.

COERCION The overcoming of a person's free will as a result of threats, promises, or undue influence.

CUSTODIAL INTERROGATION The questioning of a suspect by police while in custody.

EMPIRICAL EVIDENCE Evidence based on observation or experimentation.

EXCULPATORY EVIDENCE A statement or other evidence that tends to excuse, justify, or absolve the defendant from alleged fault or guilt.

FIFTH AMENDMENT Provides that no person shall be compelled to serve as a witness against him- or herself, be subject to trial for the same offense twice, or be deprived of life, liberty, or property without due process of law.

INCULPATORY EVIDENCE A statement or other evidence that tends to show a person's guilt in committing a criminal act.

UNDUE INFLUENCE Improper use of power that deprives an individual of freedom of choice and substitutes another's choice for the individual's own choice.

J.D.B. v. North Carolina

Youth questioned without being read his *Miranda* rights (D) v. State (P)

564 U.S. 261 (2011)

NATURE OF CASE: Appeal from state high court decision in favor of the state.

FACT SUMMARY: Police suspected J.D.B. (D), a 13-year-old seventh grade student, of breaking into two homes. Police questioned him at his school without informing him of his *Miranda* rights [*Miranda v. Arizona*, 384 U.S. 436 (1966)].

RULE OF LAW

When determining whether a suspect is in custody, thus requiring the police to inform the suspect of his *Miranda* rights, police must take into account the age of the suspect.

FACTS: Police suspected J.D.B. (D), a 13-year-old seventh grade student, of breaking into two homes. Two police officers questioned him in a room at his school in the presence of other school officials. The questioning lasted some 30–45 minutes and the police did not read J.D.B. (D) his *Miranda* rights prior to the questioning. The police officers also did not inform J.D.B. (D) he was free to leave. J.D.B. (D) confessed to the crimes. A trial court judge later found J.D.B. (D) delinquent. J.D.B. (D) appealed on the ground his statements were made while he was in custody and he was not given his *Miranda* rights. The North Carolina Supreme Court rejected his appeal on the grounds he was not in custody at the time of the questioning. His statements therefore could be used against him. J.D.B. (D) appealed to the United States Supreme Court.

ISSUE: When determining whether a suspect is in custody, thus requiring the police to inform the suspect of his *Miranda* rights, must the police take into account the age of the suspect?

HOLDING AND DECISION: (Sotomayor, J.) Yes. When determining whether a suspect is in custody, thus requiring the police to inform the suspect of his *Miranda* rights, police must take into account the age of the suspect. Whether a suspect is in custody deserving of his *Miranda* rights is an objective inquiry. The inquiry typically is whether a reasonable person in the suspect's position would understand his or her freedom to terminate the inquiry. Here, a child may sometimes feel pressured to submit to questioning when an adult would not. Also, other areas of the law, such as tort law, account for distinctions between adults and children. When reviewing one's tort liability, whether the person is an adult or a child will change the outcome of that determination. Officers are competent enough to account for a child's age when making their determination whether to give a suspect his or her *Miranda* rights. On remand, the state courts should determine whether J.D.B. (D) was in custody at the time of the questioning in light of this decision. Remanded.

DISSENT: (Alito, J.) The strength of the *Miranda* rule is that it created an objective, reasonable person test for determining custody that could be applied to everyone. The whole purpose of the test was to avoid subjective considerations of a suspect's characteristics and provide law enforcement with a clear rule to follow. Now, the majority's decision may eventually force police officers to make independent, fact intensive inquiries for each suspect based upon the suspect's age, education, employment, or prior involvement with the police. The majority also improperly relies upon tort law for support. In negligence cases, the liability determination is completed long after an incident occurred, with a thorough review of the facts by a judge or jury. In contrast, police must make their determination whether to provide *Miranda* rights quickly during an ongoing investigation.

ANALYSIS

This was a five to four Supreme Court decision, with Justice Kennedy joining Justices Sotomayor, Ginsburg, Breyer, and Kagan to reverse the state court decision. There is an ongoing confrontation within the Supreme Court over the scope of *Miranda*, with the more conservative justices seeking to limit *Miranda's* scope and the more liberal members of the Court seeking to broaden its application.

Quicknotes

***MIRANDA* RULE** A required warning given before any questioning by law enforcement authorities may take place. Individuals in custody receive warnings regarding their privilege against self-incrimination, right to remain silent, and right to be represented by an attorney.

Howes v. Fields

State official (D) v. State prisoner (P)

565 U.S. 499 (2012)

NATURE OF CASE: Appeal from affirmance of grant of habeas corpus petition to state prisoner asserting violations of his constitutional rights against self-incrimination.

FACT SUMMARY: Fields (P), a state prisoner who confessed to an out-of-prison crime after being interrogated at the prison without being told he did not have to speak to the interrogators, filed a habeas corpus petition against the State (D), contending that his constitutional rights were violated because he had not been given *Miranda* warnings, *Miranda v. Arizona*, 384 U.S. 436 (1966), notwithstanding that, according to Fields (P), the interrogation was custodial.

RULE OF LAW

An interrogation of a prisoner, in private and in isolation from the general prison population, about events outside the prison, is not a per se custodial interrogation for *Miranda* purposes.

FACTS: Fields (P), a state prisoner serving time for disorderly conduct, was escorted from his prison cell by a corrections officer to a conference room, where he was questioned by two sheriff's deputies about criminal activity he had allegedly engaged in before coming to prison. At no time was Fields (P) given *Miranda* warnings, *Miranda v. Arizona*, 384 U.S. 436 (1966), or advised that he did not have to speak with the deputies. Fields (P) was questioned for between five and seven hours; he was told more than once that he was free to leave and return to his cell; the deputies were armed, but Fields (P) remained free of restraints; the conference room door was sometimes open and sometimes shut; several times during the interview Fields (P) stated that he no longer wanted to talk to the deputies, but he did not ask to go back to his cell; Fields (P) was given food and water, but not his daily medications; and after Fields (P) confessed and the interview concluded, he had to wait an additional 20 minutes for an escort and returned to his cell well after the hour when he generally retired. After he was convicted for the crime to which he confessed, Fields (P) brought a habeas corpus action against the State (D) in federal district court under the Antiterrorism and Effective Death Penalty Act of 1996 (AEDPA), 28 U.S.C. § 2254(d)(1). The district court granted the petition, and the court of appeals affirmed, ruling that, for *Miranda* purposes, an interrogation that is held in isolation from the general prison population combined with questioning about conduct occurring outside the prison makes any such interrogation custodial per se. The United States Supreme Court granted certiorari.

ISSUE: Is an interrogation of a prisoner, in private and in isolation from the general prison population, about events outside the prison, a per se custodial interrogation for *Miranda* purposes?

HOLDING AND DECISION: (Alito, J.) No. An interrogation of a prisoner, in private and in isolation from the general prison population, about events outside the prison, is not a per se custodial interrogation for *Miranda* purposes. The court of appeals' categorical rule is unsupported by precedent and is wrong. As used in *Miranda* case law, "custody" is a term of art that specifies circumstances that are thought generally to present a serious danger of coercion. The initial step in determining whether a person is in *Miranda* custody is to ascertain, given all the circumstances surrounding the interrogation, how a suspect would have gauged his freedom of movement. However, not all restraints on freedom of movement amount to *Miranda* custody. The Court's precedents, distinguishing between restraints on freedom of movement and *Miranda* custody, have held that a break in *Miranda* custody between a suspect's invocation of the right to counsel and the initiation of subsequent questioning may occur while a suspect is serving an uninterrupted term of imprisonment. If a break in custody can occur, it must follow that imprisonment alone is not enough to create a custodial situation within the meaning of *Miranda*. At least three strong grounds support this conclusion: (1) questioning a person who is already in prison does not generally involve the shock that very often accompanies arrest; (2) a prisoner is unlikely to be lured into speaking by a longing for prompt release; and (3) a prisoner knows that his questioners probably lack authority to affect the duration of his sentence. Thus, service of a prison term, without more, is not enough to constitute *Miranda* custody. The other criteria used by the court of appeals are likewise insufficient to establish such custody. Taking a prisoner aside for questioning may necessitate some additional limitations on the prisoner's freedom of movement, but it does not necessarily convert a noncustodial situation into *Miranda* custody. Isolation may contribute to a coercive atmosphere when a nonprisoner is questioned; but questioning a prisoner in private does not generally remove the prisoner from a supportive atmosphere and may be in the prisoner's best

Continued on next page.

interest. Neither does questioning a prisoner about criminal activity outside the prison have a significantly greater potential for coercion than questioning under otherwise identical circumstances about criminal activity within the prison walls. The coercive pressure that *Miranda* guards against is neither mitigated nor magnified by the location of the conduct about which questions are asked. Here, under the circumstances, where Fields (P) was told he could leave and return to his cell at any time, and he was not physically restrained or threatened, a reasonable person would have felt free to terminate the interrogation and leave. Therefore, Fields (P) was not in *Miranda* custody. Reversed.

CONCURRENCE AND DISSENT: (Ginsburg, J.) Contrary to the majority's approach, the focus of inquiry should not be on whether there can be custody within custody, but instead on whether Fields (P) was subjected to "incommunicado interrogation...in a police-dominated atmosphere," whether he was placed, against his will, in an inherently stressful situation, and whether his freedom of action was curtailed in any significant way. Those should be the key questions, and in this case each question would receive an affirmative answer. The majority finds, critically, that Fields (P) was told he could end the questioning and return to his cell. However, the facts suggest that the interview was anything but voluntary. Fields (P) should have been informed of his rights, not merely told that he could terminate the interview and return to his cell.

ANALYSIS

In reaching its decision—with which a majority of the Supreme Court clearly disagreed—the Sixth Circuit reasoned that the Supreme Court had clearly established in *Mathis v. United States,* 391 U.S. 1 (1968), that "*Miranda* warnings must be administered when law enforcement officers remove an inmate from the general prison population and interrogate him regarding criminal conduct that took place outside the jail or prison." In the Sixth Circuit's view, the central holding of *Mathis* was that a *Miranda* warning is required whenever an incarcerated individual is isolated from the general prison population and interrogated, i.e., questioned in a manner likely to lead to self-incrimination, about conduct occurring outside of the prison. Because Fields (P) had been isolated from the general prison population and interrogated about conduct occurring in the outside world, the Sixth Circuit found that the state court's decision was contrary to clearly established federal law as determined by the Supreme Court in *Mathis.* However, the Supreme Court rejected this interpretation, stating that its precedents never clearly established a categorical rule with respect to whether the questioning of a prison inmate is custodial, and that, in fact, the Court has repeatedly declined to do so. Instead, the Court adopted a case-by-case approach to determine if *Miranda* concerns were implicated by the particular facts and circumstances of the interview to which Fields (P) was subjected.

Quicknotes

CUSTODIAL INTERROGATION The questioning of a suspect by police while in custody.

HABEAS CORPUS A proceeding in which a defendant brings a writ to compel a judicial determination of whether he or she is lawfully being held in custody.

PER SE By itself; without more; taken alone; not requiring additional evidence for proof; as a matter of law.

Rhode Island v. Innis

State (P) v. Convict with a conscience (D)

446 U.S. 291 (1980)

NATURE OF CASE: Appeal of a murder conviction.

FACT SUMMARY: On the way to the police station in a police car after his arrest, Innis (D) overheard remarks between the officers expressing concern that handicapped children in the area might find the hidden shotgun, whereupon Innis (D) told them to turn around so he could show them where he had hidden it.

RULE OF LAW

Any words or actions on the part of the police that they should know are reasonably likely to elicit an incriminating response from the suspect constitute "interrogation" under *Miranda* and bring the *Miranda* safeguards into play.

FACTS: After being arrested for murder, Innis (D) received the *Miranda* warnings, *Miranda v. Arizona*, 384 U.S. 436 (1966), and said he wanted to speak with an attorney. While being taken to the station in a police car, he overheard a conversation between the officers. "God forbid," one officer said, "that one of the students at the school for the handicapped finds a gun and hurts himself." At that point, Innis (D) told the officers to turn the car around so that he could show them where he had hidden the gun used in the murder. The gun, which was thus found, was used in evidence when Innis (D) was later convicted of murder. The Rhode Island Supreme Court reversed the conviction, holding that the officers had engaged in "interrogation" in violation of *Miranda*.

ISSUE: If the police should know that their words or actions are reasonably likely to elicit an incriminating response from the suspect, do such words or actions constitute "interrogation?"

HOLDING AND DECISION: (Stewart, J.) Yes. Any words or actions on the part of the police that the police should know are reasonably likely to elicit an incriminating response from the suspect constitute "interrogation" under *Miranda*. That is, the term "interrogation" as used in *Miranda* covers express questioning or its functional equivalent. In this particular case, the facts are that the officers engaged in an entire conversation that consisted of no more than a few offhand remarks. The Court cannot say, on that basis, that the officers should have known it was reasonably likely that Innis (D) would suddenly be moved to make a self-incriminating response to this overheard conversation. Therefore, whatever "subtle compulsion" Innis (D) experienced cannot be equated with "interrogation" bringing *Miranda* into play. Reversed.

CONCURRENCE: (Burger, C.J.) The test adopted in this case introduces new elements of uncertainty. It requires a police officer, in the brief time available, to evaluate the suggestibility and susceptibility of an accused. Even psychiatrists would normally have to employ extensive questioning and observation to make the judgment now charged to police officers. However, I concur in the result in this case because it is not inconsistent with *Miranda*.

DISSENT: (Marshall, J.) As I read the Court's definition of "interrogation" for *Miranda* purposes, I find it equivalent, for practical purposes, to my own formulation. I view the *Miranda* safeguards as applying whenever police conduct is intended or likely to produce a response from a suspect in custody. I am, however, utterly at a loss to understand how the objective standard adopted by the Court, when applied to this case, can rationally lead to the conclusion that there was no interrogation. One can scarcely imagine a stronger appeal to the conscience of a suspect than the assertion that if the weapon is not found an innocent, handicapped child will be hurt or killed.

DISSENT: (Stevens, J.) In my view, any statement that would normally be understood by the average listener as calling for a response is the functional equivalent of a direct question, whether or not it is punctuated by a question mark. The Court takes a narrower view in defining "interrogation" for *Miranda* purposes in a holding that represents a plain departure from the principles set forth in *Miranda*. It prohibits only those relatively few statements or actions that a police officer should know are likely to elicit an incriminating response, when statements that appear to call for a response from the suspect, as well as those that are designed to do so, should be considered interrogation. What the Court does in this decision is to narrow the scope of protection afforded a suspect. However, even if the Court's definition of "interrogation" is assumed to be the proper standard, the officers should have known that their appeal to the conscience of the suspect was likely to elicit an incriminating response. Thus, under either definition of the term, "interrogation" occurred in violation of *Miranda*.

ANALYSIS

In *Harryman v. Estelle*, 616 F.2d 879 (5th Cir. 1980), Harryman was arrested as a burglary suspect. A search of his person revealed a condom containing white

Continued on next page.

powder tucked under the waistband of his trousers. The officer, who later claimed he spoke out of shock and surprise, asked, "What is this?" to which Harryman answered: "Oh, you know what it is. It is heroin." Noting that the rigidity of the *Miranda* rules and the way they are to be applied is recognized as the decision's greatest strength, the court of appeals found *Miranda* had been violated by this interchange between officer and suspect. In its opinion, the court stated, "it is enough to decide that what the officer said could reasonably have had the force of a question on the accused."

Quicknotes

CUSTODIAL INTERROGATION The questioning of a suspect by police while in custody.

PRIVILEGE AGAINST SELF-INCRIMINATION A privilege guaranteed by the Fifth Amendment to the U.S. Constitution in a criminal proceeding for communications made by an accused and protecting an accused or witness from having to give testimony that may incriminate him- or herself.

Pennsylvania v. Muniz

State (P) v. Individual convicted of driving while intoxicated (D)

496 U.S. 582 (1990)

NATURE OF CASE: Appeal from conviction for driving while intoxicated, on the grounds that the convict's constitutional right against self-incrimination was violated.

FACT SUMMARY: Muniz (D), who was convicted of driving while intoxicated, contended that evidence of incriminating statements he made prior to being advised of his *Miranda* rights, *Miranda v. Arizona*, 384 U.S. 436 (1966), should not have been admitted at his trial.

RULE OF LAW

During a custodial interrogation, the response to the question "Do you know what the date was of your sixth birthday?" is testimonial and, therefore, excludable from evidence if made prior to the giving of *Miranda* warnings.

FACTS: Muniz (D) was arrested for driving while under the influence of alcohol. Without being advised of his *Miranda* rights, *Miranda v. Arizona*, 384 U.S. 436 (1966), he was taken to a booking center where, as was the routine practice, he was told that his actions and voice would be videotaped. He then answered seven questions regarding his name, address, height, weight, eye color, date of birth, and current age, stumbling over two responses. He was also asked, and was unable to give, the date of his sixth birthday. In addition, he made several incriminating statements while he performed physical sobriety tests and when he was asked to submit to a breathalyzer test. He refused to take the breathalyzer test and was advised, for the first time, of his *Miranda* rights. Both the video and audio portions of the tape were admitted at trial, and he was convicted. The United States Supreme Court held that Muniz's (D) incriminating utterances during the sobriety and breathalyzer tests were not prompted by an interrogation within the meaning of *Miranda* and should not have been suppressed. The Court also ruled that the seven routine booking questions fell outside of *Miranda* protection because they were asked for record-keeping purposes only, and therefore fell within a "routine booking question" exception that exempts from *Miranda's* coverage questions to secure biographical data necessary to complete booking or pretrial services. The Court then addressed the question of whether the sixth birthday question and Muniz's (D) slurred speech were admissible.

ISSUE: During a custodial interrogation, is the response to the question "Do you know what the date was of your sixth birthday?" testimonial and, therefore, excludable from evidence if made prior to the giving of *Miranda* warnings?

HOLDING AND DECISION: (Brennan, J.) Yes. During a custodial interrogation, the response to the question "Do you know what the date was of your sixth birthday?" is testimonial and, therefore, excludable from evidence if made prior to the giving of *Miranda* warnings. The privilege against self-incrimination does not protect a suspect from being compelled to produce "real or physical evidence," but rather protects an accused only from being compelled to testify against himself, or otherwise provide the government with evidence of a testimonial or communicative nature. To be testimonial, an accused's communication must itself, explicitly or implicitly, relate a factual assertion or disclose information. Only then is a person compelled to be a witness against himself. As regards Muniz's (D) slurred speech and lack of muscular control or coordination, those are not testimonial. It has long been held that a suspect's body or other real or physical evidence does not come within the privilege. The privilege is a bar against compelling communications or testimony, but that compulsion which makes a suspect or accused the source of real or physical evidence does not violate the privilege. On the other hand, Muniz's (D) answer to the sixth birthday question was incriminating, not just because of his slurred delivery, but also because of his answer's content; the trier of fact could infer from Muniz's (D) answer (that he did not know the proper date) that his mental state was confused. The question, thus, is whether the incriminating inference of mental confusion is drawn from a testimonial act or from physical evidence. Here, the question is not whether a suspect's impaired mental faculties can fairly be characterized as an aspect of his physiology, but rather whether Muniz's (D) response to the sixth birthday question that gave rise to the inference of such an impairment was testimonial in nature. It is the extortion of information from the accused—the attempt to force the accused to disclose the contents of his own mind—that implicates the privilege against self-incrimination clause. Unless some attempt is made to secure a communication—written, oral, or otherwise—upon which reliance is to be placed as involving the accused's consciousness of the facts and the operations of his mind in expressing it, the demand made upon him is not a testimonial one. Here, the sixth birthday question solicited a testimonial response. When he was asked if he knew the date of his sixth birthday, Muniz (D) was placed in a position the Fifth Amendment was designed to protect against. Given that he could either

Continued on next page.

not remember that date, or calculate it, he was confronted with the choice of incriminating himself by admitting that he did not then know the date of his sixth birthday, or answering untruthfully by reporting a date that he did not then believe to be accurate (an incorrect guess would be incriminating as well as untruthful). Therefore, the incriminating inference of impaired mental faculties stemmed, not just from the fact that Muniz (D) slurred his response, but also from a testimonial aspect of that response. [The disposition of this issue, and the case, is not presented in the casebook extract.]

CONCURRENCE AND DISSENT: (Rehnquist, C.J.) The sixth birthday question here was an effort on the part of the police to check how well Muniz (D) was able to do a simple mathematical exercise. Indeed, had the question related only to the date of his birth, it presumably would have come under the *Miranda* "booking exception." If the police could permissibly require Muniz (D) to use his body to demonstrate the level of his physical coordination, there is no reason why they should not have been able to require him to speak or write to determine his mental coordination and how much his mental processes were affected by his consumption of alcohol.

ANALYSIS

The Court here was attempting, among other things, to draw a line between physical and testimonial evidence in the context of self-incrimination. This was not the first time the Court has grappled with this issue. In *Schmerber v. California,* 384 U.S. 757 (1966), the Court held that a person suspected of driving while intoxicated could be forced to provide a blood sample, because that sample was "real or physical evidence" outside the scope of the privilege and the sample was obtained in a manner by which the person's testimonial capacities were in no way implicated. The Court in that case also acknowledged that the Fifth Amendment, for the same reason, offers no protection against compulsion to submit to fingerprinting, photographing, or measurements, to write or speak for identification, to appear in court, to stand, to assume a stance, to walk, or to make a particular gesture. Similarly, a suspect may be compelled to participate in a lineup and to repeat a phrase provided by the police. As Chief Justice Rehnquist's dissent points out, however, it is not always clear when a response to a question during a custodial interrogation is testimonial, since, as he observes, an answer to a question that merely tests mental function could be considered physical evidence, in the same category as responses to tests designed to determine a suspect's physical coordination. Notwithstanding Chief Justice Rehnquist's plausible objection, the Court has held that answers to psychological questions posed to a defendant to determine competency to stand trial are testimonial (*see, Estelle v. Smith,* 451 U.S. 454 (1981)).

Quicknotes

CUSTODIAL INTERROGATION The questioning of a suspect by police while in custody.

TESTIMONIAL EVIDENCE A person's statement or testimony about something he or she witnessed or experienced; it is offered to prove a matter asserted.

New York v. Quarles

State (P) v. Gun owner (D)

467 U.S. 649 (1984)

NATURE OF CASE: Appeal from order to suppress evidence.

FACT SUMMARY: The trial court granted Quarles's (D) motion to suppress a statement he made to police before being given his *Miranda* warnings, *Miranda v. Arizona*, 384 U.S. 436 (1966).

RULE OF LAW

Police need not give *Miranda* warnings where the need for such warnings is outweighed by the need to protect the public safety.

FACTS: Two New York police officers were approached by a woman who said she had just been raped by a large Black man who was armed and who had just entered a supermarket. The police entered the market and apprehended Quarles (D) after a short chase. Officer Kraft frisked him, while three other officers surrounded him and discovered he was wearing an empty shoulder holster. After handcuffing him, Kraft asked Quarles (D) where the gun was. Quarles (D) told him, and after the gun was retrieved, he was placed under arrest and given his *Miranda* rights, *Miranda v. Arizona*, 384 U.S. 436 (1966). In his trial for criminal possession of a weapon, Quarles (D) successfully moved to suppress the gun and the statement on the basis that at the time the statement was made he had not been given his *Miranda* warning. The State (P) appealed, contending the need to protect public safety outweighed the need to protect Quarles's (D) *Miranda* rights, thereby eliminating the need to read them in this case. The court of appeals affirmed, and the United States Supreme Court granted certiorari.

ISSUE: Must *Miranda* warnings be given where the need for them is outweighed by public safety concerns?

HOLDING AND DECISION: (Rehnquist, J.) No. Police need not give *Miranda* warnings where concern for public safety outweighs the need for the warnings. In this case, the police were placed in a situation where, in order to protect the people in the supermarket, they had to find a gun they had reason to believe was in the vicinity of the suspect. Under these circumstances, concern for public safety outweighed Quarles's (D) immediate invocation of his Fifth Amendment right against compelled self-incrimination. Therefore, the evidence should not have been suppressed. Reversed.

CONCURRENCE AND DISSENT: (O'Connor, J.) *Miranda* is now the law and the Court has not provided sufficient justification for departing from it or for blurring its now clear strictures. Accordingly, the initial statement taken from Quarles (D) should be repressed. A "public safety" exception unnecessarily blurs the edges of the clear line heretofore established and makes *Miranda's* requirements more difficult to understand. In some cases, police will benefit because a reviewing court will find that an exigency excused their failure to administer the required warnings. But in other cases, police will suffer because, though they thought an exigency excused their noncompliance, a reviewing court will view the "objective" circumstances differently and require exclusion of admissions thereby obtained. The result will be a fine-spun new doctrine on public safety exigencies incident to custodial interrogation, complete with the hair-splitting distinctions that currently plague our Fourth Amendment jurisprudence.

DISSENT: (Marshall, J.) Quarles (D) clearly was in custody and was interrogated without being advised of his *Miranda* rights. Therefore, the evidence must be suppressed. The questioning of Quarles (D) was coercive. The police questioned him in the middle of the night in the rear of an empty supermarket. His hands were handcuffed behind his back, and he was surrounded by four armed officers. The irony of today's majority decision is that the safety of the public can be protected without Fifth Amendment abridgement.

ANALYSIS

This case illustrates the Supreme Court's adoption of a public safety exception to the requirement that a suspect in custody be informed of his rights to remain silent and to have counsel present during questioning. Even if the evidence were suppressed under *Miranda v. Arizona*, 384 U.S. 436 (1966), it could be admissible under the inevitable discovery doctrine of *Nix v. Williams*, 467 U.S. 431 (1984).

Quicknotes

CERTIORARI A discretionary writ issued by a superior court to an inferior court in order to review the lower court's decisions; the U.S. Supreme Court's writ ordering such review.

Continued on next page.

CUSTODIAL INTERROGATION The questioning of a suspect by police while in custody.

***MIRANDA* WARNINGS** Specified warnings that must be communicated to a person prior to a custodial interrogation; in the absence of the communication of such warnings, any communications made during the interrogation are inadmissible at trial.

PRIVILEGE AGAINST SELF-INCRIMINATION A privilege guaranteed by the Fifth Amendment to the U.S. Constitution in a criminal proceeding for communications made by an accused and protecting an accused or witness from having to give testimony that may incriminate him- or herself.

STOP AND FRISK A brief, nonintrusive stop requiring the police officer to have a reasonable suspicion that a crime has been committed or is contemplated being committed based on specific and articulable facts and involving a search for a concealed weapon that is conducted by patting down the clothes of the person.

Duckworth v. Eagan

State (P) v. Convicted murderer (D)

492 U.S. 195 (1989)

NATURE OF CASE: Review of reversal of conviction for attempted murder.

FACT SUMMARY: Eagan (D) confessed to attacking a woman after being advised by police that a lawyer would be appointed for him "if and when" he went to court.

RULE OF LAW

Informing a suspect that an attorney would be appointed for him "if and when you go to court" does not render *Miranda* warnings inadequate.

FACTS: Eagan (D), prior to being interrogated for murder, was given a form that contained, inter alia, the warning that he had the right to the presence and advice of a lawyer even if he could not afford one. The waiver form also stated that "We have no way of giving you a lawyer, but one will be appointed for you, if you wish, if and when you go to court." Eagan (D) signed the waiver and gave an exculpatory statement. The next day, he was again questioned and read a different form containing standard *Miranda* warnings. He signed it and gave an incriminating statement. At trial both statements were introduced. Eagan (D) was convicted. The court of appeals reversed, holding that the first form failed to comply with *Miranda*, 384 U.S. 436 (1966), because it linked Eagan's (D) right to counsel with a future event. The State (P) appealed.

ISSUE: Does informing a suspect that an attorney would be appointed for him "if and when you go to court" render *Miranda* warnings inadequate?

HOLDING AND DECISION: (Rehnquist, C.J.) No. Informing a suspect that an attorney would be appointed for him "if and when you go to court" does not render *Miranda* warnings inadequate. *Miranda* merely requires that a suspect be told that "he has a right to the presence of an attorney, and that, if he cannot afford an attorney, one will be appointed for him prior to any questioning if he so desires." This Court has held that no "precise formulation" or "talismanic incantation" is required. Because *Miranda* warnings do not constitute constitutional rights but are measures designed to protect the right against compulsory self-incrimination, the inquiry is simply whether the warnings reasonably convey to a suspect his rights as required by *Miranda*. The "if and when you go to court" language did not link the right to appointed counsel to a future point in time after the interrogation, but accurately described the procedure for appointment of counsel in Indiana and anticipated the commonly asked question of when the suspect would obtain counsel. The initial warnings given to Eagan (D) in their totality therefore satisfied the *Miranda* requirements, and Eagan's (D) exculpatory explanation as well as the knife and clothing were properly admitted at trial. Reversed.

DISSENT: (Marshall, J.) *Miranda* emphasized that the offer to provide appointed counsel prior to questioning must be "clear and unequivocal." Eagan (D) was never told that questioning would actually be delayed until a lawyer was appointed, "if and when" he went to court. As a result, Eagan (D) could easily have concluded from the "if and when" caveat that only those who can afford an attorney have the right to have one present before answering any questions. Even a suspect with legal acumen would be inclined to interpret the "if and when" language to mean that no lawyer would be provided until trial, and that if he is never taken to court, his right to an attorney never attaches at all. The threat of an indefinite deferral of interrogation constitutes an effective means by which the police can pressure a suspect to speak without the presence of counsel and therefore violates *Miranda*.

ANALYSIS

Arguments concerning the substance of *Miranda* warnings are uncommon, with most of the litigation arising from the warning that anything a suspect says "can and will" be used against the suspect in court. Formulations warning that what a suspect says "might," "can," or "could" be used against the suspect have been held inadequate by the Fifth, Seventh, and Ninth Circuits. A formulation warning that the suspect's utterances could be used "for or against" the suspect has also been rejected as misleading. *Commonwealth v. Singleton*, 439 Pa. 185, 266 A.2d 753 (1970).

Quicknotes

INTER ALIA Among other things.

***MIRANDA* WARNINGS** Specified warnings that must be communicated to a person prior to a custodial interrogation; in the absence of the communication of such warnings, any communications made during the interrogation are inadmissible at trial.

RIGHT TO COUNSEL Right conferred by the Sixth Amendment that the accused shall be provided effective legal assistance in a criminal proceeding.

Moran v. Burbine

Court (P) v. Murder convict (D)

475 U.S. 412 (1986)

NATURE OF CASE: Appeal from reversal of denial of habeas corpus in state criminal proceeding.

FACT SUMMARY: While being interrogated by police, an attorney wishing to represent Burbine (D) called the police, a fact not conveyed to Burbine (D) by the police.

RULE OF LAW

A voluntary confession obtained by police who fail to inform a defendant that an attorney attempted to contact him is not an invalid intrusion upon the defendant's *Miranda* rights.

FACTS: Burbine (D) was arrested on suspicion of breaking and entering, and murder. Burbine (D) did not request an attorney. His sister obtained one to represent him, and the attorney called the police station, informing the police that she wished to represent him. The police informed the attorney that Burbine (D) was not to be further questioned that night. Nonetheless, Burbine (D) was later interrogated, after having expressly waived his *Miranda* rights, *Miranda v. Arizona*, 384 U.S. 436 (1966), following a proper warning. Burbine (D) confessed to the murder. The confession was admitted at trial, and Burbine (D) was convicted. After exhausting state appeals, Burbine (D) petitioned for federal habeas corpus. The district court declined to grant habeas corpus, but the court of appeals reversed.

ISSUE: Is a voluntary confession obtained by police who fail to inform a defendant that an attorney attempted to contact him an invalid intrusion upon the defendant's *Miranda* rights?

HOLDING AND DECISION: (O'Connor, J.) No. A voluntary confession obtained by police who fail to inform a defendant that an attorney attempted to contact him is not an invalid intrusion upon the defendant's *Miranda* rights. A *Miranda* waiver is valid if it is voluntary and intelligently made. A failure to be informed of an attorney's attempts at contact in no way diminishes one's ability to knowingly waive a right, which Burbine (D) did. Had Burbine (D) requested an attorney, matters would be different, but Burbine (D) never did so. Police are not under a duty to provide a defendant with a steady stream of information not requested. The benefits of burdening the police with such a duty would be minimal and would come at the cost of making it much harder to obtain confessions, something in which society has a strong interest. Since no constitutional right was violated, the conduct of the police, while not exemplary, did not call for reversal of the conviction. Reversed.

DISSENT: (Stevens, J.) As the attorney was, in effect, an agent of Burbine (D), the deception practiced upon her was in fact a deception upon Burbine (D), which necessarily invalidated the "intelligent" and "knowing" aspect of the waiver of his rights.

ANALYSIS

Besides the Fifth Amendment issue, the Court also discussed Sixth and Fourteenth Amendment concerns. The Sixth Amendment argument was dismissed because Burbine (D) had not yet been formally charged. With regard to the Fourteenth Amendment, the Court concluded that the police conduct was not fundamentally unfair, a conclusion with which the dissent took issue.

Quicknotes

FIFTH AMENDMENT Provides that no person shall be compelled to serve as a witness against him- or herself, be subject to trial for the same offense twice, or be deprived of life, liberty, or property without due process of law.

FOURTEENTH AMENDMENT Declares that no state shall make or enforce any law that shall abridge the privileges and immunities of citizens of the United States; no state shall deny to any person within its jurisdiction the equal protection of the laws.

HABEAS CORPUS A proceeding in which a defendant brings a writ to compel a judicial determination of whether he or she is lawfully being held in custody.

***MIRANDA* RULE** A required warning given before any questioning by law enforcement authorities may take place. Individuals receive warnings regarding their privilege against self-incrimination, right to remain silent, and right to be represented by an attorney.

SIXTH AMENDMENT Provides the right to a speedy and public trial by impartial jury, the right to be informed of the accusation, the right to confront witnesses, and the right to have the assistance of counsel in all criminal prosecutions.

Berghuis v. Thompkins

State (D) v. Convicted criminal (P)

560 U.S. 370 (2010)

NATURE OF CASE: Appeal from reversal of denial of habeas corpus request.

FACT SUMMARY: After Thompkins (P) was advised of his *Miranda* rights, *Miranda v. Arizona*, 384 U.S. 436 (1966), Thompkins (P) did not expressly say he wanted to remain silent, did not want to talk with the police, or wanted an attorney. Eventually, toward the end of a three-hour interrogation during which Thompkins (P) was largely silent, he answered "yes" when asked if he prayed to God to forgive him for the shooting of victim who had died. Thompkins (P) was found guilty of murder and sentenced to life without parole. In his habeas corpus petition, Thompkins (P) argued that he had invoked his Fifth Amendment right to remain silent, that he had not waived that right, and that his inculpatory statements were involuntary.

RULE OF LAW

(1) A criminal suspect's silence during an interrogation does not invoke his right to remain silent.
(2) A criminal suspect waives his right to remain silent when he knowingly and voluntarily makes a statement to the police.
(3) The police are not required to obtain a waiver of a criminal suspect's *Miranda* rights before interrogating him.

FACTS: After advising respondent Thompkins (P) of his rights, in full compliance with *Miranda v. Arizona*, 384 U.S. 436 (1966), detective Helgert and another officer interrogated him about a shooting in which one victim died. At no point did Thompkins (P) say that he wanted to remain silent, that he did not want to speak with the police, or that he wanted an attorney. He refused, however, to sign a written acknowledgment that he had been advised of or understood his *Miranda* rights. He was largely silent during the three-hour interrogation, but near the end, he answered "yes" when asked if he prayed to God to forgive him for the shooting. He moved to suppress his statements, claiming that he had invoked his Fifth Amendment right to remain silent, that he had not waived that right, and that his inculpatory statements were involuntary. The trial court denied the motion, the state's intermediate court affirmed, and the state's highest court denied review. The jury found Thompkins (P) guilty, and he was sentenced to life in prison without parole. The district court denied his subsequent habeas request, reasoning that Thompkins (P) did not invoke his right to remain silent and was not coerced into making statements during the interrogation, and that it was not unreasonable for the state's intermediate appellate court to determine that he had waived his right to remain silent. The court of appeals reversed, holding that the state court was unreasonable in finding an implied waiver of Thompkins's (P) right to remain silent. The United States Supreme Court granted certiorari.

ISSUE:

(1) Does a criminal suspect's silence during an interrogation invoke his right to remain silent?
(2) Does a criminal suspect waive his right to remain silent when he knowingly and voluntarily makes a statement to the police?
(3) Are the police required to obtain a waiver of a criminal suspect's *Miranda* rights before interrogating him?

HOLDING AND DECISION: (Kennedy, J.)

(1) No. A criminal suspect's silence during an interrogation does not invoke his right to remain silent. Thompkins's (P) silence during the interrogation did not invoke his right to remain silent. A suspect's *Miranda* right to counsel must be invoked "unambiguously." If the accused makes an "ambiguous or equivocal" statement or no statement, the police are not required to end the interrogation, or ask questions to clarify the accused's intent. There is no principled reason to adopt different standards for determining when an accused has invoked the *Miranda* right to remain silent and the *Miranda* right to counsel. Both standards protect the privilege against compulsory self-incrimination by requiring an interrogation to cease when either right is invoked. The unambiguous invocation requirement results in an objective inquiry that "avoid[s] difficulties of proof and . . . provide[s] guidance to officers" on how to proceed in the face of ambiguity. Had Thompkins (P) said that he wanted to remain silent or that he did not want to talk, he would have invoked his right to end the questioning. He did neither, and therefore did not invoke his right to remain silent.
(2) Yes. A criminal suspect waives his right to remain silent when he knowingly and voluntarily makes a statement to the police. Thompkins (P) waived his right to remain silent when he knowingly and voluntarily made a statement to police. A waiver must be "the product of a free and deliberate choice rather than intimidation, coercion, or deception"

Continued on next page.

and "made with a full awareness of both the nature of the right being abandoned and the consequences of the decision to abandon it." Such a waiver may be "implied" through a "defendant's silence, coupled with an understanding of his rights and a course of conduct indicating waiver." If the State (D) establishes that a *Miranda* warning was given and that it was understood by the accused, an accused's uncoerced statement establishes an implied waiver. The record here shows that Thompkins (P) waived his right to remain silent. First, the lack of any contention that he did not understand his rights indicates that he knew what he gave up when he spoke. Second, his answer to the question about God is a "course of conduct indicating waiver" of that right. Had he wanted to remain silent, he could have said nothing in response or unambiguously invoked his *Miranda* rights, ending the interrogation. That he made a statement nearly three hours after receiving a *Miranda* warning does not overcome the fact that he engaged in a course of conduct indicating waiver. Third, there is no evidence that his statement was coerced. He does not claim that police threatened or injured him or that he was fearful. The interrogation took place in a standard-sized room in the middle of the day, and there is no authority for the proposition that a three-hour interrogation is inherently coercive. The fact that the question referred to religious beliefs also does not render his statement involuntary.

(3) No. The police are not required to obtain a waiver of a criminal suspect's *Miranda* rights before interrogating him. Thompkins (P) argues that, even if his answer to Helgert could constitute a waiver of his right to remain silent, the police were not allowed to question him until they first obtained a waiver. However, a rule requiring a waiver at the outset would be inconsistent with precedent holding that courts can infer a waiver "from the actions and words of the person interrogated." Any waiver, express or implied, may be contradicted by an invocation at any time, terminating further interrogation. When the suspect knows that *Miranda* rights can be invoked at any time, he or she can reassess his or her immediate and long-term interests as the interrogation progresses. After giving a *Miranda* warning, police may interrogate a suspect who has neither invoked nor waived *Miranda* rights. Thus, the police were not required to obtain a waiver of Thompkins's (P) *Miranda* rights before interrogating him. Reversed.

DISSENT: (Sotomayor, J.) Under the majority's decisions, criminal suspects must now unambiguously invoke their right to remain silent—which, counterintuitively, requires them to speak. At the same time, suspects will be legally presumed to have waived their rights even if they have given no clear expression of their intent to do so. Those results are not supported by *Miranda* or subsequent precedent and are inconsistent with the fair-trial principles on which those precedents are grounded. The question whether a suspect has validly waived his right is "entirely distinct" as a matter of law from whether he invoked that right. The questions are related, however, in terms of the practical effect on the exercise of a suspect's rights. A suspect may at any time revoke his prior waiver of rights, or guard against the possibility of a future finding that he implicitly waived his rights, by invoking the rights and thereby requiring the police to cease questioning. Thus, analytically, the first question should be whether Thompkins (P) waived his right to remain silent. Precedent places a heavy burden on the prosecution to show waiver, and the presumption is that the suspect did not waive his rights. Waiver may not be presumed merely because a confession was eventually obtained. Here, the circumstances of the interrogation show that Thompkins (P) never waived his right to remain silent. He never expressly waived that right, and his refusal to sign even an acknowledgment that he understood his *Miranda* rights evinces, if anything, intent not to waive those rights. So does his silence during the interrogation for nearly three hours. Essentially, his course of conduct did not manifest waiver. Thus, it is objectively unreasonable to conclude the prosecution met its "heavy burden" of proof on a record "consisting of three one-word answers, following two hours and 45 minutes of silence punctuated by a few largely nonverbal responses to unidentified questions." By so concluding, however, the majority turns long-standing *Miranda* precedent on its head and significantly dilutes its protections and lowers the prosecution's hitherto high burden of proof. Because *Miranda* and its precedents perceive custodial interrogation to be inherently coercive, requiring proof of a course of conduct beyond the inculpatory statements themselves is critical to ensuring that those statements are voluntary admissions and not the dubious product of an overborne will. Because Thompkins (P) should prevail on his waiver argument, the issue of whether he invoked his right to remain silent should not have been reached, as it was by the majority. Nonetheless, even as to Thompkins's (P) argument that in any event his conduct invoked his right to remain silent, the majority is wrong in holding that a suspect must expressly invoke that right by speaking. Such a novel clear-statement rule for invocation invites police to question a suspect at length—notwithstanding his persistent refusal to answer questions—in the hope of eventually obtaining a single inculpatory response which will suffice to prove waiver of rights. Contrary to the majority's reasoning, there has been a precedential distinction between protections involving the right to counsel and the right to remain silent. The appropriate rule is that when a suspect's conduct is sufficiently unambiguous as

Continued on next page.

to invocation, the police must scrupulously honor that conduct. While this does not provide a bright-line rule, as does the majority's clear-statement rule, the police nonetheless have been following the prior fact-specific rule for over three decades and no evidence has been presented that the status quo has proved unworkable. The clear-statement rule is also a poor fit for the right to silence, since advising a suspect that he has a "right to remain silent" is unlikely to convey that he must speak (and must do so in some particular fashion) to ensure the right will be protected. By contrast, telling a suspect "he has the right to the presence of an attorney, and that if he cannot afford an attorney one will be appointed for him prior to any questioning if he so desires," implies the need for speech to exercise that right. Moreover, if a suspect's conduct or statements are ambiguous, it is not an undue burden to have the police ask questions clarifying the suspect's intent, such as "Do you want to talk to us?" Such an approach is a more faithful application of precedents than the majority's clear-statement approach.

ANALYSIS

Prior to this decision, courts had to grapple with doctrinal questions of what it took to make a legally valid invocation of, or waiver of, *Miranda* rights. If a suspect's conduct fell between these extremes, there was also the issue of what was acceptable police conduct. The *Thompkins* decision has seemingly done away with those issues. Now, where the police have given the suspect the proper *Miranda* warnings and the suspect understands those warnings and has not been coerced, until the moment when the suspect clearly invokes one of his *Miranda* rights, the police may continue to seek a waiver of those rights, and, even absent a clear waiver, as soon as the suspect says anything to the police he will be held to have impliedly waived his rights.

Quicknotes

FIFTH AMENDMENT Provides that no person shall be compelled to serve as a witness against him- or herself, be subject to trial for the same offense twice, or be deprived of life, liberty, or property without due process of law.

HABEAS CORPUS A proceeding in which a defendant brings a writ to compel a judicial determination of whether he or she is lawfully being held in custody.

INCULPATORY EVIDENCE A statement or other evidence that tends to show a person's guilt in committing a criminal act.

***MIRANDA* RULE** A required warning given before any questioning by law enforcement authorities may take place. Individuals in custody receive warnings regarding their privilege against self-incrimination, right to remain silent, and right to be represented by an attorney.

***MIRANDA* WARNINGS** Specified warnings that must be communicated to a person prior to a custodial interrogation; in the absence of the communication of such warnings, any communications made during the interrogation are inadmissible at trial.

Davis v. United States

Convicted murderer (D) v. Federal government (P)

512 U.S. 452 (1994)

NATURE OF CASE: Appeal from a conviction for unpremeditated murder.

FACT SUMMARY: After waiving his *Miranda* rights and talking to investigators, a suspect ambiguously requested the assistance of counsel and then made additional incriminating statements.

RULE OF LAW

After a suspect has waived his *Miranda* rights and talked to law-enforcement officers, the officers may keep questioning him unless and until he unambiguously asserts his right to counsel.

FACTS: Several pieces of evidence led investigators to suspect one sailor, Davis (D), in the homicidal death of another sailor. The agents eventually interviewed Davis (D) at their office after reading him his *Miranda* rights, 384 U.S. 436 (1966), and securing his waiver of the rights specified in the *Miranda* warnings. About ninety minutes later, Davis (D) said, "Maybe I should talk to a lawyer." The agents stopped their questioning and tried to clarify whether Davis (D) was asking for the assistance of counsel. Davis (D) unequivocally stated, "No, I don't want a lawyer." The agents again reminded him of his rights to remain silent and to counsel, and the questioning resumed. After another hour, Davis (D) said, "I think I want a lawyer before I say anything else." The questioning stopped at that time. At his court-martial, Davis (D) moved to suppress the statements he had made to the investigators. The Military Judge denied the motion, reasoning that Davis (D) did not unequivocally assert his right to counsel before he made the statements he tried to suppress. Davis (D) was convicted on one specification of unpremeditated murder, and the Court of Military Review affirmed the conviction on appeal. Davis (D) sought further review in the United States Supreme Court.

ISSUE: After a suspect has waived his *Miranda* rights and talked to law-enforcement officers, may the officers keep questioning him unless and until he unambiguously asserts his right to counsel?

HOLDING AND DECISION: (O'Connor, J.) Yes. After a suspect has waived his *Miranda* rights and talked to law-enforcement officers, the officers may keep questioning him unless and until he unambiguously asserts his right to counsel. Under *Edwards v. Arizona*, 451 U.S. 477 (1981), a suspect who is lawfully being questioned but who later asserts his right to counsel may not be questioned further unless he is permitted the assistance of counsel or he himself reinitiates questioning. This subsequent assertion of the right to counsel must be unambiguous; if it is ambiguous, as it was here, then the questioning need not cease, and any incriminating statements may be introduced in evidence at trial against the suspect. Some disadvantage could conceivably keep some suspects from clearly asserting their right to counsel. The best safeguard against that outcome, though, is *Miranda* itself and its goal of ensuring only knowing and intelligent waivers of the rights to remain silent and to counsel. Prudence suggests that law-enforcement officers should try to clarify a suspect's intentions in the face of an ambiguous invocation of the right to counsel. That practice, however, is not constitutionally required. Affirmed.

CONCURRENCE: (Souter, J.) The majority correctly concludes that the Constitution permits law-enforcement officers to ask follow-up questions to ascertain a suspect's intent when he ambiguously asserts his right to counsel. But the majority incorrectly holds further that investigators need not stop their investigative questioning to ascertain whether a suspect intended to assert his right to counsel. This Court's precedents, a majority of courts that have decided the question and even many law-enforcement agencies all argue persuasively for requiring such a follow-up inquiry.

ANALYSIS

As the Court's 9–0 vote on the result in *Davis* strongly suggests, it is perfectly reasonable to require normally rational, intelligent adults to assert their right to counsel with sufficient clarity for law-enforcement officers to know when their substantive questioning must cease. On the other hand, Justice Souter's concurrence in *Davis* also introduces a question that has long simmered in U.S. constitutional law—whether the Constitution should be read to impose affirmative duties on governments and their actors, as *Miranda* itself did by requiring law-enforcement officers to advise suspects of their rights to remain silent and to counsel. Justice Souter would require law-enforcement officers to ask follow-up questions in the face of ambiguous assertions of the right to counsel; the *Davis* majority, following the general rule in U.S. constitutional law, would not impose that additional burden on law-enforcement officers.

Continued on next page.

Quicknotes

***MIRANDA* WARNINGS** Specified warnings that must be communicated to a person prior to a custodial interrogation; in the absence of the communication of such warnings, any communications made during the interrogation are inadmissible at trial.

RIGHT TO COUNSEL Right conferred by the Sixth Amendment that the accused shall be provided effective legal assistance in a criminal proceeding.

WAIVER The intentional or voluntary forfeiture of a recognized right.

Maryland v. Shatzer

State (P) v. Convicted child abuser (D)

559 U.S. 98 (2010)

NATURE OF CASE: Appeal from state high court decision in favor of the state.

FACT SUMMARY: Police suspected that Shatzer (D), an inmate at a state correctional facility, had sexually abused his own son. Police questioned him but ended the inquiry when Shatzer (D) invoked his right to an attorney. Two and a half years later, police questioned him again and Shatzer (D), after waiving his right to an attorney, made incriminating statements.

RULE OF LAW

When a criminal suspect who had previously invoked his right to an attorney is then released from custody for a period of 14 days, his subsequent waiver of his right to an attorney at a follow-up interrogation shall be deemed valid.

FACTS: Police suspected that Shatzer (D), an inmate at a state correctional facility, had sexually abused his own son. Police questioned him but ended the inquiry when Shatzer (D) invoked his right to an attorney. Two and a half years later, police questioned him again and Shatzer (D), after waiving his right to an attorney, made incriminating statements. Police questioned him again a few days later. Shatzer (D) again waived his right to counsel, agreed to take a polygraph test, and then failed the test. After conviction at the state trial court level for various charges relating to sexual abuse, the Maryland Supreme Court eventually overturned Schatzer's (D) conviction. It did so on the grounds that no break in custody occurred between the original questioning and the follow-up questioning. Accordingly, once Shatzer (D) had invoked his right to an attorney, the police were not allowed to continue asking him on multiple occasions whether he would decline to invoke that right. The State (P) appealed.

ISSUE: When a criminal suspect who had previously invoked his right to an attorney is then released from custody for a period of 14 days, shall his subsequent waiver of his right to an attorney at a follow-up interrogation be deemed valid?

HOLDING AND DECISION: (Scalia, J.) Yes. When a criminal suspect who had previously invoked his right to an attorney is then released from custody for a period of fourteen days, his subsequent waiver of his right to an attorney at a follow-up interrogation shall be deemed valid. Under prior case law, police have been prevented from constantly questioning a criminal suspect whether he had decided to forego his right to an attorney. However, when a suspect has been released from custody for a long enough period of time, there is little reason to believe his change of heart regarding his right to counsel is due to police coercion. The suspect has been given time to consult with his attorney or his friends and family. Accordingly, the suspect's decision to waive his right to an attorney is likely due to his understanding that cooperation would be more beneficial. The Court also now holds that the appropriate length of time between such custodial interrogations is 14 days. This two-week period will allow the defendant time to get reacclimated to life, consult with an attorney or family members, and make further deliberations as how to proceed. Reversed.

CONCURRENCE: (Thomas, J.) The majority is correct that in this case, Shatzer's (D) release back into prison for two and a half years between interrogations certainly constituted a break in custody. However, the Court's arbitrary decision to apply a 14-day rule finds no basis in this Court's prior Fifth Amendment jurisprudence.

CONCURRENCE: (Stevens, J.) The majority correctly found that a break in custody occurred in this case, allowing Shatzer (D) to validly waive his right to an attorney at the subsequent interrogation. The problem with the new 14-day rule is that when the police fail to provide indigent defendants with counsel after an initial request, those defendants may ultimately believe the police lied to them and that they really have no right to an attorney.

ANALYSIS

A constant refrain in search and seizure law or the law regarding custodial inquiries is the goal of providing clear guidelines to law enforcement. This goal was clearly the main reason behind the judicially created 14-day period between interrogations. Opponents of the rule favor individual, case-by-case review of such incidents.

Quicknotes

CUSTODIAL INTERROGATION The questioning of a suspect by police while in custody.

Salinas v. Texas

Suspect (D) v. State (P)

570 U.S. 178 (2013)

NATURE OF CASE: Certiorari review to resolve lower court's division on prosecution's use of privilege assertion.

FACT SUMMARY: Salinas (D) voluntarily arrived at the police station for questioning in a homicide. He was aware he was a suspect. He was not in custody and was not given the *Miranda* warnings, *Miranda v. Arizona*, 384 U.S. 436 (1966). Prosecutors later used his silence in response to a particular question as indication of his guilt.

RULE OF LAW

A witness must expressly claim the Fifth Amendment privilege against self-incrimination during noncustodial police questioning.

FACTS: The police requested Salinas (D) come to the station for questioning as a suspect in a homicide. Salinas (D) voluntarily went to the station and was free to leave at any time. He was not given any *Miranda* warnings, *Miranda v. Arizona*, 384 U.S. 436 (1966). Salinas (D) answered questions until the police asked if his shotgun would match the shells recovered at the scene. Salinas (D) looked down and did not answer the question. The prosecutor later used Salinas's (D) silence as evidence of his guilt. The United States Supreme Court granted certiorari review to resolve split in the lower courts on the issue of prosecution's use of defendant's assertion of privilege during noncustodial police questioning as part of its case-in-chief. Salinas (D) did not invoke privilege during his questioning, so the Court does not reach that issue.

ISSUE: Must a witness expressly claim the Fifth Amendment privilege against self-incrimination during noncustodial police questioning?

HOLDING AND DECISION: (Alito, J.) Yes. A witness must expressly claim the Fifth Amendment privilege against self-incrimination during noncustodial police questioning. The privilege is an exception to the government's right to everyone's testimony. Express invocation is not required at a criminal defendant's own trial when the defendant refuses to take the stand or if government coercion makes the forfeiture of the privilege involuntary. Neither exception applies here. Salinas (D) seeks a new exception for silent witnesses facing official suspicions. In *Berghuis v. Thompkins*, 560 U.S. 370 (2010), this Court held the defendant failed to invoke the privilege when, post-*Miranda* warnings, he remained silent for two hours and 45 minutes. Salinas (D) only was momentarily silent. Silence is insufficient to put police on notice of the witness's reliance on Fifth Amendment privilege. Salinas (D) argues it would be unfair to require an unschooled witness to understand the legal technicalities of invoking the Fifth Amendment privilege. The Fifth Amendment, however, does not permit an unqualified right to remain silent and the courts are permitted to evaluate the reasons for the silence. Establishing Salinas's (D) proposed rule would require officers to ascertain when silence became expressive conduct and that is unworkable.

CONCURRENCE: (Thomas, J.) The prosecutor's comments regarding Salinas's (D) silence did not compel Salinas (D) to give self-incriminating testimony, so his claim would fail even if he had invoked the privilege. This Court decided in *Griffin v. California*, 380 U.S. 609 (1965), the prosecutor could not comment on a defendant's refusal to testify. That decision lacked foundation and should not be extended here to apply to comments on silence.

DISSENT: (Breyer, J.) The Fifth Amendment prohibits the prosecutor from commenting on the witness's silence during police questioning. To allow comment on silence directly or indirectly puts the witness in an impossible predicament. If the witness remains silent, that might be used as evidence of consciousness of guilt. If the witness answers, he might provide incriminatory information. *Berghuis* is beside the point. In that case, the Court held he waived his privilege as to the later statements, not as to his silence. The circumstances surrounding Salinas's (D) silence indicated Salinas (D) was invoking the privilege. The plurality struggles because the "explicit statement" rule is a serious obstacle to those unaware of such linguistic detail. The right question is whether the circumstances and the individual's silence indicate an exercise of the Fifth Amendment privilege. Here, the answer is yes.

ANALYSIS

Salinas was a closely watched case because it may have added to the instructions law enforcement are required to provide to suspects facing questioning. It instead confirmed a suspect's silence may be used as evidence of consciousness of guilt at trial unless the suspect expressly invoked the privilege. The burden remains on the suspect to know what words to say to fully protect himself against self-incrimination.

Continued on next page.

Quicknotes

CASE-IN-CHIEF The portion of a proceeding where the party with the burden of proof presents evidence to support his or her case.

FIFTH AMENDMENT Provides that no person shall be compelled to serve as a witness against him- or herself, be subject to trial for the same offense twice, or be deprived of life, liberty, or property without due process of law.

***MIRANDA* WARNINGS** Specified warnings that must be communicated to a person prior to a custodial interrogation; in the absence of the communication of such warnings, any communications made during the interrogation are inadmissible at trial.

Dickerson v. United States

Bank robber (D) v. Federal government (P)

530 U.S. 428 (2000)

NATURE OF CASE: Appeal from denial of motion to suppress statement based on *Miranda* violation.

FACT SUMMARY: Dickerson (D) sought to suppress a statement he made while in an FBI field office prior to being given his *Miranda* warnings, *Miranda v. Arizona*, 384 U.S. 436 (1966).

RULE OF LAW

When a decision of the court involves interpretation and application of the Constitution, Congress may not legislatively supersede such decision.

FACTS: Dickerson (D) was indicted for bank robbery and conspiracy to commit bank robbery. Before trial he moved to suppress a statement he made at an FBI field office, on the grounds he had not received *Miranda* warnings, *Miranda v. Arizona*, 384 U.S. 436 (1966), before being interrogated. The district court granted the motion, and the Government (P) took an interlocutory appeal to the court of appeals, which reversed, stating that § 3501 was satisfied since the statement was made voluntarily. Dickerson (D) appealed.

ISSUE: Where a decision of the court involves interpretation and application of the Constitution may Congress legislatively supersede such decision?

HOLDING AND DECISION: (Rehnquist, C.J.) No. Where a decision of the court involves interpretation and application of the Constitution, Congress may not legislatively supersede such decision. *Miranda* and its progeny govern the admissibility of statements made during custodial interrogation in both state and federal courts. Section 3501 provides that the admissibility of a custodial suspect's statements should depend on whether they are voluntarily made. Prior to *Miranda*, the admissibility of a suspect's confession was evaluated under a voluntariness test. The requirement of voluntariness was based on the Fifth Amendment right against self-incrimination and the Due Process Clause of the Fourteenth Amendment. The Court's decisions in *Miranda* and *Malloy* changed the focus of the due process inquiry. In *Malloy v. Hogan*, 378 U.S. 1 (1964), the Court held that the Fifth Amendment's self-incrimination clause is incorporated into the Due Process Clause of the Fourteenth Amendment and this applies to the states. In *Miranda*, the Court recognized that the coercion inherent in custodial interrogation makes it difficult to determine whether a statement is voluntary or involuntary and heightens the risk of self-incrimination. Section 3501 was enacted two years after the decision in *Miranda* and was intended by Congress to overrule the Court's decision in that case. The issue is whether Congress has the constitutional authority to do so. While Congress retains the ultimate authority to modify or set aside any judicially created rules of evidence and procedure that are not required by the Constitution, it may not legislatively supersede the Court's decisions that interpret and apply the Constitution. *Miranda* is a constitutional decision. The Court specifically stated that it was intended "to explore some facets of the problems . . . of applying the privilege against self-incrimination to in-custody interrogation and to give concrete constitutional guidelines for law enforcement agencies and courts to follow." The decision is otherwise replete with references to constitutional rules and standards. *Miranda* announced a constitutional rule that Congress may not supersede legislatively. Reversed.

DISSENT: (Scalia, J.) *Marbury v. Madison*, 1 Cranch 137 (1803), held that an Act of Congress will not be enforced if what it prescribes violates the Constitution. The majority opinion fails to state, however, that what § 3501 prescribes, the use of a voluntary confession at trial, violates the Constitution.

ANALYSIS

The Court also relies on the principle of stare decisis as weighing heavily against overruling *Miranda*, since *Miranda* warnings have become "embedded in routine police practice to the point where the warnings have become part of our national culture." Justice Scalia rejects such rationale on the basis that the court rules are both "mutable and modifiable" and that they "must make sense."

Quicknotes

CUSTODIAL INTERROGATION The questioning of a suspect by police while in custody.

INTERLOCUTORY APPEAL The appeal of an issue that does not resolve the disposition of the case but is essential to a determination of the parties' legal rights.

STARE DECISIS Doctrine whereby courts follow legal precedent unless there is good cause for departure.

Chavez v. Martinez

Police officer (D) v. Initiator of § 1983 suit (P)

538 U.S. 760 (2003)

NATURE OF CASE: Appeal from refusal of federal court of appeals to grant qualified immunity to police officer in a § 1983 suit against him.

FACT SUMMARY: Martinez (P) brought a § 1983 suit against Chavez (D), a patrol officer, for interrogating him in the hospital during emergency medical treatment for life-threatening gunshot wounds, arguing that such conduct violated his Fifth Amendment protection against self-incrimination.

RULE OF LAW
The Fifth Amendment protection against self-incrimination applies only in criminal cases.

FACTS: During a police altercation, an officer shot Martinez (P) five times, causing life-endangering injuries. Chavez (D), a patrol officer, arrived on the scene and accompanied Martinez (P) to the hospital where he continuously interrogated Martinez (P) during medical treatment, despite Martinez's (P) statements to the officer, "I don't know," "I am choking," "I am dying, please," and "I don't want to die." Although Martinez (P) was never charged with a crime and his answers were never used against him in any criminal prosecution, he brought a § 1983 suit, arguing, inter alia, that Chavez (D) had violated his Fifth Amendment privilege against self-incrimination. The federal court of appeals held that Chavez (D) was not entitled to a defense of qualified immunity because he violated Martinez's (P) clearly established constitutional rights. Chavez (D) appealed.

ISSUE: Does the Fifth Amendment protection against self-incrimination apply only in criminal cases?

HOLDING AND DECISION: (Thomas, J.) Yes. The Fifth Amendment protection against self-incrimination applies only in criminal cases. The Fifth Amendment requires that no person shall be compelled "in any criminal case" to be a witness against himself. This Court fails to see how Martinez (P) can allege a violation of this right since he was never prosecuted for a crime, let alone compelled to be a witness in a criminal case. A "criminal case" at the very least requires the initiation of criminal proceedings. Although conduct by law enforcement officials prior to trial may ultimately impair that right, a constitutional violation occurs only at trial. Here, Martinez (P) was never made to be a "witness" against himself because his statements were never admitted as testimony against him in a criminal case. Nor was he ever placed under oath and exposed to the cruel trilemma of self-accusation, perjury, or contempt. Rules designed to safeguard a constitutional right do not extend the scope of the constitutional right itself, just as violations of judicially crafted prophylactic rules do not violate the constitutional rights of any person. Even assuming, arguendo, that the persistent questioning of Martinez (P) somehow deprived him of a liberty interest, this Court cannot agree with Martinez's (P) characterization of Chavez's (D) behavior as "egregious" or "conscience shocking" since medical personnel were able to treat Martinez (P) throughout the interrogation and Chavez (D) did not interfere with the medical treatment. Reversed.

CONCURRENCE: (Souter, J.) Martinez (P) has not here been able to make the "powerful showing," subject to a realistic assessment of costs and risks, necessary to expand protection of the privilege against compelled self-incrimination to the point of the civil liability he asks this Court to recognize.

CONCURRENCE: (Scalia, J.) Without violation of the actual right protected by the text of the Self-Incrimination Clause, the § 1983 action is doomed.

CONCURRENCE AND DISSENT: (Stevens, J.) The interrogation was the functional equivalent of an attempt to obtain an involuntary confession from a prisoner by torturous methods. As a matter of law, that type of brutal police conduct constitutes an immediate deprivation of the prisoner's constitutionally protected interest in liberty.

CONCURRENCE AND DISSENT: (Kennedy, J.) A constitutional right arises the moment torture or its close equivalents are brought to bear. Constitutional protection for a tortured suspect is not held in abeyance until some later criminal proceeding takes place.

CONCURRENCE AND DISSENT: (Ginsburg, J.) The Self-Incrimination Clause applies at the time and place police use severe compulsion to extract a statement from a suspect.

ANALYSIS

As the *Chavez* decision makes clear, the text of the Self-Incrimination Clause cannot support a view that the mere use of compulsive questioning, without more, violates the Constitution.

Continued on next page.

Quicknotes

INTER ALIA Among other things.

LIBERTY INTEREST A right conferred by the Due Process Clauses of the state and federal constitutions.

QUALIFIED IMMUNITY An affirmative defense relieving officials from civil liability for the performance of activities within their discretion so long as such conduct is not in violation of an individual's rights pursuant to law as determined by a reasonable person standard.

REASONABLE PERSON STANDARD The standard of care exercised by one who possesses the intelligence, education, knowledge, attention, and judgment required by society of its members when governing behavior; the standard applies to a person's judgment when determining breach of a duty under the theory of negligence.

Brewer v. Williams (Williams I)

Court (P) v. Mental patient (D)

430 U.S. 387 (1977)

NATURE OF CASE: Appeal of a conviction of murder.

FACT SUMMARY: Williams (D) was convicted of murder based on a confession obtained during a custodial trip.

RULE OF LAW

Police questioning of a suspect without the presence of known counsel during a critical stage of the proceedings is violative of the Sixth and Fourteenth Amendments?

FACTS: Williams (D), an escaped mental patient, killed a 10-year-old girl. Williams (D) subsequently contacted a lawyer in Des Moines and informed him that he was in Davenport and was willing to surrender to the police in Des Moines who were searching for him. The attorney informed the police, and they sent a car to Waterloo to return him to Des Moines under a warrant issued for his arrest. The attorney informed both the police and his client that under no circumstances was Williams (D) to say anything. Williams (D), in the meantime, had been arrested in Davenport and hired counsel there to represent him at the arraignment on the murder charge. His attorney requested permission to accompany Williams (D) on the trip to Des Moines but was refused permission. The attorney warned both Williams (D) and the police that there was to be no conversation during the trip concerning the crime as Williams (D) was represented by counsel who had informed Williams (D) to remain silent. During the first part of the trip, Williams (D) repeatedly refused to speak unless counsel was present. One of the detectives then began to play on Williams's (D) religious beliefs, pleading with him to reveal the dead girl's whereabouts so that she could obtain a Christian burial. Williams (D) finally revealed the whereabouts of the body after confessing to the crime. Williams (D) appealed the admissibility of his confession after conviction. Williams (D) alleged, among other things, that the tactics used to obtain the confession violated his right to counsel.

ISSUE: Is police questioning of a suspect without the presence of known counsel during a critical stage of the proceedings violative of the Sixth and Fourteenth Amendments?

HOLDING AND DECISION: (Stewart, J.) Yes. Police questioning of a suspect without the presence of known counsel during a critical stage of the proceedings is violative of the Sixth and Fourteenth Amendments. The Sixth and Fourteenth Amendments grant an accused the right to the presence of counsel during all critical stages of proceedings. First, this was a critical stage. Williams (D) had a warrant issued for his arrest and had already been arraigned in Davenport on the charge. The police officers knew that he was represented by counsel; that he had been informed not to speak; that Williams (D) told them he would not speak without counsel present. Williams (D) had pleaded not guilty to the charge. There are no grounds present herein that establish that Williams (D) knowingly, intelligently, and voluntarily waived his rights. The state bears the heavy burden of establishing that once rights have been invoked by the defendant/accused, that they have been waived. No clear and convincing evidence of such a waiver is present herein. While the crime is abhorrent, we must reverse the conviction and remand for a new trial. The judgment of the court of appeals is affirmed.

DISSENT: (Burger, C.J.) After at least five warnings from two attorneys, Williams (D) voluntarily led the police to where the body was buried. There was no coercion or threats. Williams (D) was prompted solely on the simple statement by the detective. In my mind, this would constitute a voluntary waiver of known rights. The exclusionary rule should not be arbitrarily applied to nonegregious police conduct.

DISSENT: (White, J.) The voluntary confession of Williams (D), made without threats or coercions of a known right, is conclusive evidence of a waiver.

DISSENT: (Blackmun, J.) This was not an example of purposeful police conduct. The trip was necessary to transport Williams (D) to Des Moines. Merely making a Christian plea on behalf of the family seems to me not unreasonable and is simply not the type of coercion for which a reversal should be granted.

ANALYSIS

While both the Fifth Amendment and the Sixth Amendment seek to protect a criminal defendant from illegal interrogation, the significant difference between the Sixth Amendment right to counsel and the Fifth Amendment right against self-incrimination is that the Sixth Amendment right attaches after the initiation of formal proceedings. The right to counsel applies to any adversarial proceeding, as well as to noncustodial settings such as eliciting information from a suspect who is

Continued on next page.

free on bail. This right may be waived only if the waiver is knowing, voluntary, and intelligent. The state has the burden of establishing waiver.

Quicknotes

CUSTODIAL INTERROGATION The questioning of a suspect by police while in custody.

Patterson v. Illinois

Subject of a post-indictment interrogation (D) v. State (P)

487 U.S. 285 (1988)

NATURE OF CASE: Appeal from Illinois Supreme Court in favor of the State (P).

FACT SUMMARY: After being indicted for murder, Patterson (D) voluntarily waived his right to counsel and made statements implicating himself in the murder.

RULE OF LAW

Interrogation of a criminal defendant after indictment does not violate the Sixth Amendment right to counsel as long as the defendant knowingly and voluntarily waives his right to counsel at that stage.

FACTS: Patterson (D) and two others allegedly beat a rival gang member who later died as a result of his injuries. After a jury indicted Patterson (D), Patterson (D) inquired aloud to a police officer as to why another person was not indicted because "he did everything." The police officer then handed a *Miranda* waiver form to Patterson (D), read the form aloud to him, and had Patterson (D) initial the form. The form made Patterson (D) aware of his right to counsel and the consequences of any statement he might make to the police. Patterson (D) then gave a detailed statement to the police officer regarding his involvement with the murder. Later in the same day, Patterson (D) read, signed, and reviewed another *Miranda* form with an Assistant District Attorney assigned to the case. After this, Patterson (D) gave additional damaging statements to the prosecutor. At trial, Patterson (D) moved to suppress. The trial court and the Illinois Supreme Court found the statements were admissible and that Patterson (D) had voluntarily waived his right to counsel. Patterson (D) appealed.

ISSUE: Does interrogation of a criminal defendant after indictment violate the Sixth Amendment right to counsel where the defendant knowingly and voluntarily waives his right to counsel at that stage?

HOLDING AND DECISION: (White, J.) No. Interrogation of a criminal defendant after indictment does not violate the Sixth Amendment right to counsel as long as the defendant knowingly and voluntarily waives his right to counsel at that stage. First, Patterson's (D) argument that the police were barred from interrogating him after his indictment is incorrect. Our prior cases have held that once a defendant requests counsel, police cannot interrogate him unless the defendant initiates further communication. That is precisely what occurred here. Second, Patterson's (D) waiver of his Sixth Amendment right to counsel was valid. For a waiver to be valid, the waiver must be knowing and intelligent. On these facts, Patterson's (D) waiver satisfied those requirements. Twice the State (P) informed Patterson (D) of his right to counsel. Moreover, the forms also informed him that his statements could be used against him. Patterson (D) has also not identified any additional information that the police should have provided to him. Lastly, we hold that the *Miranda* warnings that suffice at the arrest stage also suffice for the interrogations at the post-indictment phase. The value of counsel at this questioning phase is minimal as opposed to the right to counsel at the trial stage. Therefore, the defendant may validly waive his Sixth Amendment right to counsel at the post-indictment phase. Affirmed.

DISSENT: (Stevens, J.) This Court should make a bright-line rule that once a jury indicts a defendant, the prosecutor who will try the case against the defendant should not be able to question the defendant without the presence of counsel. In civil litigation, once a complaint is filed, it is unethical to contact an opposing party without the presence of the party's attorney. The same rule should apply, with even more force, on the criminal side. The defendant's adversary, the prosecutor, cannot adequately provide the defendant with the advice that he can remain silent if he chooses. After jury empanelment at the trial stage, this Court would no doubt disallow contact between the prosecutor and the defendant. The same should hold true for contacts after the criminal complaint is filed.

ANALYSIS

Note that Justice Blackmun's dissent appears to agree with the majority's view that post-indictment interrogations are not completely barred. However, in effort to limit the majority's holding, Justice Blackmun emphasized that he would only allow post-indictment interrogations when the accused initiates the further contact. Several state courts have disagreed with this decision on state constitutional grounds.

Quicknotes

BRIGHT-LINE RULE A legal rule of decision to help resolve ambiguous issues simply and in a straightforward manner, sometimes sacrificing equity for certainty.

Continued on next page.

INDICTMENT A formal written accusation made by a prosecutor and issued by a grand jury, charging an individual with a criminal offense.

SIXTH AMENDMENT Provides the right to a speedy and public trial by impartial jury, the right to be informed of the accusation, the right to confront witnesses, and the right to have the assistance of counsel in all criminal prosecutions.

WAIVER The intentional or voluntary forfeiture of a recognized right.

Montejo v. Louisiana

Convicted murderer (D) v. State (P)

556 U.S. 778 (2009)

NATURE OF CASE: Appeal from a state high court decision upholding murder conviction.

FACT SUMMARY: At his arraignment on murder charges, the court appointed Montejo (D) counsel, although he did not specifically request it. Later that day, after police informed him of his *Miranda* rights, *Miranda v. Arizona*, 384 U.S. 436 (1966), without the presence of his counsel, Montejo (D) wrote a letter of apology to the murder victim's wife. Prosecutors successfully used the letter against Montejo (D) at trial.

RULE OF LAW

When a court automatically appoints counsel for an indigent defendant or when the defendant has requested counsel, there is no longer a presumption that any subsequent waiver of the defendant's right to counsel will be involuntary.

FACTS: At his arraignment for murder charges, the court appointed counsel for Montejo (D). He did not specifically request counsel at the hearing, but instead remained silent. Later that day and without the presence of his counsel, two police detectives asked if Montejo (D) would help them locate the murder weapon. The officers read Montejo (D) his *Miranda* rights, *Miranda v. Arizona*, 384 U.S. 436 (1966), and Montejo (D) agreed to join the officers. On the trip, Montejo (D) wrote an apology letter to the victim's wife. At trial, prosecutors successfully used the letter against Montejo (D), who was convicted. The court then sentenced Montejo (D) to death. The Louisiana Supreme Court upheld the conviction on the grounds that Montejo (D), informed of his *Miranda* rights, validly waived his right to an attorney before drafting the letter. Montejo (D) appealed to the United States Supreme Court.

ISSUE: When a court automatically appoints counsel for an indigent defendant or when the defendant has requested counsel, is there any longer a presumption that any subsequent waiver of the defendant's right to counsel will be involuntary?

HOLDING AND DECISION: (Scalia, J.) No. When a court automatically appoints counsel for an indigent defendant or when the defendant has requested counsel, there is no longer a presumption that any subsequent waiver of defendant's right to counsel will be involuntary. A prior decision from this court, *Michigan v. Jackson*, 475 U.S. 625 (1986), held that police could not initiate interrogation of a criminal defendant once he has requested an attorney. The Court now overrules that decision as unworkable. Many states, such as Louisiana, automatically appoint counsel for indigent defendants without even giving them the opportunity to request counsel. Therefore, the *Jackson* rule does not even apply in those states. Rather than confuse the issue, it is better to do away with the decision and rely upon other decisions that already provide criminal defendants with protection from coerced interrogations. Under prior case law, any suspect subject to a custodial interrogation must be advised of his right to have a lawyer present and may request one. Also, once a suspect invokes his right to an attorney, the interrogation must cease. No subsequent interrogation may commence until an attorney is present. While these decisions rely upon the Fifth Amendment right to counsel as opposed to the Sixth Amendment right, the justifications supporting them apply equally once a suspect is charged with a crime. A waiver of these rights is valid both for Fifth and Sixth Amendment purposes. The case is remanded to the state courts for a determination of whether Montejo (D) requested counsel when the officers approached him to accompany them on their search for the murder weapon. Reversed and remanded.

DISSENT: (Stevens, J.) The majority misinterprets *Michigan v. Jackson*, 475 U.S. 625 (1986), and grossly undervalues stare decisis. Thus, the police interrogation in this case clearly violated Montejo's (D) Sixth Amendment right to counsel, which attaches during the initiation of adversary judicial criminal proceedings, including post-arraignment interviews with law enforcement officers. If a defendant is entitled to protection from police-initiated interrogation under the Sixth Amendment when he merely requests a lawyer, he is even more obviously entitled to such protection when he has secured a lawyer. Indeed, the Court has already recognized as much. Once an attorney-client relationship has been established through the appointment or retention of counsel, as a matter of federal law the method by which the relationship was created is irrelevant: The existence of a valid attorney-client relationship provides a defendant with the full constitutional protection afforded by the Sixth Amendment. The majority's decision to overrule *Jackson* rests on its assumption that *Jackson's* protective rule was intended to "prevent police from badgering defendants into changing their minds about their rights," just as the rule adopted in *Edwards v. Arizona*, 451 U.S. 477 (1981), was designed to prevent police from coercing unindicted suspects into revoking their requests for counsel

Continued on next page.

at interrogation. Operating on that limited understanding of the purpose behind *Jackson's* protective rule, the majority concludes that *Jackson* provides no safeguard not already secured by this Court's Fifth Amendment jurisprudence. However, the *Jackson* rule was not founded upon Fifth Amendment considerations, and the majority's analysis flagrantly misrepresents *Jackson's* underlying rationale. *Jackson* did not mention any anti-badgering considerations, and it rested upon the Sixth Amendment right to counsel that is granted to all indicted defendants. Although the rules adopted in *Edwards* and *Jackson* are similar, *Jackson* did not rely on the reasoning of *Edwards* but remained firmly rooted in the unique protections afforded to the attorney-client relationship by the Sixth Amendment. Thus, once *Jackson* is placed in its proper Sixth Amendment context, the majority's justifications for overruling the decision crumble. The majority pays lip service to the principles of stare decisis, and the reasons it invokes to overrule *Jackson* are founded on its blatant misreading of *Jackson* and its rationale. The majority also looks only to the Louisiana Supreme Court's decision to determine that that court's interpretation of the *Jackson* rule is unworkable, instead of properly asking whether the *Jackson* rule as applied for the past quarter century has proved easily administrable. In fact, amici who are lawyers and judges with extensive experience in law enforcement and prosecution argue persuasively that *Jackson's* bright-line rule has provided law enforcement officers with clear guidance, allowed prosecutors to quickly and easily assess whether confessions will be admissible in court, and assisted judges in determining whether a defendant's Sixth Amendment rights have been violated by police interrogation. Regarding the reliance interests involved, the majority, again as a result of its misreading of *Jackson,* fails to identify the correct reliance interest; contrary to the majority's interpretation, the reliance interest is not that of law enforcement, but rather of the public in knowing that counsel, once secured, may be reasonably relied upon as a medium between the accused and the power of the state. That interest lies at the heart of the Sixth Amendment's guarantee and is surely worthy of greater consideration than it is given by the majority. Even if *Jackson* had never been decided, it would be clear that Montejo's (D) Sixth Amendment rights were violated under pre-*Jackson* precedents. Under the undisputed facts of this case, there is no sound basis for concluding that Montejo (D) made a knowing and valid waiver of his Sixth Amendment right to counsel before acquiescing in police interrogation following his 72-hour hearing. Because police questioned Montejo (D) without notice to, and outside the presence of, his lawyer, the interrogation violated Montejo's (D) right to counsel. The majority avoids confronting the serious Sixth Amendment concerns raised by the police interrogation in this case by assuming that Montejo (D) validly waived his Sixth Amendment rights before submitting to interrogation. It does so by summarily concluding that "doctrines ensuring voluntariness of the Fifth Amendment waiver simultaneously ensure the voluntariness of the Sixth Amendment waiver;" thus, because Montejo (D) was given *Miranda* warnings prior to interrogation, his waiver was presumptively valid. Ironically, while the majority faults *Jackson* for blurring the line between this Court's Fifth and Sixth Amendment jurisprudence, the majority commits the same error by assuming that the *Miranda* warnings given in this case, designed purely to safeguard the Fifth Amendment right against self-incrimination, were somehow adequate to protect Montejo's (D) more robust Sixth Amendment right to counsel. Instead, the Court has recognized that because the Sixth Amendment's protection of the attorney–client relationship extends beyond *Miranda's* protection of the Fifth Amendment right to counsel, there will be cases where a waiver that would be valid under *Miranda* will not suffice for Sixth Amendment purposes—this is just such a case. Because *Miranda* warnings do not hint at the ways in which a lawyer might assist her client during conversations with the police, the warnings prescribed in *Miranda,* while sufficient to apprise a defendant of his Fifth Amendment right to remain silent, are inadequate to inform an unrepresented, indicted defendant of his Sixth Amendment right to have a lawyer present at all critical stages of a criminal prosecution. The inadequacy of those warnings is even more obvious in the case of a represented defendant. The commencement of a criminal proceeding changing a suspect into a criminal defendant is a significant moment. Defendants must be fully aware of the ramifications of a waiver of the right to counsel at that stage. Because the administration of *Miranda* warnings was insufficient to ensure Montejo (D) understood the Sixth Amendment right he was being asked to surrender, the record provides no basis for concluding that he validly waived his right to counsel, even in the absence of *Jackson's* enhanced protections. Accordingly, the police interrogation violated Montejo's (D) constitutional right to counsel.

ANALYSIS

The Fifth Amendment right to counsel applies to suspects in custody prior to indictment. The Sixth Amendment right arises once judicial proceedings have begun against a defendant. This decision essentially does away with the bright-line rule of *Michigan v. Jackson,* 475 U.S. 625 (1986), which held that any waiver by a charged defendant of the right to counsel after defendant requests it must be involuntary and thus invalid.

Continued on next page.

Quicknotes

FIFTH AMENDMENT Provides that no person shall be compelled to serve as a witness against him- or herself, be subject to trial for the same offense twice, or be deprived of life, liberty, or property without due process of law.

SIXTH AMENDMENT Provides the right to a speedy and public trial by impartial jury, the right to be informed of the accusation, the right to confront witnesses, and the right to have the assistance of counsel in all criminal prosecutions.

Texas v. Cobb

State (P) v. Convicted murderer (D)

532 U.S. 162 (2001)

NATURE OF CASE: Murder case.

FACT SUMMARY: Cobb (D) argued that his conviction for capital murder should be reversed on the basis that his confession should have been suppressed since it was elicited in violation of his Sixth Amendment right to counsel.

RULE OF LAW

The Sixth Amendment right to counsel does not extend to crimes that are "factually related" to those that have actually been charged.

FACTS: Cobb (D) gave a written statement confessing to the burglary of his neighbor's house and was indicted. He later confessed to the killing of his neighbor's wife and daughter, which he had previously denied. He was convicted of capital murder for the murder of more than one person in the course of a criminal transaction and sentenced to death. He appealed, contending that his confession should be suppressed because it was obtained in violation of his Sixth Amendment right to counsel. The court of criminal appeals reversed and remanded, concluding that the right to counsel had attached on the capital murder charge when Cobb (D) was charged with the burglary because the two crimes were "factually interwoven," even though he had not yet been charged with murder.

ISSUE: Does the Sixth Amendment right to counsel extend to crimes that are "factually related" to those that have actually been charged?

HOLDING AND DECISION: (Rehnquist, C.J.) No. The Sixth Amendment right to counsel does not extend to crimes that are "factually related" to those that have actually been charged. The Sixth Amendment right of counsel is offense-specific and cannot be invoked once for all future prosecutions since it does not attach until a prosecution has commenced. This Court has held that a defendant's statements regarding offenses for which he had not been charged were admissible notwithstanding the attachment of his Sixth Amendment right to counsel on other charged offenses. Some courts, however, had craved an exception for crimes that are "factually related" to a charged offense. We decline to support this view. However, we do hold that the Sixth Amendment right to counsel, when it attaches, does encompass offenses that even if not formally charged would be considered the same offense under the *Blockburger* test, *Blockburger v. United States*, 284 U.S. 299 (1932). The test to be applied to determine whether there is more than one offense is whether each provision requires proof of a fact that the other does not. As defined by Texas law, capital murder and burglary are not the same offense under *Blockburger*. Thus, the police were not barred from interrogating Cobb (D) regarding the murders and his confession was admissible. Reversed.

CONCURRENCE: (Kennedy, J.) Note that the court reached its conclusion without approving of the decision in *Michigan v. Jackson*, 475 U.S. 625 (1986). This is wise since I believe the reasoning in that case was questionable. It is difficult to see the utility of a rule that invalidates a confession obtained after a voluntary waiver of the suspect's *Miranda* rights, *Miranda v. Arizona*, 384 U.S. 436 (1966).

DISSENT: (Breyer, J.) This case focuses on the meaning of the word "offense." The Court's definition undermines Sixth Amendment protections while doing nothing to further effective law enforcement. The majority's rule permits law enforcement to question those charged with a crime without first approaching counsel, by asking questions about any other related crime not charged in the indictment.

ANALYSIS

The *Blockburger* test adopted here has also been applied to determine the scope of the Fifth Amendment's double jeopardy clause, prohibiting multiple or successive prosecutions for the same "offense." The Court extends such test to the Sixth Amendment's "offense" reasoning that there is no constitutional difference between the meanings of the term in either context.

Quicknotes

BURGLARY Unlawful entry of a building at night with the intent to commit a felony therein.

FIFTH AMENDMENT Provides that no person shall be compelled to serve as a witness against him- or herself, be subject to trial for the same offense twice, or be deprived of life, liberty, or property without due process of law.

Continued on next page.

***MIRANDA* RULE** A required warning given before any questioning by law enforcement authorities may take place. Individuals receive warnings regarding their privilege against self-incrimination, right to remain silent, and right to be represented by an attorney.

MURDER The unlawful killing of a person, either with deliberation and premeditation or by conduct demonstrating a reckless disregard for human life.

SIXTH AMENDMENT Provides the right to a speedy and public trial by impartial jury, the right to be informed of the accusation, the right to confront witnesses, and the right to have the assistance of counsel in all criminal prosecutions.

Miller v. Fenton

Convicted murderer (P) v. State official (D)

796 F.2d 598 (3d Cir. 1986)

NATURE OF CASE: On remand of federal habeas corpus proceeding, consideration of voluntariness of confession.

FACT SUMMARY: Miller (P), who had confessed to murder, contended in his habeas corpus petition that the interviewing officer's misrepresentations, promises, and other psychological manipulations rendered the confession involuntary.

RULE OF LAW

Where the totality of circumstances, including a suspect's susceptibility to interrogation pressures and the interviewing officer's demeanor and statements, indicate that the suspect's will was not overborne during a custodial interview, the suspect's confession is "voluntary" and, therefore, admissible in a criminal prosecution of the suspect.

FACTS: Miller (P), a 32-year old with some high school education, was the prime suspect in a murder. Miller (P), who had previously been in prison for past crimes, waived his *Miranda* rights, *Miranda v. Arizona*, 384 U.S. 436 (1966), when he was taken into custody, and interviewed by officer Boyce. The interview was videotaped. Boyce made no threats and engaged in no physical coercion of Miller (P), and, throughout the interview, Boyce assumed a friendly, understanding manner and spoke in a soft tone of voice. Boyce lied to Miller (P) about the timing of the victim's death, and about other evidence that the police had. He repeatedly assured Miller (P) that he was sympathetic to him and wanted to help him unburden his mind. At different points in the interview, Boyce told Miller (P) that he believed Miller (P) had committed the crime, but also that Miller (P) was not a criminal who should be punished, but a sick individual who should receive help. Boyce assured Miller (P) that he was sincerely understanding and that he wished to help Miller (P) with his problem. Boyce also appealed to Miller's (P) conscience and described the importance of Miller's (P) purging himself of the memories that must be haunting him. After around an hour, Miller (P) confessed and immediately thereafter collapsed in a state of shock, with a blank look on his face. Prior to trial, Miller (P) moved to suppress the confession, but the state trial court denied the motion. The state's intermediate appellate court reversed, finding that Boyce's psychological pressure was coercive. The state's highest court reversed and reinstated the conviction, finding that the confession had been voluntary. On federal habeas corpus, the federal district court likewise determined that the confession was voluntary, and the court of appeals affirmed, deferring to the state's highest court's finding. The United States Supreme Court reversed and remanded, holding that on federal habeas a confession's voluntariness is a matter for independent federal appellate determination. On remand, the court of appeals reconsidered Miller's (P) confession in light of these standards.

ISSUE: Where the totality of circumstances, including a suspect's susceptibility to interrogation pressures and the interviewing officer's demeanor and statements, indicate that the suspect's will was not overborne during a custodial interview, is the suspect's confession "voluntary" and, therefore, admissible in a criminal prosecution of the suspect?

HOLDING AND DECISION: (Becker, J.) Yes. Where the totality of circumstances, including a suspect's susceptibility to interrogation pressures and the interviewing officer's demeanor and statements, indicate that the suspect's will was not overborne during a custodial interview, the suspect's confession is "voluntary" and, therefore, admissible in a criminal prosecution of the suspect. Here, Boyce did not physically coerce Miller (P), and instead assumed a sympathetic posture, holding himself out as Miller's (P) friend. Although Boyce provided Miller (P) with some untrue information concerning the victim's death, Boyce also told Miller (P) that he wanted to help him. The only issue is whether Boyce's method of interrogation constituted psychological manipulation of such magnitude that it rendered Miller's (P) confession involuntary. Psychological ploys may play a part in the suspect's decision to confess, but so long as that decision is a product of the suspect's own balancing of competing considerations, the confession is voluntary. Miller (P) was not overly susceptible to such ploys, given that he was a mature adult who had served time in prison and knew the consequences of confessing, and who had been given *Miranda* warnings. The interrogation itself was not overly long. Although Boyce's supportive, encouraging manner was an interrogation tactic aimed at winning Miller's (P) trust and making him feel comfortable about confessing, and thus was deceptive, such an approach is recognized as a permissible interrogation tactic. Additionally, although a lie told to a detainee about an important aspect of the case may affect the voluntariness of the confession, the effect of the lie must be analyzed in the context of all the circumstances of the interrogation. Here, Boyce's lie to Miller (P) about the victim's death did not seem to have

Continued on next page.

an impact on Miller (P), who remained impassive upon hearing it. Boyce's statements that Miller (P) was not a criminal, but rather a mentally ill individual not responsible for his actions, and Boyce's promises to help Miller (P) raise a more serious question about the voluntariness of the confession. By telling Miller (P) that he was not responsible for anything he might have done, Boyce may have been understood to be making an implied promise to Miller (P) that Miller (P) would not be prosecuted, or that if he were prosecuted Boyce would aid him in presenting the insanity defense. Similarly, the promises of psychiatric help might have suggested to Miller (P) that he would be treated, rather than prosecuted. If these promises, implicit and explicit, tricked Miller (P) into confessing, his confession may have been involuntary. To determine whether Boyce's promises affected the voluntariness of Miller's (P) confession, it must be determined how manipulative these tactics in fact were, and whether they overbore his will. At no time did Boyce assert that Miller (P) would not be prosecuted, or that he could successfully avail himself of an insanity defense. Also, Boyce's statements could be understood not as promises of leniency, but merely as a means of convincing Miller (P) that Boyce understood him and was sympathetic to him. Boyce never stated that anyone but he thought Miller (P) was "not a criminal," nor did he state that he had any authority to affect the charges brought against Miller (P). Moreover, Miller (P) made comments throughout the interview that showed that he understood that he was the subject of a routine police interrogation rather than an encounter with a compassionate friend. He also indicated that he was aware that a confession could result in a conviction, and, throughout the interview, he maintained a guarded and suspicious attitude. Based on the totality of these circumstances, it seems that Miller (P) confessed of his own free will, and that he made an uncoerced decision to unburden his inner tensions and to acknowledge his guilt. Boyce's manner and his statements may have stirred this urge in Miller (P), but they did not produce psychological pressure strong enough to overbear the will of a mature, experienced man who was suffering from no mental or physical illness and was interrogated for less than an hour at a police station close to his home. The confession was voluntary.

DISSENT: (Gibbons, J.) A review of the interview shows that Boyce was not truly sympathetic to Miller (P) but was just focused on obtaining a confession. Such review also shows that the first 30 minutes of the interview were full of Boyce's lies and promises, directed to Boyce's sole objective of getting that confession. There is nothing in the record from which it can be inferred that Miller's (P) abandonment of his self-interested denials of involvement in the homicide was the product of any other influence. The majority opinion describes Boyce's conduct as if he were a confessor, offering solace under the seal of the confessional, or a psychiatrist offering relief from anxiety under the shelter of a physician-patient privilege, rather than what he was—a wily interrogator determined to break down Miller's (P) resistance by lies and false promises. The majority's treatment of the police tactics leading to Miller's (P) collapse is about as fair as those tactics. Confession may be good for the soul, but it was Miller's (P) freedom, not his soul, that was at stake, and it was his freedom, not his soul, that interested Boyce. The majority also fails to account for Miller's (P) collapse into a catatonic state and his transportation to a hospital as relevant circumstances in its totality-of-the-circumstances analysis. This most telling of all indications as to the effect on Miller (P) of Boyce's tactics is simply ignored by the majority; based on this event, it is inconceivable that the majority can honestly represent that Miller (P) was not suffering from mental or physical illness. And, unless the majority identifies some other reason for Miller's (P) abrupt abandonment of his self-interested denials of guilt than the psychological coercion exercised by Boyce, what other cause is left? The effect on Miller (P) of Boyce's relentless psychological pressure was cumulative. Although the majority is correct in its general approach, its method of ascertaining the effects of Boyce's interrogation tactics on Miller (P) by attempting to place itself in Miller's (P) position, and thereby evaluate the impact of Boyce's promises and lies, is flawed. It cannot be known what effects those promises and lies had on Miller's (P) will. Instead, what we can know is that when, as in this case, the record reveals a series of repeated promises of psychological help and assurances that the suspect will not be punished, the confession, as a matter of law, must be held to be coerced. Any other rule leads to the kind of subjective speculation that the majority engages in. Instead, looking at the totality of the circumstances, Miller's (P) confession must be declared inadmissible as a violation of Miller's (P) Fifth Amendment right to remain silent.

ANALYSIS

According to the majority in this case, many criminals experience an urge during interrogation to own up to their crimes. Here, according to the majority, Boyce's tactics may have stirred up that urge in Miller (P) but did not overbear his free will in confessing, given his age, experience, and attitude during the interview. On the other hand, the court acknowledged that Boyce's method of interrogation might have overborne the will of another detainee, for example, a young, inexperienced person of lower intelligence than Miller (P), or a person suffering from a painful physical ailment. It might have overcome the will of Miller (P) himself if the interrogation had been longer or if Miller (P) had been refused

Continued on next page.

food, sleep, or contact with a person he wished to see. Moreover, if Miller (P) had made remarks that indicated that he truly believed that the state would treat him leniently because he was "not responsible" for what he had done or that he believed that he would receive psychiatric help rather than punishment, his confession might not have been "voluntary." According to the dissent, however, the majority opinion carefully selected among the totality of the circumstances to which it chose to refer, took statements out of context, ignored the sole purpose of the interrogating officer, and attached no significance to strong evidence that Miller's (P) will was overborne. The case thus illustrates how differently different judges may interpret the same set of facts when conducting a totality of circumstances analysis.

Quicknotes

TOTALITY OF THE CIRCUMSTANCES TEST Standard that focuses on all the circumstances of a particular case, instead of individual factors.

VOLUNTARY CONFESSION A voluntary statement made by a person charged with the commission of a criminal offense, acknowledging his guilt in respect to the charged offense.

Colorado v. Connelly

State (P) v. Murder suspect (D)

479 U.S. 157 (1986)

NATURE OF CASE: [The nature of case is not stated in casebook excerpt.]

FACT SUMMARY: Connelly (D) argued that the murder confession he made while severely mentally ill to a uniformed police officer should be set aside as involuntary under the Due Process Clause.

RULE OF LAW

Coercive police activity is a necessary predicate to the finding that a confession is not "voluntary" within the meaning of the Due Process Clause of the Fourteenth Amendment.

FACTS: Connelly approached a uniformed police officer and simply announced without prompting he had killed someone. The officer gave him *Miranda* warnings, *Miranda v. Arizona*, 384 U.S. 436 (1966); Connelly (D) said he understood his rights and wanted to talk. A detective arrived, gave another set of *Miranda* warnings and asked Connelly (D) "what he had on his mind" whereupon Connelly (D) admitted to killing a woman and took the officers to the location of the killing. The officers did not perceive that Connelly (D) was suffering from mental illness. Subsequently when Connelly (D) moved to suppress his statements, expert testimony revealed he was suffering from chronic schizophrenia and was in a psychotic state at least as of the day before he confessed, and that God's voice told him to either confess or commit suicide. The trial court suppressed Connelly's statements as "involuntary", and the Colorado Supreme Court upheld the decision.

ISSUE: Is coercive police activity a necessary predicate to the finding that a confession is not "voluntary" within the meaning of the Due Process Clause of the Fourteenth Amendment?

HOLDING AND DECISION: (Rehnquist, C.J.) Yes. Coercive police activity is a necessary predicate to the finding that a confession is not "voluntary" within the meaning of the Due Process Clause of the Fourteenth Amendment. Due process cases have properly focused upon the crucial element of police overreaching. Absent police conduct causally related to the confession, there is simply no basis for concluding that any state actor has deprived a criminal defendant of due process of law. As interrogators have turned to more subtle forms of psychological persuasion, courts have found the mental condition of the defendant to be a more significant factor in the "voluntariness" calculus. Nevertheless, this fact does not justify a conclusion that a defendant's mental condition, by itself and apart from its relation to official coercion, should ever dispose of the inquiry into constitutional "voluntariness." Thus, while as here, Connelly's (D) mental condition was surely relevant to his susceptibility to police coercion, this does not conclude the inquiry. A statement rendered by one in the condition of Connelly (D) might be proved to be quite unreliable, but this is a matter to be governed by the evidentiary laws of the forum and not by the Due Process Clause of the Fourteenth Amendment. Reversed.

DISSENT: (Brennan, J.) The Court's failure to recognize all forms of involuntariness or coercion as antithetical to due process reflects a refusal to acknowledge free will as a value of constitutional consequence. Due process derives much of its meaning from a conception of fundamental fairness that emphasizes the right to make vital choices voluntarily. This right requires vigilant protection if we are to safeguard the values of private conscience and human dignity.

ANALYSIS

Through judicial interpretation, due process has been held to require a pre-trial judicial hearing on the due process issue on the theory that a jury cannot be expected to make a fair and reliable finding on this question during the trial of the guilt issue. In this regard, it is the prosecutor who bears the burden of proof by a preponderance of the evidence that the defendant's confession does not violate due process.

Quicknotes

BURDEN OF PROOF The duty of a party to introduce evidence to support a fact that is in dispute in an action.

DUE PROCESS CLAUSE Language in the Fifth and Fourteenth Amendments to the U.S. Constitution providing that no person shall be deprived of "life, liberty, or property, without due process of law."

FOURTEENTH AMENDMENT Declares that no state shall make or enforce any law that shall abridge the privileges and immunities of citizens of the United States; no state shall deny to any person within its jurisdiction the equal protection of the laws.

***MIRANDA* WARNINGS** Specified warnings that must be communicated to a person prior to a custodial interrogation; in the absence of the communication of such warnings, any communications made during the interrogation is inadmissible at trial.

United States v. Patane

Federal government (P) v. Possessor of illegal firearm (D)

542 U.S. 630 (2004)

NATURE OF CASE: Appeal from suppression of physical evidence in a criminal case.

FACT SUMMARY: When a police officer seized Samuel Patane's (D) pistol from his bedroom during an arrest, after being given Patane's (D) permission to do so, Patane (D) was subsequently indicted for possession of an illegal firearm. Pantane (D) argued that since he was not given full *Miranda* warnings, *Miranda v. Arizona*, 384 U.S. 436 (1966), the pistol should be suppressed as a "physical fruit" of the poisonous tree.

RULE OF LAW

The Self-Incrimination Clause is not violated by the admission into evidence of the physical fruit of a voluntary statement.

FACTS: Upon arresting Samuel Patane (D) at his residence for violating a restraining order, a police officer attempted to advise Patane (D) of his *Miranda* rights, *Miranda v. Arizona*, 384 U.S. 436 (1966), but got no further than the right to remain silent. At that point, Patane (D) interrupted, asserting that he knew his rights, whereupon the warnings were not completed. The police officer asked Patane (D) about an illegal Glock pistol he believed Patane (D) possessed. Pantane (D) told the police officer the pistol was in his bedroom and gave permission to seize it. Pantane (D) was indicted for possession of the pistol. The court of appeals affirmed the district court's suppression of the pistol, and the Government (P) appealed.

ISSUE: Is the Self-Incrimination Clause violated by the admission into evidence of the physical fruit of a voluntary statement?

HOLDING AND DECISION: (Thomas, J.) No. The Self-Incrimination Clause is not violated by the admission into evidence of the physical fruit of a voluntary statement. The police do not necessarily violate *Miranda* rights by negligent or even deliberate failures to provide a suspect with the full panoply of *Miranda* warnings. Potential violations occur, if at all, only upon the admission of unwarned statements into evidence at trial. At that point, the exclusion of unwarned statements is a complete and sufficient remedy for any perceived *Miranda* violation. Thus, unlike unreasonable searches under the Fourth Amendment or actual violations of the Due Process Clause or the Self-Incrimination Clause, there is, with respect to mere failures to warn, nothing to deter. There is therefore no reason to apply the "fruit of the poisonous tree" doctrine. It is not for this Court to impose its proffered police practices on either federal law enforcement officials or their state counterparts. Characterization of *Miranda* as a constitutional rule does not lessen the need to maintain the closest possible fit between the Self-Incrimination Clause and any judge-made rule designed to protect it. Here, there is no such fit because the introduction of the nontestimonial fruit of a voluntary statement (the pistol) does not implicate the Self-Incrimination Clause. The admission of such fruit presents no risk that a defendant's coerced statements will be used against him or her at a criminal trial. There is simply no need to extend (and therefore no justification for extending) the prophylactic rule of *Miranda* to this context. Reversed.

CONCURRENCE: (Kennedy, J.) In light of the important probative value of reliable physical evidence, it is doubtful that exclusion can be justified by a deterrence rationale sensitive to both law enforcement interests and a suspect's rights during an in-custody interrogation.

DISSENT: (Souter, J.) In closing their eyes to the consequences of giving an evidentiary advantage to those who ignore *Miranda*, the majority adds an important inducement for interrogators to ignore the rule in that case. While there is a price for excluding evidence, the Fifth Amendment is worth a price.

DISSENT: (Breyer, J.) The "fruit of the poisonous tree" doctrine should be extended to cases such as this.

ANALYSIS

As *Patane* makes clear, the *Miranda* rule is not a code of police conduct, and police do not necessarily violate the Constitution (or even the *Miranda* rule, for that matter) by mere failures to warn. Because various prophylactic rules (including the *Miranda* rule) necessarily sweep beyond the actual protections of the Self-Incrimination Clause, the Supreme Court has consistently taken the position that any further extension of these rules must be justified by its necessity for the protection of the actual right against compelled self-incrimination. It is for this reason, for example, that statements taken without *Miranda* warnings (though not actually compelled) can be used to impeach a defendant's testimony at trial.

Continued on next page.

Quicknotes

CUSTODIAL INTERROGATION The questioning of a suspect by police while in custody.

FRUIT OF POISONOUS TREE Doctrine that evidence obtained as a result of illegal procedures is tainted and is usually inadmissible at trial.

***MIRANDA* RULE** A required warning given before any questioning by law enforcement authorities may take place. Individuals in custody receive warnings regarding their privilege against self-incrimination, right to remain silent, and right to be represented by an attorney.

***MIRANDA* WARNINGS** Specified warnings that must be communicated to a person prior to a custodial interrogation; in the absence of the communication of such warnings, any communications made during the interrogation are inadmissible at trial.

Missouri v. Seibert

State (P) v. Murder suspect (D)

542 U.S. 600 (2004)

NATURE OF CASE: Appeal from reversal of a murder conviction.

FACT SUMMARY: Patrice Seibert (D) argued that since her murder confession was obtained by the police technique of interrogating in successive, unwarned and warned phases, known as "question-first," the requirements of *Miranda v. Arizona*, 384 U.S. 436 (1966), were violated.

RULE OF LAW

The police technique of interrogating in successive, unwarned and warned phases violates the requirements of *Miranda*.

FACTS: In questioning Patrice Seibert (D), a murder suspect, the police interrogator employed a widely used interrogation technique known as "question-first" in which the interrogator questions the suspect first, then gives the *Miranda* warnings, *Miranda v. Arizona*, 384 U.S. 436 (1966), and then repeats the questioning until the interrogator obtains the confession or incriminating statement which the suspect has already previously provided. After employing this technique of interrogating in successive, unwarned and warned phases, Seibert (D) confessed to murder prior to her warnings and then again after being given the warnings. The trial court suppressed Seibert's (D) pre-warning confession but admitted her post-warning confession. She was convicted of murder. The Missouri Supreme Court reversed, holding that here where the interrogation was "nearly continuous," the second statement was clearly "the product of the invalid first statement" and should have been suppressed. Missouri (P) appealed.

ISSUE: Does the police technique of interrogating in successive, unwarned and warned phases violate the requirements of *Miranda*?

HOLDING AND DECISION: (Souter, J.) Yes. The police technique of interrogating in successive, unwarned and warned phases violates the requirements of *Miranda*. *Miranda* addressed interrogation practices likely to disable an individual from making a free and rational choice about speaking and held that a suspect must be "adequately and effectively" advised of the choice the Constitution guarantees. The object of the "question-first" technique here utilized against Seibert (D) was to render *Miranda* warnings ineffective by waiting for a particularly opportune time to give them, after the suspect had already confessed. Just as no talismanic incantation is required to satisfy *Miranda's* strictures, it would be absurd to think that mere recitation of the litany suffices to satisfy *Miranda* in every conceivable circumstance. The issue when interrogators question first and warn later is thus whether the warnings reasonably convey to a suspect his *Miranda* rights. Unless the warnings could place a suspect who has just been interrogated in a position to make an informed choice as to whether to speak, there is no practical justification for accepting the formal warnings as compliance with *Miranda*, or for treating the second stage of interrogation as distinct from the first, unwarned and inadmissible segment. By any objective measure, applied to circumstances exemplified here, it is likely that if the interrogators employ the technique of withholding warnings until after interrogation succeeds in eliciting a confession, the warnings will be ineffective in preparing the suspect for successive interrogation, close in time and similar in content. Accordingly, the question-first tactic effectively threatens to thwart *Miranda's* purpose of reducing the risk that a coerced confession would be admitted. Affirmed.

CONCURRENCE: (Breyer, J.) Courts should exclude the "fruits" of the initial unwarned questioning unless the failure to warn was in good faith.

CONCURRENCE: (Kennedy, J.) Not every violation of *Miranda* requires suppression of the evidence obtained. The scope of the *Miranda* suppression remedy depends on a consideration of whether admission of the evidence under the circumstances would frustrate *Miranda's* "central concerns and objectives."

DISSENT: (O'Connor, J.) Because here the isolated fact of the interrogating officer's intent could not have had any bearing on Seibert's (D) capacity to comprehend and knowingly relinquish her right to remain silent, it could not by itself affect the voluntariness of her confession.

ANALYSIS

As the Supreme Court makes clear in *Seibert*, the reason for the increased popularity of the question-first method of interrogation is to obtain a confession the suspect would not make if he understood his rights at the outset. The underlying police assumption, which is accurate, is that with one confession in hand before the warnings, the interrogator can usually count on getting a duplicate. It is unrealistic, explained the Court, to treat two bouts of integrated and proximately conducted

Continued on next page.

questioning as independent interrogations subject to independent evaluation simply because *Miranda* warnings formally punctuate them in the middle.

Quicknotes

CUSTODIAL INTERROGATION The questioning of a suspect by police while in custody.

***MIRANDA* RULE** A required warning given before any questioning by law enforcement authorities may take place. Individuals in custody receive warnings regarding their privilege against self-incrimination, right to remain silent, and right to be represented by an attorney.

***MIRANDA* WARNINGS** Specified warnings that must be communicated to a person prior to a custodial interrogation; in the absence of the communication of such warnings, any communications made during the interrogation are inadmissible at trial.

CHAPTER 11

Lineups, Showups, and Other Pre-Trial Identification Procedures

Quick Reference Rules of Law

	PAGE
1. *Manson v. Brathwaite.* Independent indicia of reliability will allow admissibility of a witness whose original police identification was based on suggestive identification techniques.	*164*

Manson v. Brathwaite

Court (P) v. Heroin dealer (D)

432 U.S. 98 (1977)

NATURE OF CASE: Appeal from the reversal of a conviction for the sale of narcotics.

FACT SUMMARY: Glover, a police officer, after describing the man who had sold him heroin, was given a photograph of the suspect for identification purposes.

RULE OF LAW

Independent indicia of reliability will allow admissibility of a witness whose original police identification was based on suggestive identification techniques.

FACTS: Glover, an undercover policeman, purchased heroin from Brathwaite (D). During the purchase, which took several minutes, Glover was no more than two or three feet from him. Glover returned to headquarters and described the individual whom he had seen in great detail. From the description, another officer pulled a picture of Brathwaite (D) from their files. Glover saw the photograph two days later and promptly identified Brathwaite (D) as the seller. The photograph and identification were subsequently admitted at trial without objection. Brathwaite (D) was found guilty and was sentenced to prison. Fourteen months later, Brathwaite (D) challenged the photographic identification on the grounds that it was too suggestive, thereby rendering the identification itself per se excludable. The court of appeals reversed the conviction holding that independent indicia of reliability could not overcome the suggestibility of the identification technique.

ISSUE: Will independent indicia of reliability allow admissibility of a witness whose original police identification was based on suggestive identification techniques?

HOLDING AND DECISION: (Blackmun, J.) Yes. Independent indicia of reliability will allow admissibility of a witness whose original police identification was based on suggestive identification techniques. The circuits have split over whether a per se rule should apply to excluding identification based on suggestive identification procedures. Some favor per se exclusion. Others take each case separately in order to determine if the identification would be otherwise reliable, and, if so, allowing it in evidence. We think the latter theory is correct. To hold otherwise would exclude relevant information from the jury merely because of improper police procedure. The case-by-case approach will be a deterrent to the police and will prevent the guilty from being freed. The linchpin in this area is the independent reliability of the identification. Here, we have a trained police officer who viewed Brathwaite (D) closely for two to three minutes from a short distance. Glover then described Brathwaite (D) in detail shortly thereafter. The pictorial identification was two days later. All of this indicates independent reliability based on a trained observer, prompt identification, and a reasonable opportunity to view the suspect. Independently reliable identifications need not be excluded to satisfy due process requirements. Reversed.

DISSENT: (Marshall, J.) In this case, the Court disregards distinctions in analysis developed in previous decisions and fashions a rule that is not supported by precedent. The use of a single picture on the presentation of a single suspect is inherently suggestive.

ANALYSIS

The per se rule is used to discourage police abuses. The majority appears to indicate that nonpolice witnesses will be less likely to survive an ad hoc, case-by-case, approach because they are more prone to misidentification since they are not trained observers. The stress on them is also deemed greater, which may cause faulty identifications. No hard and fast rules can be developed in this area, but the Court apparently focuses on: (1) the length of time in which the accused was viewed; (2) the nature of the witness; (3) the circumstances; (4) the length of time between the incident and the identification; and (5) the ability to give an initial description of the accused.

Quicknotes

PROCEDURAL DUE PROCESS The constitutional mandate that if the state or federal government acts so as to deny a citizen of a life, liberty, or property interest, the person is first entitled to notice and the right to be heard.

CHAPTER 12

Investigation by Subpoena

Quick Reference Rules of Law

PAGE

1. *Boyd v. United States.* A defendant cannot be compelled to produce incriminating documents. *166*

2. *United States v. R. Enterprises, Inc.* Where a subpoena is challenged on relevancy grounds, a motion to quash must be denied unless there is no reasonable possibility that the materials being sought will produce information relevant to the general subject of the grand jury's investigation. *167*

3. *United States v. Dionisio.* Both the initial compulsion of a person to appear before a grand jury and a subsequent directive to make a voice recording are not unreasonable seizures within the meaning of the Fourth Amendment. *168*

4. *Fisher v. United States.* The Fifth Amendment does not protect against compelled production of a taxpayer's papers if such production would not involve testimonial self-incrimination. *169*

5. *United States v. Hubbell.* (1) The Fifth Amendment privilege against self-incrimination protects a witness from being compelled to disclose the existence of incriminating documents that the government is unable to describe with reasonable particularity. (2) If a witness produces such documents pursuant to a grant of immunity, such immunity prevents the government from using them to prepare criminal charges against him. *170*

Boyd v. United States

Illegal importer (D) v. Federal government (P)

116 U.S. 616 (1886)

NATURE OF CASE: Appeal of forfeiture action.

FACT SUMMARY: Using evidence secured through force from Boyd (D), the Government (P) seized property illegally imported.

RULE OF LAW

A defendant cannot be compelled to produce incriminating documents.

FACTS: Using a statute validating the practice, a government attorney obtained an order mandating that Boyd (D) produce an invoice covering certain imported glass that the Government (P) suspected had been illegally imported. Using the invoice as evidence, the Government (P) seized the glass and confiscated it. Boyd (D) appealed, contending the production order was unconstitutional.

ISSUE: Can a defendant be compelled to produce incriminating documents?

HOLDING AND DECISION: (Bradley, J.) No. A defendant cannot be compelled to produce incriminating documents. The Fourth Amendment protects citizens against unreasonable searches and seizures. The forcible production of one's papers is much like forced testimony, which is clearly prohibited by the Fifth Amendment. In either case, such governmental conduct constitutes an excessive intrusion of the Government (P) into an individual's realm of protected liberty and cannot be permitted. Reversed.

CONCURRENCE: (Miller, J.) The Fourth Amendment is not involved here, as no search or seizure occurs. However, forced document production is tantamount to self-incrimination.

ANALYSIS

In its application of the Fourth and Fifth Amendments, *Boyd* is no longer good law. Compelled document production has long since ceased to be considered a Fourth Amendment issue. As far as the Fifth Amendment is concerned, document production is no longer equated with compelled testimony.

Quicknotes

FIFTH AMENDMENT Provides that no person shall be compelled to serve as a witness against him- or herself, be subject to trial for the same offense twice, or be deprived of life, liberty, or property without due process of law.

FOURTH AMENDMENT Provides that persons be secure as to their person and private belongings against unreasonable searches and seizures

PRIVILEGE AGAINST SELF-INCRIMINATION A privilege guaranteed by the Fifth Amendment to the U.S. Constitution in a criminal proceeding for communications made by an accused and protecting an accused or witness from having to give testimony that may incriminate him- or herself.

United States v. R. Enterprises, Inc.

Federal government (P) v. Pornography company (D)

498 U.S. 292 (1991)

NATURE OF CASE: Appeal from a partial grant of motions to quash subpoenas by a grand jury investigating interstate transportation of obscene materials.

FACT SUMMARY: After R. Enterprises, Inc. (D) and two other companies were served with subpoenas duces tecum in connection with a grand jury investigation, they moved to quash the subpoenas on the grounds that the materials sought were irrelevant to the grand jury's investigation.

RULE OF LAW

Where a subpoena is challenged on relevancy grounds, a motion to quash must be denied unless there is no reasonable possibility that the materials being sought will produce information relevant to the general subject of the grand jury's investigation.

FACTS: Three companies, including R. Enterprises, Inc., (D) that distributed adult and sexually oriented materials were served with subpoenas duces tecum in connection with a grand jury investigation into allegations of interstate transportation of obscene materials. The grand jury sought a variety of corporate books and records and, from one company, videotapes that had been shipped to retailers. All three companies moved to quash the subpoenas, arguing that the materials requested were irrelevant to the investigation. The district court denied the motions. The court of appeals, however, quashed the business records subpoenas issued to R. Enterprises (D) and one other company. The Government (P) appealed. The court of appeals reversed on the grounds of the Fourth Amendment.

ISSUE: Where a subpoena is challenged on relevancy grounds, must a motion to quash be denied unless there is no reasonable possibility that the materials being sought will produce information relevant to the general subject of the grand jury's investigation?

HOLDING AND DECISION: (O'Connor, J.) Yes. Where a subpoena is challenged on relevancy grounds, a motion to quash must be denied unless there is no reasonable possibility that the materials being sought will produce information relevant to the general subject of the grand jury's investigation. The burden of showing unreasonableness must be on the recipient who seeks to avoid compliance. Where a challenging party does not know the general subject of the investigation, a court may be justified in requiring the Government (P) to reveal that information before requiring the party to carry its burden of persuasion. Here, however, there is no doubt that R. Enterprises (D) knew the subject of the grand jury investigation. Because the district court could have concluded on the facts that there was a reasonable possibility that the information requested was relevant to the investigation, it correctly denied the motions to quash. Thus, the judgment of the court of appeals is reversed.

CONCURRENCE: (Stevens, J.) The trial court need only inquire into the relevance of subpoenaed materials after the moving party has initially demonstrated to the court that he or she has some valid objection to compliance. In the grand jury context, the law enforcement interest will almost always prevail, and the documents must be produced. However, it should not be suggested that the deferential relevance standard formulated here will govern decisions in every case, no matter how intrusive or burdensome the request.

ANALYSIS

Many of the rules and restrictions that apply at a trial do not apply in grand jury proceedings. This is especially true of evidentiary restrictions. The Court rejected the use of the standard applied by the court of appeals, set out by the Supreme Court in *United States v. Nixon*, 418 U.S. 683 (1974), since that standard of relevancy, admissibility, and specificity was established in the trial context. In announcing the instant rule, the Court referred to Federal Rule of Criminal Procedure 17(c), which governs subpoenas duces tecum issued in federal criminal proceedings.

Quicknotes

GRAND JURY A group summoned to investigate, inform, and accuse persons of crimes when sufficient evidence exists to do so.

QUASH To vacate, annul, void.

SUBPOENA DUCES TECUM A court mandate compelling the production of documents under a witness's control.

United States v. Dionisio

Federal government (P) v. Subpoenaed defendant (D)

410 U.S. 1 (1973)

NATURE OF CASE: Appeal from judgment for civil contempt.

FACT SUMMARY: Dionisio (D) refused to give voice exemplars to the grand jury.

RULE OF LAW

Both the initial compulsion of a person to appear before a grand jury and a subsequent directive to make a voice recording are not unreasonable seizures within the meaning of the Fourth Amendment.

FACTS: Approximately 20 persons, including Dionisio (D), were subpoenaed before the grand jury to give voice exemplars for comparison with recorded conversations taken pursuant to a court-ordered surveillance. Dionisio (D) refused to give a voice exemplar, claiming protection under the Fourth and Fifth Amendments. The district judge ordered Dionisio (D) to give a voice exemplar. When Dionisio (D) refused, he was held in civil contempt and was committed to custody until he obeyed the order or until the expiration of 18 months. The court of appeals reversed on the grounds of the Fourth Amendment.

ISSUE: Are both the initial compulsion of a person to appear before a grand jury and a subsequent directive to make a voice recording unreasonable seizures within the meaning of the Fourth Amendment?

HOLDING AND DECISION: (Stewart, J.) No. Both the initial compulsion of a person to appear before a grand jury and a subsequent directive to make a voice recording are not unreasonable seizures within the meaning of the Fourth Amendment. First, a subpoena to appear before a grand jury is not a seizure of the person. It is the obligation of every person to appear and give evidence before the grand jury. It is an orderly, lawful process without social stigma and under the supervision of a judge. The fact that 20 people were subpoenaed for the same reason is constitutionally irrelevant. Second, the order to give a voice exemplar was not a seizure under the meaning of the Fourth Amendment. What a person knowingly exposes to the public is not protected. Physical characteristics of voice, as opposed to content of conversations, are not reasonably expected to be private. Therefore, there is no need for the grand jury to determine reasonableness prior to ordering the exemplar where there is no other Fourth Amendment violation. To require would impede the grand jury's proper function. Reversed.

DISSENT: (Marshall, J.) The only recognized exception in prior cases from Fourth Amendment coverage involved grand jury subpoenas requiring individuals to appear and testify. There is no basis for extending that exception when we move beyond the realm of grand jury investigations limited to testimonial inquiries, as in this case. The danger that law enforcement officials may seek to usurp the grand jury process to secure incriminating evidence from a suspect through the simple expedient of a subpoena arises and would, if the Fourth Amendment were held inapplicable here, allow law enforcement to accomplish indirectly what it would not be able to constitutionally accomplish directly.

ANALYSIS

In *Davis v. Mississippi*, 394 U.S. 721 (1969), the Court held that an unlawful seizure could not be used to obtain fingerprints to be used to determine whether a person is the suspected criminal. *Dionisio* allows the grand jury to do exactly that on the rationale that subpoena is not a seizure and that voice prints are not a seizure. The grand jury is thus in position to gain real evidence from a potential defendant prior to any finding of probable cause.

Quicknotes

CIVIL CONTEMPT CITATION One party's failure to comply with a court order requiring that party to undertake an action for the benefit of another party to the action.

EXPECTATION OF PRIVACY Requirement that in order to invoke the Fourth Amendment's protection against unreasonable searches and seizures, the individual must have a reasonable expectation of privacy in respect to the location searched or thing seized.

GRAND JURY A group summoned to investigate, inform, and accuse persons of crimes when sufficient evidence exists to do so.

SUBPOENA A court-issued mandate to compel a witness to appear at trial.

Fisher v. United States

Income tax violator (D) v. Federal government (P)

425 U.S. 391 (1976)

NATURE OF CASE: Action to enforce an Internal Revenue Service summons.

FACT SUMMARY: The Internal Revenue Service sought to compel Fisher's (D) attorney to turn over accountant's worksheets, tax returns, and accountant-client correspondence Fisher (D) had obtained from his accountant and turned over to his attorney when it looked as if an income tax case against Fisher (D) might arise.

RULE OF LAW

The Fifth Amendment does not protect against compelled production of a taxpayer's papers if such production would not involve testimonial self-incrimination.

FACTS: The Internal Revenue Service (IRS) was investigating Fisher (D) for possible civil or criminal liability under the federal income tax laws. Thus, Fisher (D) went to his accountant and recovered the accountant's worksheets, and he retained copies of the tax returns and the accountant's copies of correspondence between the accounting firm and Fisher (D). Fisher (D) turned them over to his attorney, but the IRS issued a summons directing the attorney to produce those documents. The attorney refused, and the Government (P) began enforcement actions. Fisher's (D) attorney basically argued that the Fifth Amendment's protection against self-incrimination precluded forced production of these documents.

ISSUE: Does the Fifth Amendment protect against compelled production of a taxpayer's papers if such production would not involve testimonial self-incrimination?

HOLDING AND DECISION: (White, J.) No. The Fifth Amendment protects against compelled production of a taxpayer's papers only if such production would involve testimonial self-incrimination, which it would not under the circumstances of this particular case. It protects against "compelled self-incrimination," not the disclosure of private information. The attorney-client privilege applies only to documents in the hands of an attorney that would have been privileged in the hands of the client by reason of the Fifth Amendment, and the documents sought would not have been privileged in Fisher's (D) hands under the Fifth Amendment. Thus, they must be produced.

CONCURRENCE: (Brennan, J.) While I agree the privilege against compelled self-incrimination did not protect the papers in this case, I feel the court's opinion does not adequately stress the protection secured by the privilege against compelled production of one's private books and papers.

ANALYSIS

One law review note takes a similar position to that expressed by Justice Marshall, who wrote a concurring opinion in *Fisher* that is not included in the casebook excerpt. It argues that this case and another similar one mean that "no zone of privacy now exists that the government cannot enter to take an individual's property for the purpose of obtaining criminal information." Note, 76 *Mich. L. Rev.* 184, 209-11 (1977).

Quicknotes

ATTORNEY-CLIENT PRIVILEGE A doctrine precluding the admission into evidence of confidential communications between an attorney and the client made in the course of obtaining professional assistance.

PRIVILEGE AGAINST SELF-INCRIMINATION A privilege guaranteed by the Fifth Amendment to the U.S. Constitution in a criminal proceeding for communications made by an accused and protecting an accused or witness from having to give testimony that may incriminate him- or herself.

United States v. Hubbell

Federal government (P) v. Criminal (D)

530 U.S. 27 (2000)

NATURE OF CASE: Grant of writ of certiorari to review conditional plea agreement and court of appeals decision.

FACT SUMMARY: Pursuant to a subpoena and a grant of immunity from prosecution, Hubbell (D) produced documents to the Independent Counsel (P). A grand jury later returned an indictment against Hubbell (D) after the Government (P) presented evidence based on the same documents Hubbell (D) produced.

RULE OF LAW

(1) The Fifth Amendment privilege against self-incrimination protects a witness from being compelled to disclose the existence of incriminating documents that the government is unable to describe with reasonable particularity.

(2) If a witness produces such documents pursuant to a grant of immunity, such immunity prevents the government from using them to prepare criminal charges against him.

FACTS: Hubbell (D) pled guilty and was sentenced to prison. In the plea agreement, Hubbell (D) agreed to provide information about matters related to the Whitewater investigation. While Hubbell (D) was serving his sentence, the Independent Counsel (P) served him (D) with a subpoena requesting the production of certain documents. Hubbell (D) refused, invoking his Fifth Amendment right against self-incrimination. The Government (P) obtained a court order directing Hubbell (D) to produce the documents under a grant of immunity. The documents were then produced. A second prosecution arose out of information gained from these documents. The district court dismissed the indictment, holding that the evidence was derived from the testimonial aspects of the immunized act of producing documents. The court of appeals vacated that judgment and remanded for the lower court to hold a hearing to establish the extent of the Government's (P) independent knowledge of the documents. On remand, the Government (P) entered a conditional plea bargain with Hubbell (D) and the United States Supreme Court granted the government's (P) request for a writ of certiorari.

ISSUE:

(1) Does the Fifth Amendment privilege against self-incrimination protect a witness from being compelled to disclose the existence of incriminating documents that the government is unable to describe with reasonable particularity?

(2) If the witness produces such documents pursuant to a grant of immunity, does such immunity prevent the government from using them to prepare criminal charges against him?

HOLDING AND DECISION:

(1) Yes. The Fifth Amendment privilege against self-incrimination protects a witness from being compelled to disclose the existence of incriminating documents that the government is unable to describe with reasonable particularity.

(2) Yes. If the witness produces such documents pursuant to a grant of immunity, such immunity prevents the government from using them to prepare criminal charges against him. Thus, although a person may be compelled to provide documents, even though they may contain incriminating evidence, the Fifth Amendment protects a witness from the prosecution using this incriminating information, whether it was derived directly or indirectly from the compelled production of documents. Hubbell's (D) action of producing hundreds of documents was the first step in a chain of evidence that led to his own prosecution. The documents were produced only under a grant of immunity and a district court order. Compliance under these circumstances cannot then be turned against him. The indictment against Hubbell (D) must be dismissed. Affirmed.

DISSENT: (Rehnquist, C.J.) The judgment of the court of appeals should be reversed in part, for the reasons given by Judge Williams in his dissenting opinion in that court, 167 F.3d 552 (C.A.D.C. 1999).

CONCURRENCE: (Thomas, J.) This decision involves the act-of-production doctrine that provides that those who are compelled to produce incriminating physical evidence pursuant to a subpoena may invoke the Fifth Amendment privilege as a bar to production when the act of producing the evidence would contain testimonial features. The Fifth Amendment may be broader than this doctrine, however, and protect against compelled production of any incriminating evidence. The Fifth Amendment provides that no person shall be compelled in any criminal case to be a witness against himself.

Continued on next page.

Witness has been defined as "a person who provides testimony." This definition restricts the Fifth Amendment. Witness also means a person who gives or furnishes evidence. Therefore, a person who responds to a subpoena by producing documentation is also a witness. I remain open to a reconsideration of this definition.

ANALYSIS

In its holding, the court of appeals likened the use of the contents of the produced documents to the use of data gathered from a forced blood draw or compelled handwriting exemplar. The difference, however, may be that the forced blood draws and the giving of handwriting samples are usually not done under grants of immunity.

Quicknotes

CERTIORARI A discretionary writ issued by a superior court to an inferior court in order to review the lower court's decisions; the U.S. Supreme Court's writ ordering such review.

IMMUNITY FROM PROSECUTION Statutory protection from prosecution afforded to a witness in exchange for his or her testimony.

CHAPTER 13

Pretrial Release

Quick Reference Rules of Law

PAGE

1. *United States v. Salerno.* The Bail Reform Act, allowing for the denial of bail upon a showing that the defendant presents a risk of danger, is constitutional. *174*

United States v. Salerno

Federal government (P) v. RICO violator (D)

481 U.S. 739 (1987)

NATURE OF CASE: Appeal from denial of bail.

FACT SUMMARY: Salerno (D) contended the Bail Reform Act violated his constitutional rights by allowing a denial of bail based on his potentially dangerous activities.

RULE OF LAW

The Bail Reform Act, allowing for the denial of bail upon a showing that the defendant presents a risk of danger, is constitutional.

FACTS: Salerno (D) was charged with violation of the Racketeer Influenced and Corrupt Organizations Act (RICO). Salerno (D) was denied bail after a hearing resulted in a finding that no release conditions would reasonably ensure the safety of any person and the community. Salerno (D) appealed, contending that the Bail Reform Act was unconstitutional on its face as a violation of the Due Process Clause of the Fifth Amendment and the Eighth Amendment prohibition against excessive bail. The court of appeals reversed, and the United States Supreme Court granted certiorari.

ISSUE: Is the Bail Reform Act, allowing for the denial of bail upon a showing that the defendant presents a risk of danger, constitutional?

HOLDING AND DECISION: (Rehnquist, C.J.) Yes. The Bail Reform Act, allowing for the denial of bail upon a showing that the defendant presents a risk of danger, is constitutional. Detention is not punishment. The Bail Reform Act is regulatory, not punitive. The regulatory goal was to protect the public and people close to the trial from potentially harmful individuals. Thus, the regulatory goal was directly related to its means. The Government's (P) interest in preserving safety may outweigh an individual's right to freedom. Thus, some circumstances exist wherein application of the Bail Reform Act is constitutional. Thus, it is not invalid on its face. Reversed.

DISSENT: (Marshall, J.) This statute punishes a person for the commission of a perceived future crime. Incarceration is punishment. Thus, the Bail Reform Act is unconstitutional.

DISSENT: (Stevens, J.) Pretrial commission for future dangerousness is unconstitutional.

ANALYSIS

The traditional basis for determining if bail is available is whether there is a risk of flight. That is, whether there is a risk that the defendant will not show up for court proceedings. The higher the possibility of flight—usually based on the severity of the crime—the higher the bail. A person is considered innocent until proven guilty; thus, pretrial detention walks a thin constitutional line.

Quicknotes

EIGHTH AMENDMENT Prohibits the imposition of excessive bail, fines, and cruel and unusual punishment.

PROCEDURAL DUE PROCESS The constitutional mandate that if the state or federal government acts so as to deny a citizen a life, liberty, or property interest, the person is first entitled to notice and the right to be heard.

REGULATORY POWER Power granting authority pursuant to statute to a government agency or body to govern a particular area.

RICO Racketeer Influenced and Corrupt Organization Act; federal and state statutes enacted for the purpose of prosecuting organized crime.

CHAPTER 14

The Decision Whether to Prosecute

Quick Reference Rules of Law

	PAGE
1. *United States v. Armstrong.* A criminal defendant bringing a selective-prosecution claim must make a credible showing of different treatment of similarly situated persons in order to obtain discovery in support of the claim.	*176*

United States v. Armstrong

Federal government (P) v. Federal law violator (D)

517 U.S. 456 (1996)

NATURE OF CASE: Review of dismissal of an indictment for possession of crack cocaine and federal firearms offenses.

FACT SUMMARY: After charges were brought against him for violating federal drug laws, Armstrong (D), alleging that he was selected for prosecution because he was Black, brought a motion for discovery in support of his selective-prosecution claim or for dismissal of the indictment.

RULE OF LAW

A criminal defendant bringing a selective-prosecution claim must make a credible showing of different treatment of similarly situated persons in order to obtain discovery in support of the claim.

FACTS: Armstrong (D) was arrested for violation of federal drug and firearms laws. Armstrong (D) alleged he had been selected for prosecution because he was Black and filed a motion for dismissal of the charges or for discovery of Government (P) documents regarding its prosecution of similar defendants. The district court granted the discovery motion and dismissed the indictment when the Government (P) would not comply with discovery. The court of appeals reversed but then, upon hearing the case en banc, affirmed the district court's order of dismissal. The United States Supreme Court granted certiorari.

ISSUE: Must a criminal defendant bringing a selective-prosecution claim make a credible showing of different treatment of similarly situated persons in order to obtain discovery in support of the claim?

HOLDING AND DECISION: (Rehnquist, C.J.) Yes. A criminal defendant bringing a selective-prosecution claim must make a credible showing of different treatment of similarly situated persons in order to obtain discovery in support of the claim. Under Federal Rule of Criminal Procedure 16, which controls discovery in a criminal case, a defendant must show some evidence of disparate treatment—similar to the requirement under equal protection claims. Here, Armstrong (D) did not make such a showing. Thus, the district court's dismissal of the case was improper. Reversed and remanded.

DISSENT: (Stevens, J.) While the defendant did not make a strong enough showing to merit discovery, the district court did not abuse its discretion in requiring some response from the United States (P) Attorney's Office.

ANALYSIS

The Court notes that the test for obtaining discovery for a selective-prosecution claim should be similar to that of an equal protection claim. Recall that to successfully pursue an equal protection claim, the claimant must show both a discriminatory effect and a discriminatory purpose. In order to show a discriminatory effect, the claimant must also show that similarly situated persons (but of a different race or religion) were not prosecuted. From this equal protection language, the Court developed the test in this case.

Quicknotes

CERTIORARI A discretionary writ issued by a superior court to an inferior court in order to review the lower court's decisions; the U.S. Supreme Court's writ ordering such review.

DISCOVERY Pretrial procedure during which one party makes certain information available to the other.

DISCRIMINATORY IMPACT The effect of an action that affects one group of persons more significantly than another; insufficient to prove discriminatory intent on its own.

DISCRIMINATORY PURPOSE Intent to discriminate; must be shown to establish an Equal Protection violation.

EN BANC The hearing of a matter by all the judges of the court, rather than only the necessary quorum.

EQUAL PROTECTION Guarantee under the Fourteenth Amendment to the U.S. Constitution that the government must treat each person or class of persons the same as it treats other persons or classes of persons in like circumstances.

CHAPTER 15

The Preliminary Hearing

Quick Reference Rules of Law

	PAGE
1. *State v. Clark.* To support a binding over for trial, the prosecution must present sufficient evidence only to support a reasonable belief that an offense has been committed and that the defendant committed it.	*178*

State v. Clark

State (P) v. Alleged forgers (D)

Utah Sup. Ct., 20 P.3d 300 (2001)

NATURE OF CASE: State's appeal from the quashing of a binding over for trial.

FACT SUMMARY: When Clark (D) and Smith (D) were bound over for trial, the district court quashed the binding over.

RULE OF LAW

To support a binding over for trial, the prosecution must present sufficient evidence only to support a reasonable belief that an offense has been committed and that the defendant committed it.

FACTS: Clark (D) and Smith (D) were charged with forgery and bound over for trial by a magistrate. The binding over was quashed by the district court on grounds the State (P) failed to meet its evidentiary burden at the preliminary hearing, and the State (P) appealed.

ISSUE: To support a binding over for trial, must the prosecution present sufficient evidence only to support a reasonable belief that an offense has been committed and that the defendant committed it?

HOLDING AND DECISION: (Durrant, J.) Yes. To support a binding over for trial, the prosecution must present sufficient evidence only to support a reasonable belief that an offense has been committed and that the defendant committed it. Unlike a motion for a directed verdict, this evidence need not be capable of supporting a finding of guilt beyond a reasonable doubt. Instead, the quantum of evidence necessary to support a binding over is less than that necessary to survive a directed verdict motion. Specifically, there is no principled basis for attempting to maintain a distinction between the arrest warrant probable cause standard and the preliminary hearing probable cause standard. The "reasonable belief" standard has the advantage of being more easily understood while still allowing magistrates to fulfill the primary purpose of the preliminary hearing, namely, ferreting out groundless and improvident prosecutions. Here, the district court, by dismissing the forgery charges because the State (P) failed to demonstrate the defendants had acted with the requisite intent, wrongly applied the directed verdict standard. Viewed in the light most favorable to the prosecution, the facts presented here were sufficient to meet the reasonable belief standard, since the facts revealed that the defendants attempted to cash a forged check at local banks mere hours after the check was reported stolen. When cashiers told defendants they were seeking approval to cash the check, defendants abandoned the forged check and left the bank. Reversed.

ANALYSIS

As the *Clark* decision notes, notwithstanding that the evidence to a binding over will be viewed in the light most favorable to the prosecution, to prevail at a preliminary hearing the prosecution must still produce believable evidence of all the elements of the crime charged.

Quicknotes

BINDING OVER The imprisonment of a criminal defendant in order to guarantee the defendant's appearance at a criminal trial.

DIRECTED VERDICT A verdict ordered by the court in a jury trial.

PROBABLE CAUSE A reasonable basis for believing that a crime has been committed.

QUANTUM An essential amount; a modicum of the required degree.

REASONABLE BELIEF A reasonable basis for believing that a crime is being or has been committed.

REASONABLE DOUBT Enough doubt on the part of jurors to acquit a defendant based on the absence of evidence.

CHAPTER 16

Grand Jury Review

Quick Reference Rules of Law

	PAGE
1. *Costello v. United States.* An indictment returned by a legally constituted and unbiased grand jury, if valid on its face, is enough to call for trial of the charge on the merits, regardless of the fact the only evidence before the grand jury is hearsay.	*180*
2. *United States v. Williams.* A federal court may not dismiss an otherwise valid indictment for failure of the prosecution to disclose substantial exculpatory evidence to the grand jury.	*181*

Costello v. United States

Grand jury indictee (D) v. Federal government (P)

350 U.S. 359 (1956)

NATURE OF CASE: Petition for certiorari after conviction of income tax invasion.

FACT SUMMARY: Three investigating officers were the only witnesses before the grand jury that indicted Costello (D). They had no firsthand knowledge of the transactions upon which their computations were based. Hence, the indictment was based solely on hearsay.

RULE OF LAW

An indictment returned by a legally constituted and unbiased grand jury, if valid on its face, is enough to call for trial of the charge on the merits, regardless of the fact the only evidence before the grand jury is hearsay.

FACTS: At Costello's (D) trial, the Government (P) called 144 witnesses and introduced 368 exhibits, all of which related to business transactions and expenditures by the Costellos (D). Three government agents, whose investigations had produced the evidence used against Costello (D) at trial, summarized the evidence already introduced, and introduced computations showing, if correct, that the Costellos (D) had received far greater income than they had reported. The three agents were the only witnesses before the grand jury. Costello (D) moved to dismiss the indictment on the ground that the only evidence before the grand jury was hearsay since the officers had no firsthand knowledge of the transactions upon which their computations were based. The trial court refused to dismiss the indictment and Costello (D) was convicted. The court of appeals affirmed.

ISSUE: Is an indictment returned by a legally constituted and unbiased grand jury, if valid on its face, enough to call for traial of the charge on the merits, regardless of the fact that the only evidence before the grand jury is hearsay?

HOLDING AND DECISION: (Black, J.) Yes. An indictment returned by a legally constituted and unbiased grand jury, if valid on its face, is enough to call for trial of the charge on the merits, regardless of the fact the only evidence before the grand jury is hearsay. Neither the Fifth Amendment nor any other constitutional provision prescribes the kind of evidence upon which grand juries must act. The grand jury convenes as a body of lay people, free from technical rules. If indictments could be challenged on the ground that there was inadequate or incompetent evidence before the grand jury, a great delay would result, since before a trial on the merits, an accused could insist on a kind of preliminary trial to determine the adequacy and competency of the evidence before the grand jury. Perhaps most important, such a change would run as a body not hampered by rigid procedural or evidential rules. An indictment returned by a legally constituted and unbiased grand jury, if valid on its face, is enough to call for trial of the charge of the merits. The Fifth Amendment requires nothing more. Costello's (D) conviction is affirmed.

CONCURRENCE: (Burton, J.) In this case, substantial and rationally persuasive evidence apparently was presented to the grand jury. Hence, the indictment should be sustained. However, if it is shown that the grand jury had before it no such evidence upon which to base its indictment, that indictment should be quashed.

ANALYSIS

Depending upon its scope, *Costello* may (or may not) reflect the majority position among those states that regularly prosecute by indictment. In many states, courts will dismiss an indictment upon a showing that there was no sworn witness or legal documentary evidence before the grand jury. In several states, courts have held an indictment is also subject to attack when based solely on the testimony of an incompetent witness. Most indictment states, however, will go no further. An indictment will not be dismissed even if issued solely upon hearsay testimony, and in some jurisdictions, indictments regularly are based entirely upon a summary of investigative reports presented by a single officer or the prosecuting attorney.

Quicknotes

GRAND JURY A group summoned to investigate, inform, and accuse persons of crimes when sufficient evidence exists to do so.

HEARSAY An out-of-court statement made by a person other than the witness testifying at trial that is offered in order to prove the truth of the matter asserted.

TRIAL ON THE MERITS A judicial examination of the facts, evidence, and issues brought before the judge or jury pursuant to jurisdictional laws and rules.

United States v. Williams

Federal government (P) v. Federal statute violator (D)

504 U.S. 36 (1992)

NATURE OF CASE: Appeal from dismissal of an indictment.

FACT SUMMARY: The court of appeals, agreeing with the district court, dismissed an indictment against Williams (D) since the Government (P) failed to disclose substantial exculpatory evidence in its possession to the grand jury.

RULE OF LAW

A federal court may not dismiss an otherwise valid indictment for failure of the prosecution to disclose substantial exculpatory evidence to the grand jury.

FACTS: After a federal grand jury indicted Williams (D) for violating a federal statute, the Tenth Circuit Court of Appeals, agreeing with the district court, granted Williams's (D) motion to dismiss the indictment on the grounds that the Government (P) failed to disclose to the grand jury substantial exculpatory evidence in its possession. The Government (P) appealed.

ISSUE: May a federal court dismiss an otherwise valid indictment for failure of the prosecution to disclose substantial exculpatory evidence to the grand jury?

HOLDING AND DECISION: (Scalia, J.) No. A federal court may not dismiss an otherwise valid indictment for failure of the prosecution to disclose substantial exculpatory evidence to the grand jury. Federal courts "may, within limits, formulate procedural rules not specifically required by the Constitution or . . . Congress" that deal strictly with their power to control their "own" procedures. See *U.S. v. Hasting*, 461 U.S. 499, 505 (1983). Moreover, this "supervisory power" may be used in the grand jury context, but only to proscribe misconduct before the grand jury, which amounts to a violation of one of those carefully drafted and approved rules that ensure the integrity of the grand jury's functions. In the instant case, since failure of the Government (P) to disclose substantial exculpatory evidence before the grand jury does not amount to a violation of one of the above rules, its indictment may not be dismissed. Reversed and remanded.

DISSENT: (Stevens, J.) A United States Attorney is the representative not of an ordinary party but of a sovereign whose obligation to govern impartially is compelling and whose interest in a criminal prosecution is not that it shall win a case, but that justice shall be done. It is as much such attorney's duty to refrain from improper methods calculated to produce a wrongful conviction as it is to use every legitimate means to bring about a just one. A federal prosecutor has this exact same duty to protect fundamental fairness when presenting evidence to a grand jury.

ANALYSIS

In *U.S. v. John Doe, Inc. I*, 481 U.S. 102 (1987), the Supreme Court held that a government attorney who was involved in a grand jury proceeding may use information obtained during that proceeding in a subsequent civil proceeding in which he is involved, without a disclosure order under Rule 6(e). The Court also upheld a disclosure order. Discussing the requirement of "particularized need," it said generally that "the question that must be asked is whether the public benefits of the disclosure . . . outweigh the dangers created by the limited disclosure requested." 481 U.S. 102, 113.

Quicknotes

EXCULPATORY EVIDENCE A statement or other evidence that tends to excuse, justify, or absolve the defendant from alleged fault or guilt.

GRAND JURY A group summoned to investigate, inform, and accuse persons of crimes when sufficient evidence exists to do so.

CHAPTER 17

The Charging Instrument

Quick Reference Rules of Law

	PAGE
1. *Russell v. United States.* The sufficiency of an indictment is to be measured by two criteria: (1) whether the indictment contains the elements of the offense intended to be charged so as to sufficiently apprise the defendant of what he must be prepared to defend against, and (2) in case any other proceedings are taken against him for a second offense, whether the record shows with accuracy to what extent he may plead a former conviction or acquittal.	*184*
2. *United States v. Resendiz-Ponce.* An indictment for an "attempt" crime is not constitutionally defective if it does not specify an overt act that the defendant has taken in furtherance of the defendant's criminal goal.	*185*

Russell v. United States

Grand jury indictee (D) v. Federal government (P)

369 U.S. 749 (1962)

NATURE OF CASE: Appeal from conviction under federal law of refusing to answer questions when summoned before a congressional subcommittee.

FACT SUMMARY: A grand jury indictment failed to identify the subject under congressional inquiry at the time Russell (D), a witness, was interrogated.

RULE OF LAW

The sufficiency of an indictment is to be measured by two criteria: (1) whether the indictment contains the elements of the offense intended to be charged so as to sufficiently apprise the defendant of what he must be prepared to defend against, and (2) in case any other proceedings are taken against him for a second offense, whether the record shows with accuracy to what extent he may plead a former conviction or acquittal.

FACTS: Russell (D) and other witnesses were indicted by a grand jury for refusing to answer certain questions when summoned before a congressional subcommittee. The indictments stated only that the questions to which answers were refused "were pertinent to the question then under inquiry" by the subcommittee. Motions to quash the indictments, on the grounds they failed to state the subject under investigation, were denied. Russell (D) and the other defendants were convicted under a federal law that stated that prosecutions under it could be initiated only by grand jury indictment.

ISSUE: Where witnesses have been indicted, under federal law, for failure to answer questions when summoned by a congressional investigatory body, must the indictment identify the subject under inquiry at the time of the defendant's alleged default or refusal to answer?

HOLDING AND DECISION: (Stewart, J.) Yes. Where witnesses have been indicted, under federal law, for failure to answer questions when summoned by a congressional investigatory body, the indictment must identify the subject under inquiry at the time of the defendant's alleged default or refusal to answer. By invoking the aid of the federal courts in dealing with reluctant witnesses, Congress conferred upon the courts the duty to provide individuals prosecuted for this statutory offense every safeguard accorded other types of criminal defendants. There can be criminality here only if: (1) the witness refused to answer a question that pertained to the subject then under investigation by the body; and (2) the pleadings so showed this. Although convictions will not be overturned because of minor, technical deficiencies in an indictment that do not prejudice the accused, care must still be taken. The indictments involved here satisfied the requirement that Russell (D) and the other defendants would not be re-indicted for the same offense since the precise questions asked them were given. However, the indictments are fatally defective for failing to sufficiently apprise them of what they must be prepared to meet. An indictment must do more than simply repeat the language of the criminal statute. It must, in precise terms, inform the accused with reasonable certainty, of the nature of the accusation against him. A corollary purpose of requiring specificity in the indictment is to inform a court of the facts alleged so to enable it to decide whether they are sufficient in law to suppose a conviction. A court, or prosecutor, should not have to guess what was in the mind of the grand jury at the time it returned the indictment. Reversed.

ANALYSIS

It has been generally held that a charging instrument indictment, or information must fulfill three functions: (1) notice, to enable the defendant to adequately mount a defense; (2) protection against additional prosecutions stemming from the same defense (double jeopardy); and (3) enable a court to judge whether the government's case is based upon a valid interpretation of the offense charged (judicial review). A court satisfies the judicial review function when it determines that the charging instrument sets out the essential elements of the offense. When the instrument has been found to be defective in not setting out all the requisite elements, the ruling is said to be based on the notice function. *Russell* suggests, perhaps, a fourth function—that the defendant not be tried upon a theory or evidence different than the one embraced in the charging instrument.

Quicknotes

GRAND JURY A group summoned to investigate, inform, and accuse persons of crimes when sufficient evidence exists to do so.

INDICTMENT A formal written accusation made by a prosecutor and issued by a grand jury, charging an individual with a criminal offense.

QUASH To vacate, annul, void.

United States v. Resendiz-Ponce

Federal government (P) v. Illegal alien (D)

549 U.S. 102 (2007)

NATURE OF CASE: Appeal from reversal of conviction of illegally attempting to reenter the United States.

FACT SUMMARY: The United States (P) contended that Resendiz-Ponce's (D) conviction for illegally reentering the country should not have been overturned merely because his indictment failed to allege a specific overt act that he committed in seeking reentry, and that such omission was subject to harmless-error review.

RULE OF LAW

An indictment for an "attempt" crime is not constitutionally defective if it does not specify an overt act that the defendant has taken in furtherance of the defendant's criminal goal.

FACTS: Resendiz-Ponce (D), a Mexican citizen, was charged with the crime of attempting to reenter the United States, in violation of 18 U.S.C. § 1326, after having been twice deported. The district court denied his motion to have the indictment dismissed because it did not allege a specific overt act that he committed in seeking reentry, which he contended was an essential element of the crime of attempting to reenter the United States after deportation. The Government (P) did not disagree that an individual cannot be guilty of attempted reentry under § 1326(a) unless (1) he commits an overt act qualifying as a substantial step toward completing his goal or (2) the indictment fails to set forth each element of the crime that it charges. Instead, it contended the indictment that actually issued implicitly alleged Resendiz-Ponce (D) engaged in the necessary overt act by alleging that he "attempted" to enter the country. In reversing, the court of appeals held that the indictment's omission of an overt act was a fatal flaw not subject to harmless-error review. The United States Supreme Court granted certiorari.

ISSUE: Is an indictment for an "attempt" crime constitutionally defective if it does not specify an overt act that the defendant has taken in furtherance of the defendant's criminal goal?

HOLDING AND DECISION: (Stevens, J.) No. An indictment for an "attempt" crime is not constitutionally defective if it does not specify an overt act that the defendant has taken in furtherance of the defendant's criminal goal. Resendiz-Ponce's (D) indictment was not defective, and, therefore, the harmless-error issue does not have to be reached. First, not only does "attempt" as used in common parlance connote action rather than mere intent, but, more importantly, as used in the law for centuries, it encompasses both the overt act and intent elements. Thus, an indictment alleging attempted reentry under § 1326(a) need not specifically allege a particular overt act or any other component part of the offense. It was enough for the indictment to point to the relevant criminal statute and allege that Resendiz-Ponce (D) "intentionally attempted to enter the United States...." An indictment has two constitutional requirements: First, it must contain the elements of the offense charged and fairly inform a defendant of the charge against which he must defend, and, second, it must enable him to plead an acquittal or conviction in bar of future prosecutions for the same offense. Here, the use of the word "attempt," coupled with the specification of the time and place of the alleged reentry, satisfied both. Resendiz-Ponce's (D) argument that the indictment would have been sufficient only if it alleged any of three overt acts performed during his attempted reentry—that he walked into an inspection area; that he presented a misleading identification card; or that he lied to an inspector—is rejected because individually and cumulatively those acts were all part of a single course of conduct constituting "attempt" of reentry. Although it is true that some crimes must be charged with greater specificity than an indictment parroting a federal criminal statute's language, this is not one of those crimes. Therefore, there was no infirmity in the present indictment, which complied with Fed. R. Crim. P. 7(c)(1), which provides that an indictment "must be a plain, concise, and definite written statement of the essential facts constituting the offense charged." Reversed and remanded.

DISSENT: (Scalia, J.) Because an "attempt" to commit a crime involves both intent and an overt act of some kind toward commission of the crime, it logically follows that when the Government (P) indicts for attempt to commit a crime, it must allege both the intent and the action taken. Otherwise, the rule that an indictment must allege all the elements of the charged crime would be violated—as it was here. It is not enough, as the majority indicates, to say that in "common parlance" attempt connotes both intent and action. That is irrelevant, since all elements of a crime must be set forth in an indictment, whether or not they are somehow connoted. Moreover, the majority is probably incorrect that "attempt" conveys with precision what conviction of that crime requires. A jury could misinterpret "attempt" to only require intent plus a small step of action, versus the significant step required by law. The majority's sweeping statement that "attempt" has had

Continued on next page.

a uniform meaning in law for centuries is likewise irrelevant and most likely incorrect because the definition of "attempt" has not been consistent through the ages, and, in any event—regardless of how static the elements of a crime have remained—this has not excused the inclusion of all the elements of that crime in an indictment. If the majority's reasoning was followed with respect to all crimes, it would lead to a revolution in the requirements of an indictment. Also, as a matter of logic, attempt is a lesser included crime of a completed crime. Therefore, contrary to the majority's assertion, it is not illogical to dismiss an indictment charging "attempt" because it fails to allege an overt act even though a defendant indicted only for a completed offense can be convicted of attempt without the indictment's ever mentioning an overt act. Attempt does not need to be separately charged when it is part of a charge of a completed offense, but all its elements must be specified when it alone is being charged. Finally, the Government (P) presented no evidence that mere recitation of the word "attempt" in attempt indictments has been the traditional practice. Because the indictment was deficient that goes to the next issued that was raised but avoided by the majority—whether such deficiency was structural error as held by the court of appeals; in short, it was.

ANALYSIS

Fed. R. Crim. P. 31(c) provides that a defendant may be found guilty of "an attempt to commit the offense charged; or . . . an attempt to commit an offense necessarily included in the offense charged, if the attempt is an offense in its own right." Fed. R. Crim. P. 31(c)(2)-(3). The majority found that this rule supported its position that if a defendant indicted only for a completed offense can be convicted of attempt under Rule 31(c) without the indictment ever mentioning an overt act, it would be illogical to dismiss an indictment charging "attempt" because it fails to allege such an act. Justice Scalia clearly disagreed.

Quicknotes

ATTEMPT An effort or try, combined with the act falling short of the goal intended.

HARMLESS ERROR An error taking place during trial that does not require the reviewing court to overturn or modify the trial court's judgment in that it did not affect the appellant's substantial rights or the disposition of the action.

INTENT The state of mind that exists when one's purpose is to commit a criminal act.

OVERT ACT An open act evidencing an intention to commit a crime.

CHAPTER 18

The Location of the Prosecution

Quick Reference Rules of Law

PAGE

1. *United States v. Rodriguez-Moreno.* Venue in a prosecution for using or carrying a firearm during and in relation to any crime of violence in violation of 18 U.S.C. § 924(c)(1) is proper in any district in which the crime was committed, even if the firearm was carried in a single district only. *188*

United States v. Rodriguez-Moreno

Federal government (P) v. Kidnapper (D)

526 U.S. 275 (1999)

NATURE OF CASE: Appeal from conviction of kidnapping and carrying a firearm during and in relation to a crime of violence under 18 U.S.C. § 924(c)(1).

FACT SUMMARY: The Government (P) appealed from the reversal of a kidnapping conviction by the court of appeals on the basis that § 924(c)(1) was not violated since the defendant used a firearm in Maryland only and the kidnapping occurred in New Jersey.

RULE OF LAW

Venue in a prosecution for using or carrying a firearm during and in relation to any crime of violence in violation of 18 U.S.C. § 924(c)(1) is proper in any district in which the crime was committed, even if the firearm was carried in a single district only.

FACTS: During a drug transaction taking place in Houston, a New York drug dealer stole 30 kilograms of a Texas drug distributor's cocaine. The distributor hired Rodriguez-Moreno (D) and others to find the dealer and to hold captive the middleman in the transaction, Avendano. Rodriguez-Moreno (D) and his codefendants were tried jointly and charged with conspiring to kidnap Avendano, kidnapping Avendano, and using a firearm in relation to kidnapping Avendano, in violation of 18 U.S.C. § 924(c)(1). Rodriguez-Moreno (D) moved to dismiss for lack of venue, contending that venue was proper only in Maryland, the only place where the Government (P) had proved that he actually used the gun. The district court denied the motion and convicted defendants, and the court of appeals reversed.

ISSUE: Is venue in a prosecution for using or carrying a firearm during and in relation to any crime of violence in violation of 18 U.S.C. § 924(c)(1) proper in any district in which the crime was committed, even if the firearm was carried in a single district only?

HOLDING AND DECISION: (Thomas, J.) Yes. Venue in a prosecution for using or carrying a firearm during and in relation to any crime of violence in violation of 18 U.S.C. § 924(c)(1) is proper in any district in which the crime was committed, even if the firearm was carried in a single district only. Here the statute provides that "Whoever, during and in relation to any crime of violence . . . for which he may be prosecuted in a court of the United States, uses or carries a firearm, shall, in addition to the punishment provided for such crime of violence . . . be sentenced to imprisonment for five years. . . ." The court of appeals looked to the verbs of the statute to determine the nature of the substantive offense. While the verb test has value as an investigative tool, it cannot be applied to the exclusion of other relevant statutory language. To prove the § 924(c)(1) violation, the Government (P) was required to show the defendants used a firearm, committed all acts necessary to be subject to punishment for kidnapping in a court of the United States, and used the gun "during and in relation to" the kidnapping of Avendano. Defendants argue that for venue purposes the New Jersey kidnapping was irrelevant to the Maryland firearm crime since a gun was not used during the New Jersey crime. Several circuits have defined kidnapping as a unitary crime that once begun does not end until the victim is free. Section 924(c)(1) does not define a "point-in-time" offense when a firearm is used during and in relation to a continuing crime of violence. Reversed.

DISSENT: (Scalia, J.) The issue here is whether the defendant's alleged act of using a firearm during and in relation to a kidnapping occurred; since it occurred only in Maryland, then venue is only proper there.

ANALYSIS

"The locus delicti of the charged offense must be determined from the nature of the crime alleged and the location of the acts constituting the crime." *United States v. Cabrales*, 524 U.S. 1 (1998). First, the court must identify the conduct.

Quicknotes

VENUE The specific geographic location over which a court has jurisdiction to hear a suit.

CHAPTER 19

Joinder and Severance

Quick Reference Rules of Law

PAGE

1. *People v. Merriman.* Joinder of offenses in the same class or connected in the commission of the crime is not an abuse of discretion unless there is a reasonable probability the jury was influenced by the joinder in its verdict of guilt. *190*

2. *United States v. Dixon.* The Double Jeopardy Clause does not permit subsequent prosecution of an offense that has already been the basis of criminal contempt proceedings. *191*

3. *Ashe v. Swenson.* The doctrine of collateral estoppel is embodied in the Fifth Amendment guarantee against double jeopardy, so that an acquittal based on a factual issue that is also presented as an essential element of a second charge bars trial on that charge. *193*

4. *Schaffer v. United States.* Where the joinder of trials of multiple defendants is based on a charge of conspiracy, the failure of the conspiracy charge does not automatically mandate severance of the trials on the remaining substantive counts. *195*

5. *Gray v. Maryland.* Redacted confessions that replace the proper name with an obvious blank, the word "delete," a symbol, or similarly notify the jury that a name has been deleted violate a defendant's Sixth Amendment rights if introduced into evidence insulated from cross examination. *197*

People v. Merriman

State (P) v. Convicted murderer (D)

Cal. Sup. Ct., 60 Cal. 4th 1, 332 P.3d 1187 (2014)

NATURE OF CASE: Appeal from conviction for murder and sexual offenses.

FACT SUMMARY: Merriman (D) was charged with sexual assault and murder among many other charges. At trial Merriman (D) sought to sever the murder charge from all other charges, but the trial court denied his motion. Merriman (D) claims the denial was an abuse of discretion.

RULE OF LAW

Joinder of offenses in the same class or connected in the commission of the crime is not an abuse of discretion unless there is a reasonable probability the jury was influenced by the joinder in its verdict of guilt.

FACTS: The grand jury indicted Merriman (D) on 25 counts, including sexual offenses against Robyn G., Billie B, and Katrina; murder of Katrina; resisting arrest; and possessing a controlled substance. Merriman (D) later was indicted on five additional charges related to witness tampering from the first grand jury investigation. The prosecution filed its pretrial motion to consolidate the two indictments and the trial court granted the motion. The defense filed its pretrial motion to sever the murder count from all other charges. The trial court severed trial on drug-and firearm-possession charges and with five charges related to Merriman's (D) being under the influence. The rest of the charges remained joined with the murder charge for trial. [Merriman (D) filed for post-conviction relief.]

ISSUE: Is joinder of offenses in the same class or connected in the commission of the crime an abuse of discretion?

HOLDING AND DECISION: (Cantil-Sakauye, C.J.) No. Joinder of offenses in the same class or connected in the commission of the crime is not an abuse of discretion unless there is a reasonable probability the jury was influenced by the joinder in its verdict of guilt. Section 954 authorizes joinder of different offenses if they were connected in their commission or if they are in the same class of offenses. Here, the joinder meets the statutory requirements because the sexual offenses and murder charges are assaultive crimes and in the same class. Evading arrest and witness tampering are connected with defendant's wish to avoid criminal liability for Katrina's murder. The drug offense occurred at the time of the commission. Merriman (D) argues the trial court had discretion to sever the charges even if joinder was statutorily appropriate. The evidence, however, would have been admissible at a separate murder trial, so the trial court was justified in refusing to sever. The sexual assaults would have been admissible pursuant to Evidence Code § 1108 to show propensity. The probative value of the assaults was substantial. The prejudicial value did not outweigh the probative value. While the sexual assaults were demeaning, they paled in comparison to the horrendous nature of the murder. The fact Merriman (D) had not yet been convicted of the sexual assaults against Robyn G. and Bille B. does not tip the scales in his favor. The circumstances surrounding Merriman's (D) flight from the police and subsequent standoff in a bystander's home demonstrates consciousness of guilt for Katrina's murder. The defense can challenge the inference the evidence suggests, but offering other reasons for fleeing from the police does not require the trial court to sever the resisting arrest counts from the murder count. The crime allegedly was committed for the benefit of a criminal street gang and the witness tampering again shows consciousness of guilt. Merriman (D) argues that the evidence offered in support of the witness tampering counts included highly inflammatory evidence of his White supremacist gang membership and perverse relationship with his mother. Those facts were developed at trial, though, and the trial court could not have abused its discretion in failing to sever at pretrial. The court considers whether there was "gross unfairness" as a result of joinder. The crimes would have been admissible at a separate murder trial and the jury was instructed to consider each crime separately. There is no reasonable probability that the joinder of counts tainted the jury's verdicts in this case. Affirmed.

ANALYSIS

Joinder of like crimes and related offenses is a more efficient method of trial, but it does leave open a question of prejudice to the accused. The greater number of charges and the descriptions of multiple crimes may persuade, even unconsciously, a jury to find guilt for at least one of the charges whereas separate trials could have very different outcomes.

Quicknotes

ABUSE OF DISCRETION A determination by an appellate court that a lower court's decision was based on an error of law.

JOINDER The joining of claims or parties in one lawsuit.

PROBATIVE Tending to establish proof.

United States v. Dixon

Federal government (P) v. Double jeopardy appellant (D)

509 U.S. 688 (1993)

NATURE OF CASE: Consolidated appeals cases from ruling barring subsequent criminal prosecution in one and allowing it in the other.

FACT SUMMARY: Both Dixon (D) and Foster (D), who were convicted of criminal contempt in connection with alleged underlying criminal conduct, argued that the Double Jeopardy Clause barred any subsequent criminal prosecution on charges arising out of the same criminal conduct.

RULE OF LAW

The Double Jeopardy Clause does not permit subsequent prosecution of an offense that has already been the basis of criminal contempt proceedings.

FACTS: Dixon (D) was arrested for second-degree murder. The form by which he was released on bond specified that he was not to commit "any criminal offense" and warned that any violation of the conditions of release would subject him "to revocation of release, an order of detention, and prosecution for contempt of court." While awaiting trial, Dixon (D) was arrested and indicted for possession of cocaine with intent to distribute. He was found guilty of criminal contempt and sentenced to 180 days in jail. The trial court later granted Dixon's (D) motion to dismiss the cocaine indictment on double jeopardy grounds. Foster (D) violated a civil protection order (CPO), requiring that he not "molest, assault, or in any manner threaten or physically abuse" his wife. He was held in contempt for numerous violations of the CPO. The court found Foster (D) guilty beyond a reasonable doubt of four counts of criminal contempt, acquitted him on other counts, and sentenced him to 600 days imprisonment. The U.S. Attorney's office later obtained an indictment charging Foster (D) with simple assault, threatening to injure another, and assault with intent to kill. Foster (D) moved to dismiss, claiming a double jeopardy bar to all counts. The trial court denied the double jeopardy claim. The Government (P) appealed in *Dixon*, while Foster (D) appealed the trial court's denial of his motion. After consolidating the two cases, the court of appeals ruled that both subsequent prosecutions were barred by the Double Jeopardy Clause. The Government (P) appealed.

ISSUE: Does the Double Jeopardy Clause permit subsequent prosecution of an offense that has already been the basis of criminal contempt proceedings?

HOLDING AND DECISION: (Scalia, J.) No. The Double Jeopardy Clause does not permit subsequent prosecution of an offense that has already been the basis of criminal contempt proceedings. This protection applies both to successive punishments and to successive prosecutions for the same criminal offense. This Court has concluded that where the two offenses for which the defendant is punished or tried cannot survive the "same-elements" test, the double jeopardy bar applies. The same-elements test inquires whether each offense contains only elements contained in the other; if so, they are the "same offense" and double jeopardy bars additional punishment and successive prosecution. If not, they are not the same offense, and there is no double jeopardy bar. Dixon's (D) cocaine possession, although an offense under the D.C. Code, was not an offense under the contempt statute until a judge incorporated the statutory drug offense into his release order. Here, where the contempt sanction was imposed for violating the order through commission of the incorporated drug offense, the later attempt to prosecute Dixon (D) for the drug offense resembles the double jeopardy situation. Criminal contempt, at least in its nonsummary form, "is a crime in every fundamental respect." Because Dixon's (D) drug offense did not include any element not contained in his previous contempt offense, his subsequent prosecution violated the double jeopardy clause. The foregoing analysis obviously applies to the indictment against charging Foster (D) with assault, based on the same event that was the subject of his prior contempt conviction for violating the provision of the CPO forbidding him to commit simple assault. Thus, the subsequent prosecution for assault is barred. However, the remaining four counts of assault with intent to kill and threats to injure or kidnap are not barred. Each of those offenses contained a separate element, and the test for double jeopardy was not met. Thus, both Dixon's (D) subsequent prosecution for cocaine possession and Foster's (D) subsequent prosecution for simple assault violate the Double Jeopardy Clause and are barred. Affirmed [as to *Dixon*]. Affirmed in part; reversed in part [as to *Foster*].

CONCURRENCE AND DISSENT: (Rehnquist, C.J.) A defendant who is guilty of possession with intent to distribute cocaine or of assault has not necessarily satisfied any statutory element of criminal contempt. Nor can it be said that a defendant who is held in criminal contempt

Continued on next page.

has necessarily satisfied any element of those substantive crimes. The offenses for which Dixon (D) and Foster (D) were prosecuted in this case cannot be analogized to greater and lesser included offenses; hence, they are separate and distinct for double jeopardy purposes.

CONCURRENCE AND DISSENT: (White, J.) The Double Jeopardy Clause bars prosecution for an offense if the defendant already has been held in contempt for its commission. Thus, the subsequent prosecutions in both *Dixon* and *Foster* were impermissible as to all counts.

CONCURRENCE AND DISSENT: (Souter, J.) Both the prosecution of Dixon (D) and the prosecution of Foster (D) on all counts against him should be barred by the Double Jeopardy Clause.

ANALYSIS

The same-elements test was first enunciated by the court in *Blockburger v. United States*, 284 U.S. 299 (1932), and is commonly referred to as the *Blockburger* test. In arriving at its ruling in the instant case, the majority overruled its recent decision in *Grady v. Corbin*, 495 U.S. 508 (1990), which held that in addition to passing the *Blockburger* test, a subsequent prosecution must satisfy a "same-conduct" test to avoid the double jeopardy bar. The *Grady* test provided that if, to establish an essential element of an offense charged in that prosecution, the government would prove conduct that constituted an offense for which the defendant had already been prosecuted, a second prosecution may not be had. In the majority's view, *Grady* was not only wrong in principle but had already proved inconsistent in application.

Quicknotes

CONTEMPT Conduct that interferes with the proper administration of justice by a court or legislature.

DOUBLE JEOPARDY A prohibition against a second prosecution for the same offense after an acquittal or conviction for that offense in a prior proceeding or against multiple punishments for the same offense.

Ashe v. Swenson

Convicted robber (D) v. State official (P)

397 U.S. 436 (1970)

NATURE OF CASE: Petition for writ of habeas corpus after conviction of robbery.

FACT SUMMARY: Three or four men robbed six men and stole and fled in one of the victims' cars. Each alleged robber was charged with seven separate offenses. Ashe (D) was acquitted on the robbery charge as to one of the victims. At that trial, the state's proof that the robbery had occurred and that the alleged victim was one of the victims was unassailable, but the evidence that Ashe (D) was one of the robbers was weak. At a second trial for the robbery of a second victim, Ashe (D) was convicted. Ashe (D) contended that collateral estoppel was one of the elements of the Fifth Amendment guarantee against double jeopardy, so that his conviction at the second trial was unconstitutional

RULE OF LAW

The doctrine of collateral estoppel is embodied in the Fifth Amendment guarantee against double jeopardy, so that an acquittal based on a factual issue that is also presented as an essential element of a second charge bars trial on that charge.

FACTS: Three or four men robbed six men who were playing poker and stole and fled in one of the victims' cars. (It was never clear whether there were three or four robbers.) Three men were arrested near the abandoned stolen car. Ashe (D) was arrested separately some distance away. Each of the four was charged with six robbery counts and the theft of the car. At Ashe's (D) trial for the robbery of Knight, proof the armed robbery had occurred and Knight had been a victim was unassailable. The state's evidence that Ashe (D) had been one of the robbers was weak, and the jury found Ashe (D) not guilty. Six weeks later, Ashe (D) was brought to trial for the robbery of Roberts. Ashe (D) moved to dismiss, but his motion was not granted. The witnesses at the second trial were for the most part the same as those at the first trial, but their testimony on Ashe's (D) identification was much stronger. The victim whose identification testimony had been negative at the first trial was not called at the second trial. The jury found Ashe (D) guilty, and he was sentenced to 35 years. Ashe (D) then brought a habeas corpus proceeding in federal court on the ground that the second trial has violated his constitutional right not to be twice put in jeopardy. The United States Supreme Court granted certiorari.

ISSUE: Is the doctrine of collateral estoppel embodied in the Fifth Amendment guarantee against double jeopardy, so that an acquittal based on a factual issue that is also presented as an essential element of a second charge bars trial on that charge?

HOLDING AND DECISION: (Stewart, J.) Yes. The doctrine of collateral estoppel is embodied in the Fifth Amendment guarantee against double jeopardy, so that an acquittal based on a factual issue that is also presented as an essential element of a second charge bars trial on that charge. Collateral estoppel means that when an issue of ultimate facts has once been determined by a valid and final judgment, that issue cannot be litigated again between the same parties in any future lawsuit. Although first developed in civil litigation, the doctrine has long been held applicable in criminal cases. Where a previous judgment of acquittal was based upon a general verdict, as is usually the case, the court must examine the records of the prior proceedings to determine whether a rational jury could have grounded its verdict upon any issue other than the one which the defendant seeks to foreclose from consideration. Typically, this requires the court to take into account the pleadings, evidence, charge, and other relevant matters, and conclude whether a rational jury could have grounded its verdict on an issue other than that which the defendant seeks to foreclose from consideration. The inquiry must be set in a practical frame and viewed with an eye to all the circumstances of the proceedings. Looking to the record here, there is no indication that the first jury could have rationally based its verdict on a finding that the robbery did not occur or that Knight had not been a victim. The only rationally conceivable issue in dispute before the jury was whether Ashe (D) had been one of the robbers. The jury, by its verdict, found that he had not. The federal rule of law, therefore, would make a second prosecution for the robbery of Roberts wholly impermissible. The ultimate question, then is whether this established federal rule is an element of the Fifth Amendment's guarantee against double jeopardy. We hold that it is. It is clear that the State (P) would be precluded from bringing Ashe (D) to a second trial for Knight's robbery. From a constitutional perspective, the situation is no different here, even though the second trial related to another victim of the same robbery. The name of the victim has no bearing on whether Ashe (D) was one of the robbers. Accordingly, the doctrine of collateral estoppel is embodied in the Fifth Amendment guarantee against double jeopardy. The State (P) could not constitutionally bring Ashe (D) before a second jury to decide

Continued on next page.

whether he was one of the robbers after a first jury had already held that he was not. Reversed and remanded.

CONCURRENCE: (Brennan, J.) I agree with the majority's holding. However, even if collateral estoppel were not applicable here, the Double Jeopardy Clause bars the second trial, since the two prosecutions grew out of one criminal episode. The Double Jeopardy Clause requires the prosecution, except in most limited circumstances, to join at one trial all charges against a defendant that grow out of a single criminal act, occurrence, episode, or transaction. This "same transaction" test enforces the ancient prohibition against multiple prosecutions and also promotes the justice, economy, and convenience that result from consolidation in one lawsuit of all issues arising out of a single transaction or occurrence.

DISSENT: (Burger, C.J.) Nothing in the language or any of the gloss previously placed on the Double Jeopardy Clause remotely justifies the majority's treatment of the collateral estoppel doctrine. The essence of the concurring opinion is that all that occurred in this case was one transaction or episode. For me it demeans the dignity of the human personality and individuality to talk of a "single transaction" in the context of six separate assaults on six individuals.

ANALYSIS

Ashe deprives the prosecution of a major tactical advantage in trying separately, closely related offenses arising from a single transaction. The effect of the collateral estoppel doctrine is to prevent the prosecutor from "treating the first trial as no more than a dry run for a second prosecution" on a second charge. With this tactic eliminated, the prosecutor may find less advantage in separate prosecutions in such situations. In *Harris v. Washington,* 404 U.S. 55 (1971), the Court held that the constitutional guarantee applies, irrespective of whether the jury considered all relevant evidence, and irrespective of the state's good faith in bringing successive prosecutions. There a bomb sent through the mail killed Burdick and the defendant's son. After his acquittal on a charge of murdering Burdick, the defendant was charged with murdering his son. It was contended that the issue of identity had not been fully litigated because the trial judge had wrongly excluded a threatening letter written by the defendant.

Quicknotes

COLLATERAL ESTOPPEL A doctrine whereby issues litigated and determined in a prior proceeding are binding upon all subsequent litigation between the parties regarding that issue.

DOUBLE JEOPARDY A prohibition against a second prosecution for the same offense after an acquittal or conviction for that offense in a prior proceeding or against multiple punishments for the same offense.

ULTIMATE FACT A fact upon which a judicial determination is made and which is inferred from the evidence presented at trial.

Schaffer v. United States

Prejudiced conspirator (D) v. Federal government (P)

362 U.S. 511 (1960)

NATURE OF CASE: Appeal from criminal conviction.

FACT SUMMARY: The defendants were charged with conspiracy and with individual substantive crimes. At the close of the prosecution's case, the defendants moved successfully for dismissal of the conspiracy charge. They now contend that continued joinder of the individual cases was unduly prejudiced.

RULE OF LAW

Where the joinder of trials of multiple defendants is based on a charge of conspiracy, the failure of the conspiracy charge does not automatically mandate severance of the trials on the remaining substantive counts.

FACTS: The Schaffers (D), along with three others named Stracuzza, were charged with transporting stolen property across state lines. The Stracuzzas were also charged with separate interstate shipments involving two other individuals at separate times. All seven were also charged with conspiracy to commit the individual crimes charged and were tried in a joint trial. At the close of the prosecution's case, the seven moved for an acquittal on the conspiracy charge. The motion was granted on the basis that no connection, other than the common participation of the Stracuzzas, was shown between the Schaffers (D) and the other individual defendants. However, the motion for acquittal on the substantive crimes was denied along with a motion to sever the trials of the defendants. Upon submission of the substantive counts to the jury on a detailed charge, each petitioner was found guilty, fined, and sentenced to prison. [The court of appeals affirmed the convictions, finding that no prejudice existed by reason of the joint trial. The United States Supreme Court granted certiorari.]

ISSUE: Where the joinder of trials of multiple defendants is based on a charge of conspiracy, does failure of the conspiracy charge automatically mandate severance of the trials on the remaining substantive counts?

HOLDING AND DECISION: (Clark, J.) No. Where the joinder of trials of multiple defendants is based on a charge of conspiracy, the failure of the conspiracy charge does not automatically mandate severance of the trials on the remaining substantive counts. The trial was properly joined at the outset under Rule 8(b) of the Fed. R. Crim. P., and any severance thereafter was controlled by Rule 14, which provides for separate trials where it appears that a defendant is prejudiced by such joinder. The remaining substantive charges involved an almost identical outline with only the names of the particular defendants and the destination of the stolen goods being different in each count. The trial court was meticulously fair in pointing out to the jurors that evidence against one defendant could in no way be considered against another. This caveat was repeated in the charge to the jury. The trial judge did not abuse the discretion vested in him as to severance, since no prejudice can be shown by the trial record. While the trial judge must be particularly sensitive to the possibility of prejudice in cases such as these, we cannot hold as a hard and fast rule that the failure of a conspiracy charge that forms the basis for joinder must automatically result in severance of the trial on the remaining charges. There was no misjoinder.

DISSENT: (Douglas, J.) While the initial charge of conspiracy was a proper foundation for joinder under Rule 8(b), the failure of proof of that charge removes the basis for joinder. This Court has previously held that joinder is not proper where the only connection between multiple defendants charged with similar offenses is the participation of one defendant in all the charged crimes. The possibility of prejudice by transferred inference of guilt is too strong to allow a joint trial. Showing of prejudice in such an instance is difficult, no matter how strong the possibility. The only sure way to protect against the subtle bond of guilt and attendant prejudice is to sever the trials. This circumstance is distinguishable from the case where both the conspiracy and substantive charges go to the jury and acquittal is rendered on the conspiracy charge but not on the substantive charge.

ANALYSIS

Two critical views were expressed toward this decision. In one, the commentator found that an unscrupulous prosecutor might frame a totally groundless conspiracy charge to support joinder to save the time and expense of separate trials. Since bad faith on the part of the prosecutor is difficult to prove, actual misjoinder may be allowed to persist. Another commentator found that the dissent's view might very well be self-defeating. Since the trial judge may be very reluctant to dismiss and sever after failure of the conspiracy charge, he might

Continued on next page.

very well refuse such dismissal and submit that charge to the jury, confident of an acquittal on that charge.

Quicknotes

ACQUITTAL The discharge of an accused individual from suspicion of guilt for a particular crime and from further prosecution for that offense.

CONSPIRACY Concerted action by two or more persons to accomplish some unlawful purpose.

JOINDER The joining of claims or parties in one lawsuit.

Gray v. Maryland

State (P) v. Accused murderer (D)

523 U.S. 185 (1998)

NATURE OF CASE: Appeal of a criminal conviction for murder.

FACT SUMMARY: When a jury convicted Gray (D) of murder following a trial at which a co-defendant's redacted confession had been introduced, Gray (D) appealed, claiming that his constitutional rights had been violated.

RULE OF LAW

Redacted confessions that replace the proper name with an obvious blank, the word "delete," or a symbol, or that similarly notify the jury that a name has been deleted violate a defendant's Sixth Amendment rights if introduced into evidence insulated from cross examination.

FACTS: Gray (D) and a co-defendant were both indicted for murder. Gray's (D) motion for a separate trial was denied, and Gray (D) was convicted after the co-defendant's redacted confession incriminating Gray (D) was introduced at the joint trial with a limiting instruction. Gray (D) appealed the verdict, claiming that under *Bruton v. United States*, 391 U.S. 123 (1968), his Sixth Amendment rights had been violated.

ISSUE: Do redacted confessions that replace the proper name with an obvious blank, the word "delete," or a symbol, or that similarly notify the jury that a name has been deleted violate a defendant's Sixth Amendment rights if introduced into evidence insulated from cross examination?

HOLDING AND DECISION: (Breyer, J.) Yes. Redacted confessions that replace the proper name with an obvious blank, the word "delete," or a symbol, or that similarly notify the jury that a name has been deleted violate a defendant's Sixth Amendment rights if introduced into evidence insulated from cross examination. Under *Bruton*, the introduction at trial of the powerfully incriminating extrajudicial statements of a co-defendant, who does not testify and cannot be cross-examined, violates a defendant's Sixth Amendment rights. The introduction of the redacted confession of Gray's (D) co-defendant with the blank prominent on its face "facially incriminated" Gray (D). There were no questions of policy to be considered here since the connection of the defendant to the confession did not depend on the introduction of other evidence later in the trial. This case was not like *Richardson v. Marsh*, 481 U.S. 200 (1987), where the confession of the co-defendant had been redacted, eliminating all reference to his co-defendant and any indication that anyone else at all was implicated in the crime, and becoming incriminating only when linked to other evidence. The powerfully incriminating effect of an out-of-court accusation creates a special, and vital, need for cross examination. Redactions that simply replace a name with a blank, leave statements that, considered as a class, so closely resemble *Bruton*'s unredacted statements that, in our view, the law must require the same result. Reversed.

DISSENT: (Scalia, J.) The court's extension of *Bruton* to name-related confessions "as a class" will seriously compromise society's compelling interest in finding, convicting, and punishing those who violate the law. The Court's analogizing of "deleted" to a physical description that clearly identifies the defendant does not survive scrutiny. By "facially incriminating," we have meant incriminating independent of other evidence introduced at trial. The issue is not whether the confession incriminated Gray (D), but whether the incrimination was so "powerful" that we must depart from the normal presumption that the jury follows its instructions. It was not, and the line for departing from the ordinary rule at the facial identification of the defendant makes more sense than drawing it anywhere else.

ANALYSIS

Since the redacted confession in this case referred directly to the "existence" of the nonconfessing co-defendant, the court found more similarities with *Bruton* than with *Richardson*. In *Bruton*, the confession was held to be "incriminating on its face," while in *Richardson*, the confession became incriminating only by inference, and only when "linked" to other evidence. This "linkage" has proved problematic in other cases where the effect of a confession cannot be predicted until after the introduction of all the evidence.

Quicknotes

CROSS EXAMINATION The interrogation of a witness by an adverse party either to further inquire as to the subject matter of the direct examination or to call into question the witness's credibility.

LIMITING INSTRUCTION Directions given by a judge to the jury prior to deliberation to consider or ignore a piece

Continued on next page.

of evidence. Counsel can request the court give a limiting instruction.

REDACT To edit or revise a document.

SIXTH AMENDMENT Provides the right to a speedy trial by impartial jury, the right to be informed of the accusation, the right to confront witnesses, and the right to have the assistance of counsel in all criminal prosecutions.

CHAPTER 20

Speedy Trial and Other Speedy Disposition

Quick Reference Rules of Law

PAGE

1. *Barker v. Wingo.* The determination of whether a defendant has been deprived of his Sixth Amendment right to a speedy trial must be made on a case-by-case basis by balancing the following four factors: (1) length of delay, (2) reason for delay, (3) the defendant's assertion of his right, and (4) prejudice to the defendant. *200*

2. *United States v. Lovasco.* To prosecute a criminal defendant following investigative delay does not deprive him of due process, even if his defense might have been somewhat prejudiced by the lapse of time. *202*

Barker v. Wingo

Murder convict (D) v. Court (P)

407 U.S. 514 (1972)

NATURE OF CASE: Petition for certiorari of a murder conviction.

FACT SUMMARY: Although Barker (D) made no objections during the first four years of a five-year delay between his arrest and conviction for murder, he subsequently claimed that his right to a speedy trial had been violated.

RULE OF LAW

The determination of whether a defendant has been deprived of his Sixth Amendment right to a speedy trial must be made on a case-by-case basis by balancing the following four factors: (1) length of delay, (2) reason for delay, (3) the defendant's assertion of his right, and (4) prejudice to the defendant.

FACTS: On July 20, 1958, an elderly couple was murdered. Shortly afterwards, Silas Manning and Willie Barker (D) were arrested as suspects. On September 15, they were indicted, counsel was appointed on September 17, and Barker's (D) trial was set for October 21. However, Barker (D) was not brought to trial for more than five years after his arrest due to numerous continuances by the prosecution. Initially, the continuances were for the purpose of first convicting Manning, against whom the Commonwealth had a stronger case, to assure his testimony at Barker's (D) trial (i.e., to eliminate problems of self-incrimination). However, Manning was not convicted until 1962. Afterwards, Barker's (D) trial was delayed another seven months due to the illness of the chief investigating officer in the case. During these continuances, Barker (D) was free for all but ten months in jail, and he made no objections during the first four years of delay. However, Barker (D) objected to the last few continuances, and, at his trial, he moved for dismissal on the basis that his Sixth Amendment right to a speedy trial had been violated. This motion was denied, and Barker (D) was convicted of murder. Upon appeal to the Kentucky Court of Appeals, the conviction was affirmed. Barker (D) then petitioned for habeas corpus in the United States District Court. Upon denial of that petition, he appealed to the Court of Appeals for the Sixth Circuit. Upon affirmance of his conviction, Barker (D) brought a petition for certiorari.

ISSUE: Is a delay of five years between the arrest and trial of a defendant a violation per se of his Sixth Amendment right to a speedy trial?

HOLDING AND DECISION: (Powell, J.) No. A delay of five years between the arrest and trial of a defendant is not a violation per se of the defendan'ts right to a speedy trial. The determination of whether a defendant has been deprived of his Sixth Amendment right to a speedy trial must be made on a case-by-case basis by balancing the following four facts: (1) length of delay, (2) reason for delay, (3) the defendant's assertion of his right, and (4) prejudice to the defendant. Since the deprivation of the right to a speedy trial does not per se prejudice the ability of an accused to defend himself, it is impossible to state "with precision" when the right has been denied. Each factor, therefore, must be separately analyzed. First, it is true that a long delay before trial is more likely to be justified for a serious, complex crime (e.g., murder) than for a simple one. Here, however, the delay of more than five years was extreme by any standard. Second, it is true that a delay in bringing an accused to trial may be justified by a showing of some strong reason for it. Here, however, there was a strong reason for delay (i.e., illness of the chief investigator) for only seven months of the five-year delay. Although some additional delay might also have been necessary to acquire Manning as a witness, over four years was clearly unreasonable. Third, it is true that failure to assert the right to a speedy trial will not constitute a waiver of that right, unless it is found to be an "intentional relinquishment or abandonment of a known right." Here, however, it is obvious that Barker (D) did not want a trial at all, hoping, rather, that the delays would ultimately result in dismissal of the charges against him. Fourth, it is true that the prejudice that results from a delay of a defendant's trial must be evaluated in the light of those interests that a speedy trial was designed to protect (i.e., prevention of "oppressive pre-trial incarceration," minimization of anxiety and concern of the accused, and limitation on the possibility that the defense will be "impaired"). Here, however, prejudice was minimal. Although Barker (D) was prejudiced to some extent by spending some time in jail and by living for years under "a cloud of suspicion," none of his witnesses died or became unavailable. In conclusion, the facts that Barker (D) did not want a trial and was not prejudiced by the delay outweigh the unjustified length of delay. Judgment affirmed.

ANALYSIS

This case illustrates (1) the discretion available (through the balancing test) to the courts in determining when the right to a speedy trial has been violated and (2) the

Continued on next page.

emphasis on the desire of an accused to have a speedy trial. Note that an accused "waives" the right to a speedy trial if he flees the state after arraignment or requests postponement of his trial. Note, also, that the right to a speedy trial attaches only after a person is accused (i.e., indicted or arrested) so that it is not violated by a police delay in filing charges. However, if such a delay was purposeful, due process requires dismissal of the charges.

Quicknotes

BALANCING TEST A court's balancing of an individual's constitutional rights against the state's right to protect its citizens.

PRIVILEGE AGAINST SELF-INCRIMINATION A privilege guaranteed by the Fifth Amendment to the U.S. Constitution in a criminal proceeding for communications made by an accused and protecting an accused or witness from having to give testimony that may incriminate him- or herself.

PROCEDURAL DUE PROCESS The constitutional mandate that if the state or federal government acts so as to deny a citizen of a life, liberty, or property interest, the person is first entitled to notice and the right to be heard.

SIXTH AMENDMENT Provides the right to a speedy and public trial by impartial jury, the right to be informed of the accusation, the right to confront witnesses, and the right to have the assistance of counsel in all criminal prosecutions.

United States v. Lovasco

Federal government (P) v. Subsequent indictee (D)

431 U.S. 783 (1977)

NATURE OF CASE: Appeal from dismissal of a criminal indictment.

FACT SUMMARY: The district court dismissed the criminal indictment against Lovasco (D) due to the delay between the commission of the offense and the initiation of prosecution.

RULE OF LAW

To prosecute a criminal defendant following investigative delay does not deprive him of due process, even if his defense might have been somewhat prejudiced by the lapse of time.

FACTS: Although the offenses of possessing firearms stolen from the U.S. mail and dealing in firearms without a license allegedly occurred between July 25 and August 31, 1973, Lovasco (D) was not indicted for those crimes until March 6, 1975. The initial report noted that Lovasco (D) told Government (P) agents just one month after the alleged commission of the crimes that he had possessed and sold five of the stolen guns. By that time, there was also strong evidence linking him to the remaining three weapons. However, the agents were unable to confirm or refute his claim that he had found the guns in his car when he returned to it after visiting his son, a mail handler, at work. Little additional information was uncovered in the 17 months that followed before the initiation of prosecution. Thus, the district court granted Lovasco's (D) motion to dismiss the indictment on the ground that the unreasonable and unnecessary delay in initiating prosecution had prejudiced his defense and thus violated his due process rights. Evidence showed that the two witnesses whom Lovasco (D) claimed would have helped his defense had died, one within nine months and the other more than a year after the initial investigative report on the crimes was completed.

ISSUE: Does prosecuting a criminal defendant following investigative delay deprive him of due process, even if his defense might have been somewhat prejudiced by the lapse of time.

HOLDING AND DECISION: (Marshall, J.) No. Even if a defendant's defense is somewhat prejudiced by the lapse of time between commission of the crimes and initiation of prosecution, prosecuting a defendant following investigative delay does not deprive him of due process. Proof of actual prejudice is a necessary prerequisite to and makes a due process claim concrete and ripe for adjudication, but it does not make the claim automatically valid. The determining question is whether compelling a particular defendant to stand trial after delay in a particular case violates those "fundamental conceptions of justice that lie at the base of our civil and political institutions." *Mooney v. Holohan*, 294 U.S. 103, 112 (1935). It does not in cases like this. Reversed.

ANALYSIS

The court is careful not to say that prejudicial pre-accusation delay could never be a due process violation. This may prove most important in the future, since the Sixth Amendment right to a speedy trial has been found inapplicable to pre-indictment delays.

Quicknotes

PROCEDURAL DUE PROCESS The constitutional mandate that if the state or federal government acts so as to deny a citizen of a life, liberty, or property interest, the person is first entitled to notice and the right to be heard.

RIPENESS A doctrine precluding a federal court from hearing or determining a matter unless it constitutes an actual and present controversy warranting a determination by the court.

CHAPTER 21

Pretrial Discovery and Related Rights

Quick Reference Rules of Law

	PAGE
1. *Williams v. Florida.* A notice-of-alibi rule is not violative of the Fifth and Fourteenth Amendments by compelling a defendant to be a witness against himself.	*204*
2. *Taylor v. Illinois.* A court may forbid a defense witness from testifying as a sanction for the defendant's failure to conduct pretrial discovery in good faith.	*206*
3. *United States v. Bagley.* Evidence is material and must be disclosed to the defense if there is a reasonable probability that, had the evidence been disclosed to the defense, the result of the proceeding would have been different.	*207*

Williams v. Florida

Robbery convict (D) v. State (P)

399 U.S. 78 (1970)

NATURE OF CASE: Appeal from conviction of robbery.

FACT SUMMARY: Florida law requires that a defendant submit to a limited form of pretrial discovery by the state whenever he intends to rely at trial on the defense of alibi.

RULE OF LAW

A notice-of-alibi rule is not violative of the Fifth and Fourteenth Amendments by compelling a defendant to be a witness against himself.

FACTS: Williams (D) was charged with robbery. Prior to his trial, Williams (D) sought a protective order to be excused from complying with a Florida law that requires a defendant, on written demand of the prosecution, to give notice in advance of trial if the defendant intends to claim an alibi and to furnish the prosecution with information as to the place he claims to have been and with the names and addresses of the alibi witnesses he intends to use. Williams (D) wanted to declare his intent to use an alibi but objected to further disclosure on the grounds that the rule would compel him to be a witness against himself in violation of the Fifth and Fourteenth Amendments. The rule also obligated the State (P) to notify a defendant of any rebuttal witnesses to the alibi defense the State (P) will call. Failure to comply, by either side, results in the exclusion of the defendant's alibi evidence or the State's (P) rebuttal evidence. When Williams's (D) motion for the protective order was denied, he complied with the rule. On the morning of his trial, the State (P) interviewed Mrs. Scotty, Williams's (D) chief alibi witness. At trial, Mrs. Scotty gave testimony that contradicted her pretrial statements. The State (P) also furnished a rebuttal witness. Williams (D) was convicted.

ISSUE: Is a notice-of-alibi rule violative of the Fifth and Fourteenth Amendments by compelling a defendant to be a witness against himself?

HOLDING AND DECISION: (White, J.) No. A notice-of-alibi rule is not violative of the Fifth and Fourteenth Amendments by compelling a defendant to be a witness against himself. The rule is fair to both the defendant and the State (P) in permitting liberal discovery. The State (P) has a legitimate interest in protecting itself against eleventh hour defenses: although based on an adversary system, a trial is not yet a poker game in which players may conceal their cards at will. No pretrial statements from Mrs. Scotty were introduced at trial; her pretrial testimony was only urged to find rebuttal witnesses. A defendant is always in a dilemma whether to remain silent or present a defense that may prove disastrous. Nothing in the rule obligates the defendant to rely on an alibi or prevents him from abandoning the defense. The rule only requires that a defendant accelerate the timing of his disclosure of information that he would have revealed at trial anyway. A defendant is not entitled to await the end of the prosecution's case against him before announcing the nature of his defense any more than he can await the jury's verdict on the state's case before deciding to take the stand himself. Absent the rule, the prosecution would be entitled to a continuance at trial on the grounds of surprise; the rule thus serves to prevent a disrupted trial. Affirmed.

CONCURRENCE: (Burger, C.J.) The rule serves an added function of disposing of many cases before trial. If the prosecution interviews the defendant's alibi witnesses, and finds them to be reliable and unimpeachable, it might be strongly inclined to dismiss charges against the defendant. On the other hand, a defendant who knows that his alibi defense will be thoroughly investigated by the prosecution before trial may well be induced to change his plea.

DISSENT: (Black, J.) Before trial the defense counsel can only guess at what the state's case might be. The rule thus compels defendants with any thoughts at all of pleading alibi to be forced to disclose their intentions so as to preserve the possibility of later raising the defense—the decision goes to more than just "timing." Pretrial disclosure will adversely affect the defendant who then decides to forgo raising an alibi defense. His alibi witnesses will still help the prosecution to new leads or evidence. The rule is a clear violation of the Fifth Amendment because it requires a defendant to give information to the state that may destroy him. The entire burden of proving criminal activity rests on the state: no constitutional provision is designed to make conviction easier. The defendant need not do anything to defend or convict himself. While a criminal trial is in part a search for truth, it also is designed to protect "freedom" by ensuring that the state carries its burden. Efficiency is not a consideration. The majority's decision opens the way to compel complete

Continued on next page.

pretrial discovery of a defendant's case, and any defenses he might raise.

ANALYSIS

At the time *Williams* was decided, 15 states other than Florida had notice-of-alibi requirements of varying kinds. One such rule, in *Wardins v. Oregon*, 412 U.S. 470 (1973), was struck down because it failed to provide reciprocal discovery rights to the defendant. The Court found this omission violative of the Due Process Clause of the Fourteenth Amendment. Because exclusion of the testimony of alibi witnesses is a drastic sanction for failure on the defendant's part to comply with the rule's disclosure requirements, other sanctions have been suggested. These include (1) granting a continuance to the prosecution, (2) allowing the prosecution or court to comment on the defendant's failure to the jury, and (3) placing the defense counsel in contempt when the failure was not in "good faith."

Quicknotes

ALIBI Provable documentation of an individual's activities at the time a criminal offense was committed, thereby relieving the individual of possible guilt.

DISCOVERY Pretrial procedure during which one party makes certain information available to the other.

FIFTH AMENDMENT Provides that no person shall be compelled to serve as a witness against him- or herself, be subject to trial for the same offense twice, or be deprived of life, liberty, or property without due process of law.

FOURTEENTH AMENDMENT Declares that no state shall make or enforce any law that shall abridge the privileges and immunities of citizens of the United States; no state shall deny to any person within its jurisdiction the equal protection of the laws.

PRIVILEGE AGAINST SELF-INCRIMINATION A privilege guaranteed by the Fifth Amendment to the U.S. Constitution in a criminal proceeding for communications made by an accused and protecting an accused or witness from having to give testimony that may incriminate him- or herself.

Taylor v. Illinois

Attempted murder convict (D) v. State (P)

484 U.S. 400 (1988)

NATURE OF CASE: Appeal from conviction for attempted murder.

FACT SUMMARY: Taylor (D) contended he was deprived of his right to obtain favorable testimony by the trial court's refusal to allow a witness to testify whose identity had been withheld during pretrial discovery.

RULE OF LAW

A court may forbid a defense witness from testifying as a sanction for the defendant's failure to conduct pretrial discovery in good faith.

FACTS: Taylor (D) was charged with attempted murder. Well in advance of trial, the prosecution moved to compel a list of defense witnesses. Although Taylor's (D) attorney met with and spoke to Wormsley, he did not include this witness on the list. On the second day of trial, Taylor's (D) attorney sought to amend the list and add Wormsley, representing to the court that he (the defense attorney) had just been informed of Wormsley's existence. The court refused to allow Wormsley to testify, and Taylor (D) was convicted. Taylor (D) appealed, contending he had been deprived of his right to present favorable evidence. The appellate court affirmed, and the United States Supreme Court granted a hearing.

ISSUE: May a court forbid a defense witness from testifying as a sanction for a lack of compliance with discovery?

HOLDING AND DECISION: (Stevens, J.) Yes. A court may forbid a defense witness from testifying as a sanction for a lack of compliance with discovery. The Sixth Amendment grants defendants a right to subpoena witnesses. It does not otherwise grant a right to testimony. The Sixth Amendment cannot be used to circumvent the adversary system. The court in this case did not abuse its discretion in precluding the testimony. Judgment of the appellate court is affirmed.

DISSENT: (Brennan, J.) Precluding a criminal defense witness from testifying bears an arbitrary and disproportionate relation to the purposes of discovery, at least absent any evidence that the defendant was personally responsible for the discovery violations. Direct punitive measures, such as contempt, can be used to graduate the punishment to correspond to the severity of a discovery violation.

DISSENT: (Blackmun, J.) Specific remedies for suppression should be fashioned on a case-by-case basis.

ANALYSIS

Criminal discovery is much different from civil discovery. Criminal discovery is greatly restricted and runs heavily in favor of the defense. In civil actions, discovery is very wide and arguably favors neither party. It is generally believed that the apparent willfulness of the behavior in this case was the deciding factor in the use of the rather harsh sanction.

Quicknotes

ATTEMPT An effort or try, combined with the act falling short of the goal intended.

DISCOVERY Pretrial procedure during which one party makes certain information available to the other.

SIXTH AMENDMENT Provides the right to a speedy and public trial by impartial jury, the right to be informed of the accusation, the right to confront witnesses, and the right to have the assistance of counsel in all criminal prosecutions.

United States v. Bagley

Federal government (P) v. Criminal suspect (D)

473 U.S. 667 (1985)

NATURE OF CASE: Appeal from narcotics conviction.

FACT SUMMARY: Bagley (D) contended it was reversible error for the prosecution to fail to disclose a financial arrangement between the state and the prosecution witnesses.

RULE OF LAW

Evidence is material and must be disclosed to the defense if there is a reasonable probability that, had the evidence been disclosed to the defense, the result of the proceeding would have been different.

FACTS: Bagley (D) was arrested for narcotics and firearm violations. His attorney filed a discovery motion seeking evidence of any deals made between the prosecution and witnesses for testimony. The prosecution failed to reveal a financial arrangement with two witnesses, and Bagley (D) appealed his conviction on the ground that he was denied the right to effectively cross-examine the witnesses due to this nondisclosure. The court of appeals reversed, and the United States Supreme Court granted certiorari.

ISSUE: Must evidence be disclosed if there is a reasonable likelihood that had it been disclosed a different result would have resulted?

HOLDING AND DECISION: (Blackmun, J.) Yes. Evidence is material and must be disclosed to the defense if there is a reasonable probability that, had the evidence been disclosed to the defense, the result of the proceeding would have been different. The court of appeals held that the nondisclosure required automatic reversal. However, it made no determination regarding the materiality of the evidence so that application of the present rule could be performed. Reversed and remanded.

CONCURRENCE: (White, J.) The test of materiality does not depend upon the specificity of the defense request.

DISSENT: (Marshall, J.) A presumption of materiality should be adopted, and a rule of automatic reversal applied.

DISSENT: (Stevens, J.) While the result here is correct, a new rule of materiality should not be fashioned.

ANALYSIS

The Court in this case deemphasizes the manner in which the nondisclosure occurs in the analysis of reversible error. Previously, there were three situations analyzed separately which would provide difference levels of materiality. The first was where the prosecution knowingly introduced perjured testimony. The second was the failure to respond to a specific request. The third was where no request was made.

Quicknotes

CROSS-EXAMINATION The interrogation of a witness by an adverse party either to further inquire as to the subject matter of the direct examination or to call into question the witness's credibility.

PERJURY The making of false or misleading statements knowingly under oath.

CHAPTER 22

Guilty Pleas

Quick Reference Rules of Law

	PAGE
1. *Bordenkircher v. Hayes.* It is constitutionally permissible for a prosecutor to try to influence a defendant to accept a plea bargain by informing the defendant that more severe charges will be brought if no bargain is struck.	*210*
2. *United States v. Ruiz.* The Fifth and Sixth Amendments do not require prosecutors, before entering a plea bargain, to disclose impeachment information relating to any informants or other witnesses.	*211*
3. *Missouri v. Frye.* Counsel for criminal defendants has the duty to communicate formal offers from the prosecution with terms and conditions that may be favorable to the defendants.	*213*
4. *Santobello v. New York.* When the prosecution makes a promise regarding sentencing recommendations as an inducement to a guilty plea, the prosecutor may not renege.	*215*
5. *Class v. United States.* A guilty plea does not, by itself, bar a defendant from challenging the constitutionality of the statute of conviction on direct appeal.	*216*

Bordenkircher v. Hayes

Superintendant, Kentucky State Penitentiary (P) v. Forgery convict (D)

434 U.S. 357 (1978)

NATURE OF CASE: Appeal from a criminal conviction and penalty enhancement.

FACT SUMMARY: The prosecutor informed Hayes (D) that he would seek an indictment under the Kentucky Habitual Criminal Act if Hayes (D) did not plead guilty to the charge of uttering a forged instrument. Hayes (D) pled innocent, a jury convicted him, and his sentence was enhanced when the prosecutor initiated the Habitual Criminal indictment.

RULE OF LAW

It is constitutionally permissible for a prosecutor to try to influence a defendant to accept a plea bargain by informing the defendant that more severe charges will be brought if no bargain is struck.

FACTS: Hayes (D), who was charged with uttering a forged instrument (for $88.30), faced a sentence of two to ten years if convicted. The prosecutor offered a five-year sentence in return for a guilty plea and told Hayes (D) that refusal to take the "bargain" would result in his seeking an additional indictment under the Kentucky Habitual Criminal Act, which makes a life sentence mandatory if there are two prior felony convictions. When Hayes (D) declined the plea bargain, he was subjected to the additional indictment and sentenced to life imprisonment under the Habitual Criminal Act, after having been found guilty of the uttering charge. The two previous felonies in which Hayes (D) was involved had never resulted in his imprisonment; one was a rape charge reduced to a plea of detaining a female, and the other was a robbery conviction resulting in five years in a reformatory. Finding the prosecutor to have acted vindictively in securing the second indictment, the court of appeals reversed Hayes's (D) conviction for violation of due process of law.

ISSUE: Is it constitutionally permissible for a prosecutor to try to influence a defendant to accept a plea bargain by informing the defendant that more severe charges will be brought if no bargain is struck?

HOLDING AND DECISION: (Stewart, J.) Yes. As the constitutionality and utility of plea bargaining have been recognized, there is no bar to the prosecutor's use of the possibility of more severe charges being brought for purposes of persuading a defendant to accept a plea bargain. So long as the defendant is advised that the bringing of additional charges will accompany his refusal to bargain, the situation becomes similar to that where the prosecutor offers to drop a charge as part of the plea bargain. If plea bargaining is a recognized process, neither can be forbidden simply because the charging decision is influenced by what a prosecutor hopes to gain in plea bargaining negotiations. In accepting plea bargaining, it is implicit that there is acceptance of the notion that the prosecutor's interest is to persuade the defendant not to exercise his right to plead not guilty. So long as the prosecutor has probable cause to believe the accused committed the offense, and he properly exercises his discretion, decisions not being influenced by standards of race, religion, etc., there is no due process violation. Reversed.

DISSENT: (Blackmun, J.) Past cases indicate that prosecutorial vindictiveness resulting from a defendant's exercise of his rights is a constitutionally impermissible basis for discretionary actions. Here, it is admitted that such vindictiveness was the sole reason for the new indictment.

DISSENT: (Powell, J.) Discretion used to deter the exercise of constitutional rights is not constitutionally exercised. The prosecutor's initial failure to charge indicates his own appreciation of the unreasonableness of placing Hayes (D) in jeopardy of life imprisonment while many murderers and rapists face lighter sentences.

ANALYSIS

Brady v. United States, 397 U.S. 742 (1970), was the case in which the Court first recognized plea bargaining as a legitimate practice. While the majority here suggests that such an acceptance implies sanctioning of prosecutorial use of charging powers to influence a defendant to plead guilty, the *Brady* decision specifically states that it makes no reference to such use by the prosecutor or a similar use by the judge of his sentencing power.

Quicknotes

PLEA BARGAIN An agreement between a prosecutor and a criminal defendant that is submitted to the court for approval; it generally involves the defendant's pleading guilty to a lesser charge or count in exchange for a more lenient sentence.

United States v. Ruiz

Federal government (P) v. Drug possessor (D)

536 U.S. 622 (2002)

NATURE OF CASE: Appeal by Government (P) from the vacating of a sentencing determination.

FACT SUMMARY: Angela Ruiz (D) argued that the Constitution prohibits a defendant from waiving the right to impeachment information before the defendant can enter into a plea agreement.

RULE OF LAW

The Fifth and Sixth Amendments do not require prosecutors, before entering a plea bargain, to disclose impeachment information relating to any informants or other witnesses.

FACTS: After immigration agents found 30 kilograms of marijuana in Angela Ruiz's (D) luggage, federal prosecutors offered her a "fast track" plea bargain in return for which the Government (P) agreed to recommend a more lenient sentence than otherwise would have been mandated. Such plea bargain agreement contained detailed terms, including that the defendant waived the right to receive impeachment information relating to any informants or other witnesses. Because Ruiz (D) would not agree to this waiver, the prosecutors withdrew their bargaining offer. Despite the absence of a plea agreement, Ruiz (D) pled guilty and requested that the sentencing judge grant her the same reduced sentence she would have received if she had accepted the "fast track" plea. The judge refused; however, the federal circuit court vacated the district judge's sentencing determination, taking the position that the Constitution prohibits defendants from waiving their right to impeachment information before they enter into a plea agreement. The Government (P) appealed.

ISSUE: Do the Fifth and Sixth Amendments require prosecutors, before entering a plea bargain, to disclose impeachment information relating to any informants or other witnesses?

HOLDING AND DECISION: (Breyer, J.) No. The Fifth and Sixth Amendments do not require prosecutors, before entering a plea bargain, to disclose impeachment information relating to any informants or other witnesses. Impeachment information is special in relation to the fairness of a trial, not in respect to whether a plea is voluntary ("knowing," "intelligent," and "sufficiently aware"). Of course, the more information the defendant has, the more aware he or she is of the likely consequences of a plea, waiver, or decision, and the wiser that decision will likely be. However, the Constitution does not require the prosecutor to share all useful information with the defendant. The law ordinarily considers a waiver knowing, intelligent, and sufficiently aware if the defendant fully understands the nature of the right and how it would likely apply in general in the circumstances—even though the defendant may not know the specific detailed consequences of invoking it. It is particularly difficult to characterize impeachment information as critical information of which the defendant must always be aware prior to pleading guilty given the random way in which such information may, or may not, help a particular defendant. The degree of help that impeachment information can provide will depend upon the defendant's own independent knowledge of the prosecution's potential case—a matter that the Constitution does not require prosecutors to disclose. Furthermore, since the proposed plea agreement provides that the Government (P) will provide any information establishing the factual innocence of the defendant, that fact, along with other guilty-plea safeguards, diminishes the force of Ruiz's (D) concern that, in the absence of impeachment information, innocent individuals accused of crimes will plead guilty. Reversed.

ANALYSIS

In *Ruiz*, the Supreme Court found no decisional authority to support the Ninth Circuit position of required disclosure of impeachment witnesses. To the contrary, noted the Supreme Court, it would be difficult to distinguish, in terms of importance, (1) a defendant's ignorance of grounds for impeachment of potential witnesses at a possible future trial from (2) the varying forms of ignorance that could be at issue in any particular case.

Quicknotes

FIFTH AMENDMENT Provides that no person shall be compelled to serve as a witness against him or her self, be subject to trial for the same offense twice, or be deprived of life, liberty, or property without due process of law.

IMPEACHMENT The discrediting of a witness by offering evidence to show that the witness lacks credibility.

PLEA BARGAIN An agreement between a prosecutor and a criminal defendant that is submitted to the court for approval; it generally involves the defendant's pleading

Continued on next page.

guilty to a lesser charge or count in exchange for a more lenient sentence.

SIXTH AMENDMENT Provides the right to a speedy and public trial by impartial jury, the right to be informed of the accusation, the right to confront witnesses, and the right to have the assistance of counsel in all criminal prosecutions.

Missouri v. Frye

State (P) v. Convicted individual claiming ineffective assistance of counsel (D)

566 U.S. 134 (2012)

NATURE OF CASE: State's (P) appeal from state appellate court's decision to grant plaintiff postconviction relief.

FACT SUMMARY: Frye's (D) attorney failed to communicate to him a formal plea offer from the prosecution that included more favorable terms than the terms to which Frye (D) eventually pleaded guilty.

RULE OF LAW

Counsel for criminal defendants has the duty to communicate formal offers from the prosecution with terms and conditions that may be favorable to the defendants.

FACTS: In August 2007, Frye (D) was charged with driving with a revoked license. He had been convicted of the same offense on three other occasions. Under Missouri law, the fourth charge allowed the State (P) to charge him with a Class D felony. The felony charge carried a possible four-year prison term. In November, the prosecution sent a formal written plea offer to Frye's (D) counsel with two choices. First, the prosecutor offered a three-year sentence if Frye (D) pleaded guilty to the felony charge, without a recommendation for probation but a requirement that Frye (D) spend ten days "shock" time in jail. The second offer was to reduce the charge to a misdemeanor and have Frye (D) serve 90 days in jail. The misdemeanor charge had a possible one-year maximum sentence. The letter stated the offer would expire on December 28. Frye's (D) counsel never communicated the offer to him, and the plea offers expired. A week before his preliminary hearing on the August 2007 charge, Frye (D) was again arrested for driving with a revoked license. At a subsequent hearing, Frye (D) eventually pleaded guilty to the felony charge and the trial court sentenced him to three years in prison. Following the conviction, Frye (D) filed for postconviction relief in state court on the grounds his attorney's failure to inform him of the plea offers constituted actionable ineffective assistance of counsel. The state trial court denied his petition, but the Missouri Court of Appeals reversed, finding that Frye (D) received ineffective assistance of counsel and that Frye (D) was prejudiced thereby. The United States Supreme Court granted the State of Missouri's (D) petition for review.

ISSUE: Does counsel for criminal defendants have the duty to communicate formal offers from the prosecution with terms and conditions that may be favorable to the defendants?

HOLDING AND DECISION: (Kennedy, J.) Yes. Counsel for criminal defendants has the duty to communicate formal offers from the prosecution with terms and conditions that may be favorable to the defendants. When a defense counsel fails to communicate a plea offer to his or her client, that failure constitutes actionable ineffective assistance of counsel under the Constitution. This holding is supported by the reality that more than 94 percent of state criminal convictions are the result of guilty pleas. That is only one part of the analysis. The convicted defendant must also show the ineffective assistance of counsel caused him prejudice in the criminal proceedings. To show prejudice when an attorney fails to communicate a plea offer, the defendant must demonstrate a reasonable probability that he would have accepted the earlier plea offer had he been aware of it. Significantly, defendants must also show that the prosecution would not have canceled the plea deal or that the trial court would not have rejected the agreement. This is relevant because some states allow prosecutors the discretion to cancel a plea agreement up to the moment the agreement is accepted by the court. This further showing is also important because a defendant has no constitutional right to be offered a plea agreement and no right that the judge accepts the agreement. In the instant case, Frye (D) can show he would have accepted the offer to plead guilty to the lesser misdemeanor charge. However, Frye's (D) subsequent arrest for the same offense one week prior to his hearing complicates matters for him. It is not entirely clear that the prosecution would not have canceled the agreement based on that new arrest. Nor is it clear that the trial court would have agreed to the plea deal. Accordingly, it is appropriate to remand the case to the Missouri Court of Appeals for it to consider whether the prosecution and the trial court would have agreed to the plea offer of the lesser misdemeanor charge in light of Frye's (D) new arrest for the same offense. Remanded for consideration of state-law questions before an appeal decision.

DISSENT: (Scalia, J.) The majority improperly constitutionalizes the plea-bargaining process in criminal cases. While it is clear Frye (D) received ineffective assistance of counsel, it is not entirely clear he was prejudiced thereby. The majority's reasonability probability test is nothing more than crystal ball gazing masquerading as legal analysis. There are no cases that discuss the standard

Continued on next page.

for a prosecutor's withdrawal from a plea agreement or a trial court's authority to accept or reject a plea deal. In most states, the trial court has broad discretion to accept or reject such agreements. The judicial branch should not create precedents based upon what prosecutors and judges might have done in the past. State legislatures are better equipped to regulate the plea-bargain process, starting by imposing punishments upon a defense counsel's right to practice when counsel fails to communicate valid plea offers to his or her clients. However, in this case, Frye (D) was not prejudiced because he pleaded guilty to the felony charge after the usual colloquy with the trial court judge that assured his guilty plea was voluntary and truthful.

ANALYSIS

The majority's decision was based on the prevalent use of plea bargains in criminal prosecutions, both at the state and federal level. In addition to the 94 percent of convictions in state cases resulting from plea bargains, 97 percent of convictions in federal court are similarly the result of plea negotiations. Note that the majority's holding is narrow: where a plea offer is made, the defense counsel must communicate it to his or her clients. The Court refrained from adjudicating on any strategic decisions defense counsel may make during those plea negotiations.

Quicknotes

INEFFECTIVE ASSISTANCE OF COUNSEL A claim brought by an accused in which it must be determined whether the attorney's rendering of representation was such that the ultimate disposition of the case may not be relied upon as fair.

PLEA BARGAIN An agreement between a prosecutor and a criminal defendant that is submitted to the court for approval; it generally involves the defendant's pleading guilty to a lesser charge or count in exchange for a more lenient sentence.

Santobello v. New York

Convicted felon (D) v. State (P)

404 U.S. 257 (1971)

NATURE OF CASE: Review of sentence following plea of guilty to a felony.

FACT SUMMARY: After a prosecutor promised no recommendation regarding sentencing, as an inducement to a guilty plea, a different prosecutor did recommend a sentence.

RULE OF LAW

When the prosecution makes a promise regarding sentencing recommendations as an inducement to a guilty plea, the prosecutor may not renege.

FACTS: Santobello (D) was charged with a felony. As an inducement to plead guilty, the prosecutor promised no recommendation regarding sentencing. Santobello (D) pled guilty. At the sentencing hearing, a different prosecutor recommended the maximum sentence, which the judge imposed. Santobello (D) moved to withdraw his plea. This was denied, and the court of appeals affirmed. The United States Supreme Court granted review.

ISSUE: When the prosecution makes a promise regarding sentencing recommendations as an inducement to a guilty plea, may the prosecution renege?

HOLDING AND DECISION: (Burger, C.J.) No. When the prosecution makes a promise regarding sentencing recommendations as an inducement to a guilty plea, the prosecution may not renege. To preserve the integrity of the plea-bargaining process, due process requires the prosecution to live up to whatever promises it made to induce the guilty plea. Here, the prosecution reneged on a promise regarding sentencing. This was impermissible. [The Court then remanded to the trial court to determine whether Santobello (D) should be permitted to withdraw his guilty plea or merely be resentenced.]

CONCURRENCE: (Douglas, J.) The defendant's preference as to disposition in a case like this should be given considerable, if not controlling, weight.

CONCURRENCE AND DISSENT: (Marshall, J.) Where a defendant wishes to withdraw his plea of guilty after the prosecution reneges on a sentencing promise, he should be allowed to withdraw his plea as a matter of right.

ANALYSIS

A plea bargain is, in essence, a contract. This being so, it is logical to analogize the law of contracts to cases of broken plea bargain. This is to a large extent the rule. Differences do exist between plea bargains and typical contracts. The most important of these is that plea bargains have a constitutional dimension not usually found in contract law.

Quicknotes

FELONY A criminal offense of greater seriousness than a misdemeanor; felonies are generally defined pursuant to statute as any crime that is punishable by death or by a term of imprisonment exceeding one year.

PLEA BARGAIN An agreement between a prosecutor and a criminal defendant that is submitted to the court for approval; it generally involves the defendant's pleading guilty to a lesser charge or count in exchange for a more lenient sentence.

Class v. United States

Defendant admitting guilt pursuant to plea agreement (D) v. Federal government (P)

583 U.S. ___, 138 S. Ct. 798 (2018)

NATURE OF CASE: Appeal by defendant challenging the constitutionality of the statute of conviction after the defendant entered a guilty plea pursuant to a plea agreement.

FACT SUMMARY: Class (D), who pleaded guilty, pursuant to a written plea agreement, to possessing firearms in his vehicle on the grounds of the U.S. Capitol, sought to challenge the constitutionality of the statute of conviction.

RULE OF LAW

A guilty plea does not, by itself, bar a defendant from challenging the constitutionality of the statute of conviction on direct appeal.

FACTS: Class (D) pleaded guilty to possessing firearms in his vehicle on the grounds of the U.S. Capitol. His written plea agreement specified certain rights he waived and certain rights he could raise on appeal. However, the agreement was silent as to whether Class (D) could challenge the constitutionality of the statute of conviction. Class (D) then brought a direct appeal to challenge the constitutionality of the statute of conviction, but the court held that he could not do so because by pleading guilty, he had waived his constitutional claims. The United States Supreme Court granted certiorari.

ISSUE: Does a guilty plea, by itself, bar a defendant from challenging the constitutionality of the statute of conviction on direct appeal?

HOLDING AND DECISION: (Breyer, J.) No. A guilty plea does not, by itself, bar a defendant from challenging the constitutionality of the statute of conviction on direct appeal. This holding flows directly from the Court's precedents. In *Haynes v. United States*, 390 U.S. 85 (1968), the Court addressed a similar claim challenging the constitutionality of a criminal statute and concluded that the defendant's plea of guilty did not waive his previous constitutional claim. Then, in *Blackledge v. Perry*, 417 U.S. 21 (1974), the Court recognized that although a guilty plea bars some antecedent constitutional violations related to events (such as grand jury proceedings) that occur prior to the entry of the guilty plea, where the claim implicates the very power of the state to prosecute the defendant, a guilty plea cannot by itself bar it. Likewise, in *Menna v. New York*, 423 U.S. 61 (1975), the Court held that because the defendant's claim was that the state could not constitutionally convict the defendant, no matter how validly his factual guilt was established, his guilty plea did not bar the claim. The Court has reaffirmed the *Menna-Blackledge* doctrine's basic teaching that a plea of guilty to a charge does not waive a claim that—judged on its face—the charge is one that the state may not constitutionally prosecute, but has also held that such a claim may be foreclosed where the defendant is unable to prove the claim without contradicting the indictment and the admissions inherent in the guilty plea. Here, however, Class's (D) constitutional claims do not contradict the terms of the indictment or the written plea agreement. They are consistent with Class's (D) knowing, voluntary, and intelligent admission that he did what the indictment alleged. Those claims thus can be resolved without any need to venture beyond the record. Class (D) challenges the Government's (P) power to criminalize his (admitted) conduct and thereby calls into question the Government's (P) power to constitutionally prosecute him. A guilty plea does not bar a direct appeal in these circumstances. The Government (P) and the dissent argue that Rule 11(a)(2) of the Federal Rules of Criminal Procedure (Fed. R. Crim. P.) means that a defendant who pleads guilty cannot challenge his conviction on appeal on a forfeitable or waivable ground that he either failed to present to the district court or failed to reserve in writing. The problem with this argument is that, by its own terms, Rule 11(a)(2) itself does not say whether it sets forth the exclusive procedure for a defendant to preserve a constitutional claim following a guilty plea. At the same time, the drafters' notes acknowledge that the Supreme Court has held, in the *Menna-Blackledge* doctrine, that certain kinds of constitutional objections may be raised after a plea of guilty.

DISSENT: (Alito, J.) Neither the Constitution nor any statute or rule bars waiver of personal constitutional rights such as those raised by Class (D). To the contrary, Fed. R. Crim. P. Rule 11 makes clear that, with one exception for the *Menna-Blackledge* doctrine, a defendant who enters an unconditional plea waives all nonjurisdictional claims. Close scrutiny of *Blackledge* and *Menna*, however, reveals that their rationales are muddled and difficult to follow—and do not flow from prior precedents. *Blackledge* could be interpreted to refer to jurisdictional attacks post-guilty plea, but that would not make sense since arguments attacking a court's subject-matter jurisdiction can neither be waived nor forfeited. The case could also be seen as distinguishing between a defendant's right not to be tried, as opposed to a right not to be convicted, but the Court has indicated that even when a constitutional violation requires the dismissal of

Continued on next page.

an indictment, that does not mean that the defendant enjoyed a right not to be tried on the charges. The rule could hardly be otherwise. Most constitutional defenses and many statutory defenses, if successfully asserted in a pretrial motion, deprive the prosecution of the "power" to proceed to trial or secure a conviction. If that remedial consequence converted them all into rights not to be prosecuted, *Blackledge* would have no discernible limit. *Menna* makes even less sense in this context. The reasoning in *Menna* seems to be that a defendant who pleads guilty does no more than admit that he committed the essential conduct charged in the indictment; therefore, a guilty plea allows the litigation on appeal of any claim that is not inconsistent with the facts that the defendant necessarily admitted. If that is the correct interpretation, however, *Menna* would overrule many of the cases that it purported to distinguish, and it would contradict much that the Court had previously said about the effect of a guilty plea. When the Court returned to *Blackledge* and *Menna* in *United States v. Broce,* 488 U.S. 563 (1989), the Court essentially repudiated the theories offered in those earlier cases. The Court clarified that an unconditional guilty plea admits all of the factual and legal elements necessary to sustain a binding, final judgment of guilt and a lawful sentence, so that by entering a guilty plea, the accused is not simply stating that he did the discrete acts described in the indictment but is admitting guilt of a substantive crime. Thus, the Court concluded, a defendant's decision to plead guilty necessarily extinguishes whatever potential defenses he might have asserted in an effort to show that it would be unlawful to hold him liable for his conduct. As for *Blackledge, Broce* rejected the idea that a right not to be tried survives an unconditional guilty plea. In sum, the governing law in the present case is Rule 11 of the Federal Rules of Criminal Procedure. Under that Rule, an unconditional guilty plea waives all nonjurisdictional claims with the possible exception of the "*Menna-Blackledge* doctrine" created years ago by this Court. That doctrine is vacuous, has no sound foundation, and produces nothing but confusion.

ANALYSIS

With *Class*, the Court resolved a split among the Circuit Courts as to whether a guilty plea waives a defendant's right to challenge the constitutionality of the statute of conviction. Prior to *Class*, the Circuits were split as to whether a guilty plea waived as-applied, but not facial, challenges to the statute of conviction, whether the plea did not waive either facial or as-applied challenges, and whether the plea waived both facial and as-applied challenges. Although the Court's decision theoretically could increase the number of post-guilty plea constitutional challenges to statutes of conviction, especially since, as Justice Alito notes, roughly 95 percent of felony cases in the federal and state courts are resolved by guilty pleas, the reality is that very few convictions are set aside on the basis of the unconstitutionality of the statute of conviction. Thus, the ultimate impact of *Class* may be minimal.

Quicknotes

GUILTY PLEA A formal acknowledgment of guilt as to the commission of a criminal offense that is made by a defendant in court, after the defendant has been advised of his rights and the court finds that such plea has been made voluntarily and intelligently.

WAIVER The intentional or voluntary forfeiture of a recognized right.

CHAPTER 23

Trial by Jury and Impartial Judge

Quick Reference Rules of Law

	PAGE
1. *Taylor v. Louisiana.* The exclusion of a segment of society from jury duty is sufficient to establish a per se violation of a defendant's constitutional right to a trial by jury of his peers guaranteed under the Sixth Amendment.	*220*
2. *Batson v. Kentucky.* A prosecutor cannot use peremptory challenges to keep members of the defendant's race off the jury on the assumption that they will not be impartial.	*221*

Taylor v. Louisiana

Kidnapping convict (P) v. State (D)

419 U.S. 522 (1975)

NATURE OF CASE: Appeal from criminal conviction on the basis that the jury was unconstitutionally constituted.

FACT SUMMARY: A Louisiana statute provided that women would be exempt from jury duty unless they specifically requested to serve.

RULE OF LAW

The exclusion of a segment of society from jury duty is sufficient to establish a per se violation of a defendant's constitutional right to a trial by jury of his peers guaranteed under the Sixth Amendment.

FACTS: Louisiana enacted a statute that provided women should not be selected for jury duty unless they filed a specific request to serve. The practical effect of this provision was that women (constituting 53 percent of potential jurors) were virtually unrepresented on juries within Louisiana (D). Taylor (P) was convicted of aggravated kidnapping. Taylor (P) moved to quash the conviction on the basis that no women were available to sit on the jury that tried him. Taylor (P) claimed that this violated his right to a trial by jury of his peers (i.e., a fair cross-segment of the community). This was violative of the Sixth Amendment that was made applicable to the states under the Fourteenth Amendment to the U.S. Constitution. The motion was denied by the trial court.

ISSUE: Is the exclusion of a segment of society from jury duty sufficient to establish a per se violation of a defendant's constitutional right to a trial by jury of his peers guaranteed under the Sixth Amendment?

HOLDING AND DECISION: (White, J.) Yes. The exclusion of a segment of society from jury duty is sufficient to establish a per se violation of a defendant's right to a trial by a jury of his peers guaranteed under the Sixth Amendment. A defendant is entitled to be tried by a representative cross-section of his community. The failure to provide such a cross-section is violative of the Sixth Amendment's constitutional guarantee of a trial by jury. It does not matter that the defendant has not established discrimination, for it is immaterial. The fact that he is a man and only women are being excluded is also immaterial. A caucasian may complain that Blacks are being excluded. The blanket exemption for women has the effect of practically excluding them from jury panels. The role of women in society (i.e., mothers) is insufficient grounds for the issuance of a blanket exemption. Liberal, specific exemptions are allowed where individual facts warrant. Since the jury was unrepresentative, the conviction must be overturned. Reversed and remanded.

DISSENT: (Rehnquist, J.) The conviction should not have been overturned without a showing of prejudice. There is no sound policy ground for arbitrarily overturning this conviction.

ANALYSIS

In *Hamling v. United States*, 418 U.S. 87 (1974), the Court held that exclusion of the young through a failure to update the master jury wheel for four years was not a per se violation of the defendant's Sixth Amendment guarantees. It would require a showing of prejudice to require a reversal of the conviction. The mere fact that persons who have become eligible for jury duty have been excluded is insufficient to establish purposeful discrimination. This last fact is what differentiates *Hamling* from *Taylor*.

Quicknotes

QUASH To vacate, annul, void.

RIGHT TO JURY TRIAL The right guaranteed by the Sixth Amendment to the U.S. Constitution that in all criminal prosecutions the accused has a right to a trial by an impartial jury of the state and district in which the crime was allegedly committed.

Batson v. Kentucky

Black defendant (D) v. State (P)

476 U.S. 79 (1986)

NATURE OF CASE: Appeal of rejection of challenge to practice of exercising peremptory challenges to keep people of certain races off juries.

FACT SUMMARY: The prosecutor exercised his peremptory challenges to keep Black people off the jury in the trial of Batson (D), a Black man.

RULE OF LAW

A prosecutor cannot use peremptory challenges to keep members of the defendant's race off the jury on the assumption that they will not be impartial.

FACTS: During the jury selection process of the trial of Batson (D), the prosecutor used his peremptory challenges to disqualify all Black people from the jury. Batson (D), a Black man, argued that this constituted a violation of equal protection. The trial court rejected his contentions, and the Kentucky Supreme Court agreed. Batson (D) appealed.

ISSUE: May a prosecutor use peremptory challenges to keep members of the defendant's race off the jury on the assumption that they will not be impartial?

HOLDING AND DECISION: (Powell, J.) No. A prosecutor may not use peremptory challenges to keep members of the defendant's race off the jury on the assumption that they will not be impartial. Such generalizations are precisely what the Equal Protection Clause was meant to remove and cannot be approved, even when a time-honored practice such as peremptory challenges is concerned. If a defendant can demonstrate a pattern of racially motivated peremptory challenges in the selection of his jury, the burden falls on the prosecutor to make a legitimate explanation. Here, the prosecutor made no explanation at all. Reversed.

CONCURRENCE: (Marshall, J.) Peremptory challenges offer such a great potential for abuse that they should be abolished in the criminal justice system entirely.

DISSENT: (Burger, C.J.) Peremptory challenges are inherently based on hunches and other intangibles and one exercising them should not have to explain his or her reasons. The rule announced here can interfere with the defendant's use of peremptories if it is ever applied to him, which is likely.

DISSENT: (Rehnquist, J.) Where a party of any race may exclude members of any other race through peremptories, equal protection is not violated.

ANALYSIS

Justice Rehnquist makes an interesting argument. According to him, so long as no particular race is precluded from using peremptories to keep off the jury members of any other race, no discrimination exists. This argument obviously would be wrong in most contexts, but in as fluid an area as peremptory challenges it makes some sense, although practically speaking, Black defendants have suffered most from the practice.

Quicknotes

EQUAL PROTECTION Guarantee under the Fourteenth Amendment to the U.S. Constitution that the government must treat each person or class of persons the same as it treats other persons or classes of persons in like circumstances.

PEREMPTORY CHALLENGE A challenge issued by counsel during voir dire proceedings to refuse a jury seat to a prospective juror, for which no reason need be advanced other than the preference of counsel advocating exclusion.

CHAPTER 24

First Amendment Interests vs. Fair Trials

Quick Reference Rules of Law

	PAGE
1. *Skilling v. United States.* Pretrial publicity and community prejudice do not prevent a criminal defendant from obtaining a fair trial where the presumption of juror prejudice that these conditions create is rebutted by a showing that voir dire has been proper and thorough, so that an impartial jury has in fact been empaneled, and there is no showing that actual bias infected the jury that tried the defendant.	*224*

Skilling v. United States

Convicted criminal (D) v. Federal government (P)

561 U.S. 358 (2010)

NATURE OF CASE: Appeal from affirmance of conviction of conspiracy to commit "honest-services" wire fraud in violation of 18 U.S.C. §§ 371, 1343, and 1346.

FACT SUMMARY: Skilling (D), a former chief executive officer of the collapsed Enron Corporation who was convicted of conspiracy to commit "honest-services" wire fraud in violation of 18 U.S.C. §§ 371, 1343, and 1346 (among other crimes), contended that pretrial publicity and community prejudice prevented him from obtaining a fair trial and that the jury improperly convicted him of conspiracy to commit honest-services wire fraud.

RULE OF LAW

Pretrial publicity and community prejudice do not prevent a criminal defendant from obtaining a fair trial where the presumption of juror prejudice that these conditions create is rebutted by a showing that voir dire has been proper and thorough, so that an impartial jury has in fact been empaneled, and there is no showing that actual bias infected the jury that tried the defendant.

FACTS: Founded in 1985, Enron Corporation (Enron) grew from its headquarters in Houston, Texas, into the seventh highest revenue-grossing company in America. Skilling (D), a longtime Enron officer, was Enron's chief executive officer (CEO) for about half a year when he resigned. Less than four months later, Enron crashed into bankruptcy, and its stock plummeted in value. After an investigation uncovered an elaborate conspiracy to prop up Enron's stock prices by overstating the company's financial well-being, the Government (P) prosecuted dozens of Enron employees who participated in the scheme. In time, the Government (P) worked its way up the chain of command, indicting Skilling (D) and two other top Enron executives. These three defendants, the indictment charged, engaged in a scheme to deceive investors about Enron's true financial performance by manipulating its publicly reported financial results and making false and misleading statements. Count 1 of the indictment charged Skilling (D) with, inter alia, conspiracy to commit "honest-services" wire fraud, 18 U.S.C. §§ 371, 1343, and 1346, by depriving Enron and its shareholders of the intangible right of his honest services. Skilling (D) was also charged with over 25 substantive counts of securities fraud, wire fraud, making false representations to Enron's auditors, and insider trading. Skilling (D) moved for a change of venue, contending that hostility toward him in Houston, coupled with extensive pretrial publicity, poisoned potential jurors. He submitted hundreds of news reports detailing Enron's downfall, as well as affidavits from experts he engaged portraying community attitudes in Houston in comparison to other potential venues. The district court denied the motion, concluding that pretrial publicity did not warrant a presumption that Skilling (D) would be unable to obtain a fair trial in Houston. Despite incidents of intemperate commentary, the court observed, media coverage, on the whole, had been objective and unemotional, and the facts of the case were neither heinous nor sensational. Moreover, the court asserted, effective voir dire would detect juror bias. In the months before the trial, the court asked the parties for questions it might use to screen prospective jurors. Rejecting the Government's (P) sparer inquiries in favor of Skilling's (D) more probing and specific questions, the court converted Skilling's (D) submission, with slight modifications, into a 77-question, 14-page document. The questionnaire asked prospective jurors about their sources of news and exposure to Enron-related publicity, beliefs concerning Enron and what caused its collapse, opinions regarding the defendants and their possible guilt or innocence, and relationships to the company and to anyone affected by its demise. The court then mailed the questionnaire to 400 prospective jurors and received responses from nearly all of them. It granted hardship exemptions to about 90 individuals, and the parties, with the court's approval, further winnowed the pool by excusing another 119 for cause, hardship, or physical disability. The parties agreed to exclude, in particular, every prospective juror who said that a preexisting opinion about Enron or the defendants would prevent him or her from being impartial. Three weeks before the trial date, one of Skilling's (D) co-defendants, Causey, pleaded guilty. Skilling (D) renewed his change-of-venue motion, arguing that the juror questionnaires revealed pervasive bias and that news accounts of Causey's guilty plea further tainted the jury pool. The court again declined to move the trial, ruling that the questionnaires and voir dire provided safeguards adequate to ensure an impartial jury. The court also denied Skilling's (D) request for attorney-led voir dire on the grounds that potential jurors were more forthcoming with judges than with lawyers. But the court promised to give counsel an opportunity to ask follow-up questions, agreed that venire members should be examined individually about pretrial publicity, and allotted the defendants jointly two extra peremptory challenges. When voir dire began, after questioning the venire as a group, the court examined prospective jurors

Continued on next page.

individually, asking each about her or his exposure to Enron-related news, the content of any stories that stood out in his or her mind, and any questionnaire answers that raised a red flag signaling possible bias. The court then permitted each side to pose follow-up questions and ruled on the parties' challenges for cause. Ultimately, the court qualified 38 prospective jurors, a number sufficient, allowing for peremptory challenges, to empanel 12 jurors and 4 alternates. After a four-month trial, the jury found Skilling (D) guilty of 19 counts, including the honest-services-fraud conspiracy charge, and not guilty of nine insider-trading counts. On appeal, Skilling (D) contended that pretrial publicity and community prejudice prevented him from obtaining a fair trial. Second, he alleged that the jury improperly convicted him of conspiracy to commit honest-services wire fraud. The court of appeals determined that the volume and negative tone of media coverage generated by Enron's collapse created a presumption of juror prejudice. Stating, however, that the presumption was rebuttable, the court examined the voir dire, found it "proper and thorough," and held that the district court had empaneled an impartial jury. The United States Supreme Court granted certiorari.

ISSUE: Do pretrial publicity and community prejudice prevent a criminal defendant from obtaining a fair trial where the presumption of juror prejudice that these conditions create is rebutted by a showing that voir dire has been proper and thorough, so that an impartial jury has in fact been empaneled, and there is no showing that actual bias infected the jury that tried the defendant?

HOLDING AND DECISION: (Ginsburg, J.) No. Pretrial publicity and community prejudice do not prevent a criminal defendant from obtaining a fair trial where the presumption of juror prejudice that these conditions create is rebutted by a showing that voir dire has been proper and thorough, so that an impartial jury has in fact been empaneled, and there is no showing that actual bias infected the jury that tried the defendant. Although the Sixth Amendment and Art. III, § 2, cl. 3, provide for criminal trials in the state and district where the crime was committed, these place-of-trial prescriptions do not impede transfer of a proceeding to a different district if extraordinary local prejudice will prevent a fair trial. Thus, in the past, the Court has not hesitated to reverse convictions where the proceedings were so tainted by media prejudice that they were akin to the proceedings of a kangaroo court. However, the Court also has indicated that juror exposure to news accounts of the crime alone does not presumptively deprive a defendant of due process. In other words, prominence does not necessarily produce prejudice, and juror impartiality does not require ignorance. Thus, a presumption of prejudice attends only the extreme case. Important differences separate Skilling's (D) prosecution from those in which the Court has presumed juror prejudice. First, the Court has emphasized the size and characteristics of the community in which the crime occurred. In contrast to the small-town setting in past cases, Houston is the country's fourth most populous city. Given the large, diverse pool of residents eligible for jury duty, any suggestion that 12 impartial individuals could not be empaneled in Houston is hard to sustain. Second, although news stories about Skilling (D) were not kind, they contained no blatantly prejudicial information. Third, unlike cases in which trial swiftly followed a widely reported crime, over four years elapsed between Enron's bankruptcy and Skilling's (D) trial. Although reporters covered Enron-related news throughout this period, the decibel level of media attention diminished somewhat in the years following Enron's collapse. Finally, and of prime significance, Skilling's (D) jury acquitted him of nine insider-trading counts. Similarly, earlier instituted Enron-related prosecutions yielded no overwhelming victory for the Government (P). Given all these circumstances, it would be odd for an appellate court to presume prejudice in a case in which jurors' actions run counter to that presumption, as here. The court of appeals presumed juror prejudice based primarily on the magnitude and negative tone of the media attention directed at Enron. However, "pretrial publicity—even pervasive, adverse publicity—does not inevitably lead to an unfair trial." Here, news stories about Enron did not present the kind of vivid, unforgettable information the Court has recognized as particularly likely to produce prejudice, and Houston's size and diversity diluted the media's impact. Nor did Enron's sheer number of victims trigger a presumption. Although the widespread community impact necessitated careful identification and inspection of prospective jurors' connections to Enron, the extensive screening questionnaire and follow-up voir dire yielded jurors whose links to Enron were either nonexistent or attenuated. Finally, while Causey's well-publicized decision to plead guilty shortly before trial created a danger of juror prejudice, the district court took appropriate steps to mitigate that risk. For all these reasons, the district court did not violate the Constitution by refusing to order a change of venue. The next issue is whether actual prejudice contaminated Skilling's (D) jury. The short answer is that it did not. No hard-and-fast formula dictates the necessary depth or breadth of voir dire. Jury selection is "particularly within the province of the trial judge." When pretrial publicity is at issue, moreover, "primary reliance on the judgment of the trial court makes [especially] good sense" because the judge "sits in the locale where the publicity is said to have had its effect" and may base her evaluation on her "own perception of the depth and extent of news stories that might influence a juror." The in-the-moment voir dire affords the trial court a more intimate and immediate

Continued on next page.

basis for assessing a venire member's fitness for jury service. Skilling (D) failed to show that his voir dire fell short of constitutional requirements. The jury-selection process was insufficient, Skilling (D) maintained, because voir dire lasted only five hours, most of the district court's questions were conclusory and failed adequately to probe jurors' true feelings, and the court consistently took prospective jurors at their word once they claimed they could be fair, regardless of other indications of bias. A review of the record, however, yields a different appraisal. The district court initially screened venire members by eliciting their responses to a comprehensive questionnaire drafted in large part by Skilling (D). That survey helped to identify prospective jurors excusable for cause and served as a springboard for further questions; voir dire thus was the culmination of a lengthy process. Moreover, inspection of the questionnaires and voir dire of the seated jurors reveals that, notwithstanding the flaws Skilling (D) lists, the selection process secured jurors largely uninterested in publicity about Enron and untouched by the corporation's collapse. Whatever community prejudice existed in Houston generally, Skilling's (D) jurors were not under its sway. Skilling (D) also asserts the district court should not have accepted jurors' promises of fairness, but the district court did not have good reasons to discredit jurors' assurances of impartiality: News stories about Enron did not contain horrifying information; Houston is not, for example, a rural community; circulation figures for Houston media sources showed that not nearly everyone in Houston was reached by media reports about Enron; and Skilling's (D) seated jurors exhibited no display of unmitigated bias. In any event, the district court did not simply take venire members at their word. It questioned each juror individually to uncover concealed bias. This face-to-face opportunity to gauge demeanor and credibility, coupled with information from the questionnaires regarding jurors' backgrounds, opinions, and news sources, gave the court a sturdy foundation to assess fitness for jury service. On these facts, the voir dire did not fall short of constitutional requirements. Finally, Skilling's (D) allegation that several jurors were openly biased also fails. In reviewing such claims, the deference due to district courts is at its pinnacle. First, Skilling (D) unsuccessfully challenged only one of the seated jurors for cause. This is "strong evidence that he was convinced the [other] jurors were not biased and had not formed any opinions as to his guilt." Additionally, a review of the record reveals no manifest error regarding the empaneling of other jurors, each of whom indicated, inter alia, that he or she would be fair to Skilling (D) and would require the Government (P) to prove its case. Affirmed.

CONCURRENCE: (Alito, J.) Where there is extraordinary pretrial publicity, there is no presumption of juror prejudice. A properly conducted voir dire can ensure that the panel will be populated with impartial jurors. Trial judges can also take steps once a jury is seated to shield the jury from the media. There is no simply no way to measure the level of pretrial publicity that must be attained before a change in venue must occur.

CONCURRENCE AND DISSENT: (Sotomayor, J.) As a factual matter, the majority is incorrect about the level of hostility in Houston directed toward Enron and Skilling (D) and about the adequacy of the district court's handling of voir dire. First, the majority understates the breadth and depth of community hostility toward Skilling (D) and Enron. For example, Enron's community ties were so extensive that the entire local U.S. Attorney's Office was forced to recuse itself from the Government's (P) investigation into the company's fall. With Enron's demise affecting the lives of so many Houstonians, local media coverage of the story saturated the community. While many of the thousands of media stories were straightforward news items, many others conveyed and amplified the community's outrage at the top executives perceived to be responsible for the company's bankruptcy. Articles deriding Enron's senior executives were juxtaposed with pieces expressing sympathy toward and solidarity with the company's many victims, and the media overwhelmingly indicated that Skilling's (D) indictment was overdue when it finally occurred. Given this acute state of animus, the district court's handling of voir dire fell short of constitutional requirements. The questionnaires returned to the court indicated that more than one-third of the prospective jurors indicated that they or persons they knew had lost money or jobs as a result of the Enron bankruptcy. Two-thirds of the jurors expressed views about Enron or the defendants that suggested a potential predisposition to convict. In many instances, they did not mince words, describing Skilling (D) as "smug," "arrogant," "brash," "conceited," "greedy," "deceitful," "totally unethical and criminal," "a crook," "the biggest liar on the face of the earth," and "guilty as sin." Ultimately, numerous individuals who had made harsh comments about Skilling (D) remained in the jury pool. From this, the court of appeals determined that prejudice was to be presumed, but that this presumption was rebuttable, thus turning the concept of presumptive prejudice into a burden-shifting framework: Once the defendant musters sufficient evidence of community hostility, the onus shifts to the government to prove the impartiality of the jury. However, the Court's precedents have never treated the notion of presumptive prejudice so formalistically. Instead, they convey the commonsense understanding that as the tide of public enmity rises, so too does the danger that the prejudices of the community will infiltrate the jury. The underlying question has, therefore, always been: Do we have confidence that the jury's verdict was "induced only by evidence and argument in open court, and not by any outside influence,

Continued on next page.

whether of private talk or public print?" On one end of the spectrum, the Court has reversed, without considering the sufficiency of voir dire, a conviction where the Court found inherently prejudicial circumstances. In another case, the Court reversed the conviction where it found that voir dire did not suffice to counter the "wave of public passion" that had swept the community prior to the defendant's trial—despite the seated jurors' assurances of impartiality. In that case, the Court emphasized that a juror's word on whether he or she can be impartial is not decisive, particularly when "the build-up of prejudice [in the community] is clear and convincing." Here, the majority was correct that the prospect of seating an unbiased jury in Houston was not so remote as to compel the conclusion that the district court acted unconstitutionally in denying Skilling's (D) motion to change venue—given the size and diversity of the Houston population; the media did not present smoking-gun evidence of Skilling's (D) guilt; and the courtroom proceedings themselves never turned into a "carnival." Still, the voir dire process itself fell short of constitutional requirements. First, the district court gave short shrift to the overwhelming evidence of hostility toward Skilling (D) and Enron. Second, that court, as well as the majority, downplayed the passions Enron's demise aroused in the public, characterizing the case as "neither heinous nor sensational" because no violence was involved. Economic crimes are certainly capable of rousing public passions, particularly when thousands of unsuspecting people are robbed of their livelihoods and retirement savings. Indeed, the record was replete with examples of visceral outrage toward Skilling (D) and other Enron executives, and some Houstonians compared Skilling (D) to, among other things, a rapist, an axe murderer, and an Al Qaeda terrorist. The situation was so hostile that Skilling (D) and the other executives had to hire private security, lest the public take matters into their own hands. Also, contrary to the majority's observation, the passage of time did little to soften community sentiment. If anything, the time that elapsed between the bankruptcy and the trial made the task of seating an unbiased jury more difficult, not less. Based on these circumstances, and perhaps because the district court did not perceive the intense animosity in the community, its short voir dire fell far short of identifying and removing biased jurors. First, it did not ask questions about the effect of Causey's guilty plea on the prospective jurors. Second, the questions the court did ask were addressed in a cursory fashion, primarily eliciting "yes" or "no" responses, instead of open-ended responses. Third, the district court failed to make a sufficiently critical assessment of prospective jurors' assurances of impartiality. Although the majority insists otherwise, the voir dire transcript shows that the district court essentially took jurors at their word when they promised to be fair. Indeed, the court declined to dismiss for cause any prospective juror who ultimately gave a clear assurance of impartiality, no matter how much equivocation preceded it. Worse still, the district court on a number of occasions accepted declarations of impartiality that were equivocal on their face, as where jurors "hoped" they could presume Skilling's (D) innocence or did "not necessarily" think he was guilty. Finally, the mere fact that the jurors acquitted Skilling (D) of the insider trading charges does not necessarily indicate that they were impartial. Instead, it could just mean that there was a complete dearth of evidence to convict. For all these reasons, it is doubtful that Skilling's (D) jury was indeed free from the deep-seated animosity that pervaded the community at large.

ANALYSIS

The difficult issue in cases involving undisclosed self-dealing is the problem of proof. One reason for the court's limiting of the honest-services doctrine is that federal criminal statutes have a better chance of surviving judicial scrutiny when they are limited in scope. Here, the Court sought to limit the statute's coverage to scenarios where there exists the possibility of concrete evidence to support the alleged crime, such as a bribe or a kickback.

Quicknotes

VENIRE A list of jurors called to serve for a particular term.

VOIR DIRE A preliminary examination conducted by the court for the purpose of selecting prospective jurors to serve at trial.

CHAPTER 25

The Criminal Trial

Quick Reference Rules of Law

PAGE

1. *Presley v. Georgia.* A criminal defendant's Sixth Amendment right to a public trial is violated when the trial court excludes the public from the voir dire of prospective jurors. *230*

2. *Illinois v. Allen.* The Sixth Amendment right of an accused to be present at his own trial and confront the witnesses against him can be lost if, after a warning by the judge, he continues to conduct himself in a manner so disorderly, disruptive, and disrespectful of the court that his trial cannot be carried on with him in the courtroom. *232*

3. *Michigan v. Bryant.* Where the primary purpose of an interrogation of a witness is to allow police to respond to an ongoing emergency, statements made by a witness will not qualify as testimonial statements and the Confrontation Clause will not bar their admission at trial. *234*

4. *Griffin v. California.* The Fifth Amendment Self-Incrimination Clause implicitly forbids comment by the prosecution on an accused's failure to testify as well as instructions by the court that such failure is evidence of guilt. *236*

5. *Darden v. Wainwright.* Improper closing statements by counsel will void a conviction only if they make the trial so unfair as to violate due process. *238*

Presley v. Georgia

Convicted criminal (D) v. State (P)

558 U.S. 209 (2010)

NATURE OF CASE: Appeal from state court decision affirming holding that trial court did not violate a criminal defendant's Sixth Amendment right to a public trial when it excluded the public from the voir dire of prospective jurors.

FACT SUMMARY: Presley (D) contended that he was denied the Sixth Amendment right to a public trial when the trial court excluded the public, which constituted just Presley's (D) uncle, during the voir dire of prospective jurors.

RULE OF LAW

A criminal defendant's Sixth Amendment right to a public trial is violated when the trial court excludes the public from the voir dire of prospective jurors.

FACTS: Presley (D) was prosecuted for a crime. Prior to selecting a jury, the trial court excluded the lone courtroom observer, Presley's (D) uncle, from being present at the voir dire of prospective jurors, over defense counsel's objection. The trial court explained that there was not enough room for the public, since each of the rows would be occupied by jurors, "[a]nd his uncle cannot sit and intermingle with members of the jury panel." After being convicted, Presley (D) moved for a new trial on the grounds that his Sixth Amendment right to a public trial had been violated. The trial court denied the motion, and the State's (P) appellate courts affirmed. The United States Supreme Court granted certiorari.

ISSUE: Is a criminal defendant's Sixth Amendment right to a public trial violated when the trial court excludes the public from the voir dire of prospective jurors?

HOLDING AND DECISION: (Per curiam) Yes. A criminal defendant's Sixth Amendment right to a public trial is violated when the trial court excludes the public from the voir dire of prospective jurors. The Sixth Amendment guarantees an accused in a criminal prosecution the right to a speedy and public trial and is applicable to the states via the Due Process Clause of the Fourteenth Amendment. The Court has previously held that this right extends beyond the actual proof at trial, and that it applies during a pretrial suppression hearing. The public-trial guarantee is for the benefit of the defendant, and there is no good reason for barring the accused from raising a constitutional right that is unmistakably for the accused's benefit. Although an accused does have a right to insist that the voir dire of the jurors be public, there are exceptions to this general rule. The right to an open trial may give way in certain cases to other rights or interests, such as the defendant's right to a fair trial or the government's interest in inhibiting disclosure of sensitive information. Such circumstances will be rare, however, and the balance of interests must be struck with special care. The Court's precedents make clear that the party seeking to close the hearing must advance an overriding interest that is likely to be prejudiced, the closure must be no broader than necessary to protect that interest, the trial court must consider reasonable alternatives to closing the proceeding, and it must make findings adequate to support the closure. Trial courts are obligated to take every reasonable measure to accommodate public attendance at criminal trials, and nothing in the record shows that the trial court here could not have accommodated the public at Presley's (D) trial. Moreover, the trial court failed to identify an overriding interest likely to be prejudiced absent the closure of voir dire. The generic risk of jurors overhearing prejudicial remarks, unsubstantiated by any specific threat or incident, is inherent whenever members of the public are present during the selection of jurors. If broad concerns of this sort were sufficient to override a defendant's constitutional right to a public trial, a court could exclude the public from jury selection almost as a matter of course. There are no doubt circumstances where a judge could conclude that threats of improper communications with jurors or safety concerns are concrete enough to warrant closing voir dire, but in those cases, the particular interest, and threat to that interest, must be articulated along with findings specific enough that a reviewing court can determine whether the closure order was properly entered. However, even assuming, arguendo, that the trial court had an overriding interest in closing voir dire, it was still incumbent upon it to consider all reasonable alternatives to closure. It did not, and that is all this Court needs to decide. Reversed.

ANALYSIS

The right to a public trial also rests on the First Amendment, and such right extends beyond the accused. This First Amendment requirement is binding on the states through the Fourteenth Amendment. Prior to deciding *Presley*, the Court in *Press-Enterprise Co. v. Superior Court of Cal., Riverside Cty.*, 464 U.S. 501 (1984) (*Press-Enterprise I*), had held that the voir dire of prospective jurors must be open to the public under the First Amendment. Although the extent to which the

Continued on next page.

First and Sixth Amendment public trial rights are coextensive is an open question, the Court here concluded that there is no legitimate reason, at least in the context of juror selection proceedings, to give one who asserts a First Amendment privilege greater rights to insist on public proceedings than the accused has under the Sixth Amendment.

Quicknotes

SIXTH AMENDMENT Provides the right to a speedy and public trial by impartial jury, the right to be informed of the accusation, the right to confront witnesses, and the right to have the assistance of counsel in all criminal prosecutions.

VOIR DIRE A preliminary examination conducted by the court for the purpose of selecting prospective jurors to serve at trial.

Illinois v. Allen

State (P) v. Armed robbery convict (D)

397 U.S. 337 (1970)

NATURE OF CASE: Certiorari from reversal of a robbery conviction.

FACT SUMMARY: Allen (D) was convicted of armed robbery after he was removed from the courtroom due to his disruptive behavior.

RULE OF LAW

The Sixth Amendment right of an accused to be present at his own trial and confront the witnesses against him can be lost if, after a warning by the judge, he continues to conduct himself in a manner so disorderly, disruptive, and disrespectful of the court that his trial cannot be carried on with him in the courtroom.

FACTS: During his trial for armed robbery, Allen (D) argued with the judge continuously and in such an abusive, disruptive manner that it was impossible to carry on the trial. After repeated warnings from the judge that he would be removed, Allen (D) continued such behavior and was removed for most of his trial. Upon conviction and affirmation of the conviction by the Supreme Court of Illinois, Allen (D) brought a federal habeas corpus petition in the district court. The district court, finding no constitutional violation of Allen's (D) rights, declined to issue the writ, whereupon Allen (D) appealed to the court of appeals. The court of appeals reversed the conviction on the basis that an accused's Sixth Amendment right to "be confronted with the witnesses against him" can never be lost.

ISSUE: Where an accused is removed from his trial because of extremely disruptive behavior, after warnings by the judge that he would be removed if such behavior continued, has his right to be present at his trial been lost?

HOLDING AND DECISION: (Black, J.) Yes. The Sixth Amendment right of an accused to be present at his trial and confront the witnesses against him can be lost if, after a warning by the judge, he continues to conduct himself in a manner so disorderly, disruptive and disrespectful of the court that his trial cannot be carried on with him in the courtroom. Of course, once the right is lost, it can be reclaimed when the accused is willing to conduct himself "consistently with the decorum and respect inherent in the concept of courts and judicial proceedings." It is essential to the proper administration of justice, that trial judges be given sufficient discretion to deal with disruptive behavior to preserve our system of justice, and there are at least three constitutionally permissible ways for a judge to handle such behavior: (1) bind and gag the accused in court, (2) cite him for contempt, or (3) take him out of the courtroom until he agrees to conduct himself properly. Each of these possibilities has disadvantages and infringes to a different degree upon an accused's Sixth Amendment right to confront witnesses. Therefore, discretion must be allowed to the trial judge to determine the appropriate sanction under the circumstances. Here, the trial judge decided that it was best to remove the extremely disruptive Allen (D), and the judge did so only after repeated warnings and after telling Allen (D) that he could be present whenever he decided to act properly. This may not have been the only solution to the problem, but it was properly within the discretion of the trial judge. Under these circumstances, Allen (D) lost his right to be present throughout his trial. The judgment of the court of appeals is reversed.

ANALYSIS

This case illustrates one situation in which an accused's absence from the courtroom does not violate his Sixth Amendment right to confront the witnesses against him. Generally, this right guarantees that an accused must be present in the courtroom during any time when "testimony" is offered against him (though not necessarily during arguments on questions of law), unless he "waives" that right. Waiver not only occurs when the accused is disruptive but also, in most jurisdictions, when he voluntarily absents himself from the trial once it has started. Note, however, that if an accused is not present at the start of his trial, the court cannot proceed without him, even if his absence is deliberate. Note, finally, that the court here does not ignore the risk of prejudice to an accused, who is bound and gagged in front of a jury. Rather, the court states that this prejudice is one factor to be considered by the trial court when deciding whether such restraints should be applied or whether the disruptive accused should be removed from the court.

Quicknotes

CERTIORARI A discretionary writ issued by a superior court to an inferior court in order to review the lower

Continued on next page.

court's decisions; the U.S. Supreme Court's writ ordering such review.

HABEAS CORPUS A proceeding in which a defendant brings a writ to compel a judicial determination of whether he or she is lawfully being held in custody.

SIXTH AMENDMENT Provides the right to a speedy and public trial by impartial jury, the right to be informed of the accusation, the right to confront witnesses, and the right to have the assistance of counsel in all criminal prosecutions.

WAIVER The intentional or voluntary forfeiture of a recognized right.

Michigan v. Bryant

State (P) v. Individual (D)

562 U.S. 344 (2011)

NATURE OF CASE: Appeal from state court decision reversing conviction of an individual for murder.

FACT SUMMARY: After Bryant (D) shot victim Anthony Covington, Covington made statements before his death to the police implicating Bryant (D) as the shooter.

RULE OF LAW

Where the primary purpose of an interrogation of a witness is to allow police to respond to an ongoing emergency, statements made by a witness will not qualify as testimonial statements and the Confrontation Clause will not bar their admission at trial.

FACTS: Bryant (D) shot Covington. Police responding to a radio call found Covington and asked him what happened. Covington informed police that "Rick" Bryant (D) had shot him 25 minutes earlier through the back door of Bryant's house. The conversation between five police officers and Covington lasted five to ten minutes before an ambulance arrived and transported Covington to a hospital. He died several hours later. Police went to Bryant's (D) house and found blood and a bullet hole in the back door. At trial, the court allowed the police officers to testify as to Covington's statements regarding the identity of Bryant (D). A jury convicted Bryant (D) but the Michigan Supreme Court eventually reversed the conviction because the Confrontation Clause barred the use of Covington's statements, which that court held to be testimonial. The State (P) appealed to the United States Supreme Court.

ISSUE: Where the primary purpose of an interrogation of a witness is to allow police to respond to an ongoing emergency, do statements made by a witness qualify as testimonial statements and will the Confrontation Clause bar their admission at trial?

HOLDING AND DECISION: (Sotomayor, J.) No. Where the primary purpose of an interrogation of a witness is to allow police to respond to an ongoing emergency, statements made by a witness will not qualify as testimonial statements and the Confrontation Clause will not bar their admission at trial. To determine whether the primary purpose is to assist the police with an ongoing emergency, courts should analyze the circumstances present and the statements and actions of the parties. It is an objective test. When an emergency situation is present, statements made to resolve the emergency are given indicia of reliability, thus shielding them from cross-examination usually required by the Confrontation Clause for out of court statements. In addition to the circumstances, another factor is the informality of the questioning, including where the questioning took place. A review of both the questions and answers given during the alleged emergency situation is critical. Police officers have a duty to resolve emergency situations and serve as criminal investigators. A victim's statements often have a purpose of protecting himself, particularly when an armed assailant remains at large. Another factor is the type of dispute. If the dispute is domestic, the level of emergency may be lower. That was not the case here. The police did not know if Covington's shooter was a threat only to Covington at the time. Nor did the police know the location or motive of Bryant (D) during the police officers' questioning of Covington. The questioning was also informal and occurred in a public place. Accordingly, because the primary purpose of Covington's statements was to assist the police in resolving the emergency, the statements were not testimonials, and the Confrontation Clause did not bar their admission at trial. Reversed.

CONCURRENCE: (Thomas, J). Covington's statements were not testimonial because they occurred in an informal setting. The statements did not therefore "bear testimony" against Bryant (D). Analysis of the setting in which the statements were made is more appropriate, rather than the majority's primary purpose test.

DISSENT: (Scalia, J.) The majority's decision greatly distorts our prior Confrontation Clause jurisprudence. The focus of the inquiry should be on the intent of the declarant. Here, 25 minutes after the shooting, Covington found himself surrounded by five police officers. These five officers all asked Covington to describe what had happened, what the shooter looked like, and what events led to the shooting. The alleged "emergency situation" had ended 25 minutes earlier. It is unreasonable to think that Bryant (D) would attempt to fire upon Covington again. Covington, aware that the threat had ended, had the sole purpose of identifying his shooter to the police. Even if the perspective of the officers is taken into account, none of the officers testified that they were in danger of any imminent threat. At a minimum, the questions from the officers became investigative, thus rendering Covington's statements testimonial in nature. The majority's decision greatly expands the definition of emergency situations in violation of the Confrontation Clause. Pursuant to this decision, prosecutors and police may be able to argue that

Continued on next page.

statements given in the hours after an incident but before a suspect is arrested are not testimonial because an ongoing emergency still exists. Finally, the Court's reversion to a reliability standard has been previously rejected by this Court. Reliability of a statement does not mean it is testimonial or nontestimonial. Per the Sixth Amendment, the proper analysis is whether the statements are testimonial, not reliable. If they are testimonial, the Confrontation Clause bars the admission of such statements because the defendant has not been given the right to cross-examine.

ANALYSIS

The significance of this case is that it deals solely with the Confrontation Clause analysis. The Court remanded the case to the Michigan courts for a determination of whether the statements could be admitted through another hearsay exception, such as a dying declaration or an excited utterance. The *Crawford v. Washington*, 541 U.S. 36 (2004), decision rejected the notion that out of court statements were admissible over Confrontation Clause objections if they were shown to be reliable. Justice Scalia's dissent argued that the majority's decision was a return to the improper reliability standard.

Quicknotes

CONFRONTATION CLAUSE A provision in the Sixth Amendment to the U.S. Constitution that an accused in a criminal action has the right to confront the witnesses against him or her, including the right to attend the trial and to cross-examine witnesses called on behalf of the prosecution.

EXCITED UTTERANCE An exception to the hearsay rule for a statement relating to a startling event or condition, made while the declarant was under the stress of excitement that it caused. Fed. R. Evid. 803(2).

Griffin v. California

First-degree murder convict (D) v. State (P)

380 U.S. 609 (1965)

NATURE OF CASE: Certiorari from a murder conviction.

FACT SUMMARY: Griffin (D), during his trial for first-degree murder, did not testify on the issue of his guilt, and both the prosecutor and judge subsequently commented on this failure to the jury before it convicted him.

RULE OF LAW

The Fifth Amendment Self-Incrimination Clause implicitly forbids comment by the prosecution on an accused's failure to testify as well as instructions by the court that such failure is evidence of guilt.

FACTS: Griffin (D) refused to testify at his trial for first-degree murder, invoking the Fifth Amendment privilege against self-incrimination. Before the jury deliberated on the issue of guilt, the prosecutor commented on this failure to testify and suggested that guilt should be inferred therefrom. During instructions to the jury, the court stated that if Griffin (D) failed to explain facts within his knowledge which tended to indicate his guilt, then the jury could take that failure as "tending to indicate the truth of such evidence," but that such failure alone does not by itself "warrant an inference of guilt." Upon conviction and affirmance of that conviction by the California Supreme Court, Griffin (D) brought a petition for certiorari to the United States Supreme Court.

ISSUE: Do comments by the prosecutor on an accused's failure to testify as well as instructions by the court that such failure to testify is evidence of guilt violate the accused's Fifth Amendment privilege against self-incrimination?

HOLDING AND DECISION: (Douglas, J.) Yes. The Fifth Amendment Self-Incrimination Clause forbids such comment by the prosecution on an accused's failure to testify as well as instructions by the court that such failure is evidence of guilt. Such comment by the prosecution or court is a remnant of the "inquisitorial system of criminal justice," *Murphy v. Waterfront Comm.*, 378 U.S. 52, 55 (1964), which the Fifth Amendment protects against. Such comment penalizes the exercise of a constitutional privilege to refrain from self-incrimination and, as such, cannot be allowed. It may be true that there is a natural inference of guilt from a failure to testify as to facts within the knowledge of an accused, but the jury must make this inference on its own without comment from the court. Here, therefore, Griffin's (D) conviction must be reversed.

DISSENT: (Stewart, J.) In examining if an accused's privilege against self-incrimination has been violated, compulsion is the focus of inquiry (i.e., such privilege has only been violated if the accused was compelled to be a witness against himself). The Court, however, fails to identify any such compulsion in the comments of the court and prosecutor. First, such comments do not compel an accused's testimony by creating awareness in the jury of his failure to testify, since that failure is obvious by itself. Second, no compulsion may be assumed on the ground that the inferences drawn by the jury that has heard such comments will be detrimental to an accused, especially where the court has carefully controlled its comments. The trial court here carefully instructed the jury that Griffin's (D) failure to testify does not by itself warrant an inference of guilt. It is doubtful that a jury without such instructions would have observed such a limitation. The comment in this case was a means of articulating and rationally discussing a fact that is necessarily impressed on the jury's consciousness (i.e., the failure to testify). The state has an important interest in such discussion, which should not arbitrarily be cut off.

ANALYSIS

This case illustrates the rule applicable to "direct comment" on an accused's failure to "testify." Note, however, that it does not prevent a prosecutor from commenting on an accused's "failure to offer evidence" on critical aspects of the case. It has been held that a court's comment—that an accused's "failure to explain" possession of recently stolen property should be considered in determining whether he knew the goods were stolen—does not violate *Griffin* (*Barnes v. United States*, 412 U.S. 837 (1973)). Of course, what is considered permissible depends upon the wording of the prosecutor's comments. If he emphasizes an accused's failure to present other evidence instead of the fact that he "personally" offered no explanation, there is probably no violation of *Griffin*. Note, further, that *Griffin* does not prevent a prosecutor from commenting to a jury upon an accused's "refusal to submit to reasonable tests or examinations," the results of which would have been

Continued on next page.

admissible on the issue of guilt or innocence. Note, finally, that *Griffin* does prevent counsel for one of several co-defendants from commenting on the failure of other co-defendants to testify.

Quicknotes

PRIVILEGE AGAINST SELF-INCRIMINATION A privilege guaranteed by the Fifth Amendment to the U.S. Constitution in a criminal proceeding for communications made by an accused and protecting an accused or witness from having to give testimony that may incriminate him- or herself.

Darden v. Wainwright

Murder convict (D) v. Court (P)

477 U.S. 168 (1986)

NATURE OF CASE: Appeal of denial of habeas corpus.

FACT SUMMARY: At the guilt phase of a murder trial, the prosecution made improper closing statements concerning the crime.

RULE OF LAW

Improper closing statements by counsel will void a conviction only if they make the trial so unfair as to violate due process.

FACTS: Darden (D) was charged with a particularly vicious series of crimes, including murder. At his trial, counsel for the prosecution made various improper closing arguments that appealed to passion rather than to facts, although evidence was not misstated and no comments were made about the exercise of rights. Darden (D) was sentenced to death. This was affirmed on appeal, and the court of appeals denied habeas corpus. Darden (D) appealed.

ISSUE: Will improper closing statements by counsel void a conviction only if they make the trial so unfair as to violate due process?

HOLDING AND DECISION: (Powell, J.) Yes. Improper closing statements by counsel will void a conviction only if they make the trial so unfair as to violate due process. It is not enough to void a conviction that remarks by counsel are improper or incorrect. The relevant question is whether the remarks made the trial so unfair as to violate due process. Here, the remarks, while appealing to the passion of the jurors, did not misstate the evidence and did not comment on the exercise of constitutional rights. The trial still was fundamentally fair. Affirmed.

DISSENT: (Blackmun, J.) The prosecution in this case offered personal opinions as to guilt, injected broader issues into the trial, and used arguments designed to inflame the passions of the jury. The result of all this was an unfair trial.

ANALYSIS

The dissent did not appear to question the standard of review used by the court. Due process would appear to be the standard the dissent proposed. However, the dissent disagreed with the court's conclusion that the trial was not fundamentally unfair.

Quicknotes

PROCEDURAL DUE PROCESS The constitutional mandate that if the state or federal government acts so as to deny a citizen of a life, liberty, or property interest, the person is first entitled to notice and the right to be heard.

CHAPTER 26

Reprosecution and Double Jeopardy

Quick Reference Rules of Law

PAGE

1. *Illinois v. Somerville.* If a trial judge grants a mistrial, over the objections of the defendant, because there is a manifest necessity to grant a mistrial or to meet the ends of public justice, a second trial for the same offense does not amount to double jeopardy. *240*

2. *Renico v. Lett.* A trial judge may declare a mistrial when, considering all the circumstances, there is a high degree of necessity for doing so. *242*

3. *Oregon v. Kennedy.* Following a defendant's successful motion for a mistrial, the Double Jeopardy Clause will bar retrial only when the prosecution's objectionable conduct was done with the intent to provoke a mistrial motion. *243*

4. *United States v. Scott.* There is no violation of the Double Jeopardy Clause if the government appeals when the defendant has successfully sought to have his trial terminated without any submission to either judge or jury as to his guilt or innocence, whether it be by dismissal of the count or otherwise. *244*

5. *Lockhart v. Nelson.* When a conviction is based on evidence erroneously admitted and is reversed on appeal, the Double Jeopardy Clause does not prohibit retrial. *246*

6. *Puerto Rico v. Sánchez Valle et al.* The Double Jeopardy Clause bars Puerto Rico and the United States from successively prosecuting a single person for the same conduct under equivalent criminal laws. *247*

Illinois v. Somerville

State (D) v. Retrial defendant (P)

410 U.S. 458 (1973)

NATURE OF CASE: Appeal of a judgment granting a petition for habeas corpus on grounds of double jeopardy.

FACT SUMMARY: The judge declared a mistrial of Somerville's (P) first trial because the indictment was faulty as a consequence of the prosecutor's negligence, and Somerville (P) claimed that a second trial amounted to double jeopardy.

RULE OF LAW

If a trial judge grants a mistrial, over the objections of the defendant, because there is a manifest necessity to grant a mistrial or to meet the ends of public justice, a second trial for the same offense does not amount to double jeopardy.

FACTS: Somerville (P) was indicted by an Illinois grand jury for the crime of theft. Before any evidence was presented at his trial, the prosecuting attorney asked the court to declare a mistrial because Somerville's (P) indictment was found to be fatally defective. The defect could not be cured by an amendment and Somerville (P) could not waive the error as it was considered jurisdictional. The trial court felt that further proceedings under this indictment would be useless, and therefore declared a mistrial. Two days later, the grand jury handed down a second indictment. Somerville (P) claimed that the second trial constituted double jeopardy. The trial court rejected this contention and convicted Somerville (P), and the state appellate courts upheld the verdict. Somerville (P) then sought a writ of habeas corpus in the federal district court, but the writ was denied, and the Seventh Circuit Court of Appeals affirmed that decision. Somerville's (P) petition for certiorari was granted and the case was remanded for reconsideration in light of two recent United States Supreme Court decisions. On remand, in light of those cases, the Seventh Circuit held that Somerville's (P) petition for habeas corpus should have been granted because jeopardy had attached when the jury was impaneled and sworn in. A declaration of a mistrial by the court over Somerville's (P) objections precluded a retrial. Somerville (P) claimed that once a jury had been selected and sworn in, jeopardy attached. The United States Supreme Court granted certiorari.

ISSUE: If a trial judge grants a mistrial, over the objections of the defendant, because there is a manifest necessity to grant a mistrial or to meet the ends of public justice, does a second trial for the same offense amount to double jeopardy?

HOLDING AND DECISION: (Rehnquist, J.) No. If a trial judge grants a mistrial, over the objections of the defendant, because there is a manifest necessity to grant a mistrial or to meet the ends of public justice, a second trial for the same offense does not amount to double jeopardy. The court must consider all the circumstances in making its decision. In this case, it would have been useless to complete the first trial under the defective indictment because, on appeal, the decision would have been reversed and the case would have had to be retried. By declaring a mistrial, all parties were saved considerable time and expense. The court also pointed out that the public has an interest in seeing all trials end in either a conviction or an acquittal. The court held that even though a defendant has a valued right to have his trial completed by a particular tribunal, that right must, in some instances, be subordinated to the public's interest in fair trials ending in just judgments. Since the declaration of a mistrial implemented a reasonable state policy, Somerville's (P) interest in proceeding to verdict was outweighed by the competing and equally legitimate demand for public justice. Reversed.

DISSENT: (White, J.) The right of the defendant not to be put in double jeopardy outweighs the public's interest in fair trials, and there was no manifest necessity to grant the mistrial. Somerville (P) had the right to be tried by the jury chosen in the first trial.

DISSENT: (Marshall, J.) Here, the mistrial was a result of prosecutorial negligence. First, it is difficult to understand how negligence lends itself to manipulation. Second, the Court's precedents are controlling. Previously, the Court held that a prosecutor's negligence in calling a critical witness was insufficient to override the protections of the double jeopardy doctrine. There is no material difference as to prosecutorial negligence between failing to draft an adequate indictment and failing to call a crucial witness, so here too, the Court should have held that double jeopardy attached and should not have been overridden. Finally, the new balancing test announced by the majority is so abstract as to effectively provide no guidance to judges in deciding future cases.

ANALYSIS

This case illustrates one of the situations in which a second trial is permissible, even though jeopardy would

Continued on next page.

normally have been held to have attached at the first trial. Jeopardy attaches when the jury has been sworn in a jury trial, or when the first witness has been sworn in a trial without a jury. Usually, once jeopardy has attached, a second trial would constitute double jeopardy. Note, however, that there are several other situations in which a second trial is permissible after jeopardy has attached: (1) after a successful appeal by the defendant, (2) where a jury is unable to reach a verdict due to some "evident necessity" (e.g., death of judge or juror), (3) where there is a "hung jury," or (4) where "misconduct of a witness or a defendant" personally causes a mistrial.

Quicknotes

DOUBLE JEOPARDY A prohibition against a second prosecution for the same offense after an acquittal or conviction for that offense in a prior proceeding or against multiple punishments for the same offense.

HABEAS CORPUS A proceeding in which a defendant brings a writ to compel a judicial determination of whether he or she is lawfully being held in custody.

JEOPARDY The subjection to potential conviction and punishment in a trial for a criminal act.

MISTRIAL An erroneous or invalid trial.

Renico v. Lett

State (P) v. Individual (D)

559 U.S. 766 (2010)

NATURE OF CASE: Appeal from Sixth Circuit Court of Appeals decision in favor of the plaintiff.

FACT SUMMARY: After a nine-hour trial spread out over a week, jurors deliberated for a period of four hours. After sending a note to the trial judge referring to their inability to agree, the foreperson informed the judge that the jury would not reach a unanimous verdict. The judge then declared a mistrial.

RULE OF LAW

A trial judge may declare a mistrial when, considering all the circumstances, there is a high degree of necessity for doing so.

FACTS: After a nine-hour trial spread out over a week, jurors deliberated for a period of four hours. After four hours of deliberations, the jurors sent a note asking, "What if we can't agree? Mistrial? Retrial?" The jurors also sent a separate note stating that they had a concern their raised voices were disturbing other court proceedings. The judge then brought the jury out and asked the foreperson if the jury would be able to reach a verdict. The foreperson replied, "No, Judge." Without any objections from defense counsel or the prosecution, the judge declared a mistrial. A second jury later convicted Lett (D) of second-degree murder. Lett (D) eventually filed this petition for habeas corpus relief, which the Sixth Circuit Court of Appeals granted. The State (P) appealed to the United States Supreme Court.

ISSUE: May a trial judge declare a mistrial when, considering all the circumstances, there is a high degree of necessity for doing so?

HOLDING AND DECISION: (Roberts, C.J.) Yes. A trial judge may declare a mistrial when, considering all the circumstances, there is a high degree of necessity for doing so. The trial court judge has broad discretion to issue a mistrial. The judge is in the best position to assess whether a jury will be able to reach a verdict. Without such discretion, trial court judges would employ coercive measures that may force the jury into reaching a verdict it otherwise may not have reached. The trial judge's exercise of that discretion must be sound. The trial judge need not make any findings to support his or her decision, nor must the judge force the jury to deliberate for some time period before declaring a mistrial. Here, the jurors' notes were evidence of a significant disagreement among the jury. Moreover, the foreperson clearly answered that the jury would be unable to reach a verdict. While the judge could have used her discretion to have the jury deliberate for additional time or consulted with trial counsel before proceeding, she was under no obligation to do so. The writ of habeas corpus should be denied. Reversed.

DISSENT: (Stevens, J.) The trial judge cut off deliberations before it was evident that further deliberations would be useless. The judge did not poll the jurors, instruct the jury to conduct further deliberations, query counsel on their thoughts for proceeding forward, or make any findings on the record regarding the declaration of a mistrial. A judge has a duty to exercise sound discretion, which did not occur here.

ANALYSIS

When the standard of review is abuse of discretion, it is often difficult on appeal to overturn a decision made by a trial court judge. Appellate courts typically grant trial court judges broad discretion to make decisions based upon the conduct of the trial as it occurs in front of them. Even the majority noted the trial court judge should have instructed the jury to continue deliberations, but the judge was not required to do so.

Quicknotes

ABUSE OF DISCRETION A determination by an appellate court that a lower court's decision was based on an error of law.

HABEAS CORPUS A proceeding in which a defendant brings a writ to compel a judicial determination of whether he or she is lawfully being held in custody.

Oregon v. Kennedy

State (P) v. Retried theft convict (D)

456 U.S. 667 (1982)

NATURE OF CASE: Appeal from dismissal of prosecution for theft.

FACT SUMMARY: After being granted a mistrial, Kennedy (D) contended the Double Jeopardy Clause barred reprosecution.

RULE OF LAW

Following a defendant's successful motion for a mistrial, the Double Jeopardy Clause will bar retrial only when the prosecution's objectionable conduct was done with the intent to provoke a mistrial motion.

FACTS: Kennedy (D) was charged with theft. During redirect of a state's (P) witness, the prosecutor made certain improper comments that resulted in a mistrial. It did not appear that the prosecutor intentionally provoked the motion. Kennedy (D) was retried and convicted. Kennedy (D) appealed, contending the Double Jeopardy Clause barred retrial. The Oregon Supreme Court agreed and reversed the conviction. Oregon (P) appealed.

ISSUE: Following a defendant's successful motion for a mistrial, will the Double Jeopardy Clause bar retrial only when the prosecution's objectionable conduct was done with the intent to provoke a mistrial motion?

HOLDING AND DECISION: (Rehnquist, J.) Yes. Following a defendant's successful motion for a mistrial the Double Jeopardy Clause will bar retrial only when the prosecution's objectionable conduct was done with the intent to provoke a mistrial motion. The protection against double jeopardy is largely waived when the defendant himself moves for a mistrial. However, prosecutorial conduct may compel a defendant to move for a mistrial. There will always be an element of prejudicial prosecutorial conduct toward a defendant, so this alone does not justify barring retrial. A standard of intent by the prosecutor to provoke a mistrial motion is one easily applied. Any other standard would be very difficult to quantify. Only when the prosecutor intentionally provokes a motion should the prosecutor's conduct be such that a retrial should be barred. Reversed.

CONCURRENCE: (Powell, J.) A court should rely on objective evidence of intent.

CONCURRENCE: (Stevens, J.) Prosecutorial harassment or overreaching should also bar retrial.

ANALYSIS

It is basic constitutional law that the United States Supreme Court is the final word on federal law. Several states have adopted rules broader than that enunciated here, based on state law. Oregon (P) did so later in this action. Kennedy (D) lost the battle but won the war.

Quicknotes

DOUBLE JEOPARDY A prohibition against a second prosecution for the same offense after an acquittal or conviction for that offense in a prior proceeding or against multiple punishments for the same offense.

MISTRIAL An erroneous or invalid trial.

United States v. Scott

Federal government (P) v. Narcotics indictee (D)

437 U.S. 82 (1978)

NATURE OF CASE: Appeal from dismissals of two counts of a criminal indictment.

FACT SUMMARY: Two of the three counts in the indictment against Scott (D) were dismissed on the grounds that his defense had been prejudiced by preindictment delay, and the Government (P) sought to appeal.

RULE OF LAW

There is no violation of the Double Jeopardy Clause if the government appeals when the defendant has successfully sought to have his trial terminated without any submission to either judge or jury as to his guilt or innocence, whether it be by dismissal of the count or otherwise.

FACTS: Scott (D) successfully moved to have two of the three counts in his indictment for distributing narcotics dismissed on the ground that his defense had been prejudiced by preindictment delay. The offense allegedly occurred in September 1974, and the indictment was issued on March 5, 1975. A guilty verdict as to the third count was returned, but the Government (P) sought to appeal the dismissal of the first two counts. Concluding that any further prosecution on those counts was barred by the Double Jeopardy Clause, the appeal was dismissed, and the Government (P) then sought review of that decision only as to the first count.

ISSUE: Can the government appeal when a defendant is successful in having the trial terminated without submission to judge or jury for determination of guilt or innocence?

HOLDING AND DECISION: (Rehnquist, J.) Yes. If a defendant manages to have his trial terminated without his guilt or innocence being submitted to judge or jury, as when he successfully moved for dismissal of a charge, the government may appeal without violating the Double Jeopardy Clause. The Double Jeopardy Clause looks askance at the government's repeatedly seeking to try a person, but it does not come into play when the government is quite willing to continue a trial to conclusion, but the defendant elects to seek termination of the trial on grounds unrelated to guilt or innocence. Unlike an insanity or entrapment defense, dismissal of a charge for preindictment delay represents a legal judgment that a defendant, although criminally culpable, may not be punished because of a supposed constitutional violation. It is a termination of a trial on grounds unrelated to guilt or innocence, and the Double Jeopardy Clause is not offended when such a dismissal is appealed by the government. In such a case, it is the government which has lost its right to "one complete opportunity to convict those who have violated its laws," *Arizona v. Washington*, 434 U.S. 497, 509 (1978); the defendant has voluntarily given up, as opposed to being deprived of, his valued right to go to the first jury. Judgment reversed.

DISSENT: (Brennan, J.) The majority's attempt to draw a distinction between "true acquittals," supposedly subject to the Double Jeopardy bar of government appeals, and other final judgments, supposedly subject to the bar, favoring the accused, is unsupported in logic or policy. The definition adopted for "acquittal" is overly restrictive, as is evidenced by the attempted distinction between a dismissal based on preaccusation delay and one based on a defense of insanity or entrapment. The Double Jeopardy Clause mandates the government has just one complete opportunity to convict an accused and that retrial be barred when the first proceeding terminates in a final judgment favorable to the defendant, which is what occurred in this case. The reasons underlying preclusion of retrial after an acquittal are equally applicable to a final judgment entered on a ground "unrelated to factual innocence," so their disparate treatment is untenable. Furthermore, in this case one of the "factual elements of the offense charged" was delay. If, indeed, acquittal is resolution of some or all these elements, there was an acquittal and retrial is barred. In fact, there are few instances where defenses can be deemed unrelated to factual innocence.

ANALYSIS

Prior to this case, the Court had determined that an appeal by the government is barred by double jeopardy considerations when there is a preverdict judgment of acquittal based on the court's determination of the sufficiency of the evidence. Since the same result could be obtained by dismissing the indictment for failure to charge an offense, which would be more like a mistrial and could make appeal possible in certain circumstances, the court would be left with two options on how to treat a particular case. One option would bar government appeal and the other would not. Regarding this situation, Wright, Miller, and Cooper, 15 *Federal Practice and Procedure* § 3919 (1978) (pocket part) states: "If this conclusion is correct, it means that the trial court has discretion to control the double jeopardy consequences

Continued on next page.

of its ruling. It also means that the government must be astute to argue for a disposition that leaves it free to appeal or start over. Although it is troubling that trial judges should be left free of appellate review, procedural punctilio at least has the advantage of helping the defendant to know whether further proceedings may be possible. Even this virtue may be reduced, however, until the 'manifest necessity' standard that limits retrials after a mistrial or dismissal without the defendant's consent is elaborated in the context of defective indictments."

Quicknotes

ACQUITTAL The discharge of an accused individual from suspicion of guilt for a particular crime and from further prosecution for that offense.

MISTRIAL An erroneous or invalid trial.

Lockhart v. Nelson

State (P) v. Burglary convict (D)

488 U.S. 33 (1988)

NATURE OF CASE: Review of habeas corpus invalidating a conviction under a recidivist statute.

FACT SUMMARY: Nelson (D) was convicted under a recidivist statute, and when the conviction was shown to have been invalid, the State (P) attempted to retry him.

RULE OF LAW

When a conviction is based on evidence erroneously admitted and is reversed on appeal, the Double Jeopardy Clause does not prohibit retrial.

FACTS: Nelson (D) was convicted of burglary. Under a state recidivist statute, which required four prior felony convictions to be applicable, an enhanced sentencing hearing was held. Evidence of four prior convictions was introduced, although Nelson (D) contended one had been pardoned. Nelson was convicted under the recidivist law. In a habeas proceeding, Nelson (D) introduced proof of the pardon. The district court granted habeas. The State (P) announced an intention to retry, substituting another felony for the pardoned one. The district court held this to be barred by the Double Jeopardy Clause. The Eighth Circuit affirmed, and the United States Supreme Court granted review.

ISSUE: When a conviction is based on evidence erroneously admitted and is reversed on appeal, does the Double Jeopardy Clause prohibit retrial?

HOLDING AND DECISION: (Rehnquist, C.J.) No. When a conviction is based on evidence erroneously admitted and is reversed on appeal, the Double Jeopardy Clause does not prohibit retrial. It has long been settled that the clause does not bar retrial if a conviction is reversed on appeal. An exception to this rule has been created that where a reversal is based on insufficiency of evidence, no retrial should occur, as such a reversal is tantamount to an acquittal. However, a reversal based on the erroneous admission of evidence is not the same situation. It may be that other evidence was not introduced for tactical reasons, because of the evidence that was erroneously admitted. The prosecution is entitled to present its best case. This differs from the above exception, because there the prosecution presumably has introduced its best case and still failed to obtain a conviction. Here, the prosecution wishes to introduce evidence of another, valid conviction, and it should be permitted to do so. Reversed.

DISSENT: (Marshall, J.) The decision here seems to rest on the notion that prosecutors held back evidence, which is a questionable supposition at best.

ANALYSIS

The rule that a defendant may be retried following a reversal is relatively new. Up until the latter part of the nineteenth century, there could be one trial, one judgment, and one appeal. If exonerating evidence was later found, there was no judicial remedy. Appeals for executive clemency were much more important then, than now. There have been calls among a minority of authorities for a return to such a system.

Quicknotes

DOUBLE JEOPARDY A prohibition against a second prosecution for the same offense after an acquittal or conviction for that offense in a prior proceeding or against multiple punishments for the same offense.

HABEAS CORPUS COLLATERAL REVIEW An independent review of whether a prisoner is being lawfully imprisoned.

RECIDIVIST One who repeatedly commits crimes.

Puerto Rico v. Sánchez Valle et al.

U.S. territory (P) v. Convicted illegal firearms trafficker (D)

579 U.S. 59 (2016)

NATURE OF CASE: Appeal in prosecution for illegal firearms trafficking wherein the defendant has asserted double jeopardy on the grounds that the prosecution is a successive prosecution for the same criminal conduct by the same sovereign.

FACT SUMMARY: Sánchez Valle (D) and Gómez Vázquez (D), who were indicted in the Commonwealth of Puerto Rico (Puerto Rico) (P), a United States territory, for illegally selling firearms in violation of the Puerto Rico Arms Act of 2000, contended that the Double Jeopardy Clause should have required dismissal of their indictments after they pleaded guilty to violating analogous United States federal statutes based on the same transactions, on the theory that Puerto Rico (P) and the United States are the same sovereign for double-jeopardy purposes.

RULE OF LAW

The Double Jeopardy Clause bars Puerto Rico and the United States from successively prosecuting a single person for the same conduct under equivalent criminal laws.

FACTS: Sánchez Valle (D) and Gómez Vázquez (D) each sold a gun to an undercover police officer in the Commonwealth of Puerto Rico (Puerto Rico) (P), a United States territory. Puerto Rican prosecutors indicted them for illegally selling firearms in violation of the Puerto Rico Arms Act of 2000. While those charges were pending, federal grand juries also indicted them, based on the same transactions, for violations of analogous U.S. gun trafficking statutes. Both defendants pleaded guilty to the federal charges and moved to dismiss the pending Puerto Rico (P) charges on double jeopardy grounds. The United States Supreme Court granted certiorari to determine if the Double Jeopardy Clause applied.

ISSUE: Does the Double Jeopardy Clause bar Puerto Rico and the United States from successively prosecuting a single person for the same conduct under equivalent criminal laws?

HOLDING AND DECISION: (Kagan, J.) Yes. The Double Jeopardy Clause bars Puerto Rico and the United States from successively prosecuting a single person for the same conduct under equivalent criminal laws. Ordinarily, a person cannot be prosecuted twice for the same offense. However, under the dual-sovereignty doctrine, the Double Jeopardy Clause does not bar successive prosecutions if they are brought by separate sovereigns. Moreover, "sovereignty" in this context does not bear its ordinary meaning. This Court does not examine the extent of control that one prosecuting entity wields over the other, the degree to which an entity exercises self-governance, or a government's more particular ability to enact and enforce its own criminal laws. Rather, the test hinges on a single criterion: the "ultimate source" of the power undergirding the respective prosecutions. If two entities derive their power to punish from independent sources, then they may bring successive prosecutions. Conversely, if those entities draw their power from the same ultimate source, then they may not. Under that approach, the states are separate sovereigns from the federal government and from one another. Because states rely on "authority originally belonging to them before admission to the Union and preserved to them by the Tenth Amendment," state prosecutions have their roots in an "inherent sovereignty" unconnected to the U.S. Congress. For similar reasons, Native American tribes also count as separate sovereigns. A tribe's power to punish pre-existed the Union, and so a tribal prosecution, like a state's, is attributable in no way to any delegation of federal authority. Conversely, a municipality cannot count as a sovereign distinct from a state, because it receives its power, in the first instance, from the state. Further, and most pertinent here, this Court concluded in the early 20th century that U.S. territories—including an earlier incarnation of Puerto Rico (P) itself—are not sovereigns distinct from the United States. Going back as far as the doctrine demands—to the "ultimate source" of Puerto Rico's (P) prosecutorial power—reveals, once again, the U.S. Congress. If the dual-sovereignty doctrine hinged on measuring an entity's self-governance, the emergence of Puerto Rico (P) as a Commonwealth would have resulted in the capacity to bring the kind of successive prosecutions attempted here. However, that is not the focus of the doctrine, which does not focus on self-rule, but on the wellspring of an entity's prosecuting authority. That "ultimate" source is the U.S. Congress, which conferred the authority to create the Puerto Rico (P) Constitution, which in turn confers the authority to bring criminal charges. That makes Congress the original source of power for Puerto Rico's (P) prosecutors—as it is for the federal government's prosecutors. The island's Constitution, significant though it is, does not break the chain. Accordingly, the Double Jeopardy Clause bars both Puerto Rico (P) and the United States from prosecuting a single person for the same conduct under equivalent criminal laws.

Continued on next page.

CONCURRENCE: (Ginsburg, J.) A larger question not addressed by this case, but that should be addressed if the opportunity arises in the future, is whether the current "separate sovereigns" doctrine serves the objective of the Double Jeopardy Clause. Given that the states and the federal government are kindred systems that are part of a whole nation, it seems that permitting multiple prosecutions (by both a state and the federal government) for the same conduct is an affront to human dignity.

ANALYSIS

Justice Breyer, dissenting, disagreed that Puerto Rico (P) and the federal government share the same source of power, namely, the U.S. Congress. He explained that although to find the source of an entity's criminal law one must seek the "furthest-back source" of that power, conceptually what that means is that one traces the source of power back to a time when a previously nonexistent entity, or a previously dependent entity, became independent—at least, sufficiently independent to be considered "sovereign" for purposes of the Double Jeopardy Clause. Thus, he observes, we do not trace Puerto Rico's (P) source of power back to Spain or to Rome or to Justinian, nor do we trace the federal government's source of power back to the English Parliament or to William the Conqueror or to King Arthur. Nonetheless, in the case of Puerto Rico (P), Justice Breyer opined that Congress, in enacting the Puerto Rican Federal Relations Act (Act), determined that the political status of Puerto Rico (P) would for double jeopardy purposes subsequently encompass the sovereign authority to enact and enforce—pursuant to its own powers—its own criminal laws. Justice Breyer contended that this position is amply supported by history and the timing of the enactment of the Act, which, for example, led the United Nations to proclaim that the people of the Commonwealth of Puerto Rico (P) had achieved a new political status, and were invested with attributes of political sovereignty that clearly identified the status of self-government attained by the Puerto Rican people as that of an autonomous political entity. Additionally, he noted that Puerto Rico's (P) Supreme Court has consistently held, over a period of more than 50 years, that Puerto Rico's (P) people (and not the U.S. Congress) are the "source" of Puerto Rico's (P) local criminal laws, and that Puerto Rico's (P) legal system arises out of, and reflects, not traditional British common law (which underlies the criminal law in 49 of the 50 states), but a tradition with Spanish roots stemming from European civil codes and Roman law. Thus, to Justice Breyer, the "source" of Puerto Rico's (P) criminal law ceased to be the U.S. Congress and became Puerto Rico (P) itself, its people, and its Constitution.

Quicknotes

DOUBLE JEOPARDY A prohibition against a second prosecution for the same offense after an acquittal or conviction for that offense in a prior proceeding or against multiple punishments for the same offense.

JURISDICTION The authority of a court to hear and declare judgment in respect to a particular matter.

CHAPTER 27

Sentencing

Quick Reference Rules of Law

	PAGE
1. *Williams v. New York.* A sentencing judge may exercise wide discretion in the sources and types of evidence used to assist him in determining the kind and extent of punishment to be imposed within limits fixed by law.	*250*
2. *Apprendi v. New Jersey.* The Due Process Clause of the Fourteenth Amendment requires that any fact that increases the penalty for a crime beyond the statutory maximum must be submitted to a jury and proved beyond a reasonable doubt.	*251*

Williams v. New York

Defendant (D) v. State (P)

337 U.S. 241 (1949)

NATURE OF CASE: Appeal from a death sentence.

FACT SUMMARY: The judge imposed a death sentence for a murder conviction after a jury had recommended life imprisonment.

RULE OF LAW

A sentencing judge may exercise wide discretion in the sources and types of evidence used to assist him in determining the kind and extent of punishment to be imposed within limits fixed by law.

FACTS: Williams (D) was found guilty of murder in the first degree. The jury recommended life imprisonment. The trial judge, after considering information from the presentence investigation, imposed the death sentence. Williams (D) appealed, alleging that the judge's consideration of information obtained outside the courtroom, from persons whom Williams (D) had not been permitted to confront or cross-examine, violated his due process rights under the Fourteenth Amendment.

ISSUE: May a sentencing judge exercise wide discretion in the sources and types of evidence used to assist him in determining the kind and extent of punishment to be imposed within limits fixed by law?

HOLDING AND DECISION: (Black, J.) Yes. A sentencing judge may exercise wide discretion in the sources and types of evidence used to assist him in determining the kind and extent of punishment to be imposed within limits fixed by law. In addition to the historical basis for different evidentiary rules governing trial and sentencing procedures, there are sound practical reasons for the distinction. Modern concepts individualizing punishment have made it necessary that a sentencing judge not be denied an opportunity to obtain pertinent information by a requirement of rigid adherence to restrictive rules of evidence properly applicable to the trial. Affirmed.

DISSENT: (Murphy, J.) In our criminal courts the jury sits as the representative of the community; its voice is that of the society against which the crime was committed. A judge, even though vested with the statutory authority to do so, should hesitate indeed to increase the severity of such a community expression.

ANALYSIS

The court relied on information that Williams (D) had committed thirty other burglaries in the same areas, some to which he had confessed. His probation report revealed certain sexual activities that the judge considered to be morbid. Based on this information, the judge found Williams (D) to be a menace to society. Rule 32 of the Federal Rules of Criminal Procedure permits federal judges to consider reports made by probation officers in imposing sentences, reflecting the historical position.

Quicknotes

DISCRETION The authority conferred upon a public official to act reasonably in accordance with his or her own judgment under certain circumstances.

FIRST-DEGREE MURDER The willful killing of a person with deliberation and premeditation; first-degree murder also encompasses those situations in which a person is killed within the perpetration of, or attempt to perpetrate, specified felonies.

Apprendi v. New Jersey

Convicted accused (D) v. State (P)

530 U.S. 466 (2000)

NATURE OF CASE: Appeal from sentence.

FACT SUMMARY: Apprendi (D) contended that any fact that increases the penalty for a crime beyond the statutory maximum must be submitted to a jury and proved beyond a reasonable doubt.

RULE OF LAW

The Due Process Clause of the Fourteenth Amendment requires that any fact that increases the penalty for a crime beyond the statutory maximum must be submitted to a jury and proved beyond a reasonable doubt.

FACTS: Apprendi (D) pleaded guilty to a shooting, and at sentencing the government produced evidence that the shooting was racially motivated. The sentencing judge found evidence of racial bias by a preponderance of the evidence and imposed an enhanced sentence on basis of the hate crime law. That sentence was well above what Apprendi (D) could have received for the crime to which he pled guilty. The sentence was upheld by the New Jersey appellate court, which concluded that the state had the authority to define racial motivation as a "sentencing factor" rather than as "an element of the crime." Apprendi (D) appealed.

ISSUE: Does the Due Process Clause of the Fourteenth Amendment require that any fact that increases the penalty for a crime beyond the statutory maximum must be submitted to a jury and proved beyond a reasonable doubt?

HOLDING AND DECISION: (Stevens, J.) Yes. The Due Process Clause of the Fourteenth Amendment requires that any fact that increases the penalty for a crime beyond the statutory maximum must be submitted to a jury and proved beyond a reasonable doubt. The New Jersey procedure here challenged is an unacceptable departure from the jury tradition that is an indispensable part of our criminal justice system. At stake in this case are constitutional protections of surpassing importance: the proscription of any deprivation of liberty without due process of law and the guarantee, inter alia, of public trial by an impartial jury. Taken together, these rights indisputably entitle a criminal defendant to a jury determination that he or she is guilty of every element of the crime with which charged, beyond a reasonable doubt. In this regard, this Court does not recognize any distinction between an "element" of a felony offense and a "sentencing factor." This court has previously made clear that due process and associated jury protections extend, to some degree, to determinations that go not to a defendant's guilt or innocence, but simply to the length of his or her sentence. Reversed.

DISSENT: (O'Connor, J.) This Court has long recognized that not every fact that bears on a defendant's punishment need be charged in an indictment, submitted to a jury, and proved by the government beyond a reasonable doubt. Rather, the legislature's definition of the elements of the offense is usually dispositive.

ANALYSIS

As the Supreme Court makes clear in *Apprendi*, the historic link between verdict and judgment and the consistent limitations of judges' discretion to operate within the limits of the legal penalties highlight the novelty of a legislative scheme, such as that of New Jersey, that removes the jury from the determination of a fact that, if found, exposes the criminal defendant to a penalty exceeding the maximum he or she would receive if punished according to the facts reflected in the jury verdict alone. It is for this articulated reason that the Supreme Court emphasizes that the "reasonable doubt" requirement has such a vital role in American criminal procedure for cogent reasons. Hence, the Court requires, among other things, procedural protections in order to provide concrete substance for the presumption of innocence and to reduce the risk of imposing such deprivations erroneously.

Quicknotes

FOURTEENTH AMENDMENT DUE PROCESS CLAUSE Provides that protections mandated by the U.S. Constitution and observed by the federal government are equally applicable, and therefore must be observed by the states.

REASONABLE DOUBT Enough doubt on the part of jurors to acquit a defendant based on the absence of evidence.

CHAPTER 28

Appeals

Quick Reference Rules of Law

	PAGE
1. *North Carolina v. Pearce.* (1) The Double Jeopardy Clause does not prohibit, upon a defendant's reconviction, the imposition of a harsher sentence than that imposed after the first conviction, but whenever a judge does impose a more severe sentence upon a defendant's reconviction, the judge's reasons for doing so must be shown. (2) The Double Jeopardy Clause requires that in computing a new sentence on retrial, credit be given for that part of the original sentence already served.	*254*
2. *Chapman v. California.* A federal constitutional error may be found to be harmless where such is shown beyond a reasonable doubt.	*256*
3. *Neder v. United States.* When a trial court fails to instruct a jury on each and every element of an offense in a jury instruction, the proper review on appeal is the harmless error analysis.	*257*

North Carolina v. Pearce

State (P) v. Assault convict (D)

395 U.S. 711 (1969)

NATURE OF CASE: Petitions for writs of habeas corpus.

FACT SUMMARY: Pearce (D) obtained a reversal of his conviction. Upon retrial, he was sentenced to eight years in prison which, when added to the time he had already served, amounted to a longer total sentence than that originally imposed. Rice (D) also obtained a reversal of his conviction. Upon retrial, he was sentenced to a harsher sentence than his original sentence, and no credit was given for the time he had already served.

RULE OF LAW

(1) The Double Jeopardy Clause does not prohibit, upon a defendant's reconviction, the imposition of a harsher sentence than that imposed after the first conviction, but whenever a judge does impose a more severe sentence upon a defendant's reconviction, the judge's reasons for doing so must be shown.
(2) The Double Jeopardy Clause requires that in computing a new sentence on retrial, credit be given for that part of the original sentence already served.

FACTS: Pearce (D) was sentenced to 12 to 15 years in prison for assault with intent to rape. He obtained a reversal of his conviction. Upon retrial, he was convicted and sentenced to eight years, which, when added to the time he had already served, amounted to a longer sentence than that originally imposed. Rice (D) was sentenced to ten years in prison after pleading guilty to burglary. He obtained a reversal of his conviction. Upon his retrial, he was convicted on three of the original four counts and sentenced to a term totaling 25 years. No credit was given for the time he had already served. Pearce (D) was granted habeas corpus on the grounds that the longer sentence was unconstitutional. Rice (D) was also granted habeas corpus as it was found that the state was punishing him for his having exercised his post-conviction right of review.

ISSUE:

(1) Does the Fifth Amendment prohibit the imposition of a more severe punishment after conviction for the same offense upon retrial?
(2) Does the Fifth Amendment require that in computing a new sentence on retrial, credit must be given for that part of the original sentence already served?

HOLDING AND DECISION: (Stewart, J.)

(1) No. The Fifth Amendment does not prohibit the imposition of a more severe punishment after conviction for the same offense upon retrial. The guarantee against double jeopardy does not include restrictions upon the length of a sentence imposed upon reconviction. This rule rests upon the premise that the original conviction has, at the defendant's behest, been wholly nullified. However, it would be a flagrant violation of the Fourteenth Amendment for a state court to impose a heavier sentence upon every reconvicted defendant for the explicit purpose of punishing the defendant for his having gotten his original conviction set aside. The very threat inherent in the existence of such a policy would "chill the exercise of basic rights" by those still in prison. A court cannot put a price on an appeal, and a defendant's exercise of a right of appeal must be free and unfettered. In order to ensure the absence of a motivation to punish, whenever a judge imposes a more severe sentence upon a defendant after a new trial, the judge must affirmatively show his reasons for doing so. These reasons must be based upon objective information concerning identifiable conduct on the part of the defendant after the original proceeding.
(2) Yes. The Fifth Amendment requires that in computing a new sentence on retrial, credit must be given for that part of the original sentence already served. The Double Jeopardy Clause protects against multiple punishments as well as multiple prosecutions. This basic constitutional guarantee is violated when punishment already exacted is not fully credited in imposing sentence upon a new conviction for the same offense. In both these cases before us, no reason was offered to justify the imposition of the harsher sentence. The judgment below must be affirmed.

ANALYSIS

In *Green v. United States*, 355 U.S. 184 (1957), mentioned in one of the concurring opinions, the defendant had originally been charged with first-degree murder, but was convicted of second-degree murder. His appeal resulted in the reversal of his conviction, and he was retried on the original charge. The second jury convicted him of first-degree murder. The Supreme

Continued on next page.

Court held that double jeopardy barred conviction on that charge, since Green had already been in peril of being convicted and punished for first-degree murder at his first trial. In *Tucker v. Peyton*, 357 F.2d 115 (1966), it was held that where a prisoner serving consecutive sentences succeeded in having one of the sentences invalidated after it had been fully or partially served, the state must give credit on the sentence remaining for the time served. In *Miller v. Cox*, 443 F.2d 1019 (4th Cir. 1971), it was held that a defendant who had served 21 years on a void conviction was not entitled to credit against subsequently committed felonies.

Quicknotes

DOUBLE JEOPARDY A prohibition against a second prosecution for the same offense after an acquittal or conviction for that offense in a prior proceeding or against multiple punishments for the same offense.

FIRST-DEGREE MURDER The willful killing of a person with deliberation and premeditation; first-degree murder also encompasses those situations in which a person is killed within the perpetration of, or attempt to perpetrate, specified felonies.

HABEAS CORPUS A proceeding in which a defendant brings a writ to compel a judicial determination of whether he or she is lawfully being held in custody.

PROCEDURAL DUE PROCESS The constitutional mandate that if the state or federal government acts so as to deny a citizen of a life, liberty, or property interest, the person is first entitled to notice and the right to be heard.

SECOND-DEGREE MURDER The unlawful killing of person, without premeditation, and characterized by either an intent to kill or by a reckless disregard for human life.

Chapman v. California

Defendant who fails to testify (D) v. State (P)

386 U.S. 18 (1967)

NATURE OF CASE: Appeal from conviction of robbery, kidnapping and murder.

FACT SUMMARY: Chapman (D) and others contended that because the prosecutor committed a constitutional error by commenting on his failure to testify in his own behalf, as a matter of law such error was reversible.

RULE OF LAW

A federal constitutional error may be found to be harmless where such is shown beyond a reasonable doubt.

FACTS: Chapman (D) and others were arrested for kidnapping, robbery, and murder. None of the defendants testified at trial. The prosecution commented heavily on Chapman's (D) failure to testify, and they were convicted. While the case was on appeal, the United States Supreme Court held that it was a deprivation of a defendant's constitutional rights for the prosecution to comment on his failure to testify. Chapman (D) contended that because the error was constitutional, as a matter of law it was reversible error. The California Supreme Court held the error to be harmless. The United States Supreme Court granted review.

ISSUE: May a federal constitutional error be found to be harmless where such is shown beyond a reasonable doubt?

HOLDING AND DECISION: (Black, J.) Yes. A federal constitutional error may be found to be harmless where such is shown beyond a reasonable doubt. It must be shown beyond a reasonable doubt that a constitutional error was harmless, or such will be considered reversible. Not all federal constitutional errors are reversible. However, the highest level of proof must be presented to hold such an error harmless. It is not harmless error to effectively deprive a defendant of his right against self-incrimination. By commenting on Chapman's (D) failure to testify, the prosecution suggests that such failure is an admission of guilt. Thus, this is reversible error. Reversed.

ANALYSIS

Some commentators suggest this opinion implies that constitutional errors are, by their nature, more important errors than others. The abuse of constitutional as opposed to statutory or state common-law standards is considered fundamentally more erosive of the justice system.

Quicknotes

HARMLESS ERROR An error committed during trial that does not require the reviewing court to overturn or modify the trial court's judgment in that it did not affect the appellant's substantial rights or the disposition of the action.

Neder v. United States

Criminal (D) v. Federal government (P)

527 U.S. 1 (1999)

NATURE OF CASE: Appeal from a guilty verdict and appellate court's holding that district court committed harmless error.

FACT SUMMARY: A jury found Neder (D) guilty on various charges and a judge sentenced him (D) to 147 months in prison. The defendant appealed and the court of appeals held that the district court's failure to instruct the jury on materiality was harmless error.

RULE OF LAW

When a trial court fails to instruct a jury on each and every element of an offense in a jury instruction, the proper review on appeal is the harmless error analysis.

FACTS: Neder (D) was tried and convicted of fraud and tax offenses, and sentenced to 147 months of imprisonment, five years of supervised release, and $25 million in restitution. On appeal, the court of appeals affirmed the conviction and held that the district court erred when it failed to submit the materiality element of the tax offense to the jury. The error, however, was harmless because materiality was not in dispute, therefore, the error did not contribute to the jury's verdict. Neder (D) appealed.

ISSUE: Is the harmless error analysis appropriate in reviewing a trial court's failure to instruct a jury on each and every element of an offense?

HOLDING AND DECISION: (Rehnquist, C.J.) Yes. When a trial court fails to instruct a jury on each and every element of an offense in a jury instruction, the proper review on appeal is the harmless error analysis. Federal Rule of Criminal Procedure 52(a) states that any error, defect, irregularity, or variance that does not affect substantial rights will be disregarded. Although this rule applies to all alleged errors, there is a class of fundamental constitutional errors that goes beyond the harmless error examination. The error at issue here is a jury instruction that fails to include an element of an offense and is not an error that necessarily renders a criminal trial fundamentally unfair. The harmless error analysis is properly applied to an error as is involved in this case. The harmless error inquiry is whether it is clear beyond a reasonable doubt that a rational jury would have found the defendant guilty without the error. When an element of the offense is omitted from a jury instruction but supported by overwhelming and uncontroverted evidence, the above analysis balances society's interest in punishing the guilty and the method by which such decisions of guilt are made. Affirmed.

CONCURRENCE AND DISSENT: (Scalia, J.) A failure to include each element of the crime charged in an instruction can never be harmless error. The right to be tried by a jury necessarily means the right to have a jury determine whether one has been proved guilty of a charged offense, and that means a jury must determine all elements that were proved or not. The Court does not specify exactly how many elements of an offense can be omitted before the error is not viewed as harmless. Failure to prove one element should be treated the same as a failure to prove all elements of an offense and prevent a conviction.

ANALYSIS

Justice Stevens's concurrence noted that the Court took a narrow perspective in identifying those errors that required automatic reversal. For example, racial discrimination in the selection of grand juries is not to be tolerated, even if the defendant's guilt is later established in a fair trial with overwhelming evidence. Our Constitution and criminal justice system respect other values besides the reliability of a determination of guilt.

Quicknotes

HARMLESS ERROR An error taking place during trial that does not require the reviewing court to overturn or modify the trial court's judgment in that it did not affect the appellant's substantial rights or the disposition of the action.

MATERIALITY Importance; the degree of relevance or necessity to the particular matter.

CHAPTER 29

Post-Conviction Review: Federal Habeas Corpus

Quick Reference Rules of Law

	PAGE
1. *Stone v. Powell.* Where the state has provided an opportunity for full and fair litigation of a Fourth Amendment claim, the Constitution does not require that a state prisoner be granted federal habeas corpus relief on the ground that evidence obtained in an unconstitutional search or seizure was introduced at his trial.	*260*
2. *Wainwright v. Sykes.* One who did not comply with state procedural rules by not raising his federal claim at trial cannot obtain federal habeas corpus review of his state criminal conviction unless he shows "cause" for noncompliance and shows "prejudice" as a result of the claimed error in the original proceeding.	*261*
3. *Teague v. Lane.* Except in special circumstances, case law will not be applied retroactively in collateral review.	*263*
4. *Harrington v. Richter.* Under 28 U.S.C. Section 2254 as amended by the Antiterrorism and Effective Death Penalty Act (AEDPA) of 1996, federal habeas relief may not be granted unless it is shown that an earlier state court's decision was contrary to clearly established federal law or involved an unreasonable application of such federal law.	*264*

Stone v. Powell

Accused (D) v. State (P)

428 U.S. 465 (1976)

NATURE OF CASE: Writ for federal habeas corpus.

FACT SUMMARY: A prisoner sought habeas corpus relief on the ground that he was convicted based on evidence obtained in an illegal search or seizure.

RULE OF LAW

Where the state has provided an opportunity for full and fair litigation of a Fourth Amendment claim, the Constitution does not require that a state prisoner be granted federal habeas corpus relief on the ground that evidence obtained in an unconstitutional search or seizure was introduced at his trial.

FACTS: Stone (D) alleged that his conviction was based on evidence illegally obtained and requested habeas corpus review. After state habeas corpus proceedings, Stone (D) filed a writ for federal habeas corpus, alleging violation of Fourth Amendment rights guaranteed through the Fourteenth Amendment.

ISSUE: Where the state has provided an opportunity for full and fair litigation of a Fourth Amendment claim, does the Constitution require that a state prisoner be granted federal habeas corpus relief on the ground that evidence obtained in an unconstitutional search or seizure was introduced at his trial?

HOLDING AND DECISION: (Powell, J.) No. Where the state has provided an opportunity for full and fair litigation of a Fourth Amendment claim, the Constitution does not require that a state prisoner be granted federal habeas corpus relief on the ground that evidence obtained in an unconstitutional search or seizure was introduced at his trial. The primary justification for the exclusionary rule is the deterrence of police conduct that violates Fourth Amendment rights; the Fourth Amendment itself is not a personal constitutional right. Fourth Amendment concerns support the implementation of the exclusionary rule at trial and its enforcement on direct appeal of state court convictions. The additional contribution, if any, of the consideration of search and seizure claims of state prisoners on collateral review is small in relation to the costs. Writ denied.

DISSENT: (Brennan, J.) The Court today is ignoring the settled principle that for purposes of adjudicating constitutional claims, Congress, which has the power to do so under Article III of the Constitution, has effectively cast the district courts sitting in habeas in the role of surrogate Supreme Courts. The procedural safeguards mandated by the Congress are not admonitions to be tolerated only to the extent they serve functional purposes. Every guarantee enshrined in our Constitution is endowed with an independent vitality and value, and the Court is not free to curtail those Constitutional guarantees even to punish the most obviously guilty.

ANALYSIS

The Court has not extended the holding from this case to bar habeas corpus review of other claims based on violations of the Constitution. The Antiterrorism and Effective Death Penalty Act, enacted in 1996, limited successive habeas corpus petitions. This Act did not, however, repeal the authority of the Court to entertain original habeas corpus petitions.

Quicknotes

FOURTH AMENDMENT Provides that persons be secure as to their person and private belongings against unreasonable searches and seizures.

HABEAS CORPUS A proceeding in which a defendant brings a writ to compel a judicial determination of whether he or she is lawfully being held in custody.

SEARCH An inspection conducted in order to obtain evidence to be utilized for the prosecution of a crime.

SEIZURE Under the Fourth Amendment, the application of physical force to the body of a person, or a show of force or authority, intended to restrain a person's liberty. Also, as relates to property, the meaningful interference with an individual's possessory interests in that property. Only "unreasonable" seizures by the government are prohibited by the Fourth Amendment.

Wainwright v. Sykes

Court (P) v. Murder convict (D)

433 U.S. 72 (1977)

NATURE OF CASE: Habeas corpus challenge to a murder conviction.

FACT SUMMARY: Sykes (D) sought a review of his murder conviction via a habeas corpus proceeding, but he had failed to comply with state procedural rules in not raising the underlying claim at trial.

RULE OF LAW

One who did not comply with state procedural rules by not raising his federal claim at trial cannot obtain federal habeas corpus review of his state criminal conviction unless he shows "cause" for noncompliance and shows "prejudice" as a result of the claimed error in the original proceeding.

FACTS: Sykes (D) violated a state procedural rule by not raising at trial his claim that the incriminating statements admitted against him were involuntary because he did not understand the *Miranda* warnings, *Miranda v. Arizona*, 384 U.S. 436 (1966), that he had been given. When he was convicted in state court for murder, Sykes (D) then presented a federal habeas corpus challenge to that conviction based on the aforementioned contention. Opposing such action, Wainwright (P) argued that the rule in *Francis v. Henderson,* 425 U.S. 536 (1976), should be extended to cover this case. That rule was that federal habeas corpus review was barred absent a showing of "cause" and "prejudice" where the challenge was to the makeup of a grand jury. Sykes (D) argued that *Fay v. Noia*, 372 U.S. 391 (1963), had laid down an all-inclusive rule rendering state timely objection rules ineffective to bar review of underlying federal claims in federal habeas corpus proceedings absent a showing of "knowing waiver" or a "deliberate bypass" of the right to so object.

ISSUE: In order to obtain federal habeas corpus review of his state criminal conviction, must one who did not comply with state procedural rules in raising his federal claim at trial show "cause" for noncompliance and show "prejudice" resulting from the claimed error in the original proceeding?

HOLDING AND DECISION: (Rehnquist, J.) Yes. If one who suffered a state criminal conviction did not comply with state procedural law by bringing up his federal claim at trial, he cannot obtain federal habeas corpus review of the conviction unless he shows "cause" for noncompliance and shows "prejudice" as a result of the claimed error in the original proceeding. A state's contemporaneous objection rule is designed to ensure that constitutional claims are heard when they are fresh, not years later in a federal habeas corpus proceeding. Furthermore, to apply the "knowing waiver" or "deliberate bypass" standard, the more lenient of those suggested, would encourage "sandbagging" by lawyers who would take their chances on a not guilty verdict at trial with the intent to raise their constitutional claims in a federal habeas corpus court if their initial gamble does not pay off. The "cause" and "prejudice" rule herein adopted attempts to make the state trial on the merits the "main event" rather than a "tryout on the road." In this case, the required showing of cause was not made. Reversed and remanded with instructions to dismiss the petition for a writ of habeas corpus.

CONCURRENCE: (Stevens, J.) In applying the "deliberate bypass" standard, courts have found the client impliedly consents where, as here, his attorney decides as a tactical ploy not to raise a constitutional objection at trial. Furthermore, there is no evidence that the trial lacked fundamental fairness. So, there is no reason to allow collateral attack in this case regardless of which rule is chosen.

DISSENT: (Brennan, J.) The Court is not justified in imposing a stricter standard than the "deliberate bypass" test. It is the harshest test possible that still distinguishes between intentional and inadvertent noncompliance by counsel with procedural rules. Most procedural defaults are born of the inadvertence, negligence, inexperience, or incompetence of trial counsel; and it is unfair to make the criminal defendant accountable for the naked errors of his attorney. The mistakes of a trial attorney should be visited on the head of a federal habeas corpus applicant only when this Court is convinced that the lawyer actually exercised his expertise and judgment in his client's service, and with his client's knowing and intelligent participation, where possible.

ANALYSIS

One possible result of this case may be that defendants are pushed into making more claims based on ineffectiveness of counsel to fulfill the requirement that they show "cause." That is, a particular procedural default will simply be cited as an example of general incompetence of counsel. The effect would be merely to transform the old claims alleging deprivation of constitutional rights

Continued on next page.

to new claims alleging ineffectiveness of counsel, with all the attendant problems that will engender.

Quicknotes

HABEAS CORPUS A proceeding in which a defendant brings a writ to compel a judicial determination of whether he or she is lawfully being held in custody.

KNOWING AND INTELLIGENT WAIVER The intentional or voluntary forfeiture of a recognized right.

Teague v. Lane

Black felony convict (D) v. Court (P)

489 U.S. 288 (1989)

NATURE OF CASE: Review of denial of habeas corpus.

FACT SUMMARY: Teague (D) argued in a habeas proceeding that a post-conviction judicial decision had rendered his conviction invalid.

RULE OF LAW
Except in special circumstances, case law will not be applied retroactively in collateral review.

FACTS: Teague (D) was charged with various felonies. An all-White jury convicted Teague (D), a Black man, of attempted murder, robbery, and battery. The prosecution had used all its peremptory challenges to exclude Blacks from the jury. Teague (D) appealed, contending that this denied him due process. On appeal the conviction was upheld. Teague (D) subsequently petitioned for habeas corpus, contending that he had been entitled to a jury consisting of a cross-section of the community. The district court denied his petition on the merits, as did the court of appeals. The United States Supreme Court granted review.

ISSUE: Will case law be applied retroactively in collateral review?

HOLDING AND DECISION: (O'Connor, J.) No. Except in special circumstances, case law will not be applied retroactively. Habeas corpus provides an avenue for upsetting judgments that otherwise would be final. It is not intended to be a substitute for direct review. Both the state and criminal defendants have an interest in leaving concluded litigation in a state of repose. If new rules of constitutional law were to be applied retroactively, any litigation might be reopened if the new rule were to be applicable. Further, the purpose of habeas is that its presence creates an incentive for trial and appellate judges to conduct their proceedings in a manner consistent with established constitutional principles. To apply new principles retroactively would actually subvert this purpose. Therefore, the Court concludes that, unless the post-conviction rule announced is so fundamental to the concept of ordered liberty that it would be unconscionable not to retroactively apply it, retroactive application will not be given. A necessary corollary to this rule is that no new rule of constitutional criminal procedure should be announced in a habeas proceeding. Here, to rule as Teague (D) urges would amount to that. Therefore, without ruling on the merits of the claim, the denial of habeas must be affirmed.

CONCURRENCE: (Stevens, J.) The test adopted by the court is essentially proper. However, as to the Court's discussion of the "fundamental fairness" exception, the Court gives an excessively result-oriented analysis.

DISSENT: (Brennan, J.) The 1867 Habeas Corpus statute was, from its inception, given an extremely broad jurisdictional reach. Nothing done by Congress since has indicated a wish to narrow its reach. Further, the ruling by the Court will foreclose decision upon important constitutional issues.

ANALYSIS

The opinion in fact announces two rules, the first being that stated above and the second being that new constitutional issues cannot be announced in a habeas proceeding. The latter rule is potentially much more significant than the first. It is important to note, however, that only four justices joined the section announcing that rule, which limits its precedential value.

Quicknotes

HABEAS CORPUS A proceeding in which a defendant brings a writ to compel a judicial determination of whether he or she is lawfully being held in custody.

Harrington v. Richter

State (P) v. Individual (D)

562 U.S. 86 (2011)

NATURE OF CASE: Appeal from habeas decision in favor of the plaintiff.

FACT SUMMARY: A jury convicted Richter (D) of murder, attempted murder, and armed robbery. Richter (D) then brought a petition for habeas corpus relief directly to the California Supreme Court. That court denied his petition without full explanation.

RULE OF LAW

Under 28 U.S.C. Section 2254 as amended by the Antiterrorism and Effective Death Penalty Act (AEDPA) of 1996, federal habeas relief may not be granted unless it is shown that an earlier state court's decision was contrary to clearly established federal law or involved an unreasonable application of such federal law.

FACTS: In 1994, police in California arrived at the home of Joshua Johnson, a known drug dealer. Johnson had been shot. Another man, Klein, had also been shot and lay on a couch in the living room. Klein later died from his injuries. Johnson informed the police that two men came into his house and one of them, named Christian Branscombe, shot Johnson near the door of Johnson's bedroom. Johnson also informed the police that Richter (D) allegedly shot Klein in the living room. The police later searched Richter's (D) residence and found items stolen from Johnson's home as well as similar ammunition used in the murder of Klein. At trial, Richter's (D) attorney argued Branscombe fired at Johnson in self-defense and that Klein was shot in the crossfire by Johnson near the bedroom door. Klein was then allegedly moved to the couch. At trial, the prosecution put on expert witnesses to prove that the blood near the door was that of Johnson, and not Klein. This evidence supported Johnson's story and damaged the credibility of Richter's (D) version of events. Fifteen years after his conviction and imposition of a life sentence, Richter (D) filed a petition for habeas corpus relief at the California Supreme Court on the grounds of ineffective assistance of counsel. The basis of Richter's (D) claim was that his attorney did not call any expert witnesses of his own to rebut the expert testimony of the prosecution. The California Supreme Court denied his application with a one-line rejection of his claims. Richter (D) then filed a new habeas petition in federal district court which denied his claim. On appeal, however, the Ninth Circuit Court of Appeals reversed, holding that the California Supreme Court unreasonably applied the federal standard for ineffective assistance of counsel claims. The State (P) appealed to the United States Supreme Court.

ISSUE: Under 28 U.S.C. Section 2254 as amended by the Antiterrorism and Effective Death Penalty Act (AEDPA) of 1996, may federal habeas relief be granted only if it is shown that an earlier state court's decision was contrary to clearly established federal law or involved an unreasonable application of such federal law?

HOLDING AND DECISION: (Kennedy, J.) Yes. Under 28 U.S.C. Section 2254 as amended by the Antiterrorism and Effective Death Penalty Act (AEDPA) of 1996, federal habeas relief may not be granted unless it is shown that an earlier state court's decision was contrary to clearly established federal law or involved an unreasonable application of such federal law. First, 28 U.S.C. 2254 applies because Richter (D) is in state custody. Moving to the substantive issue, Richter's (D) burden is to show that the state court's application of the standard this court laid out in *Strickland v. Washington*, 466 U.S. 668 (1984), for ineffective assistance of counsel claims was unreasonable. The issue here is not a relitigation of whether Richter's (D) counsel actually performed at a level below the standard set in *Strickland*. This Court is not adjudicating an ineffective assistance of counsel claim under direct review. Rather, under AEDPA, the state court's review of the habeas petition is granted deference. A state court's denial of habeas relief will preclude relief in the federal courts if fair-minded jurists could disagree about the correctness of the state court's determination. A federal habeas court must consider what arguments the state court could have used to support its decision. Here, a state court could have made the determination that defense counsel reasonably decided to forgo the use of his own experts and rely upon cross examination only of the prosecution experts. Richter's (D) counsel clearly had reason to question his client's account. Use of their own expert may possibly have proved that Richter's (D) version of events was wrong. It was thus a reasonable strategic decision to instead rely upon cross-examination in the hopes of creating reasonable doubt in the minds of the jury. Because the state court's review of the *Strickland* standard was reasonable, federal courts must defer to the state courts and deny Richter's (D) habeas petition as well. Reversed and remanded.

Continued on next page.

ANALYSIS

Habeas petitioners relying upon ineffective assistance of counsel claims face a very difficult burden. The Anti-terrorism and Effective Death Penalty Act (AEDPA) of 1996 added another layer by requiring that federal courts may not grant habeas relief unless the state court decision was essentially unreasonable. As this decision noted, unreasonable is different from incorrect.

Quicknotes

RIGHT TO COUNSEL Right conferred by the Sixth Amendment that the accused shall be provided effective legal assistance in a criminal proceeding.

Glossary

Common Latin Words and Phrases Encountered in the Law

A FORTIORI: Because one fact exists or has been proven, therefore a second fact that is related to the first fact must also exist.

A PRIORI: From the cause to the effect. A term of logic used to denote that when one generally accepted truth is shown to be a cause, another particular effect must necessarily follow.

AB INITIO: From the beginning; a condition that has existed throughout, as in a marriage that was void ab initio.

ACTUS REUS: The wrongful act; in criminal law, such action as is sufficient to trigger criminal liability.

AD VALOREM: According to value; an ad valorem tax is imposed upon an item located within the taxing jurisdiction calculated by the value of such item.

AMICUS CURIAE: Friend of the court. Its most common usage takes the form of an amicus curiae brief, filed by a person who is not a party to an action but is nonetheless allowed to offer an argument supporting his or her legal interests.

ARGUENDO: In arguing. A statement, possibly hypothetical, made for the purpose of argument.

BILL QUIA TIMET: A bill to quiet title (establish ownership) to real property.

BONA FIDE: True, honest, or genuine. May refer to a person's legal position based on good faith or lacking notice of fraud (such as a bona fide purchaser for value) or to the authenticity of a particular document (such as a bona fide last will and testament).

CAUSA MORTIS: With approaching death in mind. A gift causa mortis is a gift given by a party who feels certain that death is imminent.

CAVEAT EMPTOR: Let the buyer beware. This maxim is reflected in the rule of law that a buyer purchases at his or her own risk because it is the buyer's responsibility to examine, judge, test, and otherwise inspect what he or she is buying.

CERTIORARI: A writ of review. Petitions for review of a case by the United States Supreme Court are most often done by means of a writ of certiorari.

CONTRA: On the other hand. Opposite. Contrary to.

CORAM NOBIS: Before us; a writ of error directed to the court that originally rendered the judgment.

CORAM VOBIS: Before you; a writ of error directed by an appellate court to a lower court to correct a factual error.

CORPUS DELICTI: The body of the crime; the requisite elements of a crime amounting to objective proof that a crime has been committed.

CUM TESTAMENTO ANNEXO, ADMINISTRATOR (ADMINISTRATOR C.T.A.): With will annexed; an administrator c.t.a. settles an estate pursuant to a will in which he or she is not appointed.

DE BONIS NON, ADMINISTRATOR (ADMINISTRATOR D.B.N.): Of goods not administered; an administrator d.b.n. settles a partially settled estate.

DE FACTO: In fact; in reality; actually. Existing in fact but not officially approved or engendered.

DE JURE: By right; lawful. Describes a condition that is legitimate "as a matter of law," in contrast to the term "de facto," which connotes something existing in fact but not legally sanctioned or authorized. For example, de facto segregation refers to segregation brought about by housing patterns, etc., whereas de jure segregation refers to segregation created by law.

DE MINIMUS: Of minimal importance; insignificant; a trifle; not worth bothering about.

DE NOVO: Anew; a second time; afresh. A trial de novo is a new trial held at the appellate level as if the case originated there and the trial at a lower level had not taken place.

DICTA: Generally used as an abbreviated form of obiter dicta, a term describing those portions of a judicial opinion incidental or not necessary to resolution of the specific question before the court. Such nonessential statements and remarks are not considered to be binding precedent.

DUCES TECUM: Refers to a particular type of writ or subpoena requesting a party or organization to produce certain documents in its possession.

EN BANC: Full bench. Where a court sits with all justices present rather than the usual quorum.

EX PARTE: For one side or one party only. An ex parte proceeding is one undertaken for the benefit of only one party, without notice to, or an appearance by, an adverse party.

EX POST FACTO: After the fact. An ex post facto law is a law that retroactively changes the consequences of a prior act.

EX REL.: Abbreviated form of the term "ex relatione," meaning upon relation or information. When the state brings an action in which it has no interest against an individual at the instigation of one who has a private interest in the matter.

FORUM NON CONVENIENS: Inconvenient forum. Although a court may have jurisdiction over the case, the action should be tried in a more conveniently located court, one to which parties and witnesses may more easily travel, for example.

GUARDIAN AD LITEM: A guardian appointed by the court to represent a minor or incompetent person in a legal action.

HABEAS CORPUS: You have the body. The modern writ of habeas corpus is a writ directing that a person (body) being detained (such as a prisoner) be brought before the court so that the legality of his or her detention can be judicially ascertained.

IN CAMERA: In private, in chambers. When a hearing is held before a judge in his or her chambers or when all spectators are excluded from the courtroom.

IN FORMA PAUPERIS: In the manner of a pauper. A party who proceeds in forma pauperis because of his or her poverty is one who is allowed to bring suit without liability for costs.

INFRA: Below, under. A word referring the reader to a later part of a book. (The opposite of supra.)

IN LOCO PARENTIS: In the place of a parent.

IN PARI DELICTO: Equally wrong; a court of equity will not grant requested relief to an applicant who is in pari delicto, or as much at fault in the transactions giving rise to the controversy as is the opponent of the applicant.

IN PARI MATERIA: On like subject matter or upon the same matter. Statutes relating to the same person or things are said to be in pari materia. It is a general rule of statutory construction that such statutes should be construed together, i.e., looked at as if they together constituted one law.

IN PERSONAM: Against the person. Jurisdiction over the person of an individual.

IN RE: In the matter of. Used to designate a proceeding involving an estate or other property.

IN REM: Signifies an action against the res, or thing. An action in rem is basically one that is taken directly against property, as distinguished from an action in personam, i.e., against the person.

INTER ALIA: Among other things. Used to show that the whole of a statement, pleading, list, statute, etc., has not been set forth in its entirety.

INTER PARTES: Between the parties. May refer to contracts, conveyances, or other transactions having legal significance.

INTER VIVOS: Between the living. An inter vivos gift is a gift made by a living grantor, as distinguished from bequests contained in a will, which pass upon the death of the testator.

IPSO FACTO: By the mere fact itself.

JUS: Law or the entire body of law.

LEX LOCI: The law of the place; the notion that the rights of parties to a legal proceeding are governed by the law of the place where those rights arose.

MALUM IN SE: Evil or wrong in and of itself; inherently wrong. Describes an act that is wrong by its very nature, as opposed to one which would not be wrong but for the fact that there is a specific legal prohibition against it (malum prohibitum).

MALUM PROHIBITUM: Wrong because prohibited, but not inherently evil. Describes something that is wrong because it is expressly forbidden by law but that is not in and of itself evil, e.g., speeding.

MANDAMUS: We command. A writ directing an official to take a certain action.

MENS REA: A guilty mind; a criminal intent. A term used to signify the mental state that accompanies a crime or other prohibited act. Some crimes require only a general mens rea (general intent to do the prohibited act), but others, like assault with intent to murder, require the existence of a specific mens rea.

MODUS OPERANDI: Method of operating; generally refers to the manner or style of a criminal in committing crimes, admissible in appropriate cases as evidence of the identity of a defendant.

NEXUS: A connection to.

NISI PRIUS: A court of first impression. A nisi prius court is one where issues of fact are tried before a judge or jury.

N.O.V. (NON OBSTANTE VEREDICTO): Notwithstanding the verdict. A judgment n.o.v. is a judgment given in favor of one party despite the fact that a verdict was returned in favor of the other party, the justification being that the verdict either had no reasonable support in fact or was contrary to law.

NUNC PRO TUNC: Now for then. This phrase refers to actions that may be taken and will then have full retroactive effect.

PENDENTE LITE: Pending the suit; pending litigation underway.

PER CAPITA: By head; beneficiaries of an estate, if they take in equal shares, take per capita.

PER CURIAM: By the court; signifies an opinion ostensibly written "by the whole court" and with no identified author.

PER SE: By itself, in itself; inherently.

PER STIRPES: By representation. Used primarily in the law of wills to describe the method of distribution where a person, generally because of death, is unable to take that which is left to him or her by the will of another, and therefore his or her heirs divide such property between them rather than take under the will individually.

PRIMA FACIE: On its face, at first sight. A prima facie case is one that is sufficient on its face, meaning that the evidence supporting it is adequate to establish the case until contradicted or overcome by other evidence.

PRO TANTO: For so much; as far as it goes. Often used in eminent domain cases when a property owner receives partial payment for his or her land without prejudice to his or her right to bring suit for the full amount he or she claims the land to be worth.

QUANTUM MERUIT: As much as the party deserves. Refers to recovery based on the doctrine of unjust enrichment in those cases in which a party has rendered valuable services or furnished materials that were accepted and enjoyed by another under circumstances that would reasonably notify the recipient that the rendering party expected to be paid. In essence, the law implies a contract to pay the reasonable value of the services or materials furnished.

QUASI: Almost like; as if; nearly. Essentially used to signify that one subject or thing is almost analogous to another but that material differences between them do exist. For example, a quasi-criminal proceeding is one that is not strictly criminal but shares enough of the same characteristics to require some of the same safeguards (e.g., procedural due process must be followed in a parole hearing).

QUID PRO QUO: Something for something. In contract law, the consideration, something of value, passed between the parties to render the contract binding.

RES GESTAE: Things done. In evidence law, this principle justifies the admission of a statement that would otherwise be hearsay when it is made so closely to the event in question as to be said to be a part of it, or with such spontaneity as not to have the possibility of falsehood.

RES IPSA LOQUITUR: The thing speaks for itself. This doctrine gives rise to a rebuttable presumption of negligence when the instrumentality causing the injury was within the exclusive control of the defendant, and the injury was one that does not normally occur unless a person has been negligent.

RES JUDICATA: A matter adjudged. Doctrine that provides that once a court of competent jurisdiction has rendered a final judgment or decree on the merits, that judgment or decree is conclusive upon the parties to the case and prevents them from engaging in any other litigation on the points and issues determined therein.

RESPONDEAT SUPERIOR: Let the master reply. This doctrine holds the master liable for the wrongful acts of his or her servant (or the principal for his or her agent) in those cases in which the servant (or agent) was acting within the scope of his or her authority at the time of the injury.

STARE DECISIS: To stand by or adhere to that which has been decided. The common-law doctrine of stare decisis attempts to give security and certainty to the law by following the policy that once a principle of law as applicable to a certain set of facts has been set forth in a decision, it forms a precedent that will subsequently be followed, even though a different decision might be made were it the first time the question had arisen. Of course, stare decisis is not an inviolable principle and is departed from in instances where there is good cause (e.g., considerations of public policy led the Supreme Court to disregard prior decisions sanctioning segregation).

SUPRA: Above. A word referring a reader to an earlier part of a book. (The opposite of infra.)

ULTRA VIRES: Beyond the power. This phrase is most commonly used to refer to actions taken by a corporation that are beyond the power or legal authority of the corporation.

Addendum of French Derivatives

CHATTEL: Tangible personal property.

CY PRES: Doctrine permitting courts to apply trust funds to purposes not expressed in the trust but necessary to carry out the settlor's intent.

IN PAIS: Not pursuant to legal proceedings.

PER AUTRE VIE: For another's life; during another's life. In property law, an estate may be granted that will terminate upon the death of someone other than the grantee.

PROFIT A PRENDRE: A license to remove minerals or other produce from land.

VOIR DIRE: Process of questioning jurors as to their predispositions about the case or parties to a proceeding in order to identify those jurors displaying bias or prejudice.